Inventorying Cultural Heritage Collections

Inventorying Cultural Heritage Collections

A Guide for Museums and Historical Societies

Sandra Vanderwarf and Bethany Romanowski

ROWMAN & LITTLEFIELD
Lanham • Boulder • New York • London

Published by Rowman & Littlefield
An imprint of The Rowman & Littlefield Publishing Group, Inc.
4501 Forbes Boulevard, Suite 200, Lanham, Maryland 20706
www.rowman.com

86-90 Paul Street, London EC2A 4NE

British Library Cataloguing in Publication Information Available

Library of Congress Cataloging-in-Publication Data

Names: Vanderwarf, Sandra, 1979– author. | Romanowski, Bethany, 1977– author.
Title: Inventorying cultural heritage collections : a guide for museums and historical societies / Sandra Vanderwarf and Bethany Romanowski.
Description: Lanham : Rowman & Littlefield Publishers, [2022] | Includes bibliographical references and index.
Identifiers: LCCN 2021046844 (print) | LCCN 2021046845 (ebook) | ISBN 9781538107256 (cloth) | ISBN 9781538166499 (paperback) | ISBN 9781538107263 (ebook)
Subjects: LCSH: Museum registration methods. | Museums—Collection management. | Museums—Inventory control—United States—Case studies.
Classification: LCC AM139 .V36 2022 (print) | LCC AM139 (ebook) | DDC 069/.5—dc23
LC record available at https://lccn.loc.gov/2021046844
LC ebook record available at https://lccn.loc.gov/2021046845

Contents

Preface

Over the past half-century, the critical nature of inventories has been stressed increasingly in official policies, legislation, and conventions. UNESCO's Convention on the Means of Prohibiting and Preventing the Illicit Import, Export and Transfer of Ownership of Cultural Property (1970) and Recommendation Concerning the Protection and Promotion of Museums and Collections, Their Diversity and Their Role in Society (2015) emphasize inventories as a primary means of disrupting unlawful possession, traffic, and sale of heritage and of discerning rightful ownership. In 2017, Sandra experienced this connection firsthand while leading an inventory barcode initiative with the National Museum of Mongolia under the auspices of the U.S. State Department. Heightened awareness of illicit trafficking of Mongolian heritage lent impetus to scrutiny of inventory control at state-run institutions, which gave rise to self-determined legislation mandating comprehensive inventories on a stringent schedule.

Other policies, developed in tandem with the professionalization of our field, further underscore the broader role of inventory as foundational to collections care and preservation. This is brought to bear in the American Alliance of Museums accreditation program (1971), the addition of a dedicated chapter on inventories in *Museum Registration Methods* edited by Rebecca A. Buck and Jean A. Gilmore (1998), the National Park Service's *Museum Handbook Part II* (2000), and the Smithsonian Directive 600 (2001). Sandra, a conservator by training, became acutely aware of this function of inventories during her tenure at Brooklyn Children's Museum. Over the past 120 years, the encyclopedic collection profile had evolved into an archive of collecting fashions in America, and it manifested numerous transformations in collections information documentation systems reflecting the advent of computer technology and changing professional standards. At this institution, Sandra oversaw an unprecedented federally funded 100 percent inventory, an absolute prerequisite for mobilizing a sustainable preventive conservation strategy and for perpetuating the institution's legacy of community service through innovative collections access.

These policies affirm the critical nature of inventories in theory, but our experience evidences that inventory systems aren't functioning as well as they could be and what can happen when inventories are deferred. As a registrar with New York City museums for over fifteen years, Bethany has witnessed how underdocumented collections, inaccurate collection data, and the lack of a sound inventory practice diminish an institution's ability to engage communities in meaningful dialogues through research, access, and interpretation. In 2015, she led the National September 11 Memorial & Museum's first comprehensive inventory to strengthen the recently opened institution's physical and intellectual control of the collection.

The Smithsonian Office of the Inspector General's ongoing audits, which flag inventory enhancement needs at its own collecting units, suggest that our perspectives resonate with those of the broader museum community. (One of these audits in 2011 addressed inventory practices at the Cooper Hewitt, Smithsonian Design Museum where Bethany managed the first phase of a comprehensive, multiyear inventory and collection relocation project.) In fact, the 2019 Heritage Health Information Survey, published by the Institute of Museum and Library Services, reported that finding aids—defined as inventorying or cataloging of collections—is the top preservation improvement need among U.S. collecting institutions of any type. This reality may stem in part from inadequate resource allocation and administrative deprioritization of behind-the-scenes collections work in favor of more visible activities. While this book can't solve these problems, it addresses another barrier: in tackling our inventory challenges, we struggled to find as much practical literature as we would have liked to guide our work. To this end, the book adds a substantive resource to the modest body of inventory literature. An expression of what we had hoped to find, the book aspires to streamline the work of other practitioners endeavoring to strengthen their inventory practice.

In addition to a gap in the literature, we've encountered inventories as complex time and resource-intensive project-style undertakings, which can overwhelm those charged with bringing them to fruition. In response, part I of the book approaches inventory through the lens of project management. While imperfect, this framework provides a flexible model that can be used as a tool for planning and executing inventories in a wide range of contexts. The hypothetical case of Museum A, a brew of the authors' experiences, applies project management concepts to inventory. Part II features case studies that illustrate how inventories play out in practice within the myriad contexts that make up the rich cultural heritage community. Many of these stories resulted from our research and engagement with the museum community over the past four years via an informal survey, conference presentations, and outreach to our professional networks.

Yet the case studies paired with our research attest that there is more to do beyond the scope of this book to build inventory capacity. For one, more effective, accessible technology is needed to facilitate inventories. While the book centers technology needs with chapters that scrutinize database features and barcode systems, it can't remedy this deficiency. The capacity to perform inventories is also affected by the changing technologies used to create heritage. Digital collections, discussed in chapter 13, require a different kind of documentation and expertise that are nascent in many institutions. In addition, inventories merit more attention as an element of resilience. Case studies demonstrate how an inventory can unite a community as it rebuilds in the wake of armed conflict or be a pivotal emergency response tactic that provides a sense of stability following a disaster. An inventory can also counter structural inequality by rejecting prevailing standards for naming and describing artifacts in favor of culturally accurate standards that honor the communities of origin. Our field stands to benefit from greater emphasis on inventory in such contexts, which will continue to characterize the human experience. Indeed, we finalized this manuscript during the COVID-19 pandemic, which shuttered museums everywhere. Inventory data was the first thing we reached for to support preservation, security, and access to cultural heritage on lockdown, an unprecedented scenario unforeseen by even the most seasoned practitioners.

In celebrating this collaborative effort, Sandra acknowledges all who supported her own resilience in response to COVID-19 museum unemployment, the numerous colleagues who shared generously to enrich the content of this book, and Bethany for validating and holding the vision. Bethany would like to thank her partner, friends, and family, her 9/11 Memorial Museum inventory team and colleagues, and everyone who shared their knowledge and supported her during this process. She would also like to thank Sandra for her partnership and mutual support in writing this book. Both extend special thanks to Jennifer Beetem, a point of inspiration for featuring a quipu as the cover image.

PART I

EXECUTING PROJECT-STYLE INVENTORIES

CHAPTER ONE

Centering Inventories in Museum Practice

An inventory refers to a list that features basic descriptive information about every object in the collection. Inventory is also the act of generating the list through a process of reviewing, confirming, and improving the quality and accuracy of the descriptive information.[1] Inventory data, a subset of cataloging data, typically focuses on essential information needed to access and manage objects in the collection. It often includes an object's unique identifying number, name, a brief description, its current location, and absence or presence. Inventories may also build on this data to improve collection care and documentation, for example, by capturing condition information, photographic documentation, or dimensions.

In broad strokes, inventory methodology has three prongs: a physical inspection of objects, a review of object records, and a reconciliation of discrepancies between the two. During physical inspection, inventory takers survey objects and make sure each has a corresponding record. Ideally, records are registered in a computerized database that serves as the authoritative collections information repository. As objects are inspected, inventory data is captured or confirmed in their records. Physical inspection facilitates the discovery of objects that are misplaced, separated from documentation, or unregistered. While surveying object records, staff ensure that each object has a corresponding record in the database, followed by a check to confirm the object's presence. Reviewing records identifies objects that should be in the collection that perhaps were not encountered during physical inspection. These two elements of inventory—comparing objects to records and records to objects—results in a list of the collection's contents. The third element of inventory, reconciliation, involves reviewing the list for any discrepancies between objects and records and attempts to resolve them. This includes correcting documentation errors, reconnecting objects with their records, locating misplaced objects, and deciding how to deal with discrepancies that persist after all reconciliation efforts are exhausted. The three elements of inventory—object inspection, record review, and reconciliation—may occur linearly or simultaneously to some degree.

There are various expressions of inventories, which are reviewed in this chapter. While there is no one-size-fits all approach, the aim is the same—to exercise "good collections stewardship." A common refrain in the museum field, the phrase may be regarded as a vague, catchall term used to describe any number of collections caretaking activities and aspirations. Instead, this chapter spells out how inventories are a cornerstone of good stewardship: they underpin relevant preservation, interpretation, and access strategies as well as ethical collections practices.

Types of Collection Inventories

There are several types of inventories: comprehensive, partial, spot-check, lot, and open/closed. Although their purpose is similar, the contexts in which each is most effective vary. A firm grasp of their advantages and disadvantages guides decisions about the best inventory approach in a given scenario.

Comprehensive Inventory

The most complete inventory is known as a comprehensive, 100 percent, or wall-to-wall inventory. This type of inventory entails working systematically through all spaces where collections may be encountered to document all objects owned by the museum as well as those in temporary custody, including incoming loans and acquisitions under review. A comprehensive inventory encompasses collections stored and displayed on-site, off-site, or away from museum premises for conservation or other purposes.

Comprehensive inventories are ideal because every object in the collection is surveyed, which means the results can be compared definitively against registration records to identify objects separated from documentation or records for which no object was found.[2] This type of inventory also allows a subset of cataloging data to be brought to a desired standard across the entire collection. In the wake of a disaster or in connection with initiatives such as a collection move or digitization project, comprehensive inventories are used to definitively account for collections in tandem with recovery or preparation activities. However, while comprehensive inventories are favorable, they are the most resource-intensive and time-consuming inventory application. They are often invoked exceptionally as projects or as a means of authoritatively regaining physical and intellectual control of a collection. This need often arises after a period of substandard stewardship, during which basic object information such as storage location, name, and description are unreliably documented. Inadequate collections care budgets, dysfunctional location tracking systems, or a lack of knowledge about collections documentation practices can all eventuate the need for a comprehensive inventory.

Partial Inventory

A partial inventory focuses on a portion of the collection limited in scope to some logical group, such as a discrete collection from one donor; a classification, such as paintings; a material type, such as plastics; objects on display; or objects in a circumscribed storage area. Partial inventories are sometimes integrated with other projects, such as a rehousing initiative, condition assessment, digitization, or mounting an exhibition.[3]

A benefit of partial inventories is that they break down the work of inventory into smaller, more manageable chunks that demand fewer resources than a comprehensive inventory. The main limitation of partial inventories on their own is that they represent an incomplete snapshot of the collection's contents and documentation status. Partial inventories may suggest that objects are missing when they have been misplaced or may overlook items stored or displayed in unofficial or infrequently visited locations. For example, staff inventorying records for the snuffbox collection that is stored in a designated cabinet will not encounter the one that was inadvertently moved to a neighboring storage unit and may record it as missing. Likewise, an unregistered snuffbox mistakenly placed with the silver collection will likely go undetected. Partial inventories are therefore perhaps most advantageous when they are structured to achieve a full inventory within a targeted timeframe.

Spot-Check Inventory

A spot-check inventory is a type of partial inventory that targets a representative sampling of objects, often generated randomly from object records.[4] They are an effective means of gauging the accuracy, error rate, and completeness of collection data; of periodically auditing an institution's record-keeping practices; and of evaluating data captured during a comprehensive inventory project as a quality control measure.

The effectiveness of spot-checks depends on the sample being a statistically valid cross section of the collection. Some collections management systems and spreadsheet applications can auto-generate random samples of object records. The sample is determined by collection size.[5] To conduct a spot-check inventory, users run a random sample query in the database. Each record in the query result is checked to confirm the object's presence and the accuracy and completeness of inventory data. The results are analyzed to understand the current status and effectiveness of documentation and inventory control procedures. The Smithsonian's Office of the Inspector General routinely uses spot-check inventories during audits of inventory control at its museums.[6]

The benefit of spot-check inventories is that they provide a sense of overall inventory control strengths and weaknesses without having to inventory the entire collection. A known system of regular spot-checks may also deter theft. Given its efficiency, some institutions—particularly those with expansive collections—view the random spot-check method as the most sustainable approach to routine inventory control and records accuracy maintenance. As such, their inventory practices are often largely based on this method. A limitation of the random spot-check approach is that it typically compares digitally registered records to objects. Random sample inventories would therefore not necessarily identify objects unregistered in the database or deaccessioned objects that were never dispersed if these records were excluded from the sample.

Lot Inventory

Lot or batch inventories document collections as lots, rather than at the item level. One accession number may be applied to an entire lot or subcollection instead of assigning unique numbers to each individual item. Lot inventories present a sustainable approach to registering and tracking large numbers of similar (often small) objects such as archaeological finds. For example, a group of twenty similar pottery shards from the same context may be registered as a lot under one record number. Lot inventories present institutions with a viable first step for reining in control of large groups of undocumented objects or accession backlogs. The results provide big-picture documentation needs and empower institutions to prioritize areas for item-level documentation.

Open and Closed Inventory

Open and closed describe an administrative state during inventory. During a closed inventory, collections areas are "frozen," meaning moving objects in or out of them is prohibited. This policy may be applied to some or all collections areas for the duration of the inventory. Institutions may even issue moratoriums to suspend outgoing loans, acquisitions, and other activities that require object movements until the inventory is complete. Closed inventories increase the degree of confidence in documentation accuracy in a given area at a given time. The intention is to prevent a situation where staff believe every object in a room has been surveyed only to discover (or not) that objects were moved into the room while they were away at lunch or after moving on to the next storage area. Closed inventories are also beneficial if an institution is searching for a specific object or theft is suspected. Museums with considerable collection activity may find a closed inventory unrealistic. For these institutions, a closed inventory may be more feasible when it dovetails with a collection relocation, building renovation, or other undertaking during which collection activities are already suspended.

During an open inventory, business continues as usual, and objects are transferred in and out of storage areas as needed. In open inventories, it is especially critical to exercise rigorous object location tracking procedures to diminish the risk of overlooking objects. Effective strategies include documenting location changes in the database as soon as objects are moved, using object sign-out logs, and dedicating shelves in storage as check-in/checkout staging areas for objects entering and leaving the space.

Why Inventories Are Important

Inventories are important because they are the foundation for good collections stewardship. Good stewardship presumes that an institution uses collections to support many primary functions of museums: to collect, preserve, interpret, and provide access to collections through exhibitions, programs, and research. Fulfillment of these functions flows from sound inventory practice.

Good collections stewardship also encompasses notions that govern how and why museums go about fulfilling their core functions. These notions—and the core museum functions themselves—are rooted in ethics, or moral principles that govern behavior and how activities are conducted.[7] For guidance on ethical professional conduct, museums look to organizations such as the American Alliance of Museums (AAM) and the International Council of Museums (ICOM).[8,9] Both organizations' codes of conduct maintain that museums hold their collections in trust for the public. The public trust doctrine holds that governing authorities must preserve certain natural and cultural resources for public use.[10] Gaining and maintaining public trust is key to the health of any public institution; it directly impacts community support, attendance, collection building, and funding. Both AAM's and ICOM's ethical codes hold that "inherent in public trust is a notion of stewardship that includes rightful ownership, permanence, documentation, accessibility and responsible disposal."[11] Collection inventories are thus a primary mechanism through which museums demonstrate that their values align with these notions of stewardship. Ethical practice achieved through a sound inventory policy includes compliance with laws and conventions, particularly those that address rightful ownership and respect for the preservation of natural and cultural resources on the global scale.

Lastly, good collections stewardship includes being accountable to museum stakeholders. Inventories quite literally result in an accounting of every item in a museum's permanent and temporary possession, which increases its ability to respond to public inquiries about collections. These may include questions about what collections the museum owns, the museum's rightful ownership status, whether or not an item is on exhibit or otherwise accessible, an object's historical significance and current condition, how an object was acquired or disposed of, and any other nonconfidential information. Being able to answer such questions accurately and with confidence builds the community's trust in museums as places of truth where answers can be found. Operating with accountability as a guiding principle also fosters trust among potential lenders and funders, which furthers the museum's ability to carry out its core functions.

This section takes a closer look at how inventories support preservation, interpretation, and access; help museums meet their legal and ethical commitments; and enable them to measure their performance and remain accountable.

Inventory as Conservation

Inventories support collections preservation by providing an opportunity to observe the condition of every object surveyed. This may reveal previously unknown condition issues and risks that impact preservation. While inventories may or may not include a formal condition assessment, inventories in themselves are an act of preventive conservation. They may also address or support remedial conservation needs.

Inventory as Preventive Conservation

Preventive conservation is the systematic, proactive, holistic practice of avoiding needless object damage and loss. It is the most effective and affordable approach to long-term collections preservation.[12] Preventive conservation measures interfere minimally with the materials and structures of objects. Examples of preventive conservation include "appropriate . . . actions for registration, storage, handling, packing and transportation, security, environmental management (light, humidity, pollution and pest control), emergency planning, education of staff, public awareness, [and] legal compliance."[13] Overall, preventive conservation activities aim to mitigate agents of deterioration. These agents are known, predictable factors that threaten the preservation of collections: physical forces, thieves and displacers, fire, water, pests, pollutants, light, improper temperature, improper humidity, and custodial neglect.[14] While some activities carried out with the inventory may explicitly target these threats, the act of inventory itself addresses risks posed by thieves and displacers, custodial neglect, and physical force.

How do inventories prevent theft and displacement? Institutions that regularly inventory collections are less likely to lose items through theft. If items have been taken unlawfully or displaced, routine inventories support early detection, which prevents continued loss and increases chances of recovery. The improved documentation state gained through inventory also plays a role in combating theft since undocumented or poorly documented objects are less likely to be noticed by staff if they go missing. If their absence is discovered, a lack of accessible and suitable inventory documentation impedes reporting the crime, proving rightful ownership, and recovering the property. The connection between inventory and theft was emphasized in a remarkable series of incidents resulting in a significant loss of cultural heritage held in Russian museums. In 2006, it was reported that more than 200 artifacts valued at about $5 million were missing from the State Hermitage Museum in Saint Petersburg.[15] Jewelry, icons embellished with precious gems, and enamelwork were among the items discovered missing during an inventory that began in 2005. The museum's director, Mikhail Piotrovsky, acknowledged that "years can pass between inventory checks of specific collections in the more than 1,000-room museum" and that "only several hundred thousand of the 3 million artworks at the Hermitage are registered in an electronic catalog."[16] Investigations pointed to a museum curator and her family as individuals directly involved in the thefts that occurred over several years.[17] The incident prompted President Vladimir Putin to order inventories at all Russian museums, which revealed more missing objects.[18]

Another agent of deterioration, custodial neglect, occurs when an institution is not as proactive as it could be in preserving collections or when collection documentation and care practices are out of step with current professional standards.[19] Outdated collection documentation often results in dissociation of objects from their records.[20] For example, object number labels are removed or fall off and aren't replaced, or loans and object locations aren't tracked consistently and reliably. Objects may be displaced from their intended storage environments, which are often carefully controlled for humidity, temperature, and light to minimize damage.

Consequently, objects may be discarded inadvertently, lost, or subject to unchecked, preventable deterioration. This further diminishes the objects' value due to separation from documentation confirming their context, provenance, and significance. Even in the face of increased productivity pressures and budget constraints, institutional prioritization of inventory is a critical tool for deterring deterioration and loss of objects through custodial neglect.[21]

Inventories lessen the risk of object damage from physical force, another threat, because they reduce object handling. Each time an object is handled, there's a chance it will be damaged by being dropped, bumped, or picked up with insufficient support relative to the object's weight, materials, techniques, and vulnerabilities. Inventories reduce the need for handling in a few ways. Knowing the exact location of objects eliminates the need to handle or move other objects while looking for them. Improved, accessible documentation in computerized systems further minimizes the need to inspect objects for routine information requests, such as dimensions. Many institutions take additional steps to minimize handling, such as photographic documentation and integration of basic handling aids, such as support boards, trays, and foam wedges to stabilize objects (figure 1.1).

Figure 1.1. Object handling support at the National September 11 Memorial & Museum
COURTESY 9/11 MEMORIAL & MUSEUM, PHOTOGRAPH BY BETHANY ROMANOWSKI

By nature, inventories reduce damage and loss from thieves and displacers, custodial neglect, and physical force. But inventories are also an opportune time to improve storage conditions, which can further combat several agents of deterioration. For instance, if heavy objects rest on more fragile items, they can be separated to avoid damage through physical force. Objects can be reorganized by material, size, and weight. As well, housing objects in boxes, bags, or tissue protects them from light, dust, water, fire, short temperature and humidity fluctuations, and other objects undergoing deteriorating chemical changes.

Inventory and Remedial Conservation
In addition to supporting preventive conservation, inventories offer an opportunity to observe and measure remedial conservation needs. Remedial conservation, which interferes directly and sometimes substantially with object materials and structure, is all actions "aimed at arresting current damaging processes or reinforcing their structure. These actions are only carried out when the items are in such a fragile condition or deteriorating at such a rate, that they could be lost in a relatively short time."[22] Examples of remedial conservation include "textile disinfestation, desalination of ceramics, deacidification of paper, dehydration of wet archaeological materials, stabilization of corroded metals, consolidation of mural paintings," mounting, and reversal of damaging mounts.[23] Although only trained conservators are qualified to undertake remedial conservation, inventories help museum staff identify and prioritize objects that need it. Inventory preparations may also include training staff to carry out first-level interventions that can be accomplished without putting objects at further risk. At minimum, proactive planners establish protocols for addressing pest infestations—for example, procedures for isolating textiles infested with active moth larvae to prevent the pests from consuming other textiles. In addition, planners may target removal of chemically unstable housing materials (e.g., acidic tissue paper) or isolation of chemically unstable objects (e.g., those made of nitrocellulose), to prevent these materials from accelerating deterioration of nearby objects.

Expanding Collections Access
Providing access to collections is another core museum function. Collections practitioners know that the value of a collection and its accessibility is closely connected to the accuracy and fullness of its records.[24] Without up-to-date inventory documentation, staff and the public aren't able to fully engage with or benefit from museum collections. Inventories support both physical and intellectual collections access.

Inventories expand physical access to collections by documenting where objects are located. Poor and incomplete inventory data impedes physical access to collections since the museum is unable to exhibit, study, conserve, or otherwise provide access to objects whose locations are unknown. Although objects with poor location data are often found thanks to staff memory and searches, these retrieval methods are not always successful or possible, nor are they efficient. Indeed, increased efficiency in the day-to-day work of collections staff is one of the most immediate and welcomed outcomes of an overdue inventory.

Up-to-date inventory data also enhances intellectual access to collections, which refers to the potential to understand and benefit from the object's historical and cultural significance. Fundamentally, this hinges on knowing what an object is and what it looks like in order to place it in the appropriate context. During inventory, staff confirm or capture essential data to identify and describe objects in their records. A key piece of data is an object's unique identifying number, which keeps it linked to its record where identifying information is stored. Records hold additional information, such as when and how objects were acquired, and knowledge accumulated through years of research, publication, and exhibition. Data confirmed through inventory, such as accession numbers, object names, and descriptions, is often the first level of interpretive information invoked for exhibitions, programs, and research. Inventories likewise reveal documentation deficiencies that impede intellectual access. Objects that are unidentified, difficult to describe, or sparsely documented bespeak the need for further research so people can benefit from them.

Accurate inventory data further supports intellectual access because it brings into focus the size, breadth, and depth of the collection. When this data is captured digitally, staff can analyze it in a variety of ways—at the object, donation, subcollection, or collection level—for a variety of uses. A primary use is a collection review, a critical stewardship activity. Collection reviews serve to identify gaps in collecting as well as irrelevant or redundant objects. While institutions develop collecting plans to identify the types of objects that best serve their mission and audience, collecting plans and mission statements can shift or be interpreted differently over time—the rationale behind what types of objects the institution does and does not collect may become obscured. Institutions may also engage in opportunistic collecting or lack a collecting plan entirely. Through these and other means, out-of-scope and redundant objects are a feature of most collections. Even with carefully crafted collecting plans, the collection may grow to a size that ultimately exceeds the institution's capacity to effectively store, house, or exhibit it. Accurate inventory data is an absolute prerequisite for periodically reviewing collections to identify redundant and irrelevant objects so that they can be dispersed through appropriate means. In this way, inventories support meaningful and conscientious curation as well as optimal use of storage, exhibition space, and other resources.

Finally, digitizing collections represents an ever-expanding means of increasing intellectual access to collections. One type of digitization refers to the process of capturing data about collections from paper records in a computerized database to create an authoritative, centralized source for collection documentation. Digitization also refers to imaging physical objects through digital photography, scanning, and 3D modeling or converting analog audiovisual collections to digital formats. The end goal is often to increase access to collections via an online interface. Digitization is a common product of inventories. Paper records are often entered in computerized systems in preparation for inventory, and object photography is frequently carried out in tandem with object inspection. Inventory data can also be used to identify and estimate resources for future digitization initiatives. All forms of digitization expand intellectual access for museum staff and the public.

Evaluating Performance

Conscientious museums formalize inventory policies and procedures in their collections management policy (CMP), a written document that articulates the museum's professional and ethical framework for collecting and managing collections.[25] In itself, effective policy making is an expression of institutional accountability. (Museums that lack clear inventory directives in their CMP likely underperform in this area.) When inventory policies exist, they must be carried out in order to demonstrate that an institution is meeting its own standards. A strong CMP articulates who is responsible for ensuring inventories occur and when and how they will be conducted. Inventory practice, then, is one criterion for measuring a museum's performance—how and to what degree it is fulfilling its mission.

Some museums implement a formal internal audit system as a way of evaluating whether they're operating as effectively as they could be. An example of this is seen in the Metropolitan Museum of Art's CMP. The policy delegates inventory responsibilities to individual curatorial departments, but it also requires the registrar to inventory "a limited number of works of every curatorial department" each year.[26] Inventory findings are reported to the Acquisitions Committee and may be reviewed by internal auditors.

At the Smithsonian, the Office of the Inspector General (OIG) routinely audits collecting units to assess how well they are operating and safeguarding collections. Audits involve a random sample spot-check inventory and an assessment of the results. In a 2011 audit of collections management practices at the National Museum of American History (NMAH), the OIG reported that roughly 10 percent of 2,216 objects sampled were not found. Auditors also noted that electronic records existed for only about half of the collection and that NMAH did not have an accurate count of its collections.[27] In 2013, Inspector General Dahl testified about these findings before the U.S. House of Representatives:

> [We] found that collecting units had not developed or consistently followed inventory plans. Cyclical inventories, including those of highly sensitive objects, were lacking, and inventory records were often incomplete and inaccurate. The lack of inventory controls leaves

collections objects vulnerable to loss or theft, diminishes accountability, and reduces the scholarly value of the objects.[28]

While sample size and other factors influence the usefulness and reliability of audits, such reviews must also consider how effectively the museum is operating within the context of allotted resources. During the 2011 NMAH audit, collections personnel cited a lack of adequate staffing, competing museum priorities, and poor oversight for inventory performance as factors that contributed to suboptimal performance.

Audit results—especially when they are public information—can be a powerful tool for demonstrating accountability or for refocusing institutional priorities and resources to enhance performance in this area. Furthermore, audits can play an important role in risk management because they help identify areas of concern before they become unmanageable liabilities that further erode public trust.

An institution's inventory track record is also an evaluation criterion for museums pursuing accreditation with the AAM. AAM accreditation recognizes an institution's commitment to mission achievement and fieldwide standards of best practice.[29] Candidates must complete a self-study, which asks about the museum's inventory schedule; when the institution last undertook an inventory; what information is captured; what percentage of the collection has been inventoried in the last ten years; and if not 100 percent, what the plans are for accomplishing this.[30] According to AAM, as custodians of collections held in public trust, museums should know what they have, know where it is, and take good care of it.[31] It can be difficult to measure whether a museum honors public trust when no external entity is holding the museum accountable. Thus, AAM's peer-based validation can lend credibility in this area, increasing the public's confidence as well as that of potential funders and museums considering loan requests.

Managing Risk

Risk management is the identification and prioritization of risks followed by a "coordinated and economical application of resources to reduce, monitor, and control the probability and/or impact of unfortunate events."[32] Inventories help staff identify and reduce risks to collections, the museum's financial well-being, and the health and safety of staff and visitors. They are also an economical use of resources for reducing risk given their myriad benefits. By reducing risk to the museum and the public, inventories are another expression of accountability.

To minimize risk to collections, museums make disaster preparedness plans to safeguard collections before and after events such as floods, fires, and natural disasters. These plans often include priority lists, which indicate which objects should be safeguarded first in the face of an impending disaster or prioritized for salvage after an incident occurs. Identifying priority objects in advance allows evacuation and protection plans to be developed, which may include moving objects out of the gallery or museum or using specialized crates for transport. Up-to-date inventories provide an accounting of the museum's most important objects so that reliable priority lists can be developed. Strong inventory data also ensures that accurate lists of objects affected by a disaster can be produced based on their location. These lists help to account for objects during disaster response and may also be used to prevent further damage. In the case of a fire, for instance, firefighters may be able to use less destructive firefighting techniques in areas where they know collections are stored. Following a natural disaster, armed conflict, or act of terrorism, inventories play a critical role in identifying and recovering collections that have been damaged or displaced. This impedes illicit trade and movement of cultural heritage, often associated with such events. When objects are unsalvageable, inventory documentation can assist with making replicas that reflect the objects' historic significance and aesthetic attributes.

When disasters or substantial disruptions occur, museums rely on operational continuity plans to get back up and running. These plans identify the museum's essential functions and develop strategies to ensure they can be "continued throughout, or resumed rapidly after, a disruption of normal activities."[33] Up-to-date, accessible inventories are key to continuing essential functions when disruptions occur. For example, the 2019 COVID-19 pandemic led to the abrupt closure of most museums, increasing collections security and preservation vulnerabilities. Inventory data—especially for loaned objects and objects in transit—was the first thing many collections practitioners reached for. Inventory data accessed remotely allowed staff to estimate resources needed to continue security and preservation protocols during closure. Easily accessible collection data also allowed staff to continue museum business remotely: online exhibitions and virtual programming immediately began to be researched and developed from object data stored in digital records. When museums could reopen, inventory data was used again to estimate supplies and staff hours required to assess and clean objects displayed on open mounts. In other business disruption scenarios, inventory data may be used to identify replacements for objects that have been damaged or lost so that museum programming can continue.

Inventories also protect museums from catastrophic monetary loss in the event of damage or loss of the collection. Information from inventories is used to ensure a museum's blanket insurance policy provides adequate market-value coverage for all objects in the museum's care, custody, and control up to a certain dollar amount based on probable maximum loss or the maximum loss an insurer would be expected to incur on a policy.[34] Inventories, which may also integrate object value assessments, are even more critical for institutions with scheduled policies, which cover loss and damage related only to objects listed on the schedule.[35]

Finally, inventories help museums manage risk by supporting the health and safety of museum personnel and visitors. Inventories reveal collection items that may be hazardous to people due to the object's fabrication, intended use, materials and chemical makeup, or historic conservation treatments.[36] While some hazardous materials are controlled through laws, others may be less evident. Examples of hazards in collections include acid from batteries, loaded firearms and live explosives, edged weapons or needles that may have been used, ethnographic materials embedded with toxic botanicals, mirrors and meteorological equipment containing mercury, taxidermy specimens or fur garments fumigated with arsenic, leaking wet animal specimens preserved in formaldehyde, and objects made with radioactive minerals. Some objects become hazardous as they deteriorate. For example, cellulose nitrate is a plastic used to make dolls, motion picture films, and other objects. As it ages, it becomes combustible and emits gases that are harmful to people and other objects. Inventories raise awareness of such collections so that strategies for mitigating health and safety risks to staff, visitors, and other objects can be developed. Information resulting from inventory can also guide decisions about how these objects are safely handled and stored, loaned, and used in order to protect people and shield the museum from liabilities that could arise beyond being compliant with known laws.

Compliance with Laws on the Protection of Cultural and Natural Heritage

Professional ethics say that museums are expected to manage collections in accordance with applicable laws, codes, and regulations. Inventories are central to fulfilling many of these obligations, which focus on rightful ownership of collections, the protection of cultural and natural heritage, and discouragement of illicit trade associated with looting of heritage sites or other unlawful possession of collections. In recent years, many countries have passed cultural heritage protection laws that articulate inventory requirements and procedures. In the U.S. and on the global scale, NAGPRA, CITES, and UNESCO's 1970 convention broadly influence museum collecting and collections use activities. Compliance with these measures promotes the underlying ethical aims and demonstrates a commitment to good collections stewardship.

NAGPRA

The Native American Graves Protection and Repatriation Act (NAGPRA), enacted in 1990, guarantees the rights of Indigenous tribes, people, cultures, and Native Hawaiians regarding the treatment, repatriation, and disposition of objects of cultural patrimony with which these groups can show a relationship of lineal descent or cultural affiliation.[37] The law requires that museums receiving federal funding after November 16, 1990, prepare inventories of relevant collection items, which may include human remains and sacred or funerary objects. NAGPRA inventories are itemized descriptions of each object supplemented with provenance information that documents when, how, where, and from what source objects were acquired. Inventories are shared with Indian tribes and Native Hawaiian organizations, which can request repatriation or other disposition of the objects.

Under NAGPRA, museums were required to inventory relevant holdings by November 16, 1995, five years after the law went into effect.[38] While the deadline for completing these inventories has long passed, there is evidence to suggest that some institutions have yet to fulfill these expectations.[39] Shoring up a dormant inventory procedure helps meet NAGPRA requirements while also demonstrating compliance to museum constituents.

CITES

In 1973, the International Union for Conservation of Nature drafted the Convention on International Trade in Endangered Species of Wild Fauna and Flora (CITES). The agreement restricts the movement of live and dead plant and animal specimens (and their parts) that are endangered, threatened, or internally protected.[40] The convention aims to ensure that international trade in endangered plants and animals does not threaten these species in the wild. Participating countries are responsible for implementing the convention by requiring licenses for the import and export of covered specimens. The Endangered Species Act of 1973 implemented CITES in the United States. The Act prohibits the importation, exportation, sale, trade, or shipment in interstate and foreign commerce of listed endangered species, their parts, and products made from them.[41] While the exhibition of listed species by museums isn't considered commercial activity, an affidavit and supporting material documenting the object's status must accompany shipments of relevant specimens and objects embedded with them.[42] CITES encourages parties to the agreement to regularly inventory relevant holdings and share information between other parties to the agreement.

In connection with CITES, the U.S. Fish and Wildlife Service requires a range of species-specific permits and documentation that impact the possession, transfer, or loan of specimens and items derived from them.[43] Inventories are critical to ensuring collection items are not confiscated or destroyed under these restrictions. Additional inventory documentation includes provenance information, which proves the institution's lawful acquisition, rightful ownership, date of procurement, and species identification.[44] A number of states impose similar restrictions regarding species that are endangered or protected. Conditions include annual inventory reports documenting the object's location, exhibition and display activities, and disposition of relevant collection items.

UNESCO

The United Nations Educational, Scientific and Cultural Organization (UNESCO) has drafted conventions aimed at coordinating international cooperation to preserve the world's natural and cultural heritage. UNESCO'S 1970 Convention on the Means of Prohibiting and Preventing the Illicit Import, Export and Transfer of Ownership of Cultural Property targets theft at museums and archaeological sites and trade and illegal import/export of objects of unlawful provenance or of unidentified origin. Under the convention, cultural property that has been unlawfully acquired or illegally imported is to be returned to the country of origin.[45] In the U.S., membership to the convention is expressed by the Convention on Cultural Property Implementation Act, which became law in 1983.[46] Inventory forms the basis of member states' ability to fulfill the convention's purpose: prohibiting the import or acquisition of unlawfully possessed cultural property relies upon the property being documented in the inventory of particular institutions.[47]

In 2015, UNESCO also adopted the Recommendation Concerning the Protection and Promotion of Museums and Collections, Their Diversity and Their Role in Society.[48] The recommendation affirms that museums and collections are the primary means of protecting the world's natural and cultural heritage. To this end, the recommendation spells out the critical role of inventories:

> A key component of collection management in museums is the creation and maintenance of a professional inventory and regular control of collections. An inventory is an essential tool for protecting museums, preventing and fighting illicit trafficking, and helping museums fulfill their role in society. . . . Member States should take appropriate measures to ensure that the compilation of inventories based on international standards is a priority in the museums established in the territory under their jurisdiction.[49]

From myriad perspectives, then, inventory is fundamental to effective and ethical stewardship of cultural heritage collections. Consequently, many museums acknowledge the need to enhance their inventory protocols. But mobilizing an inventory can feel daunting when the breadth, depth, and complexity of cultural collections and their contexts are considered. Inventories can also strain staffing and financial resources. While there is no best way to do inventory, there is a way to move forward in spite of all these variables. The following chapter proposes a starting point for sketching out a road map that can take inventory from an idea to a sustainable practice.

Notes

1. Office of Policy and Analysis Study Team, "Concern at the Core: Managing Smithsonian Collections, An Executive Summary," *Smithsonian Institution*, 2005, accessed June 15, 2017, https://www.si.edu/content/opanda/docs/Rpts2005/05.04.ConcernAtTheCore.Executive.pdf, vi.
2. Maureen McCormick, "Inventory," in *Museum Registration Methods*, 5th ed., ed. Rebecca A. Buck and Jean Allman Gilmore (Washington, DC: AAM Press, 2010), 301.
3. Ibid.
4. Ibid.
5. U.S. Department of the Interior, *Inventory of Museum Collections*, DOI Museum Property Directive 21 (Washington, DC: Office of Acquisition and Property Management, 2014), doi.gov/sites/doi.gov/files/migrated/museum/policy/upload/Dir-21-Collection-Inventory.pdf.
6. Cathy L. Helm, *Collections Management: The National Museum of African American History and Culture Needs to Enhance Inventory Controls Over Its Collections*, OIG-A-20-05 (Washington, DC: Office of the Inspector General, 2020), si.edu/oig/Audit_Reports.
7. *English Oxford Living Dictionaries*, s.v. "ethics," accessed June 5, 2017, https://en.oxforddictionaries.com/definition/ethics.

8. American Alliance of Museums (AAM), "Code of Ethics for Museums," *AAM*, 2000, accessed June 2, 2017, http://aam-us.org/resources/ethics-standards-and-best-practices/code-of-ethics.

9. International Council of Museums (ICOM), "ICOM Code of Ethics for Museums," *ICOM*, 2013, accessed June 5, 2017, http://icom.museum/fileadmin/user_upload/pdf/Codes/code_ethics2013_eng.pdf, 5.

10. Cornell Law School Legal Information Institute, "Public Trust Doctrine," *Cornell Law School*, 2017, accessed June 5, 2017, https://www.law.cornell.edu/wex/public_trust_doctrine.

11. American Alliance of Museums and International Council of Museums, "Code of Ethics."

12. American Museum of Natural History, "Preventive Conservation," *American Museum of Natural History*, accessed June 7, 2017, http://www.amnh.org/our-research/natural-science-collections-conservation/general-conservation/preventive-conservation/.

13. International Council of Museums (ICOM) Committee for Conservation, "Terminology to Characterize the Conservation of Tangible Cultural Heritage," *ICOM*, accessed June 7, 2017, http://www.icom-cc.org/242/about/terminology-for-conservation/.

14. Canadian Conservation Institute, "Agents of Deterioration," *Government of Canada*, 2016, accessed June 8, 2017, http://canada.pch.gc.ca/eng/1444330943476.

15. Galina Stolyarova, "Stolen Russian Museum Items Not Insured," *Washington Post*, August 1, 2006, accessed June 1, 2017, http://www.washingtonpost.com/wp-dyn/content/article/2006/08/01/AR2006080100406.html.

16. Ibid.

17. Associated Press, "Russian Police: Hermitage Curator Tried to Sell Stolen Museum Goods," *Fox News*, August 12, 2006, accessed June 1, 2017, http://www.foxnews.com/story/2006/08/12/russian-police-hermitage-curator-tried-to-sell-stolen-museum-goods.html.

18. Associated Press, "Much Art Missing from Russian Museums," *The Denver Post*, July 17, 2008, accessed June 20, 2017, http://www.denverpost.com/2008/07/17/much-art-missing-from-russian-museums/.

19. American Institute for Conservation of Historic and Artistic Works (AIC), "Ten Agents of Deterioration," *AIC Wiki*, 2014, accessed June 7, 2017, http://www.conservation-wiki.com/wiki/Ten_Agents_of_Deterioration#Custodial_Neglect.

20. Ibid.

21. R. Robert Waller and Paisley S. Cato, "Agent of Deterioration: Dissociation," *Canadian Conservation Institute*, accessed June 15, 2017, http://canada.pch.gc.ca/eng/1444924574622.

22. International Council of Museums Committee for Conservation, "Terminology to Characterize the Conservation."

23. Ibid.

24. Buck and Gilmore, *Museum Registration Methods*.

25. Rebecca A. Buck and Jean Allman Gilmore, eds., *Museum Registration Methods*, 5th ed. (Washington, DC: AAM Press, 2010).

26. "Collections Management Policy," *The Metropolitan Museum of Art*, September 8, 2020, https://www.metmuseum.org/-/media/files/about-the-met/policies-and-documents/collections-management-policy/collections-management-policy-9_8_2020.pdf?la=en&hash=5512B67EE5A7B552E4D98C8225393C65, 13.

27. Office of the Inspector General, *Collections Stewardship of the National Collections*, 1.

28. Scott S. Dahl, "Testimony of Scott S. Dahl Inspector General, Smithsonian Institution on Collections Stewardship at the Smithsonian Committee on House Administration U.S. House of Representatives," *Smithsonian Institution*, 2013, accessed June 1, 2017, http://icom.museum/fileadmin/user_upload/pdf/Codes/code_ethics2013_eng.pdf, 2–3.

29. American Alliance of Museums, "Accreditation," *American Alliance of Museums*, accessed June 7, 2017, http://www.aam-us.org/resources/assessment-programs/accreditation.

30. Ibid.

31. Merritt, *National Standards*, 26.

32. Douglas Hubbard, *The Failure of Risk Management: Why It's Broken and How to Fix It* (New Jersey: John Wiley & Sons), 46.

33. Federal Emergency Management Agency (FEMA), "Continuity of Operations: An Overview," *FEMA*, 2017, accessed June 7, 2017, https://www.fema.gov/pdf/about/org/ncp/coop_brochure.pdf.

34. Buck and Gilmore, *Museum Registration Methods*.

35. Ibid.

36. Catharine Hawks et al., *Health and Safety for Museum Professionals* (New York: Society for the Preservation of Natural History Collections, 2010).

37. U.S. Department of the Interior, "National NAGPRA," *National Park Service*, 2017, accessed June 6, 2017, https://www.nps.gov/nagpra/.

38. Marie C. Malaro and Ildiko P. DeAngelis, *A Legal Primer on Managing Museum Collections*, 3rd ed. (Washington, DC: Smithsonian Books, 2012).

39. U.S. Department of the Interior, "National NAGPRA," under Frequently Asked Questions: Our museum has never submitted a NAGPRA inventory or summary, and we are concerned that we may be out of compliance. What should we do?

40. Malaro and DeAngelis, *A Legal Primer*.

41. Ibid.

42. U.S. Fish and Wildlife Service, "Endangered Species: Permits, Frequently Asked Questions," *U.S. Fish and Wildlife Service*, 2016, accessed June 6, 2017, https://www.fws.gov/endangered/permits/faq.html.

43. U.S. Fish and Wildlife Service, "How Can I Obtain a Permit?" *U.S. Fish and Wildlife Service*, accessed June 1, 2017, https://www.fws.gov/faq/permitfaq1.html.

44. American Institute for Conservation of Historic and Artistic Works (AIC), "The Preservation of Cultural Property with Respect to U.S. Government Regulation of African Elephant Ivory," *AIC*, accessed May 1, 2017, http://www.conservation-us.org/docs/default-source/governance/position

-paper-on-government-regulation-of-ivory-(november-2015).pdf.

45. United Nations Educational, Scientific and Cultural Organization (UNESCO), "Convention on the Means of Prohibiting and Preventing the Illicit Import, Export and Transfer of Ownership of Cultural Property 1970," *UNESCO*, accessed June 6, 2017, http://portal.unesco.org/en/ev.php-URL_ID=13039&URL_DO=DO_TOPIC&URL_SECTION=201.html.

46. Bureau of Educational and Cultural Affairs, "IV. Key Provisions of the Convention on Cultural Property Implementation Act," *United States Department of State*, accessed June 7, 2017, https://eca.state.gov/cultural-heritage-center/cultural-property-protection/process-and-purpose/background.

47. United Nations Educational, Scientific and Cultural Organization, "Convention on the Means."

48. United Nations Educational, Scientific and Cultural Organization (UNESCO), "Recommendation Concerning the Protection and Promotion of Museums and Collections, Their Diversity and Their Role in Society," *UNESCO*, accessed June 7, 2017, http://portal.unesco.org/en/ev.php-URL_ID=49357&URL_DO=DO_TOPIC&URL_SECTION=201.html.

49. Ibid., lines 8 and 25.

CHAPTER TWO

Creating an Inventory Project Road Map

Chapter 1 described how comprehensive inventories are often initiated as projects to reestablish control of collections when documentation has become unreliable or in preparation for an initiative impacting collections such as digitization, a collection move, or even a disaster recovery response. Comprehensive inventories are the most complex and resource intensive to implement, and they require careful planning. To that end, this book applies basic project management concepts to project-style inventories. Referencing this framework, the chapters correspond to the three overarching phases of a project: chapters 2 to 8 address planning, chapters 9 and 10 cover execution, and chapter 11 discusses closing the inventory. This chapter kicks off the planning phase with an overview of the project scope, a key inventory planning tool. Later chapters address each scope element in detail.

The primary purpose of the planning stage is to craft an inventory project scope that presents a viable strategy for propelling the museum toward its collections stewardship goals. The project scope is a written document that outlines the inventory's objectives, deliverables, activities, timelines, and resources. As such, the scope document is also about placing boundaries to clarify what the project will and won't accomplish. During the planning phase, stakeholders may rework elements of the project scope a few times as objectives are checked against available time and resources. When stakeholders reach consensus on these elements, the result is a plan that serves as a road map they can rely on to bring the inventory to fruition and to guide the project through successful execution. The following sections review each element of this guiding document.

Objectives

The first step in forming an inventory project scope is to identify the objectives. Objectives describe the project's desired results, or what it is meant to achieve.[1] Effective objectives express precisely what stakeholders are working toward and may propose solutions to problems that keep the museum from stewarding collections as well as it could be. Generally, inventory objectives center around reining in and/or maintaining physical, intellectual, and administrative control of the collection. This involves recording or confirming the minimum amount of information necessary for managing collections. During the planning stage, staff establish inventory objectives by assessing the collection's documentation status, identifying deficiencies, and determining what is needed to bring documentation to the desired standard. They may also consider whether collections management policies or systems need adjustment to record and maintain accurate data. Factors that further shape inventory objectives include the collection profile, the collection's condition and storage environment, the museum's strategic plans, upcoming projects, and constraints such as cost and time.

Justification

Most inventory planners will need to justify the inventory to other stakeholders, and having an initial draft of objectives will help win their support. In most scenarios, buy-in is required from a number of stakeholders because they must allocate resources to the inventory, they will participate in the work, they will be the primary users of the inventory products, or it will otherwise affect their work. The project justification must persuade stakeholders that enhancing inventory control is necessary right now. Sound objectives that show how the inventory will solve problems and help the museum meet its goals are therefore critical to building a strong argument, as is showing stakeholders what's in it for them, both in dollars and sense. Furthermore, engaging with stakeholders during the planning phase is vital, as their input can strengthen the inventory objectives.

Deliverables

After gaining buy-in, stakeholders may scrutinize the initial objectives to reach consensus on the inventory's deliverables. Deliverables are the tangible or intangible products or processes that must be produced in order to achieve the project objectives.[2] They succinctly express the value and benefits the inventory will bring.

The main deliverable of any inventory is good collections data, ideally captured in a computerized database. Technically, "to inventory" and "to catalog" can be used synonymously. In practice, inventorying involves documenting a subset of cataloging data, with the presence or absence of objects at the core.[3] Defining this deliverable means quantifying and qualifying what data will be captured. While it can be tempting to aspire to document as much information as possible, the focused inventory dataset ultimately functions as the scaffolding on which to build an ongoing collections care and documentation strategy. An expansive documentation scope or one that creeps outward as the project moves along diminishes the likelihood that the inventory will achieve its objectives on time and on budget. Typically, inventory data is limited to the minimum amount of information needed to manage and account for collections. An object's unique identification number, location, brief description, object name, item count, condition, and inventory date and recorder's name are common elements of inventory datasets.

Institutions that maintain baseline inventory data may expand the information captured during an inventory episode. Additional data such as object dimensions and medium not only enrich documentation but also facilitate effective planning for other activities such as exhibitions and preservation. Still other data may be required by laws pertaining to certain types of collections or by the museum's collections management policy.

Each objective added to the project scope will call for correlating deliverables. In addition to digital inventory data, project deliverables may include upgraded collections management software, a revised inventory policy, or a barcode system. If digital photography for the entire collection is an objective, the corresponding deliverable may be TIFF files for every object stored in a digital asset management system.

Project constraints, or restrictions that define the inventory's limitations, will come into play when considering what form the inventory deliverables will take.[4] Constraints that influence deliverables are time; money; and the scope, or the sum of requirements specified to achieve the project objectives. Each constraint influences the possibilities and limitations of the others. They are an essential building block of the project scope because they influence the inventory activities, timelines, and resources.[5] As such, they determine which deliverables are viable as well as the quality of work that will produce them. Consequently, deliverables may undergo several revisions before they are finalized.

Activities and Time

Activities are the work required to produce the inventory deliverables. One of the most important things to remember is that they have timespans. Only by identifying and estimating timespans for inventory activities can planners arrive at a reasonable project duration and timeline.[6]

To produce inventory data—the primary inventory deliverable—staff survey collections areas to physically inspect objects, check them against records, and record the inventory dataset in their database records. During this process, objects are handled to confirm information, to make other objects accessible, or to tag them with their record numbers. Inventory takers also check records against objects to ensure the museum has what its records say it should have. Inventory staff further research and correct documentation discrepancies, reunite dissociated objects with their records, and search for missing objects. This data culminates in reports that paint an accurate and complete picture of the collection holdings. Inventory activities may reflect other deliverables aimed at improving collections care and access on a comprehensive scale, for example, object photography, records digitization, rehousing, storage reorganization, and marking objects with their numbers.

Identifying activities required to produce the deliverables is easier than estimating their durations. Reasonable projections are based on trial runs of the inventory activities, which reveal a sense of how much work effort is required to inventory different collections objects in different conditions and environments. The collection's documentation status, composition, condition, and storage environment are factors that influence how much time is required to carry out inventory activities. It may take longer to access and inspect ten canoes, for instance, than ten pairs of chopsticks. Likewise, crowded storage rooms, complex object constructions, and objects in unstable condition may require additional time for inspection. Given these factors, the reality is that project-style inventory activity durations often carry some inherent unknowns. But reasonable guestimates enable planners to create an activity network that projects the duration of the inventory. This provisional inventory timeline reveals whether activities must be scaled back or whether they are reasonable relative to time and budget targets.

Resources

The duration and nature of inventory activities ultimately informs what, how much, and when resources will be needed to carry out inventory activities on the anticipated timeline. Trial runs not only inform activity durations, but they also clarify which staff and nonstaff resources are needed and in what quantity. The resulting timeline also avoids resource conflict and guides spending by indicating when resources will be needed.

Ideally, inventories utilize dedicated, available staff with appropriate skill sets. Some may fulfill more than one role or acquire necessary skills through professional development training. Registrars, collections managers, museum specialists, conservators, art handlers, and curators often comprise the core inventory staff. But they will also rely on the cooperation of individuals working across various museum departments. When estimating staff needs, planners will therefore consider all human resources required so that staff can be hired or contracted and work across departments can be coordinated.

The types and amount of nonstaff resources—supplies, equipment, and infrastructure upgrades—clearly depend on the project scope. However, some basic implements for transporting, handling, and documenting objects are required for most inventory projects. Computers, databases and other software, object naming lexicons, object carts and dollies, object handling and support materials, tags, general office equipment and supplies, and housekeeping and personal protective equipment are mainstays. Inventories also require workspaces with appropriate infrastructure. The team will need adequate space for inspecting and documenting collections, which may involve removing objects from shelves or boxes and unrolling or assembling them. Other infrastructure elements that often need updating are utilities (e.g., electricity, heating, and cooling), internet and/or intranet connectivity, adequate lighting, and ventilation wherever inventory activities may occur.

The level of attention dedicated to developing the project scope underscores that sound planning is the driving force behind a "successful" inventory project. The project scope produces a road map that personnel will use to bring an inventory to fruition and to determine whether the inventory is proceeding in line with expectations during execution. When changes from the theoretical plan present themselves, as they most certainly will do, the project scope guides stakeholders toward adjustments that keep the inventory on track. At the project's closing, the project scope confirms that the inventory results satisfy stakeholders' expectations in substance and quality.

Given the pivotal role of the project scope, the following chapters take a closer look at each element: objectives, deliverables, activities, time, and resources. The hypothetical case of Museum A is woven throughout each chapter to illustrate how these project scope elements may express.

Notes

1. Kate Eby, "How to Write a S.M.A.R.T Project Objective," *Smartsheet*, last modified November 22, 2016, https://www.smartsheet.com/how-write-smart-project-objective.

2. "A Complete Guide to Deliverables in Project Management," *Kissflow*, last modified May 26, 2021, https://kissflow.com/project/project-deliverables/#:~:text=Objective%20vs%20Deliverable,the%20objectives%20to%20be%20achieved.

3. Rebecca A. Buck and Jean Allman Gilmore, *Collection Conundrums: Solving Collections Management Mysteries* (Washington, DC: American Association of Museums, 2017), 17.

4. "Constraint (Project Constraint)," *TechTarget*, accessed June 21, 2021, https://whatis.techtarget.com/definition/constraint-project-constraint.

5. Ben Aston, "A Project Management Triple Constraint Example & Guide," *The Digital Project Manager*, last modified April 23, 2019, https://thedigitalprojectmanager.com/triple-constraint/.

6. Nick Graham, *Project Management for Dummies* (Chichester: John Wiley & Sons, 2015), 95.

CHAPTER THREE

Identifying Inventory Objectives

Identifying the inventory's objectives is a good place to start when developing an inventory project scope. Objectives are concrete, measurable, and time-limited steps taken to achieve a goal. Goals, on the other hand, are abstract or aspirational statements that describe what the project will accomplish. A universal goal of inventory, for example, may be to establish, rein in, or maintain intellectual, physical, and administrative control of a collection. This vague statement tells us where we want to go, but objectives propose exactly how to get there in a given collections scenario.[1]

In any scenario, there are myriad ways to achieve the project's goals. Thus, effective objectives also establish boundaries to create a unified understanding of what the project will and will not accomplish. This, in turn, delimits all the other elements of the project scope. SMART is a well-known mnemonic acronym for creating objectives that are specific, measurable, achievable, relevant, and time-bound.[2] These characteristics ensure objectives place boundaries and achieve goals.

This chapter presents three complementary exercises to encourage the development of SMART inventory objectives. Beyond the universal goal of inventory, the first approach asks planners to consider how the objectives can serve overarching departmental or museum goals. Another approach deduces goals by assessing problems that impede inventory control; this inspires objectives that will solve them. A third approach calls for assessing the relevance of objectives by checking them against the fundamentals of inventory methodology. The final section applies a problems assessment to a hypothetical collections scenario and discusses the pros and cons of SMART objectives that might emerge.

Plugging into Overarching Goals

The overarching goals of an institution or its collections department provide a lens through which inventory planners may contextualize and shape inventory objectives. These goals may be stated in the museum's mission, strategic plan, or work plans. For instance, many museums aspire to be more inclusive. To further this goal, planners may consider focusing objectives on underdocumented collections, such as those representing women makers, to increase awareness of and access to these materials. Another common goal is to expand digital access to collections, which may be achieved with objectives that target digital photography or registration of all object records in a computerized database. Clarifying how the inventory will advance the institution's broader interests ensures objectives are relevant to the museum's circumstances, one of the SMART criteria. It also helps garner support from stakeholders whose work is indirectly tied to collections care.

Identifying Problems That Impede Inventory Control

Effective inventory objectives may also propose how to resolve problems that have resulted from, caused, or contributed to inadequate inventory control. Often, these problems stem from the documentation state (e.g., inaccurate location data). Inventory objectives may remedy these problems, for example, by capturing accurate locations for every object. However, this is a Sisyphean task unless the underlying causes of documentation deficiencies are also addressed. Sound collections management systems enable museums to know what objects are in their custody and where they are in order to provide reasonable access to them.[3] When these systems aren't working as well as they could be, problems with inventory control occur. Thus, objectives may target fixing problems that are the outcome of flawed systems as well as the systems themselves (e.g., by improving location tracking procedures).

Most likely, staff who work regularly with the collection can rattle off a list of problems associated with inadequate inventory control. In addition to soliciting feedback about these issues, full appreciation of the nature and extent of problems emerges from fact-finding exercises that target the documentation state as well as unique aspects of the collection contents and environment that deter access for inventory documentation. Within the SMART framework, these exercises support objectives that are specific and relevant by recognizing the museum's unique needs rather than naming objectives that the museum literature suggests or that other museums have undertaken, even if the goals are similar. By understanding the extent of problems, these exercises also begin to provide a sense of how potential objectives might be measured, how long they might take to achieve, and to what extent they can be accomplished with anticipated resources and timeframes.

Problems Evidenced by the Collections Documentation State

The creation and maintenance of collections data, a primary function of inventories, is critical to enjoying adequate inventory control. Problems resulting from inadequate inventory control often manifest as documentation deficiencies, which can be understood by assessing three criteria: data accessibility, completeness, and accuracy. Examining the collection's documentation state prompts planners to identify objectives that remedy documentation deficiencies and their causes.

Data Accessibility

When assessing the collection's documentation state, a primary question to ask is, what portion of the collection is or is not accessible via an authoritative computerized system? An obvious remedy to inaccessible data would be to locate and register collection records in the database. But the issue could also stem from problems with the original documentation: it may not be readily accessible or may be decentralized or disorderly, lost, nonexistent, or destroyed in a disaster. It is also possible that records haven't been digitized because a database hasn't been procured, the database doesn't meet the needs of the users, or users lack sufficient training. A backlog of unregistered objects might also stem from a clunky ingest process that initiates registration on paper forms, rather than directly in the database.

For collections that are digitally registered in a database, the quality of data also affects its accessibility. If data used to describe collections doesn't conform to a common standard, meaningful access may be lacking. For instance, while an object location may technically be correct, five different expressions of that location in the database may obscure which objects are where, or if different names are applied to similar objects, records may be excluded inadvertently from database query results. Object descriptions may be accurate but insufficient because they're too vague or too technical to identify objects and distinguish them from others. Queries that yield unreliable results or require workarounds to isolate desired information are indicators that the accessibility of digitized collections information needs enhancement.

Data inaccessibility might also manifest in routine encounters with objects that have become dissociated from their records because accession numbers have worn away, fallen off, or were never applied. Without the numbers that link objects to their records, documentation becomes inaccessible even if it exists in a database.

To identify data accessibility issues, planners may interview collections personnel, who likely know about undigitized records or other data accessibility barriers. Relevant information about inaccessible documentation may also exist as gray literature in unrealized grant proposals or annual reports in collections department files. Location spot-checks are another way to gauge data accessibility. In this exercise, staff survey a few discrete locations (e.g., a storage drawer or exhibit case) that represent different collection categories. Objects encountered can be queried in the database to get a rough sense of the percentage of objects that are unregistered while the number of dissociated objects is tracked. Data quality can also be assessed, perhaps focusing on the consistency of object names, descriptions, or storage location formats. For a rough estimate of records that are inaccessible because they're not registered in a database, the number of unregistered objects in one representative unit can be multiplied by the total number of units.

Conversely, collections documentation may be too accessible. Uncontrolled access to collections documentation increases opportunities for theft and diminishes inventory control. In this scenario, planners may incorporate into inventory objectives changes to who has permission to create, edit, and delete object records in any format.

To remedy data accessibility problems, objectives may target locating and registering records in a database. They may also address the causes of inaccessible data by establishing data standards, enacting systems for tagging or labeling objects with their numbers, or introducing protocols for originating object documentation in the database.

Incomplete Minimum Inventory Data

Documentation deficiencies may also present as incomplete minimum inventory data, or a lack of the minimum information necessary for effectively accessing and managing collections. Examples include abundant database records that hold little information beyond an object's number or lot records that represent groups of objects that merit registration at the item level. To pinpoint the extent of incomplete data in digital records, database queries can be run against location, description, or name fields to quantify the number of records with empty fields or partial information.[4] Query results can be sorted by object classification, name, department, or other criteria to identify data deficiency hot spots.

To address incomplete data, inventory objectives may focus on capturing location and other minimum inventory data for every object or updating protocols to include capturing a minimum dataset during records registration.

Inaccurate Data

Just because database fields are populated doesn't necessarily mean the information is correct. Perhaps the most common problem associated with collection data accuracy is incorrect location records. The accuracy of recorded object locations and other minimum inventory data can be tested with a random sample spot-check.[5] In this exercise, a random sample of collections records is queried in the database. Query results yield a list of objects that, theoretically, represents a cross section of the collection. Each object in the list is physically inspected and compared against the database record to check that the record number and the number on the object match exactly, the object was located in its recorded location, and the object name and description effectively identify and distinguish it from other objects. Error or accuracy rates can be calculated as a percentage of the sample size, which is believed to reflect the data accuracy of the entire body of database records from which the random sample was drawn. To ensure statistical validity, the U.S. Department of the Interior guides the determination of a random sample size (i.e., the number of records in a random sample query) relative to the sample population (i.e., the number of records from which the sample is pulled).[6]

Data inaccuracy may stem from human error or location tracking or inventory policies in need of enhancement. A buggy database or one that is poorly equipped to track object components or multiple object movements may also contribute to data accuracy issues. To address data inaccuracy, inventory objectives may focus on physically inspecting objects to confirm or correct data, upgrading a database to enhance location tracking features, or staff trainings to encourage the consistent application of documentation protocols.

Problems Posed by the Collection's Contents

An understanding of the collection's contents further clarifies problems that inventory objectives may address. Collections refers to objects the museum owns, manages, or has custody of temporarily or permanently. Assessing the collection's contents aims to quantify roughly how many and what types of objects the inventory will address, to narrow inventory priorities, and to identify objects whose characteristics deter inventory documentation.

Walkthroughs of storerooms and galleries, database research, and staff interviews can reveal the rough extent of the collection. Quantifying collections includes identifying material that may not be present in the database, such as undocumented material tucked away in a closet. Upon inspection, it may be evident that there are too many objects relative to timelines being considered for the inventory or resources dedicated to it.

It may be discovered that the characteristics of some objects have impeded staff's ability to record and maintain inventory data. Examples include objects that are oversized, unwieldy, in poor condition, or especially fragile. Other collections may feature complex constructions or components that pose safety risks. Objects made with fur, skins, and feathers, for instance, may pose health hazards due to historic pest control treatments.

Assessing the collection's contents can also highlight materials to prioritize for inventory, such as especially significant objects known to be dissociated from provenance documentation or objects of high intrinsic value that are vulnerable to theft. Still other collections, such as human remains or objects that derive from legally restricted or protected flora and fauna, may be found to require documentation beyond a minimum inventory dataset. Conversely, planners may want to focus efforts on highly redundant or unidentified objects that are underdocumented as a result of administrative deprioritization.

If these objects might be deaccessioned, a list featuring inventory data will be the starting point.

Problems Posed by the Collection Environment

Surveying the collection's contents may also reveal barriers to inventory control posed by the collections environment, which is anywhere objects live. It may include on- and off-site storage rooms, galleries, outdoor spaces, conservation laboratories, study rooms, offices, or stairwells and closets. Objectives may be needed to remedy issues that make inventory control difficult or that create unsafe spaces for people.

When formulating the objectives, any environmental conditions that pose health and safety risks to project staff are the top priority. For instance, buildings and shelving units must be structurally sound. Lighting must be adequate. Air quality issues such as naphthalene moth ball vapors or excessive dust must be mitigated. Beyond health and safety concerns, the environment where inventory activities will take place must be conducive to work. Deafening air handlers, excessive heat or cold, or lack of electricity or internet connectivity may need to be addressed.

The collection environment will also show to what extent objects are accessible for inventory. Some objects may be inaccessible because of their physical arrangement within a space. They may be piled on top of each other or blocked by storage units erected in front of them. Shelving may be too densely populated to securely access or receive objects, and storage areas may not provide sufficient space for inspecting objects.

Safety and access issues in collections environments highlight the need to prioritize worker wellness and the collections storage infrastructure. Problems in these areas may be the result of opportunistic collecting or insufficient resources dedicated to collections care. In such

Textbox 3.1

MUSEUM A'S PROBLEMS ASSESSMENT

At Museum A, the inventory project manager learns that collections staff frequently encounter objects that are unregistered in the database. Although paper records exist, they're locked in a closet, and the key must be checked out from the registrar to access them. While digging through old files, the project manager finds a binder listing unregistered objects. A quick check confirms that they don't appear to be registered in the database. Staff also inform the project manager that object locations in database records are often inaccurate. In fact, during a random sample spot-check, about 10 percent of recorded object locations were inaccurate. Some records had empty location fields or listed historic locations that became obsolete when the museum was renovated five years ago. Many records in the random sample were shell records, including only an accession number and, sometimes, an object name. In a location spot-check of a storage drawer and a few exhibition cases, numbers linking objects to their records couldn't be found for about 11 percent of the objects.

During a walkthrough of storage areas, staff pointed out several drawers storing fine art prints and paintings, material that falls outside of the museum's collecting scope. Other objects are isolated in a cabinet because they're in an advanced state of deterioration and can't be used. The project manager notices that a section of a large, carved wooden temple facade and a couple of other mystery objects are leaning against a wall. Two shelving units erected in front of them render them inaccessible. Overall, storage is very densely populated. Most objects are stored in cabinets or on open shelving, but they lack housings or storage supports and are often touching or overlapping with one another. Several items are stored on top of mobile shelving units. When staff are asked about any other spaces that may hold collections, they point to a room on another floor that they believe holds items that were deaccessioned but never dispersed. A records search indicates that the museum deaccessioned almost two hundred objects and hosted a yard sale to disperse them decades ago. A stack of Polaroid photographs found among deaccessioning documentation seems to match some of the objects in the room, but the project manager can't be certain.

A further review of records turns up a thin file titled "Inventories." The contents include a ten-year-old museum accreditation self-study that shows the museum lacks an inventory policy but plans to initiate one. Around that time, a small percentage of the collection appears to have been inventoried. A few handwritten inventory sheets are also found that date to a few years later as well as some yellowed pages bearing a type-written list of object numbers. A review of the collections management policy reveals vague inventory protocols: collections should be inventoried, and object location changes should be tracked "when possible."

a scenario, inventory objectives may target improving the collections environment so that collections can be easily and safely accessed. This might include installing lighting or electricity in a storage area, creating staging areas for object inspection, or utilizing the inventory to estimate how much storage furniture is needed to safely store the collection.

Checking Objectives against Inventory Methodology

A review of departmental or institutional goals and problems associated with inventory control is likely to generate a robust list of potential objectives or at least a list of problems the inventory may remedy. Within the SMART framework, checking this list against aspects of inventory methodology helps to narrow the list to objectives that are relevant and complementary. As described in chapter 1, inventory methodology is three pronged, involving a physical inspection of objects, a comparison of records that document the objects, and a reconciliation of discrepancies between the two (e.g., records with missing objects, objects separated from their records, and undocumented objects).

In one sense, objectives that don't reflect these core inventory elements may be considered irrelevant. For example, a collections assessment may reveal the need for object housings or a deaccession initiative. While addressing these needs is important, planners are encouraged to consider whether they are truly relevant vis-à-vis inventory methodology. A prime benefit of adequate inventory control is the ability to efficiently plan future collections projects, including object housing initiatives and collection reviews, which are distinct from inventory. Certainly, inventories that incorporate tangential activities are common. In fact, they may present the most likely means of securing support or the most efficient use of resources. Furthermore, each inventory scenario is unique, and tangential objectives may be required in order to execute the inventory. That said, narrowing the list of objectives to those that enable or implement inventory methodology optimizes the project's intended benefits.

Within the SMART framework, another aspect of relevance is to ensure that objectives are complementary or "are supporting each other and not creating conflict or tensions."[7] An argument can be made that conflict occurs when certain aspects of inventory methodology are privileged over others. While the problems and goals in a particular inventory scenario may logically demand this, sustained bias in the application of inventory methodology may create conflict or tension by perpetuating or overlooking documentation problems. This, in turn, diminishes inventory control.

To illustrate this idea, consider Museum A's situation (textbox 3.1). Given the high inaccuracy rate of recorded object locations, the inventory planner may logically focus on improving physical control of the collection. To achieve this, she may identify objectives that privilege the physical inspection of objects during which personnel will create corresponding database records and/or capture locations and other essential data in existing records. This approach, sometimes termed "objects-to-records," is effective for reining in physical control of the collection by creating accessible data that accurately describes what is in the museum's custody right now and where it is. However, this approach may deprioritize a records review and reconciliation of discrepancies; this risks overlooking records that may correspond to objects without numbers or objects that should be in the museum's custody according to its records but aren't. Nevertheless, several other scenarios may reasonably call for an approach that favors physical inspection: (a) inventory takers are documenting a collection for the first time and the resulting documentation will serve as the foundational records; (b) inventory takers are establishing control over a collection whose records are unavailable, unreliable, highly incomplete, decentralized, or destroyed in a disaster; or (c) especially significant objects are misplaced and need to be located.

Conversely, objectives and their related activities may privilege the records review aspect of inventory methodology. For example, inventory protocols may involve generating checklists from database records and checking that corresponding objects are present in their recorded locations. A records-to-objects approach is useful for auditing what the museum should have and ensuring records are present in an authoritative system. For collections that are consistently well documented, generating checklists from the database is an efficient way to conduct an inventory. But privileging the comparison of records to objects creates the possibility of overlooking objects that are present but lack database records because they are unregistered (if a full records review hasn't been completed) or incorrectly registered or were removed, misplaced, or deleted. It also decreases the chances of locating objects that are lost or misplaced. Scenarios that reasonably favor a records review include the following: (a) copious paper collection records exist, but few or none are digitized in a database; (b) objects of special interest are dissociated from provenance or acquisition documentation; and (c) collection records exist in a database, but the data is incomplete or of poor quality and queries produce unreliable results.

Clearly, the most effective inventory practice involves a comprehensive comparison of objects to records and records to objects, which allows for the fullest reconciliation of discrepancies between them. While reconciliation takes place to some degree during most inventories, inventories that favor certain aspects of the methodology preclude definitive reconciliation. As well, an approach that favors both physical inspection and a records review may deprioritize the reconciliation of discrepancies altogether. Such an outcome is illustrated by the Smithsonian Office of the Inspector General's (OIG's) audit of inventory practices at the Cooper Hewitt Smithsonian Design Museum:

> Cooper-Hewitt has demonstrated good inventory procedures . . . but did not ensure its electronic collections records stored in the collections information system . . . were updated. If museum personnel find anomalies during the collections inventory, such as objects on the shelves without corresponding collections records, or records without corresponding objects, they need to research and resolve the anomalies . . . so that the records accurately reflect the status of the objects. Although the Museum had been inventorying its collections, . . . staff had not been resolving differences found between records and objects.[8]

The OIG further emphasized the conflicts and risks associated with perpetual deprioritization of reconciliation: it "creates the appearance that objects are missing when in fact the objects may have actually been deaccessioned or assigned a temporary tracking number." This, in turn, creates the potential for duplicate records, which reduces the usefulness of records overall and "increases the risk that objects could be lost or stolen without detection."[9]

Any combination of inventory control problems, goals, resources, and time may call for objectives that reasonably privilege certain aspects of inventory methodology over others. At the same time, checking objectives against the inventory methodology can foreground truly relevant or overlooked objectives and reveal whether prevailing applications of the methodology may be causing conflict. When equal emphasis on all three elements of the methodology is unreasonable or out of reach, this awareness encourages a strategic variation of inventory practices to alleviate such conflicts. For example, Museum A may decide to focus the current inventory's objectives on a records review, ensuring that all paper records are registered in the database. This, in turn, facilitates a physical inspection of objects as the focus of a subsequent inventory.

Drafting the Objectives

To identify inventory objectives, the preceding sections proposed referencing overarching goals, analyzing problems that hinder adequate inventory control, and reviewing inventory methodology. Within the SMART framework, these exercises inspire objectives that are specific and relevant to a unique context, the institution as a whole, and to the inventory methodology. The problems analysis addresses measurability, for example, by roughly quantifying how many objects need to be registered, how many records lack location data, or how many objects need to be inventoried. These exercises may also provide a general sense of what might be achievable given available resources and time. But these latter two SMART characteristics, achievable and time-bound, can be tricky to build into objectives, especially in the early planning stages when resources and time requirements may still be undefined. Drawing on Museum A's hypothetical problems assessment, the following section presents sample objectives to facilitate a deeper discussion of how to embed achievable and time-bound elements in inventory objectives. These techniques are particularly useful for drafting initial objectives, which often evolve as other elements of the project scope are determined.

Within the SMART framework, *achievable* refers to an objective that can be accomplished utilizing available resources and time. However, these elements of the project scope may still be in the formative stages. A general guideline to keep in mind when considering achievability is to limit the number of objectives to around three.[10] Focusing on just a few objectives—not to be confused with numerous activities that may be required to achieve them—motivates planners to dedicate resources and time to the highest priorities. Following their problems assessment presented earlier, Museum A drafted some objectives, shown in textbox 3.2. In terms of achievability, one might reasonably conclude that the list is overly ambitious. One way to pare it down is to review each objective's relevance. On second thought, planners may decide that Objectives 2 and 3 include elements that are more relevant to a collection review and deaccession backlog, which are of secondary importance to establishing what the museum has and where it is. They may likewise reconsider the relevance of Objective 4, which also lacks specificity and markers for measuring progress. While rehousing has merit, one may reasonably conclude that it is a tangential objective that can also be time and resource intensive. It therefore has the potential to create tension by delaying or limiting achievement of the other objectives. Museum A's problems assessment also noted that storage was densely

Textbox 3.2

MUSEUM A'S DRAFT INVENTORY OBJECTIVES

1. The museum will create digital access to 100 percent of the collection by retrospectively registering roughly 2,000 object records in the collections database by the end of month two in a two-year project timeline.
2. The museum will determine exactly what is in the collection and where it is by physically inspecting roughly 15,000 objects and twenty-one boxes of undispersed deaccessioned material. During inspection, essential identifying information and locations will be documented in the database. This will be completed by the end of eighteen months.
3. Inventory personnel will initiate realignment of the collection with the collecting plan by flagging the following objects in the database during the eighteen-month inspection: fine art paintings, drawings and prints, and objects the museum is unable to adequately care for or use.
4. In tandem with the eighteen-month physical inspection, inventory personnel will incorporate basic object housings and storage supports.
5. Inventory staff will reunite orphaned objects with records for which no object was found. The number of objects reconciled within three months following physical inspection will be tracked.

populated. This further questions the achievability of Objective 4, since storerooms may lack the space required for integrating housings and storage supports. As an alternative, planners may opt to include object dimensions in the "essential identifying information" noted in Objective 2 to prepare for a post-inventory rehousing project.

Obviously, achievability is also linked to time required to execute the work described in the objectives. To this end, chapter 6 explores in greater detail how to estimate time requirements and set realistic timelines, for example, by piloting activities such as registering objects in the database and inspecting objects. While final objectives should be based on credible information, planners may like to consider whether granular exercises to determine timelines are worth the effort during the early planning stages. That is to say, objectives may evolve substantially in response to stakeholders who have the power to green light, veto, or reshape the project. It may therefore be more reasonable at this stage to insert general time boundaries or ballpark estimates.

Planners may begin thinking about time boundaries by identifying existing deadlines or time constraints. A scheduled building renovation or a collections move, for example, can bring deadlines into focus. In Museum A's scenario, planners intend to pursue a grant for financial sponsorship. The funding body specifies a maximum project duration of two years, which Museum A adopted as its ballpark timeframe. Museum A then sequenced its objectives in a logical order to begin estimating durations and distributing work described in the objectives across the estimated timeframe. Sequencing the objectives in the order they will be completed encourages a time-efficient approach and gives a general idea of which objectives are more or less time intensive. At Museum A, planners found that a substantial number of object records aren't registered in the database. A lot of time will be saved by registering these records first rather than stopping to do so each time an unregistered object is encountered during the physical inspection. Based on their experience, planners reasoned that with dedicated inventory staff and readily accessible records, Objective 1 can be accomplished fairly quickly. Objective 2, which encompasses the physical inspection and documentation of objects, will likely require the most time. Objective 5 (Objectives 3 and 4 were judged irrelevant) addresses reconciliation. While the full extent of documentation discrepancies will not be known until object inspection and data capture are complete, planners reason that reconciliation will take longer than retrospective registration but certainly not as long as the object inspection. In fact, the three-month period that has been assigned is rather arbitrary. In any inventory, some discrepancies may never be reconciled, and the ones that are reconcilable may require more or less time. Museum A's problems analysis revealed the potential for a significant number of dissociated objects. Thus, planners dedicated a three-month period beyond the physical inspection to allow for reconciliation to the fullest extent.

Generally speaking, it is reasonable to begin incorporating nitty-gritty calculations of time and resources required to achieve the objectives in response to increased certainty that the project will move forward. As resource and time constraints become clear, inventory planners will be positioned to determine the extent to which draft objectives are achievable and logically scale them up, down, or eliminate some altogether. This process gains momentum when the time comes to secure support for the inventory, the topic of the next chapter. SMART inventory objectives play an important role in garnering the support needed to execute the project by justifying why it's needed. But an effective strategy for securing support also includes being open to shaping objectives to appeal more strongly to the interests of key stakeholders.

Notes

1. Steven D. Peterson, Peter E. Jaret, and Barbara Findlay Schenck, "Set Goals and Objectives in Your Business Plan," *dummies*, accessed February 22, 2021, https://www.dummies.com/business/start-a-business/business-plans/set-goals-and-objectives-in-your-business-plan/.

2. Graham Yemm, *Financial Times Essential Guide to Leading Your Team: How to Set Goals, Measure Performance and Reward Talent* (Harlow: Pearson Education, 2013), 37–39.

3. The American Association of Museums, *National Standards and Best Practices for U.S. Museums* (Washington, DC: AAM Press, 2008), 44.

4. Cathy L. Helm, "Collections Management, The National Museum of African American History and Culture Needs to Enhance Inventory Controls Over Its Collections," Report No. OIG-A-20-05 (Washington, DC: Smithsonian Office of the Inspector General, 2020), www.si.edu/oig/Audit_Reports.

5. Ibid.

6. U.S. Department of the Interior, *Inventory of Museum Collections*, DOI Museum Property Directive 21 (Washington, DC: Office of Acquisition and Property Management, 2014), doi.gov/sites/doi.gov/files/migrated/museum/policy/upload/Dir-21-Collection-Inventory.pdf.

7. Yemm, *Financial Times*, 38.

8. A. Sprightley Ryan, *Collections Stewardship at the Cooper-Hewitt National Design Museum*, OIG-A-11-02 (Washington, DC: Office of the Inspector General, 2011), www.si.edu/oig/Audit_Reports, 1.

9. Ibid., 9.

10. Holly Rustick, "Goals, Objectives, and Outcomes," *Grant Writing & Funding* (blog), July 22, 2017, https://grantwritingandfunding.com/write-goals-objectives-and-outcomes-for-your-grant-proposal/.

CHAPTER FOUR

~

Winning Support for the Inventory

Activating a project-style inventory hinges on the support of numerous people and groups beyond those who are initiating it. Support manifests variously at key junctures along the inventory trajectory, from senior leadership authorization to the provision of human and financial resources. Though a recent survey discussed in this chapter cites inventory as the top preservation need at U.S. museums, securing support for them often presents enormous hurdles. There's a tendency for this behind-the-scenes work, which can be time and resource intensive, to be overshadowed by more front-facing initiatives such as exhibitions. Thus, there is especially great appreciation for supportive decision-makers and sponsors who not only validate the importance of inventories in their own right but also acknowledge that strong inventory control underpins effective and meaningful outward-facing work.

Given these challenges, the inventory's justification, or the explanation for why decision-makers should support it, is an especially critical component of the project scope. The justification must persuade others whose buy-in is essential to green light the inventory and to allocate resources to it. Effective justifications address the following questions: Why is the inventory urgently needed, and what benefits will it provide? In large part, the answers are anchored in SMART inventory objectives, discussed in chapter 3. Planners must further identify the inventory's stakeholders whose buy-in is required or highly desired to bring the project to fruition and frame the inventory's benefits to resonate with their motivations and interests. Forethought must also be given to anything that may dissuade stakeholders and how to negotiate lack of buy-in. In response to these considerations, the inventory's benefits, and often the objectives, evolve to produce a justification that has a better chance of winning support.

Why Is the Inventory Necessary Right Now?

The answer to this question, which is central to the project justification, derives directly from the exercises used to develop SMART inventory objectives, discussed in chapter 3. These exercises prompted project initiators to identify problems that discourage adequate inventory control in a given context and to articulate how these problems prevent the museum from achieving its overarching goals. These problems are why the inventory is urgently needed. This rationale may be bolstered by recognizing the urgent need for enhanced inventory control across the broader museum community. In 2019, the Institute of Museum and Library Services published survey results that gauged the health, status, and needs of America's nonliving tangible and digital heritage collections. Results showed that 73 percent of small museums and 66 percent of medium/large museums identified finding aids—defined as inventorying or cataloging of collections—as the top preservation improvement need.[1] In fact, this was deemed the top need among heritage collecting institutions of any type.[2] On an international scale, the United Nations Educational, Scientific, and Cultural Organization, the International Centre for the Study of the Preservation and Restoration of Cultural Property, and the Canadian Conservation Institute have collaborated on the joint RE-ORG initiative to raise awareness of and mitigate widespread risks stemming from inventory control and storage deficiencies.[3,4,5]

Explaining the Benefits

The inventory's benefits may be clear to project initiators. But their value must also be understood by key players whose support is needed to execute the inventory. A stakeholder analysis identifies who these key players are, which prompts planners to recognize the value of each stakeholder relationship to the inventory. This provides a sense of who has the most power over the project and positions planners to discern what benefits will be most compelling to them. Benefits described in this chapter reference a project management framework that classifies each as a business (financial) benefit, compliance benefit, maintenance benefit, or an enabling benefit (i.e., it will enable financial benefits post-inventory).[6] Admittedly, not all inventory benefits fit perfectly into one of these categories; nevertheless, this framework is useful for explaining benefits or recognizing that they need to be more appealing.

This analysis further highlights the need to engage directly with stakeholders if planners haven't already done so and tailor the inventory's objectives or products to increase their appeal and the overall impact of the project. A stakeholder analysis is also an effective tool for considering how stakeholders' interpersonal professional relationships may be leveraged to increase support.

Identifying the Stakeholders

Typically, getting an inventory off the ground requires some level of engagement with stakeholders, whether for approval, financial support, participation, collaboration, or because the inventory will affect their work in some way. Stakeholders can be thought of as any group or individual who can affect or is affected—positively or negatively—by the achievement of the inventory's objectives.[7] Stakeholders also represent the collective expertise, resources, influence, and interest in the project.[8]

To gain stakeholder buy-in, project planners need to know who the stakeholders are. One approach classifies those with an interest in or a relationship to the inventory as users, governance stakeholders, influencers, or providers.[9] Table 4.1 shows a hypothetical inventory stakeholder chart using this framework. In actuality, many of these stakeholders may fall in multiple categories. "Users" are people who are the main beneficiaries of what the inventory will produce. While an inventory may deliver a number of benefits, the primary output of any inventory is data about collections. For the sake of example, users are largely interpreted as those who will utilize the inventory's resulting data. "Governance" stakeholders may be interpreted as individuals or groups who have an interest in how collections are acquired, used, and managed and exercise oversight of the ef-

Table 4.1. Provisional Inventory Project Stakeholder Analysis

Users[1–3]	*Governance*	*Influencers*	*Providers*
Collections managers	Board of trustees	Chief executive officer/ executive director	Funding bodies, donors
Registrars	Oversight committees	Chief financial officer	Temporary inventory staff or contractors
Conservators	Auditors	Chief operating officer	Collections managers
Curators	Regulators	Other senior leadership	Registrars
Exhibition planners	Government agencies		Conservators
Communities with personal and historical connections to the collection			Curators
Communities that rely on online collections for education, scholarship, and enjoyment			Volunteers
Communities with objects held, managed, or displayed by the museum			IT personnel
Rights and reproductions managers			Database managers
Peer institutions			Software vendors

Sources adapted from:

1. Rachael Cristine Woody, "Responsible Practices for Working with Communities and Collections," *Lucidea* (blog), June 12, 2019, https://lucidea.com/blog/responsible-practices-for-working-with-communities-and-collections/.
2. Rachael Cristine Woody, "Who Are the Stakeholders in Museum Digital Projects?" *Lucidea* (blog), June 19, 2019, https://lucidea.com/blog/who-are-the-stakeholders-in-museum-digital-projects/?highlight=stakeholders.
3. Rachael Cristine Woody, "The Importance of Internal Stakeholders to the Museum CMS," *Lucidea* (blog), August 28, 2019, https://lucidea.com/blog/the-importance-of-internal-stakeholders-to-the-museum-cms/.

fectiveness and efficiency of collections management functions. They also require or oversee compliance with laws and policies, such as the museum's collections management policy or federal laws governing certain types of collections. "Providers" provide resources for the inventory, which may include financial sponsorship, human resources, and products necessary for achieving the inventory's objectives. "Influencers" are those with the power to influence decisions about the inventory and protect or change its direction.[10] Typically, this group holds the most sway in securing institution-wide support for the inventory. By organizing stakeholders in this way, planners can deduce who is able to approve or oppose the inventory and what benefits might persuade them to support the project.

What's in It for Influencers

To mobilize an inventory, approval from the museum's influencers is required. Typically, these are the highest-ranking executives in the museum who are responsible for making decisions about the museum's use of resources, about its overall operations, and for influencing and carrying out the board's strategic plans. As they are largely responsible for the museum's financial well-being, influencers are primarily interested in any business benefits—or financial gains—the inventory may bring. One way to increase chances for influencer buy-in is to incorporate cost savings into the inventory by securing financial sponsorship from a donor or a grant-funding body. In addition to covering temporary project personnel, these funds may yield cost savings by covering a percentage of salaries of permanent staff who will play a significant role in the inventory's execution, annual collections database user license and support fees, and a percentage of overhead costs. Funds may also cover supplies; equipment; and software, such as laptops, barcoding equipment, or a collections database system, that will be useful well beyond the life of the project.

Other benefits won't yield measurable financial gains but will enable other projects that could generate income post-inventory. For example, if the inventory will produce high-quality object photographs, an image-licensing program may be launched, creating a new revenue stream. If the inventory will expand online access to collections, the number of people engaging with the museum may grow, resulting in increased attendance or other financial support. Other fundraising opportunities may present in collections rediscovered by the inventory that need rehousing, conservation, or digitization. "Fund a collection" campaigns offer a way for the public to monetarily support the museum in a way that is meaningful to them.

However, not all inventories will yield financial benefits, in which case influencer buy-in will hinge on other types of benefits. Because this stakeholder group often represents the public face of the museum and sets the tone of its workplace culture, benefits that bolster the institution's public image may also interest them. For instance, by demonstrating via its website and social media channels that the museum invests in preserving and expanding access to collections, the inventory can engender "confidence . . . on the part of donors, lenders, and other constituencies" that the institution is a worthy recipient of artifact and monetary donations.[11] The institution's unique history and collections highlighted by the inventory may further offer opportunities to affirm or refashion the museum's "brand" and mission.

What's in It for Governance Stakeholders

The museum's board of directors, as its governing authority, is a key governance stakeholder in an inventory project. The board's leadership is crucial to fulfilling the museum's mission, overseeing programs and activities, and managing risks. Though they emphasize the museum's balance sheet as a measure of success, they are also responsible for establishing sound collections care and documentation policies and ensuring they are carried out.[12] At U.S. museums, matters that concern collection policy require "evidence of good-faith efforts on the part of board members to set reasonable policy, to follow policy, and to exercise reasonable oversight."[13] The board may therefore recognize the inventory's compliance benefits, which meet internally or externally imposed organizational or legal requirements. In some cases, however, board members may not be fully aware of their crucial relationship to sound collections care, which is often one of the museum's least visible functions.[14] Some board members may be new to their role or unacquainted with museum work, the collections management policy may be silent or vague regarding inventory protocols, or there may be communication gaps between board members and collections care staff. To secure support for the inventory, project planners may cultivate increased appreciation for the fundamental role of inventory among the board and reinforce their role as thought leaders and policy makers accountable for collections stewardship. Reaffirming the board's all-important role in this respect may further encourage deeper engagement or even the appointment of a member as a collections care representative.

The board of directors also develops the museum's strategic plan, which reflects a vision of where the museum is going and what it wants to achieve.[15] The museum's influencers also shape and are responsible for implementing the board's strategic goals. Inventory objectives that advance the strategic plan are thus another means of securing buy-in from the board and influencers. Examples of strategic initiatives the inventory may support include expanded digital access, improved disaster preparedness, or a collection relocation. Strategic plans may also target American Alliance of Museums accreditation; inventories satisfy a core criterion, which is to demonstrate that the museum "legally, ethically, and effectively manages, documents, [and] cares for . . . the collections."[16]

What's in It for Users

Sticking with data as the primary example of what the inventory produces, user stakeholders include registrars, collections managers, external communities, and anyone else who uses collections data. Internal users, who encompass the many staff roles noted in table 4.1, are critical because they create, discover, affirm, and/or maintain the value and significance of the collection. They do so by referencing, generating, and recording data that describes and distinguishes objects, prevents loss, enables access, underpins determination of rightful ownership, facilitates conservation, and provides the foundation for interpretation, among other contributions. Registrars and collections managers, for example, use inventory data to identify and locate objects. Curators rely on the data to develop exhibitions and strategically build the collection, and exhibition staff require it for designing object layouts and fabricating display cases. Their role in identifying inventory objectives that produce this data is critical.

For these users, inventories generate and maintain information that helps them accomplish work more efficiently and effectively. From this perspective, the inventory provides a maintenance benefit—it allows for continued or improved collections access. For registrars and collections managers especially, increased efficiency in rudimentary functions that hinge on good collections data means more time to focus on other work. While among the most significant benefits, the maintenance benefit of increased efficiency is often underappreciated by nonuser stakeholders. To explain its impact, inventory initiators may note, for example, that the registrar spends two weeks of paid time each year searching for objects lacking location data. The same concept can be applied to the number of collections inquiries that could not be fulfilled because of unreliable collection data.

Though the public may not need to be persuaded to greenlight the inventory, perhaps they should be. The public (or the museum's audience) are external users who validate the existence of the museum, which holds collections in public trust. Accurate, accessible, and complete collections inventory data enables the public to benefit from the collection to the fullest extent. Various communities within the public use the data to increase their knowledge and enjoyment, to enrich scholarship, to critique interpretation and presentation of collections, and to hold the museum accountable as its collections relate to social and environmental justice imperatives. The public further brings value to collections caretaking, access, and interpretation endeavors by enriching and improving the accuracy of collections data, identifying objects not appropriate for public consumption, or initiating repatriation requests. These users' interest in utilizing and enriching collections information may help garner support for the inventory or in some cases even demand it.

Peer institutions are likewise important external users that strengthen the collection's purpose through exhibitions and increased scholarship. They may also benefit from the inventory in less expected ways. For example, if the inventory's objectives include developing features of an open-source collections management system, the entire museum community of database users may benefit from the enhanced features. Accurate and accessible inventory data also increases opportunities for academic exchange and loans between institutions. Indeed, interaction with inventory data among professional peers and the community validates an institution as being effective and relevant.

What's in It for Providers

The value of providers is clear in that they supply the resources needed to achieve the inventory objectives at various junctures from green lighting to implementation. This includes internal and external providers of funding; human resource providers of knowledge, skills, and expertise; and vendors or manufacturers of off-the-shelf or customized products. The museum, as a provider of resources and perhaps permanent staff who will contribute significant expertise and time working on the inventory, may be the provider whose buy-in is most critical.

To secure initial approval, the museum typically must agree to provide or allocate financial and human resources to the inventory. The individuals with the authority to do this are usually influencers who, as noted earlier, are often motivated by business and enabling benefits.

Permanent staff providers, such as registrars and collections managers, are also users who may be swayed by maintenance benefits. But as providers, they must buy into taking on more work. From this perspective, permanent staff may find enabling benefits more appealing. These present when the inventory offers opportunities to develop professional skills and networks that enable career advancement. Soliciting their input about the project early and often can serve this interest.

Museum IT personnel are key permanent staff providers who may fall solely within the provider category. They will be integral to the inventory's success by maintaining hardware and software, preparing the collections database to receive inventory data, and implementing a digital asset backup protocol. While IT personnel are often enthusiastic collections technology collaborators, there are institution-wide demands on their time. Because they constantly provide resources that support everyone's work, the IT manager may essentially be an under-the-radar influencer. Offering meaningful maintenance benefits, such as updated equipment or a temporary part-time IT assistant to cover routine tasks while time is diverted to the inventory, may lock in support. Soliciting their expertise may further garner buy-in. For example, if the inventory involves implementing new technology, the IT team may advise which equipment and software will deliver the desired results but also complement or extend the usefulness of existing IT resources. This may present an enabling benefit that advances their goals.

Even after the inventory is approved, it may not become a reality without financial sponsorship from external funding bodies or donors. For public funding bodies whose job is to sponsor projects that advance cultural heritage or humanities agendas, the inventory project presents a maintenance benefit. However, these providers typically articulate key criteria of projects they're looking to fund, such as digital access initiatives or those that address a particular cultural group or geographic area. Inventory objectives must promise to meaningfully advance these providers' missions or goals. To get a better sense of what motivates them, inventory planners can research previous awardees and reach out to funders directly. These providers are often willing collaborators who will work with planners to craft a project that more persuasively serves their interests.

Many project-style inventories can't be implemented without the services of temporary staff or contractors. As the primary inventory workers, they are indispensable providers, and getting buy-in from those with the right talent can be challenging. Furthermore, these providers are likely to leave the project before it's completed if a more promising job presents. To secure temporary staff and contractors, the inventory must offer compelling financial benefits in the way of competitive compensation packages. These providers also often seek enabling benefits or experience that will strategically raise their professional profile. To this end, these providers may be attracted to job descriptions that reflect relevant and well-organized projects that reference up-to-date, professionally recognized standards.

Contractors such as software vendors are critical external providers in many inventory projects whose success relies heavily on a database that meets user needs and increases efficiency. These providers have more agency in defining the level of business benefits they expect for services such as database development. However, they also respond to inventory projects that pose an interesting challenge or that require new technical solutions that can be integrated into subsequent software versions or upgrades. This may be seen as an enabling benefit that improves their market penetration.

Negotiating Lack of Buy-In

In addition to revealing who has the most power over an inventory project, the stakeholder analysis helps identify who may not support the project and why. As a provider, the museum may view an inventory project as an unwarranted allocation of resources, while external providers may validate the need for an inventory but question the proposed methods. Influencers may worry that an inventory could jeopardize the museum's public image or their professional reputation. Anticipating the opposition's rationale helps planners strategize how to negotiate lack of buy-in. It may also reveal that the proposed objectives or means of achieving them fail to present meaningful benefits to key stakeholders. In response, an overarching strategy calls for reaffirming the value of both skeptical and supportive stakeholders, attempting to gain consensus that the inventory objectives have merit vis-à-vis the distinct stakeholder roles, and pinpointing exactly what the opposing sides disagree on. This opens the door for skeptical and supportive stakeholders to collaboratively reshape, expand, or downsize objectives to deliver the benefits necessary for buy-in.

Anticipating opposition may be less about the "what" and more about the "who." For example, planners may identify stakeholders to whom a key decision-making influencer would be most receptive when pitching the idea of an inventory project. In another scenario, the museums' human resources directors might represent low decision-making influence. However, they may use their amicable relationship with the CFO to advocate for the project if they view it as a unique opportunity to cultivate volunteers.

Unwillingness to Dedicate Resources

Most inventories will not result in financial gains or significant cost savings. Indeed, the inventory may be possible only if the museum dedicates resources to it. The CFO or other influencers authorized to approve or veto resource allocation requests may fail to appreciate how the inventory benefits the entire institution or dismiss it as a high-cost, low-yield endeavor that will siphon scarce resources away from work they deem more important. If consensus can be gained that the inventory is important, planners can acknowledge these stakeholders' expertise in resource efficiency and management and solicit suggestions for making the project more feasible. During the early planning stages, cost and time estimates may be quite general, and there may be concerns that the project will go over budget. The CFO may be receptive to scaled-down objectives that reduce expenditures or the rate of spending. For instance, planners can reconsider whether certain resource-intensive objectives, such as collections rehousing, can be tabled, or if a lengthy timeline is projected, the inventory may be viewed as more viable if it can be carried out in a series of smaller, shorter projects.

While permanent staff providers may support the inventory in theory, they may convey to influencers their reservations about the additional responsibilities, increased workloads, and disruptions of other work that the inventory presents. To secure their support, planners may invite these providers' input on the value and achievability of the inventory objectives, which may result in more realistic targets they can get behind. The inventory's objectives may be more persuasive if they promise to meet other self-determined needs. For instance, the registrar may be more inclined to manage the project if it includes collections management system upgrades or other technology to increase efficiency in inventory data management. Curators may be more willing to support the project if underdocumented collections of interest for an upcoming exhibition are targeted first. Conservators may support it if condition data will be documented or made more accessible. The inventory might further garner support if it moves projects forward that multiple providers have a stake in, such as applying for a grant to inventory, conserve, and exhibit a particular collection. On the other hand, any of these providers may be most responsive to the prospect of temporary staff support covered by the project budget.

An especially unfortunate scenario occurs if supportive influencer stakeholders are replaced by less supportive influencers after the inventory is underway. This can result in sudden priority shifts and a redirection of staff and financial resources away from the project. This has the potential to quickly derail an inventory and diminish morale. There's no easy solution to this pivot, but planners may avoid this scenario by writing into the project plan a senior leadership representative who is administratively responsible for seeing the inventory through to completion. Though taxing, diplomatic challenges to the redirection of resources away from a previously approved project can be successful. While this may involve compromise, a redirection of resources must be reflected in scaled-back objectives, a longer timeline, or lower-quality standards.

Questionable Inventory Methods

External funding bodies that acknowledge the benefits of inventory projects may nonetheless withhold support if the project proposes methods that are perceived as out of date, inefficient, or out of step with professionally recognized approaches. Financial providers, such as granting agencies, want to see that inventory planners are applying current methods, they're in dialogue with experienced peers in the professional community, and the inventory proposes an efficient and effective use of funds. Applicants may receive this feedback from proposal reviewers only with the news that the project will not be awarded funding, which means the museum will have to make modifications and reapply during the next funding cycle. In connection with this, it may also prove difficult to get buy-in from qualified temporary inventory personnel if the objectives and methods convey a lack of expertise or an unproductive use of their time and skills. To prevent this, planners can solicit critiques of proposed methodologies and seek alternate views from as many peers as possible. Engaging with past inventory project awardees, other institutions that have recently completed an inventory, or those that are in the process of executing one is an invaluable means of increasing buy-in from these crucial stakeholders.

Perceived Threat to Public Image or Professional Reputation

Influencer stakeholders may worry about negative repercussions of an inventory project because they often expose inadequacies, such as undocumented collections, misplaced objects, or expired loans. Influencers may be uneasy about the prospect of revealing problems that may have developed during their tenure, especially when the remedies require significant resources or represent thorny legal or ethical issues.[17] However, most museums encounter these issues at one time or another, and transparency is an effective approach to dealing with them. In recent years, a number of collecting institutions have taken control of how these problems are perceived by sharing stories about how they lost track of artifacts that were especially significant or even dangerous.[18,19,20,21,22,23,24,25] These stories highlight how an inventory remedied, will remedy, or would have remedied such issues. Acknowledgment of and awareness of collections stewardship challenges raised by stories like these can ultimately elevate stakeholder trust, support, and interest.

Despite best efforts, a project-style inventory may ultimately not be approved. In that case, planners must consider which aspects of the inventory may be able to proceed using existing resources. Proposed objectives will likely require significant modification, and strategies for implementing or continuing inventory control may need to shift. Chapter 11, Closing the Inventory, examines methods for maintaining collections data following a project-style inventory. These methods may also represent an alternative means of reining in or establishing control of collections when an inventory project is not possible.

When a project does receive approval to move forward, more detailed planning can begin. Objectives agreed upon with project stakeholders can now be scrutinized to determine the project deliverables, or exactly what must be produced in order to achieve the objectives. Nailing down the deliverables, the focus of the next chapter, is key to finalizing consensus about what the inventory will produce as well as the activities, time, and resources needed to produce them.

Notes

1. Institute of Museum and Library Services, *Protecting America's Collections: Results from the Heritage Health Information Survey* (Washington, DC: The Institute, 2019), 52–53.
2. Ibid., 19.
3. "Stored but Not Safe: Museum Collections Are at Risk Worldwide," *United Nations Educational, Scientific, and Cultural Organization*, accessed April 5, 2021, www.unesco.org/new/en/culture/themes/museums/unescoiccrom-re-org/.
4. "Re-Org," *International Centre for the Study of the Preservation and Restoration of Cultural Property*, accessed April 5, 2021, https://www.iccrom.org/section/preventive-conservation/re-org.
5. "RE-ORG—Collection Storage Reorganization," *Canadian Conservation Institute*, last modified December 10, 2020, www.canada.ca/en/conservation-institute/services/preventive-conservation/collection-storage-reorganization.html.
6. Nick Graham, *Project Management for Dummies* (Chichester, West Sussex: John Wiley & Sons, Ltd., 2015), 42–43, 78.
7. Sue Davies, "Stakeholder Engagement in Publicly Funded Museums: Outlining the Theoretical Context and a Proposal for Future Research," *Cultural Policy, Criticism and Management Research* 3 (July 2008), https://culturalpolicyjournal.files.wordpress.com/2011/05/sue-davies-july-2008.pdf, 4.
8. Jeanne Vergeront, "Stakeholders + Engagement," *Museum Notes* (blog), March 25, 2012, https://museumnotes.blogspot.com/2012/03/stakeholder-engagement.html.
9. Elizabeth Harrin, "4 Types of Stakeholders in Project Management," *PMTips*, August 7, 2020, https://pmtips.net/article/4-types-of-stakeholders-in-project-management.
10. Ibid.
11. Maureen McCormick, "Inventory," in *Museum Registration Methods*, 5th ed., ed. Rebecca A. Buck and Jean Allman Gilmore (Washington, DC: AAM Press, 2010), 301.
12. Ildiko Pogány DeAngelis and Marie C. Malaro, *A Legal Primer on Managing Museum Collections*, 3rd ed. (Washington, DC: Smithsonian Books, 2012), 445.
13. Ibid., 18.
14. Ibid., 445.
15. "Alliance Reference Guide: Developing a Strategic Institutional Plan," *American Alliance of Museums*, accessed April 5, 2021, https://www.aam-us.org/wp-content/uploads/2017/12/Developing-a-Strategic-Institutional-Plan-2018.pdf.
16. "Core Standards for Museums," *American Alliance of Museums*, accessed April 5, 2021, http://www.aam-us.org/resources/ethics-standards-and-best-practices/characteristics-of-excellence.
17. Peggy Smith Finch, "The Essential Collections Inventory," in *Registrars on Record: Essays on Museum Collections Management*, ed. Mary Case (Washington, DC: American Association of Museums, 1988), 150.
18. Sarah Fearing and Jack Jacobs, "Historic Society Questioned Whether Grenade Was a Replica Before Calling Police," *Daily Press*, October 25, 2016, http://www.dailypress.com/tidewater-review/news/dp-west-point-main-street-closed-after-vietnam-era-grenade-found-20161024-story.html.
19. Rebecca Rego Barry, "An Intern Saved a Museum by Finding This Revolutionary War Treasure in the Attic," *Smithsonian Magazine*, December 1, 2015, https://www.smithsonianmag.com/history/found-attic-rare-document-revolutionary-war-saved-museum-brink-financial-ruin-180957411/.
20. Ashley Hupfl, "Listen to Newly Discovered 1962 MLK Jr. Speech," *USA Today*, January 20, 2014, https://www.usatoday.com/story/news/nation/2014/01/20/found-martin-luther-king-jr-speech/4663937/.
21. David Wallis, "Golden Age of Discovery . . . Down in the Basements," *New York Times*, March 19, 2014, https://

www.nytimes.com/2014/03/20/arts/artsspecial/golden-age-of-discovery-down-in-the-basements.html.

22. Robin Wander, "A Five-Year Digitization and Inventory Project at Stanford's Cantor Arts Center Nears the Finish Line," *Stanford News*, May 4, 2015, https://news.stanford.edu/2015/05/04/digitized-cantor-collection-050415/.

23. Erin McCarthy, "11 Things Lost, Then Rediscovered, at Museums," *Mental Floss*, September 5, 2019, http://mentalfloss.com/article/60536/11-things-lost-then-rediscovered-museums.

24. Harvard University, "Acquisition of Lewis and Clark Found at Peabody," *Harvard Gazette*, January 22, 2004, https://news.harvard.edu/gazette/story/2004/01/acquisition-of-lewis-and-clark-found-at-peabody/.

25. Rachel Farkas, "Borrowed and Returned," *The Power of Play* (blog), Boston Children's Museum, September 29, 2015, https://bostonchildrensmuseum.wordpress.com/2015/09/29/borrowed-and-returned/.

CHAPTER FIVE

~

Defining the Inventory Deliverables

With support for the inventory project secured, it's time to get into the nitty-gritty of planning the work. This chapter continues the planning phase by identifying the project's deliverables. Deliverables are the tangible or intangible products or processes the project team must create to achieve the inventory's objectives. By centering deliverables, stakeholders establish consensus about what it means to have achieved the objectives at the end of the project.

What the inventory will ultimately deliver depends on many factors, including available time and resources. Indeed, two museums with identical inventory objectives may produce different deliverables or the same ones that look very different. Deliverables and their quality criteria must therefore also be defined. Planners can then sequence the deliverables in the order they will be completed to determine the inventory's activities, or the tasks that must be carried out to produce the deliverables. This informs the project's duration and required resources—information that is critical to the rest of the project planning process and may result in further changes to the deliverables.[1] In this chapter, the deliverables necessary for achieving Museum A's objectives, described in chapter 3, are identified, defined, and organized in a logical sequence in preparation for mapping out the various activities and resources needed to create them.

Identifying the Deliverables

After drafting initial inventory objectives and comparing them against SMART criteria, Museum A settled on three objectives: (a) to create digital access to 100 percent of the collection via retrospective registration, (b) to know exactly what is in the collection and where it is by inspecting each object and recording locations and essential identifying information in the database, and (c) to reconcile discrepancies between undocumented objects and records for which no object was found. This section lays out the deliverables necessary for achieving Museum A's objectives and offers definitions and quality criteria for each.

To begin identifying deliverables, planners can start by reviewing the objectives and jotting down a list of deliverables as they come to mind. To illustrate this process, the following are provisional deliverables for achieving Museum A's objectives:

1. Inventory procedures manual
2. Digital inventory data
3. Inventory-equipped database
4. Retrospective registration
5. Documentation problems list
6. Undocumented objects list
7. Missing objects list
8. Reconciled records
9. Reconciled objects
10. Final undocumented objects list
11. Lost-in-inventory list
12. Inventory list
13. Inventory summary report

While a given list may not be "wrong," taking a break from the list and returning to it later may reveal that in fact, some deliverables fall under the umbrella of another deliverable. For example, retrospective registration and the documentation problems list may be considered digital inventory data. Reconciled objects and reconciled records can be classified as reconciled discrepancies. The undocumented objects list and the missing objects list, which derive from digital inventory data, also pertain to reconciled discrepancies. And the final undocumented objects list and lost-in-inventory list are actually elements of a final inventory list. Thus, Museum A's revised provisional deliverables list may look like this:

1. Inventory procedures manual
2. Digital inventory data
3. Inventory-equipped database
4. Reconciled discrepancies
5. Inventory lists
6. Inventory summary report

Once the list feels complete, each deliverable may be defined, including the quality criteria each deliverable must meet to satisfy the objectives.[2] Taking time to define the deliverables is an essential step that will eliminate confusion among stakeholders about what the inventory will produce. It also helps ensure that each deliverable is achievable given available time and resources. For instance, the deliverable "digital inventory data" can mean a lot of things. If left undefined, staff may interpret the inventory as a full-on cataloging project, others may assume digital images will be included, while still others may arbitrarily decide which information to capture. The former could negatively affect the deliverable's achievability, while the latter might result in less useful data. Brainstorming to define deliverables with project stakeholders ensures everyone is working toward the same goal. The following sections provide definitions and quality criteria for Museum A's deliverables.

Inventory Procedures Manual

The inventory procedures manual is a document with step-by-step instructions for inventorying objects in the project scope so that all participants agree on how to produce inventory data (and other deliverables). It includes protocols for capturing inventory data and recording and reconciling documentation problems. It models records with inventory data captured to the desired standard as well as examples of anticipated documentation discrepancies and how to resolve them. It may also include instructions for capturing data in the database, running queries, and exporting reports. Brief descriptions of inventory team roles and responsibilities are also useful. Ideally, the manual is shared with colleagues for feedback, and procedures are tested to ensure clarity and logic. The manual is concise enough to be a quick reference guide over the life of the project and to expedite onboarding in the event of staff transitions.

Digital Inventory Data

Digital inventory data is the primary deliverable of any inventory. Often, the most accurate and efficient approach is to collect and enter the data directly into a database during the physical inspection of objects. The inventory dataset is a predetermined subset of cataloging information; the dataset must comprise the minimum information needed to account for objects in the collection yet still be achievable. An object's unique identifier and location are two pieces of information common to most museum inventory datasets. Datasets vary across institutions and usually include additional information such as a brief description, object name, item count, and condition. A key piece of data sometimes overlooked is an inventory record, or a logged inventory episode—data indicating that an object was inventoried and when. Useful digital inventory data meets the institution's standards for registering, cataloging, and inventorying collections. In some instances, the inventory may present the first substantive consideration of such standards, and their establishment may ultimately be a project deliverable. Chapter 6 provides a detailed discussion about determining the inventory dataset.

Museum A's objectives include registration for 100 percent of the collection; thus, digital inventory data includes creating database records for objects that lack them. This encompasses objects that are unregistered but clearly associated with accession or loan documentation as well as objects that lack any identifying numbers and/or documentation, known as undocumented objects,[3] which may be tracked with temporary numbers. These objects are registered according to professionally recognized standards and/or institutional procedures, and records feature agreed-on inventory data, as defined by the digital inventory data quality standards.

The documentation problems list, often in the form of a simple spreadsheet, is another type of digital inventory data. The list is used to queue and track the status of documentation issues encountered during the physical inspection of objects. Typically, issues recorded on the list impede capturing inventory data in the database—for example, objects that lack an identifying number or are numbered incorrectly, are unregistered in the database, or feature separate components that are undocumented, unregistered, or unnumbered. Ultimately, the list enables inventory data capture for the full scope of objects. It is also prerequisite to producing the reconciled discrepancies deliverable. After the inventory, the list serves as a record of problems encountered, reconciled, and unreconciled. The documentation problems list features an intuitive and simple layout. For example, it may feature columns for digital inventory data, a menu with standardized terms to describe the documentation problem, and a field for adding notes about it or logging updates and tracking the resolution status of problems. It may also include a menu for flagging issues that can be addressed later, such as incorrect images linked to database records or objects requiring physical numbering. Utilization of sharing platforms enables team members in different locations to update the list in real time simultaneously.

Inventory-Equipped Database

An inventory-equipped database is a computerized collections management system or other database configured to input, extract, and manipulate inventory data. Effective inventory-equipped databases have designated fields for each piece of inventory data. Check boxes, drop-down menus, and auto-populating fields may be employed to facilitate quick and standardized entry and to minimize errors. Users can also run queries and export lists from the database formatted with inventory data. Ideally, this data can be sorted by location, inventory date, recorder, object name, etc. User profiles can be created to ensure appropriate access and editing capabilities. An inventory-equipped database is also protected from loss or damage and backed up regularly to safeguard information. Along with digital inventory data, chapter 6 reviews inventory-equipped database functionalities, as these two deliverables are closely linked.

Reconciled Discrepancies

Reconciled discrepancies refers to object records and numbers that have been updated in response to resolved documentation problems encountered during and immediately following the physical inspection. Reconciliation is driven by issues on the documentation problems list, noted earlier as part of digital inventory data. It is also driven by inventory data captured or not captured in the database during inspection. For example, efforts must be made to reunite undocumented objects registered under temporary tracking numbers with legitimate records. Records that lack a logged inventory episode may represent objects that are missing, but these records might also be matched with undocumented objects, or the objects may have been overlooked. Inventory staff will attempt to reconcile these issues. Duplicate database records that have been merged, deactivated, or deleted and corrected object numbers are additional examples of reconciled discrepancies. Records and objects are reconciled following protocols established in the inventory procedures manual.

Inventory List

The inventory list is an itemized list or lists reflecting every located and unlocated object, including components, undocumented objects, and incoming and outgoing loans. The list may also feature records for dispersed and undispersed deaccessioned objects, which sometimes account for objects that appear unregistered or undocumented. It can be generated directly from the database, produced in searchable digital and printed paper formats, and formatted to display the inventory dataset and an object image if one is linked to the record.

This deliverable may also include sublists that are required for reports or that serve as references for ongoing reconciliation efforts beyond the official inventory timeline. For example, one sublist may isolate remaining undocumented objects. This list shows objects that remain dissociated from original documentation after all attempts to reconcile them have failed.

Another sublist may isolate unlocated objects. This represents all records for which objects were not found after reasonable measures have been taken to locate them or to match them with objects on the undocumented objects list.

All inventory lists are backed up according to digital preservation best practices. At least three copies of the printed list are maintained: two on-site and one off-site. The list may be printed in several sort orders (e.g., location, classification, or object number) to facilitate future reference.

Inventory Summary Report

The inventory summary report is a document that describes the inventory project by assessing its objective achievement, performance metrics, and outcomes. A comprehensive report summarizes the scope, deliverables achieved, staff, budget, vendors, acquired supplies and equipment, overall outcome, statistics, lessons learned, and other big-picture takeaways. The report can be produced in digital and printed formats and serves as a log of the institution's inventory activities.

Sequencing the Deliverables

After identifying and defining the inventory deliverables, a deliverables flowchart can be created. To create the flowchart, planners arrange the deliverables in a logical sequence that corresponds to the order in which they will be produced. The flowchart in table 5.1 shows the provisional sequence for Museum A, whose case was recapitulated earlier in this chapter, and discussed in detail in chapter 3. Each deliverable is boxed and connected with arrows that represent dependencies: the deliverable at the beginning of the arrow must be produced before the deliverable at the end of the arrow can be produced. The deliverables flowchart is an effective tool for revealing overlooked deliverables, omitting redundant or unnecessary ones, and optimizing efficiency. As such, there may be a few iterations before the optimal sequence is achieved.

Table 5.1. Museum A's Deliverables Flowchart

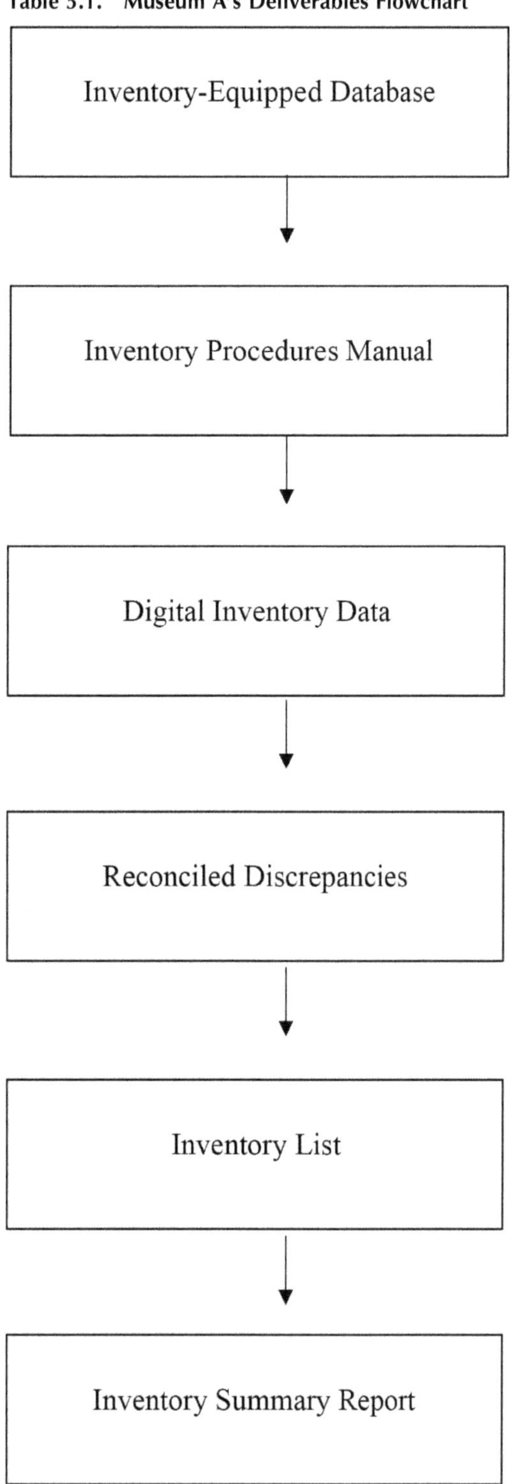

As a single uninterrupted chain, Museum A's flowchart is straightforward. But depending on several influencing factors, the flowchart may feature multiple branches that converge or diverge. For example, Museum A already has a collections database that functions well, but it would like some custom upgrades to increase data capture efficiency. These changes will influence instructions for recording inventory data in the procedures manual. As a result, the flowchart shows the manual as dependent on completion of the inventory-equipped database. In most inventories, a few minimal preparations are necessary to render a database inventory equipped, for example, updating the location hierarchy and drop-down menus or creating user profiles. If Museum A only needed to implement such minor changes, the deliverables flowchart would look a little different. "Inventory procedures manual" would not depend on "Inventory-equipped database." Instead, they would appear adjacent and unconnected, with their respective arrows both pointing to "Digital inventory data," which depends on the completion of both. Of course, the deliverables flowchart becomes increasingly complex when the project promises deliverables such as object photography or rehousing. With a clear understanding of how the approach works in a basic inventory, it will be easier to consider how additional deliverables can be integrated into the sequence.

During this exercise, it's easy to get sidetracked with observations that relate to a deliverable's activities. It's important to remember that *deliverables* are what must be produced by the end of the project to achieve the inventory objectives, while *activities* are everything project personnel must do, or the steps they must follow, to produce the deliverables. Planners may observe that some activities pertaining to a dependent deliverable can initiate before the predecessor deliverable is complete. For example, "reconciled discrepancies" can start during "digital inventory data." That is to say, as soon as issues are noted on the documentation problems list (part of "Digital inventory data"), project staff may begin reconciling straightforward discrepancies. But this doesn't change the order in which the deliverables will be completed: "Digital inventory data" must still be completed before "Reconciled discrepancies" can be completed. Ultimately, the deliverables flowchart is the scaffolding planners will build on to determine the inventory activities and timeline (and beyond that, the required resources). As such, observations about activities will come in handy later on. Before finalizing the deliverables flowchart, inventory planners may like to turn to chapter 6 to deepen understanding and consensus around the core project deliverable, digital inventory data, as well as the inventory-equipped database. Those who are comfortable with the deliverables flowcharts they've drafted may turn to chapter 7, which addresses the next step: planning activities and time. This chapter further illustrates the distinction and relationship between deliverables and activities.

Notes

1. Nick Graham, *Project Management for Dummies* (Chichester: John Wiley & Sons, 2015), 75.
2. Ibid., 85.
3. Rebecca A. Buck and Jean Allman Gilmore, *Collection Conundrums: Solving Collections Management Mysteries* (Washington, DC: American Association of Museums, 2017), 17.

CHAPTER SIX

Deliverables Spotlight: Inventory Data and Databases

Chapter 5 identified digital data as the main deliverable of any inventory project. To optimize the data's usefulness, museums establish minimum inventory datasets and agree on quality standards for producing the data. Inventory data also needs a place to go so that inventory personnel can access, input, and extract the data efficiently. In keeping with this, chapter 5 also identified an inventory-equipped database as a deliverable. A database that is inventory equipped is configured to efficiently manage data in a way that also satisfies quality standards. Consequently, inventory planners must consider how each element of the dataset might manifest in a given database. In addition to exploring these particulars, this chapter broadly overviews pros and cons of different types of database systems as well as database features that best facilitate effective data capture and retrieval. This discussion serves as a starting point for practitioners tasked with selecting or enhancing a database for inventory execution. For practitioners considering a barcode system to expedite inventory data capture, chapter 12 provides an in-depth discussion of relevant data and database considerations. Those preparing to inventory collections featuring digital objects may turn to chapter 13 for an overview of databases and digital preservation metadata.

Establishing the Minimum Inventory Dataset

During an inventory, a subset of cataloging information—here termed the minimum inventory dataset—is captured or confirmed in a database. Before initiating an inspection of objects, inventory planners must define the minimum dataset inventory takers will record for each object. The minimum dataset is aptly named: it must be achievable with respect to time and resource constraints while still capturing the minimum amount of information needed to account for objects.

Table 6.1 compares minimum inventory datasets used by several cultural heritage preservation authorities. If these datasets have been interpreted correctly, only two pieces of data appear as elements in every dataset: object number and object location. The content, care, and use of collections vary, which is one reason datasets across museums and even across subcollections at the same institution may differ. Dataset variations may also be tied to other activities—a conservation survey, for example—occurring in tandem with the inventory. An institution's strategic plan or collections care goals can also shape the dataset. For instance, if a collection relocation or rehousing is anticipated, dimensions may be an essential piece of data. Inventory datasets also evolve over time, which may be evidenced by past inventory protocols. Most likely, they will continue to evolve as an institution's records accuracy and depth improve, as professional standards change, and as museums become more attuned to the expectations of accountability and access asserted by the communities they serve or represent.

While all data in table 6.1 is fundamental collections information, the importance of sticking with the dataset decided on by project planners is worth mentioning. Presumably, planners select the most salient data for advancing collections care goals in their unique context at a given time. Sticking with the dataset also helps ensure the inventory is completed on time and on budget and that the agreed-on objectives are achieved. That said, expanding the dataset may be justifiable in some instances. For example, hard-to-access objects may ex-

Table 6.1. Comparison of Minimum Inventory Datasets

Data	*Smithsonian Institution*			*U.S. Department of the Interior*	
	Office of Policy and Analysis[1]	*Office of the Inspector General*[2]	*Spectrum 5.0*[3]	*Directive 21*[4]	*National Park Service*[5]
Object number					
Location					
Brief description			Or photo		
Object name/title					
Object found/not found					
Item count					
Inventory taker name					
Inventory date					
Condition					
Current owner and entry record if not your collection					
Dimensions					
Inventory method				Physical or transaction based*	
Record present/absent					
Catalog completion status					
Controlled property status**					
Accuracy of "other data"					

*A transaction-based inventory occurs if staff performed any transaction that involved physical inspection of that object anytime during the inventory cycle period.
**National Park Service classifies as controlled property incoming loans; museum firearms; type specimens; objects valued over $1,000; or objects especially vulnerable to theft, loss, and damage.

Sources adapted from:
1. Smithsonian Institution Office of Policy and Analysis Study Team, *Concern at the Core: Managing Smithsonian Collections Executive Summary* (Washington, DC: Smithsonian Office of Policy and Analysis, 2005), soar.si.edu/report/concern-core-managing-smithsonian-collections-executive-summary-april-2005, vi.
2. Cathy L. Helm, *Collections Management: The National Museum of African American History and Culture Needs to Enhance Inventory Controls Over Its Collections*, OIG-A-20-05 (Washington, DC: Office of the Inspector General, 2020), si.edu/oig/Audit_Reports, 8.
3. Collections Trust, "Spectrum 5.0 UK Collections Management Standard, Inventory—Suggested Procedure," 2017, accessed October 1, 2020, collectionstrust.org.uk/resource/inventory-suggested-procedure/.
4. U.S. Department of the Interior, *Inventory of Museum Collections*, DOI Museum Property Directive 21 (Washington, DC: Office of Acquisition and Property Management, 2014), doi.gov/sites/doi.gov/files/migrated/museum/policy/upload/Dir-21-Collection-Inventory.pdf, 5.
5. National Park Service, *Museum Handbook Part II: Museum Records* (Washington, DC: National Center for Cultural Resources, 2000), nps.gov/orgs/1345/cr-publications.htm, 4:1–4:17.

temporaneously merit a higher level of documentation given the effort required to physically inspect them. Leeway to veer from the agreed-upon dataset must be considered judiciously.

Establishing Data Quality Standards

Once the minimum inventory dataset is determined, a unified understanding of quality standards for generating and recording the data is critical to ensuring its usefulness. Useful data is accurate and consistent with agreed-upon quality criteria. It is also captured in dedicated fields in a database, enabling users to efficiently discover, retrieve, sort, and share it. Inventory planners may find that data quality standards are not in place or they need updating. Reviewing current practices will reveal adjustments to data quality standards that may be necessary.

Typically, standards for recording collections data are broken down into three categories: structure, value, and content.[1] Data *structure* standards—also known as data element sets or schemas—refer to a fixed list of information containers (i.e., database fields) that comprise a catalog record. The Dublin Core Metadata Element Set and Categories for the Description of Works of Art are two examples of data structure standards. During inventory, existing or planned schemas may need modification or expansion to ensure each piece of data has a dedicated field.

Data *value* standards refer to controlled vocabularies, thesauri, or sets of descriptive terms used to populate fields included in cataloging schemas. These standards ensure a unified understanding of terminology and help database users quickly find what they're looking for. Object name is one example of data that is typically standardized during inventory through the use of a controlled vocabulary. Variously named construction helmets, for instance, may be standardized to "hard hat."

Data *content* standards refer to syntax and format guidelines for populating fields that may or may not utilize a controlled vocabulary. For example, a museum preparing to inventory its tool collection may adjust its object description content standard to ensure that records include an explanation of the tools' function. Cataloging Cultural Objects (CCO) is one widely referenced data content standard.[2] The CCO and the Canadian Heritage Information Network (CHIN) are useful online resources for learning more about data standard typologies.[3]

Mobilizing an Inventory-Equipped Database

Equipping a database for inventory may mean selecting, developing, or modifying a system to receive and extract data. This involves scrutinizing how the dataset and quality criteria will manifest in the system. This section presents a broad overview of database types. Then quality standards for common dataset elements are discussed and correlated with database preparation considerations. This includes where to put data as well as how to promote efficient data capture, security, and preservation. A review of database functions for retrieving inventory data rounds out the discussion. Table 6.2 may serve as a preliminary checklist to keep in mind during the database selection process or during a scripted walkthrough of a database presented by a vendor.

Overview of Database Types

Museums already using a database for day-to-day collections management will generally benefit from using the same system for the inventory. In other situations, it may be up to the project manager to research and select a new database that will receive imported data or be used to document the collection digitally for the first time. In either scenario, the database may need modification for better or faster data entry. The project budget, scope, timeline, deliverables, IT support resources, user skills, collection size, and other databases currently in use will guide the selection. While researching options, it's helpful to understand the differences between various database types, such as flat file, relational, general purpose, purpose built, and open source.

Flat File versus Relational Databases

Flat file databases store information in a single table, more or less like a spreadsheet application does. While easy to use and economical, there are some cons associated with using flat file databases to capture and manage inventory data. Because all information is held in one table, data that is duplicated across many records—such as storage location—must be repeated in each record's location field. This requires more effort and increases risk of inconsistencies and errors. Some spreadsheet applications mitigate this drawback by supporting the creation of multiple tables that can be linked to fields in a main data entry table. For example, the database manager could create a table populated with the location authority, link it to the "location" column in the main data entry table, and add a drop-down menu to enable users to enter location data in a consistent format. Another downside to flat file databases is that they have limited querying power, so they may be satisfactory for inventorying only smaller collections of a few thousand objects or less. Because they are more accessible, a flat file database may be acceptable for museums that haven't yet acquired a dedicated collections management system. Capturing data directly in a readily available flat file database with the intention to migrate the data to a more robust system later could be the most feasible way forward in some scenarios.

Relational databases, such as The Museum System and PastPerfect, manage data more efficiently than flat file databases. "Instead of the entire record being stored on a single table, several tables contain fields that store unique field data occurrences (e.g., each occurrence is stored only once)."[4] The tables link, or relate, to each other through shared fields, such as a record number, name, or location. Any field in an object record using data already stored in the database references the field in the related table instead of storing the same data again,[5] which thus eliminates extensive data duplication.[6] Relational databases are preferred for large collections, as they are generally more efficient and can perform more complex query and reporting functions. Relational databases that are purpose-built collections management systems are typically more expensive. However, more affordable, general-purpose databases, such as FileMaker Pro, can also be built as effective relational databases for collections management.

The searchability of relational databases depends on well-defined data being entered consistently in dedi-

Table 6.2. Checklist for Preparing an Inventory-Equipped Database

Object number	• Can the database ensure that a unique object number be assigned to all object records? • Can the system prevent users from assigning the same number twice (i.e., creating duplicate records)? • Does the system support user-assigned object numbers? • Can the system archive previous or alternate object numbers? • Can the system support accession numbers in various formats? • Does the database support numbering parts of objects with letters (i.e., 2019.2.1a and 2019.2.1b) and objects that are parts of sets or portfolios with extending numbers (i.e., 2019.2.1.1 and 2019.2.1.2)? • Does the database feature an object component tracking function? • How are object numbers queried?
Location	• Are bulk location transactions supported? How? • Does the location tracking function employ a location hierarchy? Can it be edited and developed? • Does the location tracking function record an object's location, date of move, purpose of move, and mover's name? • Does the database archive past locations? • Can object components and objects that are parts of sets or portfolios be assigned separate storage locations? • Are options for move purpose customizable?
Brief description	• Can the object's description be entered in a designated field?
Object name	• Does the system feature free-text fields for entering object names? • Are there fields designated for former/obsolete names? • Are controlled vocabularies built into the system or can they be "plugged" in? • Can controlled vocabularies be edited and developed in the software?
Item count	• Is there a field for entering item count that is restricted to numerals?
Inventory record: object located/not located, inventory taker's name, inventory date	• Are bulk inventory transactions supported? How? • Can the database record the outcome of object inspection, including whether an object was located, the recorder's name, and the date? How? Can data such as date and recorder's name be standardized/selected from a drop-down menu? • Can this information be captured via a location transaction? • Can the database archive past inventory activities?
Condition	• Can the database accommodate designated fields, drop-down menus, or checkboxes for recording object condition and the date of observation?
Data entry screens	• Can data entry shortcut screens be configured to capture the dataset more efficiently?
Retrieving inventory data	• Can users query inventory-specific fields, such as location and inventoried/uninventoried records, with parameters such as date range? Can queries be run against any field? • Does the database support keyword/wildcard and word stem search for querying information on any field? • Can users build custom queries and report templates? • Can queries be exported to word processing and spreadsheet software? • Can query results be sorted and edited? • Can query results be printed?
Security controls	• Can profiles be created to restrict users' ability to read, edit, create, and delete information? • Does the database maintain an audit trail of all changes made?
Data backup plan	• What database features support storing, backing up, and recovering data?

cated fields; when performing a query, users generally have to select what fields they believe their data is in. This arrangement presumes that all users are familiar with the database's data, terms, and structure and that the database is populated perfectly with no errors. This improbable scenario means that searches may yield too many, too few, or unhelpful results. Thus, relational databases that support queries based on keyword and text, stemming, and wildcard searches allow for greater discovery.[7] Queries by keyword or text allow search engine–style searches, which is especially useful for searching free-text fields such as object description. Word stemming automatically strips the user's query term of punctuation, accent marks, and common prefixes and suffixes to search by the root of a word. Wildcard searches enable users to query an incomplete term or partial sequence of characters when the full sequence is unknown. These capabilities come into play often when inventory takers are attempting to identify objects with no number or partial numbers or to match an object with descriptive information.

General Purpose versus Purpose-Built Collections Management Database

General purpose relational databases—those not designed with collections management in mind—are an economical option that has worked well for many institutions. Microsoft Access and FileMaker Pro, for example, can usually be configured to meet inventory needs. In addition to accessibility, such databases can be built from the ground up with the collection's unique needs in mind. However, they come with a steep learning curve and require a significant time investment and a strong operational continuity plan. As with any database, resources and know-how will be required to maintain and develop them over time.[8]

On the other hand, purpose-built collections management systems are inherently configured with collections management functions and data standards options in mind. Developers typically offer training and technical support as well as assistance with data migration from old systems and regular software upgrades as part of a purchased package. These systems may also be enhanced through customization or via a menu of optional add-on functions. However, they can be cost prohibitive with significant fees for initial setup and annual service agreements based on the number of users, customizations, continued upgrades, and professional development trainings. As well, poorly executed data migrations may require years of work to clean up. While purpose-built systems generally require much less development than general-purpose ones, even users of the flashiest collections management systems may find that modification or even substantial development is required to prepare the database to meet an institution's inventory needs. In other words, it shouldn't be assumed that these systems are inventory equipped in their off-the-shelf state.

Purpose-built collections management databases can also be open source, meaning their source code is freely available to be used and modified by anyone.[9] CollectionSpace, CollectiveAccess, and Arches are a few open-source systems that have emerged in recent years. Open-source systems are appealing because they're free and highly customizable, and they promote collaboration and sharing. Software developments made or commissioned by one user are included in subsequent free upgrades that benefit all users. While the database itself is technically free, a museum needs in-house personnel with expertise to manage, maintain, and develop it. Otherwise, it will depend on contracting external vendors to fulfill these functions. Furthermore, if an open-source platform isn't widely adopted or falls out of favor, collaborators and service providers may vanish.

The number and variety of computerized collections databases has proliferated in recent years. This development is not unwelcomed, but it may make the task of procuring or developing a database feel overwhelming. Choosing a database requires extensive research and consideration of additional factors beyond functionality, such as collection type, long-term costs, platform, and support resources. Fortunately, resources for choosing and upgrading a database have also increased. Kozak's guide to selecting a collections management system offers additional considerations.[10] CHIN's more detailed Collections Management System Criteria Checklist includes extensive functionality descriptions, requirements to consider, numerous vendor profiles, database system descriptions, and user evaluations.[11] In recent years, CHIN also convened a collections management software task force in partnership with the American Association for State and Local History to support institutions navigating this process. Collections Trust, an organization that develops the international collections management standard known as Spectrum, also offers a tool for identifying systems that support Spectrum inventory procedures and other protocols.[12] To qualify as Spectrum compliant, software applications undergo a review to ensure they accommodate every piece of data needed to document collections according to the Spectrum standard.

Applying Quality Standards to the Dataset and Database

How do data quality standards apply to the inventory dataset, and how are they expressed in the database? Referencing table 6.1, this section reviews the most common pieces of inventory data: object number, location, brief description, object name, item count, inventory record, and condition. Quality standards and parallel considerations for preparing an inventory-equipped database ready to receive data are also considered. Although "standards" connotes prescriptive guidelines, the application of standards can vary from institution to institution based on resources, unique mandates of the collection, and needs of the community the museum serves. An institution may adopt existing standards to promote data quality or modify them or, in some cases, may develop its own.

Object Number
An object number is typically an accession or catalog number. It is a unique identifier that links an object to its record, distinguishes it from other objects, and enables effective information tracking. Data content standards require that object numbers be unique and not repeated with other objects, except in cases of lot registration when a group of similar objects is tracked with a single record number.[13] Effective systems for assigning object numbers are logical, standardized, and consistently applied. The so-called trinomial system is a widely used format incorporating three numbers that represent three pieces of information. In this system, the accession number 2017.1.2 represents an object that was accessioned in 2017, that is part of the first acquisition of 2017, and is the second object in the acquisition to be registered. Many institutions also structure numbering formats to indicate the status of an object, for example, whether an object is accessioned (e.g., 2017.1.2), on loan to the museum (e.g., L2017.1.2), or in temporary custody (e.g., T2017.1.2) while being considered for acquisition.[14]

In addition to shoring up these numbering protocols, inventory planners must establish standards for numbering objects that have been dissociated from their records. Encountering this material—often referred to as undocumented objects[15]—is a typical inventory occurrence. Implementing a temporary numbering protocol allows undocumented objects to be tracked until they're reunited with their legitimate or original record numbers. Temporary numbering systems often feature a prefix such as NN for "no number," X for "unknown," or T for "temporary." Sticking with the trinomial format, a temporary object number may be expressed as NN2017.0.3. This indicates that the object is undocumented, that it was encountered in 2017, that the acquisition source is unknown (indicated by the zero), and that it was the third undocumented object registered that year. Whatever the chosen format, prefixes must be unique to distinguish undocumented objects from other object categories. When prefixes are used, it's best to keep them short, use them judiciously, avoid using letters easily confused with numbers (e.g., I or O), and apply the system consistently.

Standards also guide toward adopting a numbering system that indicates relationships when separate parts comprise a whole object. Extending a numbering format to indicate that items are separate components of the same object helps signal and preserve this relationship. A teapot is a classic example of an object that may be made of more than one component: teapot and lid. Other part/whole relationships include pairs (e.g., shoes), sets (e.g., a tea service), or portfolios. Components of the same object or parts of a set may be stored in separate locations or have different conservation treatment and exhibition histories. Thus, an expandable numbering system that allows for individual tracking of separable parts is a critical inventory consideration. One approach to numbering multicomponent objects is to add a letter suffix: a pair of shoes or a teapot may be numbered 2017.1.2ab (teapot, 2017.1.2a, and lid, 2017.1.2b). For objects that are parts of sets or portfolios, a fourth number may append the trinomial: the number 2017.1.2.1-17 may represent prints 2017.1.2.1, 2017.1.2.2, etc., that comprise a portfolio of seventeen prints. For complex sets of objects, the four-part system and letter suffixes are sometimes used together to document each item in the set and separable parts that comprise each item. If a teapot is part of a tea service 2017.1.2.1-11, the teapot may be numbered 2017.1.2.1ab.

While objects are accounted for most effectively by registration at the item level, sometimes it makes sense to register a group of objects as a lot under one number. A box of potsherds from the same archaeological context and a bag of mixed dollhouse accessories are examples of objects that might be registered as lots, at least initially. As an example, 11.6.4 represents a lot of nails. If objects are eventually separated from the lot, the four-part numbering extension may also be used to track them. If five nails are separated from the lot for exhibition, they may be registered as "components" of the original lot record as 11.6.4.1-5. If five potsherds are separated from the lot because it is determined they comprise a separate vessel, this numbering format may also be used to register them as a distinct object, rather than as a component of a lot.

Many documentation systems reflect legacy numbering protocols. A question that often arises in connection with inventory is, should objects that were numbered differently than our current system be renumbered? Generally, the answer is no, unless a legacy number is incorrect or a duplicate. Renumbering is time consuming and creates numerous opportunities for mistakes, oversights, and confusion. It's more important for each object to have a unique identifying number than it is for objects to be perfectly registered following the same format.

While object numbering systems have been covered generally in the literature, they continue to be an aspect of inventory that can quickly disrupt momentum. Formalizing a content standard for object numbering prior to the inventory's execution phase will spare the team hours of debate about how numbers should be assigned. Once decisions have been made, drawing up a decision tree for deploying the numbering system can be a useful tool. Resources such as *Museum Registration*

Methods provide additional guidance for how to assign object numbers.[16]

In databases, object numbers are typically entered in designated free-text fields, which are populated when an object record is created. Inventory personnel may encounter objects marked with multiple numbers, a result of defunct registration systems or numbers assigned by previous owners. Ideally, the database schema also includes dedicated fields for entering these former or alternate numbers. Recording alternate numbers allows users to discover the object by querying a legacy number in addition to its current number. One caveat for database shoppers is that some systems don't restrict the creation of a record using the same number twice and some databases are designed to automatically assign record numbers.

One of the trickiest aspects of preparing an inventory-equipped database is determining how multicomponent objects can be tracked effectively. During inventory, personnel aim to account for each object component and part of a set. This is especially challenging when parts of the same object or set are stored or displayed in different locations. Several collections management systems facilitate tracking components or parts of sets by configuring the database to nest "child" records within a master, or "parent," record. The parent record features fields used to record information about the object as a whole. Nested child records feature fields for tracking information unique to the components, such as identifying number, location, and inventory record. However, many databases are deficient in component tracking features. One workaround is to create parent records for each component so that different locations can be recorded. Generally, this method is cumbersome and inefficient. However, it may be appropriate for multicomponent objects of high intrinsic value.

Depending on the overall collections documentation state, time, and resources, project managers may consider limiting the application of component registration protocols during inventory. Because registering components in a database can take a great deal of time, the most efficient approach may be to register them individually only when they are found in different locations. A point to consider is that even when components have been recorded faithfully in child records, the database configuration may increase the likelihood of overlooking them when recording an inventory episode, in query results, or in reports exported from the database.

The searchability of object number fields also merits scrutiny. Among the most significant time-saving features is the ability to perform bulk queries. This enables users to enter numerous, random object numbers in a query field and retrieve records in one transaction instead of querying them one by one. Unfortunately, many databases lack this feature, offer it only as a paid add-on, or lack an elegant expression of it. Another consideration is whether a database offers the option to include alternate and component number fields in object number queries. Wildcard and stemming-type queries are also important time-savers. For example, all undocumented objects may be queried and isolated using the designated prefix followed by the wildcard symbol (e.g., NN*), a partial accession number can be queried to locate its record, and queries of component numbers will retrieve the parent record.

Location

Object locations are typically recorded using a data content standard that reflects a standardized location naming system, also called a location authority or hierarchy. These systems define all spaces where objects may be encountered. Standardizing how locations are described, formatted, and punctuated ensures they are easily understood and recorded and reliably queried. Location hierarchies often feature levels of discrete locations that describe an object's location from general to specific (table 6.3). Effective location names are specific enough to enable staff to locate an object within a few minutes. In addition to describing where objects are, the hierarchy may include a "location" for objects whose

Table 6.3. Provisional Location Hierarchy

Level	*Discrete Location*				
1	Museum name, address			Off-site address	Lost in inventory
2	Storeroom A	Gallery 4	Conservation Lab	Room M12	
3	Row 3	Left Wall	Table 1	Crate 7	
4	Shelving Unit 1				
5	Shelf D				
6	Box 9				

whereabouts are unknown. A standardized term such as "lost in inventory" or "not located" can be added to the location hierarchy to designate the object's provisional missing status.

During inventory, physical locations are labeled using terminology that matches the location hierarchy exactly. Location naming systems can be supported by room-level diagrams that show locations and their names. This is especially useful for display areas, as it may not be realistic to physically label spaces with their location name.

While a correctly recorded location is most important, recording additional data when objects are moved is recommended as a security measure. This includes the date of the move, the person who moved the object, and the reason for moving it. The date format, names of movers, and reasons for moves (e.g., conservation, research, exhibition, or storage) are also standardized. Adding "inventory" to the list of reasons for moving an object is one way to indicate that objects were located during inventory. This type of location transaction can serve as the inventory record; the transaction is used to confirm an object's location rather than change it.

Inventory-equipped databases make it easy to account for objects, query objects by storage location, and print inventory lists. Before initiating object inspection in a particular area, the database must be populated with the relevant location names in the hierarchy. These are typically entered in databases via a function known as a location authority. Often, each level in the hierarchy has its own field with sublocations nested below it. For example, to enter a location, a building may be selected, followed by a room in the building, followed by a storage unit in the room, and so on. The date of the move can be configured to auto-populate, while fields corresponding to mover names and the reason for the move may feature drop-down menus. Ideally, the same location tracking features are available for parent records and child records used to track components.

One feature sometimes overlooked is whether the database has a system for archiving an object's location history, an important security measure. While location logs kept by hand in the past may have been inefficient, they inherently resulted in a retraceable location history. In an ill-equipped database, that information may disappear each time a new location transaction is recorded unless a system for archiving the information is in place. Many museum-specific systems automatically archive past locations as updates are made, while others don't. Working out a method for recording previous locations in the database is recommended, as objects may be moved more than once during the inventory or away from their "inventoried" location throughout the course of the project.

A final important feature to consider is whether the database supports bulk move transactions. For instance, some systems allow users to move entire storage containers and their contents or several items selected from search results in one transaction. As with some barcode systems, a bulk move feature may also express as the ability to scan numerous random object numbers to a selected location. Bulk move capabilities can shave days off a project where personnel would otherwise have to update locations record by record.

Brief Description

Conventional approaches to describing objects vary based on discipline and object type. But inventory descriptions don't always need to conform to expert standards in the absence of proficiency in a particular field. Most critical is that an object's description helps identify and distinguish it from other items in the collection. Data content standards for descriptions captured during the inventory may include describing any of the following characteristics:[17]

- Overall shape or form
- Function
- Manufacturing technique
- Material or material class
- Texture
- Color, using standard names
- Design details or motifs
- Marks, labels, and inscriptions
- Condition issues

Cheat sheets can provide prompts for describing objects consistently, such as from top to bottom or from exterior to interior. Inventory takers may also like to consult online museum or auction catalogs to utilize descriptive terms that are widely used and easily understood. It's worth reiterating that the minimum inventory dataset is a subset of cataloging data; full cataloging is rarely part of an inventory's scope. In the interest of keeping the inventory on schedule, content standards for object descriptions may underscore brevity.

In databases, object descriptions are generally entered in designated free-text fields. While the format for describing objects is freer than for other data, users must be able to query this information separately from other data.

Object Name

Inventories are an optimal time to record and update object names using standardized terms and formats. Ideally, object names are chosen according to a data value standard, which is rarely deviated from to ensure consistency and help database users quickly find what they are looking for. Because many words may accurately describe the same object, these standards suggest "preferred" terms to be used in place of "non-preferred" terms.[18] They also organize terms in hierarchies featuring names progressing from general to specific. This ensures a standardized name is used even if the inventory taker has general knowledge of an object.

Among the most well-known value standards for naming objects are the Getty Research Institute's *Art & Architecture Thesaurus Online* (AAT) and *The Revised Nomenclature for Museum Cataloging* ("Chenhall's," after the author of the original version). More recently, a U.S. and Canadian task force integrated Chenhall's with a formerly used Canadian nomenclature and a visual dictionary to produce *Nomenclature for Museum Cataloging*. The CHIN website is another resource that links to several discipline- and language-specific authorities for object names and other data.[19] While all these are open-source online resources, a factor to consider is that some are web dependent, while others are downloadable for use offline.

Different nomenclatures are best suited to different collection types. For example, Chenhall's is often favored for history collections, while the AAT is used heavily by institutions that contextualize objects as art. While adopting an existing nomenclature supports work that has already been done and accepted as standard by the museum community,[20] existing nomenclatures may be unsuitable for some collections. For one, the nomenclature may be culturally inaccurate. Some established nomenclatures are working to remedy this, while other collecting institutions are creating new vocabularies to classify and name collections with cultural accuracy. In other cases, established nomenclatures may need only minor adjustments to meet collections documentation needs.

Object names are typically entered in a dedicated free-text field in the database, which is populated after referencing the nomenclature. In some databases, the object name field can be linked to the nomenclature, allowing users to search for and select terms from a menu. Some databases have an additional field(s) for retaining obsolete terms used to name objects or for capturing the object name in the language of the maker. Many museums consider these important aspects of the objects' historiography. To ensure these terms are searchable, staff may wish to retain obsolete terminology in a field designated for alternate object names.

Item Count

At the most basic level, an aim of inventory is to know how many objects are in the collection. Capturing item count in database records is especially important when objects are registered as lots or sets. Database considerations for capturing item count are simple—a designated field restricted to numerals is required. However, the meaning of the term "item count" may cause confusion, so the content standard for this piece of data needs to be well defined and illustrated. For instance, will a set of prints be counted as separate items? Will a teapot with a lid be counted as one or two items? Consistency when assigning item counts is paramount. In addition to producing accurate collection totals, these numbers can influence collections care planning. For instance, while shoes may only ever be worn as a pair, staff may like to be alerted to two separate items when quantifying conservation work or insurance values.[21]

Inventory Episode Record: Object Located/Not Located, Inventory Taker Name, Inventory Date

Data describing the outcome of object inspection (i.e., whether an object was located, who performed the inspection, and when) comprise the record for an inventory episode. Capturing this information enables database users to confirm, track, measure, and easily generate reports about inventory activity. There are many methods for recording inventory episodes. Capturing the information with a location transaction in the database, described earlier, is one way. Another is to enter the information in a main cataloging table or a linked table designated for inventory documentation. The content standard for the inventory record will describe the chosen approach. Whether the object was found may be indicated with a checkbox or drop-down option, with drop-down or free-text fields for entering the name of the recorder, and a standardized field for the date.

When thinking about how the inventory record will be captured in the database, query and bulk transaction capabilities again come into play. Implementing a function for recording inventory in bulk for groups of objects, rather than record by record, enables data capture to proceed efficiently. A final consideration is how the database will archive inventory episodes and whether it can record subsequent inventories. Even the most sophisticated collections management systems may lack a feature for recording whether an object was found during inventory; development in this area may therefore be required.

Condition

While monitoring object condition is imperative, it can be challenging to distill condition observations into useful, brief data for inventory. Inventorying a heterogeneous collection exacerbates this challenge, as does the subjectivity and experience of the inventory takers. However, recording condition during inventory may catch an issue that would otherwise go unnoticed for decades, and observations recorded during inventory may very well be the only condition information ever captured for the vast majority of collections objects. Furthermore, the inventory itself may discover a condition issue, such as pest infestation, or cause an issue if damage occurs while handling. Working with conservation professionals to determine an effective condition documentation protocol is therefore worthwhile.

A straightforward approach for capturing condition data is to record brief observations of damage as part of the object description using standardized terminology or in a designated free-text condition field, accompanied by a date entry. At minimum, this creates baseline information for staff examining the object in the future. Another approach is to work with a conservator to define a condition rating system and to train inventory personnel in its application. A system may be as basic as "stable" or "unstable" to isolate objects that may not be handled without causing damage or that require immediate intervention. The U.S. Department of the Interior uses a "good, fair, poor" rating system, with each rating clearly defined.[22] Standard ratings may appear in a drop-down menu in a dedicated condition field along with a field featuring a menu of reasons for the rating and a date. Alternatively, a condition entry may be expressed as a checkbox-style

Textbox 6.1

RECORDING CONDITION DURING INVENTORY AT THE NATIONAL SEPTEMBER 11 MEMORIAL & MUSEUM

While preparing for the first comprehensive inventory at the 9/11 Memorial Museum, the project team decided it would capture baseline condition data for the collection. Prior to the inventory, collections were surveyed for condition on an as-needed basis, usually before being exhibited or loaned. The inventory represented the first attempt to record baseline condition information for the collection as a whole. Information about the level of dust present on a portion of the collection, produced by the building collapses at the World Trade Center and the Pentagon, would also be recorded. The Museum preserves visible dust on museum objects as an important visual aspect of their historical significance. Recording the level of dust present was important to collections staff for a few reasons. First, dust level influences how objects are safely handled, housed, and displayed, from the perspectives of preservation and health and safety. The dust level may also play a role in an object's interpretation or prioritization for conservation assessment and treatment. Finally, the quantity of dust present impacts testing procedures for dust-implicated objects. The Museum tests objects originating from the New York City and Washington, DC, crash sites for contaminants commonly found in dust produced by the collapsed buildings. Objects originating from the sites but displaying no visible dust may be cleaned prior to contaminant testing to mitigate occurrences of testing, cleaning, and retesting if contaminants are detected.

For the survey, two types of data were captured. The first was free-text descriptive information about an object's observed condition. The second was condition information captured using checkboxes and a rating system. For each object, in the database's main cataloging table, a checkbox was used to flag objects that "need conservation assessment." Inventory takers used discretion to determine when flagging an object for assessment was appropriate. If the assessment box was checked, the condition issue was described in the condition report table in a free-text condition description field. Following this, in the condition report table's object condition section, checkboxes were used to indicate whether objects were "stable," "moderately stable," or "unstable." In the handling section, checkboxes were used again to record whether objects were "safe to handle" or "unsafe to handle." A third set of checkboxes were used to describe objects originating from Ground Zero or the Pentagon as having "heavy dust," "light/medium dust," or "no dust." The combined use of checkboxes and free-text fields to record baseline condition data allowed staff to query and isolate object records for interpretation considerations as well as future assessment, testing, treatment, and rehousing initiatives.

menu of conservation terms describing damage; this prompts inventory takers to look for and check off specific condition indicators. This format can be a very effective planning tool for future conservation projects, as isolated condition issues can be queried and quantified.

Data Entry "Shortcut" Screens

Usually, elements of the inventory dataset are stored across several database tables. This means a lot of time may be spent clicking through screens to record the dataset for each object. Some databases allow users to design a data entry screen, or "shortcut" form. These forms feature the fields relevant to the inventory dataset in a single screen. As the form is filled, data in the corresponding tables is automatically populated. Especially for large collections, time saved by a data entry screen will likely justify adding this feature to the inventory-equipped database checklist.

Extracting Inventory Data

Throughout the inventory, the database will be used to capture as well as to extract data. Queries are used to retrieve and analyze information about individual objects or groups of objects. Effective querying relies on discrete data elements residing in purpose-built, searchable fields, as described in the data standards. Anticipating what type of information will be useful enables project planners to design queries that can be utilized from the very beginning of the project. Handy inventory queries include searches for all objects registered in the database, all objects in a particular location, objects inventoried, objects inventoried by date/date range, objects not inventoried or not located, objects with no location recorded, and random sample selection.

Often, queries must be exported as reports, whether for spot-checking data accuracy, reporting on inventory progress, or generating the inventory's final deliverables. While queries can be exported to spreadsheets, specially designed report templates can be considered to display, sort, and export query results in more useful formats. The inventory report template may feature a thumbnail image of the object and the inventory dataset organized in a logical, easy-to-read layout (figure 6.1). An added design feature would itemize components of parent records. Once designed, it's helpful to record in the inventory procedures manual exactly how queries are performed and exported as reports.

Security Controls

To protect collection data and confidential information, effective databases feature capabilities to guard against "unauthorized changes or deletion, accidental or intentional."[23] One security feature is the ability to create database user profiles linked to log-on credentials; the profiles define which data a user has permission to read, edit, create, and delete. Preparing an inventory-equipped database includes considering which fields and functions inventory personnel will be authorized to access and designing or assigning user profiles accordingly. Restricting editing permissions to the inventory dataset has the added benefit of keeping data capture focused. A second important security feature is an audit trail, which records and enables authorized users to review changes made to a record, who made them, and when.

Data Backup Plan

The database used for the inventory should be configured so that data is backed up in alignment with the institution's digital stewardship plan. Backup schedules differ between institutions and may be based on the frequency of changes made in the system. For an inventory, when large amounts of data are captured and changed, a daily backup is recommended. In addition to regular backups, the National Digital Stewardship Alliance

Object Number	Object Name	Description	Inventory 2022	Date Inventoried	Entered By	Object Image	Storage Location
1983.170.1	Hard Hat	Hard hat featuring an American flag emblem applied with blue, red and silver metallic paint.	Located	January 24 2022	Joshua Chavez		Site → Museum → Storage Room 1 → Unit 4 → Shelf C → Box-338
1994.207.1	Hard Hat	Blue plastic hard hat, size medium. Manufactured by All Safe Company.	Located	March 28 2022	Joshua Chavez	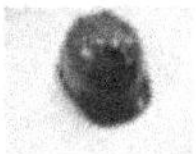	Site → Museum → Storage Room 1 → Unit 5 → Shelf C → Box-98

Figure 6.1. Provisional Inventory Report Template Generated by the CollectiveAccess Database. BETHANY ROMANOWSKI

recommends storing a minimum of two complete copies of data that are not colocated.[24] The institution's IT personnel and the database developer may collaborate on data backup protocols.

While there's a lot to consider, consensus around the two core deliverables of digital inventory data and the inventory-equipped database underpins an effective inventory plan. This decision-making process must acknowledge both the needs expressed in the project objectives and available resources and time. As such, what it means to produce digital inventory data and an inventory-equipped database may undergo revision throughout the project scope planning process. To this end, the next chapter addresses how to identify the activities required to produce each deliverable and how to estimate their durations. This culminates in a provisional inventory timeline that will further determine resource needs and give planners a sense of whether the deliverables or their quality criteria must be adjusted.

Notes

1. Anne J. Gilliland, "Setting the Stage," in *Introduction to Metadata*, 3rd ed., Murtha Baca (Los Angeles: Getty Publications, 2016), http://www.getty.edu/publications/intrometadata/setting-the-stage/.
2. Murtha Baca et al., eds., "Cataloging Cultural Objects: A Guide to Describing Cultural Works and Their Images," Visual Resources Association, accessed January 3, 2021, http://vraweb.org/wp-content/uploads/2018/08/CatalogingCulturalObjectsFull.pdf.
3. Canadian Heritage Information Network, Government of Canada, "Collections Documentation Standards," accessed January 3, 2021, https://www.canada.ca/en/heritage-information-network/services/collections-documentation-standards.html.
4. Susan Fishman-Armstrong, "Incorporation of Barcode Capabilities to Existing Museum Databases," Master's thesis (Texas Tech University, 2000), accessed February 2, 2020, https://ttu-ir.tdl.org/bitstream/handle/2346/13041/31295015930455.pdf?sequence=1, 15–17.
5. Ibid.
6. Suzanne Quigley, updated and expanded by Perian Sully, "Computerized Systems," in *Museum Registration Methods*, 5th ed., ed. Rebecca A. Buck and Jean Allman Gilmore (Washington, DC: AAM Press, 2010), 161.
7. Emily Nedell Tuck, "CCO as a Metadata Standard for the Retrieval of Museum Cataloging Records: A Critical Review," Museum of Fine Arts Houston, 2014, accessed January 3, 2021, https://www.academia.edu/5685687/CCO_as_a_Metadata_Standard_for_the_Retrieval_of_Museum_Cataloging_Records_A_Critical_Review_Dec_2009?auto=download.
8. Quigley and Sully, "Computerized Systems," 164.
9. opensource.com, "What Is Open Source?" accessed January 3, 2021, https://opensource.com/resources/what-open-source.
10. Zenobia Kozak, "How Do We Select a Collections Management System?" History Associates, accessed January 3, 2021, https://www.historyassociates.com/wp-content/uploads/2020/02/ARTICLE-How-Do-We-Select-a-Collections-Management-System.pdf.
11. Julie Kemper, "AASLH Announces Collections Management Software Task Force," American Association of State and Local History, accessed January 3, 2021, https://aaslh.org/cms-task-force/.
12. Collections Trust, "Choose Collections Software," accessed January 3, 2021, https://collectionstrust.org.uk/software/.
13. Collections Trust, "Guidance on Bulk Accessioning," accessed January 3, 2021, https://collectionstrust.org.uk/wp-content/uploads/2018/11/Guidance-on-bulk-accessioning-2019.pdf.
14. Collections Trust, "Cataloging," Spectrum 5.0, accessed January 3, 2021, https://326gtd123dbk1xdkdm489u1q-wpengine.netdna-ssl.com/wp-content/uploads/2017/11/Cataloguing.pdf.
15. Rebecca A. Buck and Jean Allman Gilmore, *Collection Conundrums: Solving Collections Management Mysteries* (Washington, DC: American Association of Museums, 2017), 17.
16. John E. Simmons and Toni M. Kiser, "Numbering," in *Museum Registration Methods*, 6th ed., ed. John E. Simmons and Toni M. Kiser (London: Rowman & Littlefield, 2020), 216–19.
17. National Park Service, "Appendix C: Cataloging Guidelines," *NPS Museum Handbook*, Part II, accessed January 3, 2021, https://www.nps.gov/museum/publications/MHII/mh2appc.pdf.
18. Quigley and Sully, "Computerized Systems," 173.
19. Canadian Heritage Information Network, "Vocabulary (Data Value Standards)," accessed January 3, 2021, https://www.canada.ca/en/heritage-information-network/services/collections-documentation-standards/chin-guide-museum-standards/vocabulary-data-value.html.
20. Quigley and Sully, "Computerized Systems," 174.
21. Gallery Systems, "Bridging the Object/Component Divide," accessed January 7, 2021, https://www.gallerysystems.com/bridging-the-object-component-divide/.
22. U.S. Department of the Interior, *Cataloging Museum Collections*, DOI Museum Property Directive 20 (Washington, DC: Office of Acquisition and Property Management, 2016), www.doi.gov/museum/policy/Museum-Directives, 4.
23. Suzanne Quigley, updated and expanded by Christina Linclau, "Computer Systems and Data Management," in *Museum Registration Methods*, 6th ed., ed. John E. Simmons and Toni M. Kiser (Lanham, MD: Rowman & Littlefield, 2020), 191.
24. National Digital Stewardship Alliance, "Levels of Digital Preservation," accessed January 3, 2021, https://ndsa.org//activities/levels-of-digital-preservation/.

CHAPTER SEVEN

Planning the Activities and Timelines

This chapter continues to reference basic project management theory to facilitate planning an inventory scope document, using Museum A's case to illustrate the process. Previously, Museum A developed inventory objectives, which the staff then used to identify project deliverables. The deliverables were ordered logically to produce a deliverables flowchart. This chapter builds on the flowchart to produce an inventory project activity network. An activity network is a diagram that maps out the tasks required to produce each deliverable, shows the order of their completion, and determines how long the inventory will take.[1] In this sense, it provides a bird's-eye view of the entire project.

To create the inventory activity network, planners determine, sequence, and estimate durations for the activities required to produce each deliverable. The activity sequences for all deliverables are then integrated based on the dependent relationships between them, and activity duration estimates are used to estimate the length of the entire inventory. At this juncture, planners with existing time targets can immediately discern whether the project scope's deliverables and/or activities are reasonable or must be scaled back to align with expected or preferred time constraints. The activity network calculations help determine exactly where the project must or can be adjusted in order to meaningfully reduce the project length. Planners can also see where activity sequences can be manipulated to make more efficient use of time, which increases resource efficiency in the long run. Finally, the network also eliminates some guesswork by revealing how long an activity can be delayed or prolonged without delaying the entire project.

For those who like charts and systems as a way of organizing and visualizing work, the activity network is a particularly worthwhile planning tool that can be used throughout the inventory project. Admittedly a little tricky at times, its usefulness makes it well worth the time it takes to create it. Ultimately, it functions as a north star that also lends peace of mind and confidence to planners gearing up to execute an inventory for the first or tenth time, for those asked to validate their project plans, or for those responding to inevitable unforeseen changes.

Identifying Activities to Produce Each Deliverable

To create an activity network, the first step is to brainstorm the activities necessary for producing each inventory deliverable. Referencing Museum A's deliverables flowchart developed in chapter 5, table 7.1 integrates the required activities. Because activity networks read from left to right, the diagram is placed on its side, resulting in an early framework for the activity network.[2] It can be tempting to list activities on a granular level, which may result in a very long list. Taking a break and returning to the list later may reveal that some activities or even deliverables are actually subtasks of a greater activity or subproducts of another deliverable. While important to note, many subtasks don't need to be listed here; the goal is to include a level of detail adequate for the planning and visualizing process. Further observations about the level of detail necessary and the relationships between activities and deliverables will naturally result in tweaks throughout the activity network building process.

Table 7.1. Museum A's Inventory Activities Integrated with the Provisional Deliverables Flowchart

Inventory-equipped Database (DB)	→	Inventory Procedures Manual	→	Digital Inventory Data	→	Reconciled Discrepancies	→	Inventory List	→	Inventory Summary Report
Identify dataset, queries, reports needed Identify DB changes needed Engage DB developer Implement DB backup plan Await changes Test changes Create user profiles Update location authority Design queries Design reports		Draft procedures for inspecting objects & capturing data in DB Draft procedures for logging documentation problems Draft procedures for reconciling discrepancies Test & update inventory procedures		Train staff Register known unregistered records Inspect objects & capture data in DB Log documentation problems Register unregistered & undocumented objects encountered Tag undocumented objects with temporary numbers Audit data		Generate missing objects report from DB Generate undocumented objects report from DB Reconcile missing & undocumented objects Resolve other discrepancies on documentation problems list		Generate inventory list(s) from DB Archive inventory list		Assess objective achievement, performance metrics, outcomes Write report

Sequencing the Activities

The next step in building the activity network is to sequence the activities required to produce each deliverable. Sequencing the activities is like sequencing the deliverables, where dependent relationships informed the order in which they will be produced.[3] Now, dependencies between each deliverable's activities are considered: within each deliverable box, the relevant activities are also boxed and connected with arrows, which indicate a dependency and help determine a logical and efficient activity sequence.[4]

Three types of activity dependency relationships are used in Museum A's case. The finish-to-start dependency, represented with straight arrows as in the deliverables flowchart, is most common.[5] It indicates that the activity at the beginning of the arrow must finish before the activity at the end of the arrow can start (table 7.2). If two arrows point to an activity, both preceding activities must finish before the dependent activity can begin. Likewise, if arrows extend from a predecessor activity to multiple successor activities, the latter can't start until the former is finished.

The second type of dependency used is start-to-start, which indicates that as soon as the activity at the beginning of the arrow gets started, the activity at the end of the arrow can begin. Start-to-start dependencies are expressed with a two-legged arrow bent at a ninety-degree angle; the vertical leg extends from the bottom left corner of the predecessor activity box and bends to terminate at the center left side of the dependent activity box (table 7.3).

With a lead-time dependency, the third type used here, the activity at the end of the arrow can start only after the activity at the beginning of the arrow has been going for some time. Lead-time dependencies are also visualized with an arrow bent at a ninety-degree angle, but the vertical leg extends from the bottom center of the predecessor activity (table 7.3). The amount of lead time, five days in this example, is noted above the horizontal leg.

While there are a couple of other dependency relationships readily found in the project management literature, the following section illustrates the use of these three dependencies in the context of sequencing the activities for producing Museum A's inventory deliverables. Activity dependency decisions and the resulting sequences may be influenced by several factors, including logic, best practice, requirements, preference, and staff resources. In connection with this, a few assumptions about Museum A's project staff must be made. The institution has a full-time registrar, collections manager, and IT professional, and it intends to hire two temporary full-time inventory technicians.

Inventory-Equipped Database

All the activity dependencies for producing the inventory-equipped database are finish-to-start (table 7.2). Museum A already has a collections management system in place that will be used to record inventory data; however, the exact information to be recorded and where it will be entered hasn't been determined. To begin, the registrar and collections manager, with input from other stakeholders, will define the minimum inventory dataset and identify the queries and reports needed to input, extract, and manipulate the data. To ensure the database is ready to receive data, they will then analyze the system to assess whether there are sufficient dedicated fields for recording data or more efficient ways of capturing information are needed. From this, a list of desired system updates will be generated.

With assistance from IT, Museum A is now ready to hire a database developer and initiate a dialogue about how and whether desired updates to the collections management system can be achieved, expected turnaround times, costs, and budget. With the developer on board, the registrar will send the change requests and await their completion. That the team will have to wait for changes to be implemented is obvious; however, including it as an activity emphasizes that waiting on vendors can be a time-consuming aspect of preparing the database.

While awaiting database changes, IT will have time to perform any associated system updates to back up the database at appropriate intervals given the high volume of data entry that will occur during the project. When database changes are complete, the developer, IT, and the registrar will test the changes, and IT and the registrar will test the backup system.

Next, the collections manager will create user profiles that provide appropriate database access to the project team. The manager will then confirm that discrete locations for storing, preparing, treating, staging, and displaying collections have a corresponding entry in the database. Meanwhile, the registrar will design necessary queries and reports, and the inventory-equipped database activity sequence will be complete.

Inventory Procedures Manual

As shown in table 7.4, the activity sequence for producing the inventory procedures manual is also straightforward, and all the dependencies are also finish-to-start.

Table 7.2. Museum A's Inventory-Equipped Database Activity Sequence

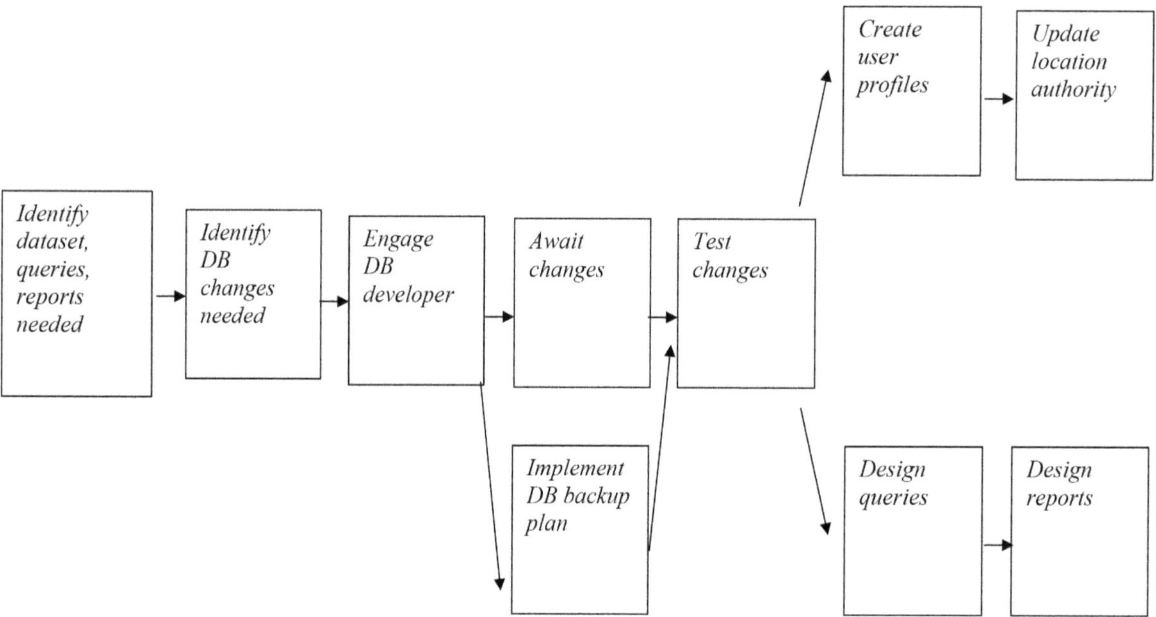

(For now, the gray arrows extending from activities in "inventory-equipped database" to activities in "inventory procedures manual" can be ignored—they'll be discussed later in the chapter.) Now, someone can begin drafting procedures for inspecting objects and capturing data in the database, logging documentation problems, and resolving documentation discrepancies. Procedures will be tested by inventorying a few objects in different parts of the collection, and any necessary updates to the procedures will be made.

Digital Inventory Data

To produce digital inventory data, the registrar and collections manager will train the inventory technicians to use the database and execute inventory procedures. Staff will also be trained to handle objects in accordance with institutional policy and health and safety guidelines.

While formulating their objectives, Museum A identified a substantial group of accession records known to be unregistered in the database. After training, the registrar, collections manager, and technicians will crash "register known unregistered records"; that is, all staff resources will be directed to retrospective registration of records in the database as a way of completing this activity as efficiently as possible. After this activity, the registrar will update the technicians' and collections manager's database user profiles to preclude new records registration, which will be relegated to the registrar for the rest of the project. By performing retrospective registration first, the technicians can inventory the objects as soon as they're encountered during physical inspection instead of logging them as unregistered on the documentation problems list and awaiting registration.

With this task complete, the technicians will begin physically inspecting objects to capture inventory data directly in the database. As soon as data capture begins, the technicians will also start logging any documentation problems they encounter, shown with a start-to-start dependency arrow (table 7.3). On the documentation problems list, they'll record numbering discrepancies, any additional unregistered objects, and undocumented objects encountered that impede inventory data capture in the database. Some discrepancies may be addressed immediately, while trickier problems remain on the list for later review. As soon as unregistered and undocumented objects are noted, the registrar can create database records for them to allow the technicians to circle back and record inventory data. As well, as undocumented objects are registered under numbers that denote their dissociated status, they can be tagged with temporary tracking numbers. All these activities are likewise shown with start-to-start dependencies in table 7.3.

This sequence, like other deliverables' activity sequences, may be different even if the context is the same. For example, as an alternative, if Museum A anticipates a very high number of undocumented objects but suspects that legitimate numbers for them can be found, undocumented objects may be addressed a little differently. This is because registering a lot of objects under temporary numbers represents significant extra work if the objects are likely to be reconciled with legitimate

Table 7.3. Museum A's Digital Inventory Data Activity Sequence

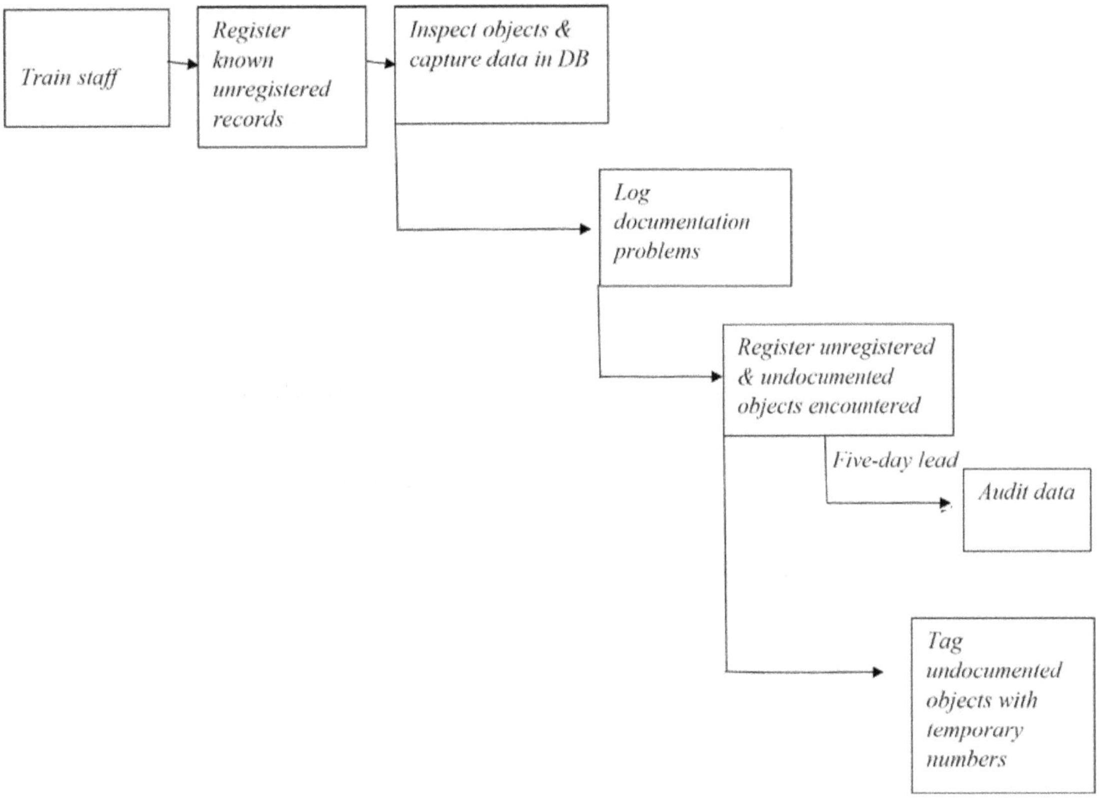

Train staff → *Register known unregistered records* → *Inspect objects & capture data in DB*

→ *Log documentation problems*

→ *Register unregistered & undocumented objects encountered*

Five-day lead → *Audit data*

→ *Tag undocumented objects with temporary numbers*

records. As well, many databases lack an elegant record merging function, which can complicate records reconciliation when duplicate records for the same object exist (i.e., one registered under the legitimate number and another under the temporary number). In this case, rather than registering undocumented objects under temporary numbers, once all objects have been inspected, the documentation problems list can be sorted to group all undocumented objects together. The undocumented objects can then be reconciled with items on the missing objects list. Once this is complete, inventory data can be captured in the legitimate records and the objects reconciled. At this juncture, remaining undocumented objects can be registered in the database under a temporary tracking number. While this sequence may prove more efficient in some scenarios, a pitfall to this approach is that critical collections data is decentralized. There are two data repositories: the database and the documentation problems list used to track undocumented objects. If the project is waylaid or there are staff changes, the list may be misplaced, forgotten, or deprioritized, and the undocumented objects will be absent from the database. Aside from each approach's pros and cons, that this alternate sequencing can just as easily be represented in an activity network shows its flexibility as a planning tool.

Returning to table 7.3, after data capture and its related start-to-start activities have been underway for some time, the registrar and collections manager will begin auditing the data to ensure it is captured to the agreed-on standard. This activity is shown with a lead-time dependency arrow and a lead time of five days. It's reasonable to audit the data early to discern where additional training or feedback would be beneficial; once the team is in the groove, auditing can occur less frequently.

Reconciled Discrepancies

After all objects have been inspected and the data collected, the registrar and a technician can query all database records that lack an inventory episode and export results into a missing objects report. Similarly, an undocumented objects list can be generated by querying the database for objects tracked with temporary numbers and exporting the results into a report. The registrar and technicians will then compare the missing objects list to the undocumented objects list to see whether any matches can be made. Reconciling missing and undocumented objects includes updating records for matched objects, perhaps deleting duplicate records, and tagging objects with correct numbers. The team will further research objects that remain unmatched with records in a final attempt to unite them with documentation. They will likewise search for any remaining missing objects one final time before recording unlocated objects as "lost in inventory" in the database. All these activities are shown with finish-to-start dependency arrows (table 7.4).

Meanwhile, the collections manager and the other technician will review the documentation problems list to resolve other discrepancies that at least, initially, do not derive from a missing or undocumented status; this activity, of course, depends on the previous deliverable being finished but not on the other activities in the "reconciled discrepancies" sequence. Resolving other discrepancies means annotating the documentation problems list and/or updating database records to reflect the outcome—whether reconciled or unreconciled after reasonable efforts—and tagging reconciled objects with correct numbers.

Inventory List

The inventory list(s) is created by querying the database and exporting a report that includes every located and lost-in-inventory object, including components, undocumented objects, and incoming and outgoing loans along with the inventory dataset where present. The list may also feature records for dispersed and undispersed deaccessioned objects. Once the list is created, multiple copies will be archived in digital and paper formats (table 7.4).

Inventory Summary Report

To produce the inventory summary report, the registrar and collections manager will assess to what extent inventory objectives were achieved, performance metrics, and outcomes. The summary report will then be written, submitted, and archived for future reference (table 7.4).

Identifying Activity Dependencies across Dependent Deliverables

In building the activity network, so far, each deliverable has been treated independently in terms of its activity dependencies. For the inventory execution to reflect this, a museum would initiate the activities of a dependent deliverable only after all activities of its predecessor deliverable were complete. In reality, certain activities in a dependent deliverable may often occur in tandem with an activity in a predecessor deliverable. Or, an activity of a dependent deliverable absolutely cannot proceed until a particular activity within its predecessor deliverable is complete. To visualize this interconnectedness, planners will now consider activity dependencies between one deliverable and any dependent deliverables directly connected to it with an arrow (table 7.4). Museum A benefits from integrating the activity sequences in this way. For one, a roadmap emerges to show how the inventory will play out with logistic accuracy. Two, the process brings into focus where time and resources could be used more efficiently. A third benefit is that planners will be able to approximate the length of the entire project timeline.

Starting at the beginning of the network, each deliverable's activities are considered in relation to the activities of any dependent deliverables—those to which they are directly connected with an arrow. For example, the deliverables sequence says that the "inventory-equipped database" must finish before the "inventory procedures manual" can start (table 7.1). However, Museum A discerns that some activities in "inventory procedures manual" can begin after some activities in "inventory-equipped database" are finished or underway. For example, once activities up to "engage DB developer" are complete, the collections manager has enough information and time while awaiting changes to start drafting the inventory procedures manual. At the same time, the registrar can work with IT to implement the database backup plan. Thus, table 7.4 shows a dependency arrow extending from "engage DB developer" to "draft procedures for inspecting objects and capturing data." Because "inventory-equipped database" activities really must be complete before the project team can "test and update inventory procedures," it follows that an arrow extends from the last activities in "inventory-equipped database" to the last activity of "inventory procedures manual."

Sticking to the deliverable arrow pathways, activity dependencies from one deliverable to the next dependent deliverable are straightforward until "log documentation problems" within "digital inventory data." One start-to-start dependency arrow extends from this activity all the way to "resolve other discrepancies on documentation problems list" within the dependent deliverable "reconciled discrepancies." Staff can start this activity as soon as they start logging documentation problems, but the activity can't be completed until after all the digital inventory data has been collected and documentation problems logged.

While identifying activity dependencies across deliverables connected with an arrow, planners may realize previously overlooked dependencies or may discern that some activities fall under the umbrella of another deliverable. This may require further adjustments to the deliverables list, activities, and/or sequences to achieve the most efficient and logical plan. This often streamlines, rather than complicates, the network.

Once all dependencies are penciled in, the original deliverables flowchart—the deliverables boxes and their dependency arrows—essentially recede, leaving planners with the activity network that serves as the project road map. Table 7.5 shows Museum A's resulting activity network. The next section discusses how to use the network to calculate the length of the inventory project, one of the most valuable aspects of the diagram.

Estimating Activity Durations

With the sequencing of each deliverable's activities and the dependencies between them established, planners are now ready to add time estimates to each activity to show how long it will take to produce each deliverable. In turn, this will inform the entire project's duration—the true power of the activity network.

To accomplish this, planners must have informed ideas about how long it will take to complete each inventory activity. Developing these estimates, however, is one of the trickiest aspects of planning an inventory. Inexperience, a lack of precedence to refer to, little knowledge about the documentation status of the collection, or external dependencies—such as relying on a database developer to implement upgrades—increase the degree of uncertainty about time estimates. Although estimating the duration of an inventory isn't easy, there are a number of things to consider to encourage realistic estimates. These include the following:

- How much work effort it takes to do an activity
- Staff availability to do it
- The experience and expertise of the staff
- Whether more than one person can work simultaneously on the activity
- Available resources such as space, supplies, and equipment needed to carry out the activity[6]

Planners may also consider incorporating a certain percentage of contingency time into durations to offset delays due to staff turnover, resource unavailability, staff leave, or unforeseen setbacks.

Literature for estimating inventory durations is scarce. After all, the circumstances of every inventory are unique. Still, some have tried to produce useful data around inventory work rates. For example, in 2001, Willpower Information Management Consultants surveyed museums in the United States, the United Kingdom, and Australia.[7] They asked, among other things, how long it took to catalog objects at the inventory level per person, per day. A day was assumed to be six hours of work dedicated to cataloging activity. For objects that had preexisting records, eight respondents reported a typical daily rate ranging from 20 to 1,000 objects. However, 1,000 was exceptional; the highest typical rate among the other seven respondents was 250. Two respondents reported inventorying 30 and 165 objects per day, respectively, if creating a new database record was required. Several uncontrolled factors influenced these rates, including whether they carried out supplementary activities such as photography. While efforts to quantify the time it takes to inventory objects is appreciated and perhaps interesting to compare to one's own projections, the wide-ranging result of this survey limits its usefulness for estimating inventory activity durations. On the other hand, it emphasizes that myriad variables and activities making up any given inventory project result in widely variable durations.

An effective way to estimate inventory activity durations is to reference the museum's previous inventory projects. If records from past inventories exist, paging through old files and talking with staff can yield helpful information; estimates for the inventory's duration can be extrapolated and adjusted for the current project's variables. Conferring with colleagues who manage similar collections about their inventory experiences can also provide insight.

Though not feasible for every activity, the most realistic projections are based on trial inventory runs that include the project's activities carried out with resources expected to be on hand. For the most accurate estimates, different parts of the collection are inventoried for a few hours. Practicing the inventory will reveal how long it takes to inventory loose works on paper, compared to rolled textiles, compared to objects on open shelving. Multiplying the time it takes to inventory a single rolled textile by the number of rolled textiles in the collection will provide a rough sense of how much time will be needed to inventory the entire collection of rolled textiles, and so forth. For a more or less homogeneous collection stored in a standardized way, another approach is to track how long it takes to inventory objects located on a particular shelf. That time can be multiplied by the number of shelves. This method can also be used to roughly estimate how long it will take to inventory undocumented collections where the contents and number of objects is unknown or create database records for objects that lack them.

Known time constraints, such as a scheduled collection move or a grant deadline, may place limits on

Table 7.4. Museum A's Activity Dependencies across Dependent Deliverables

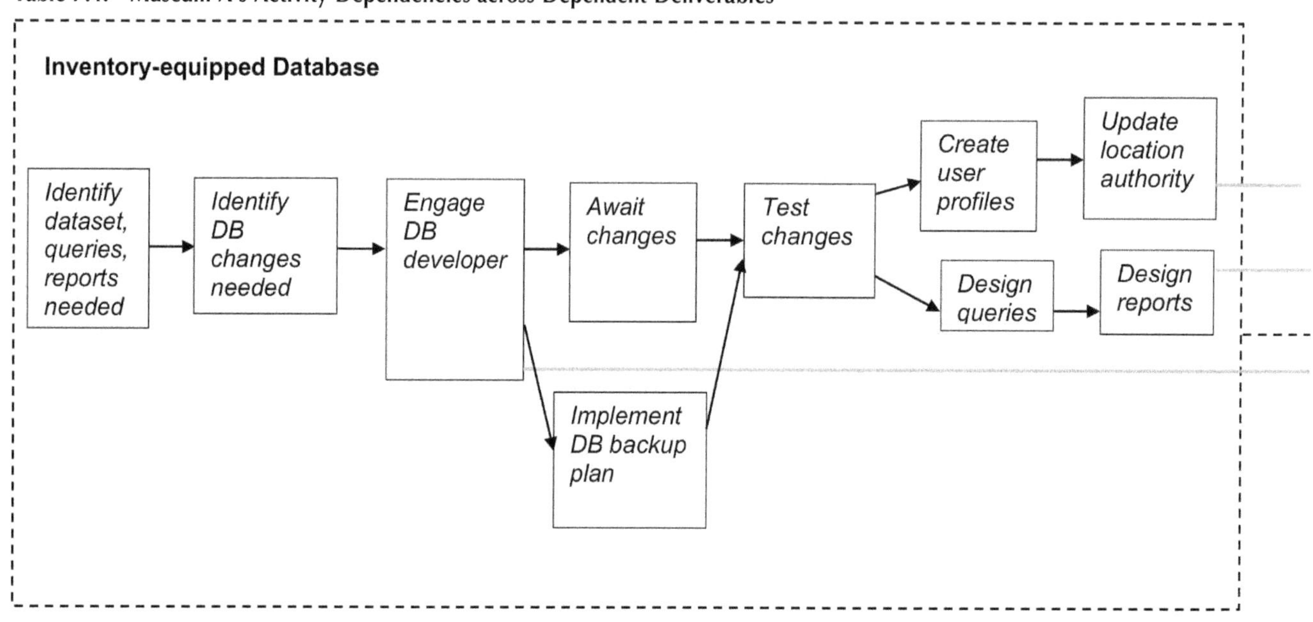

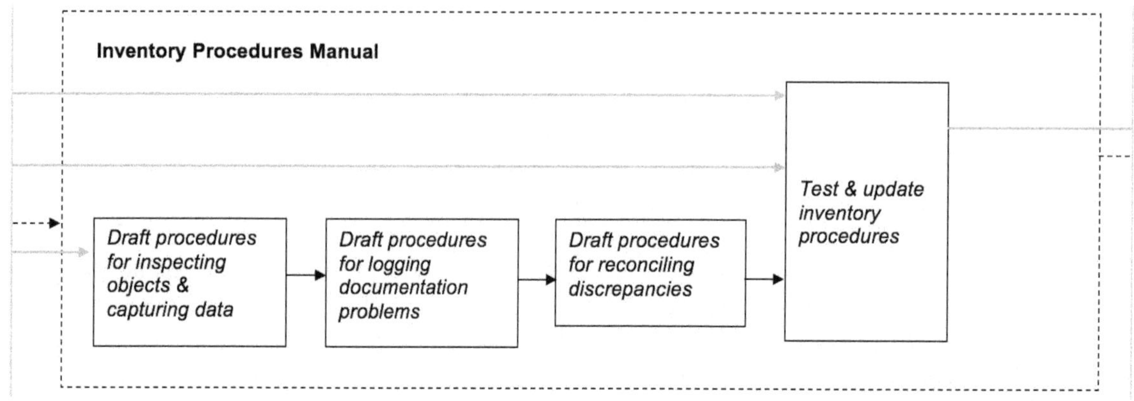

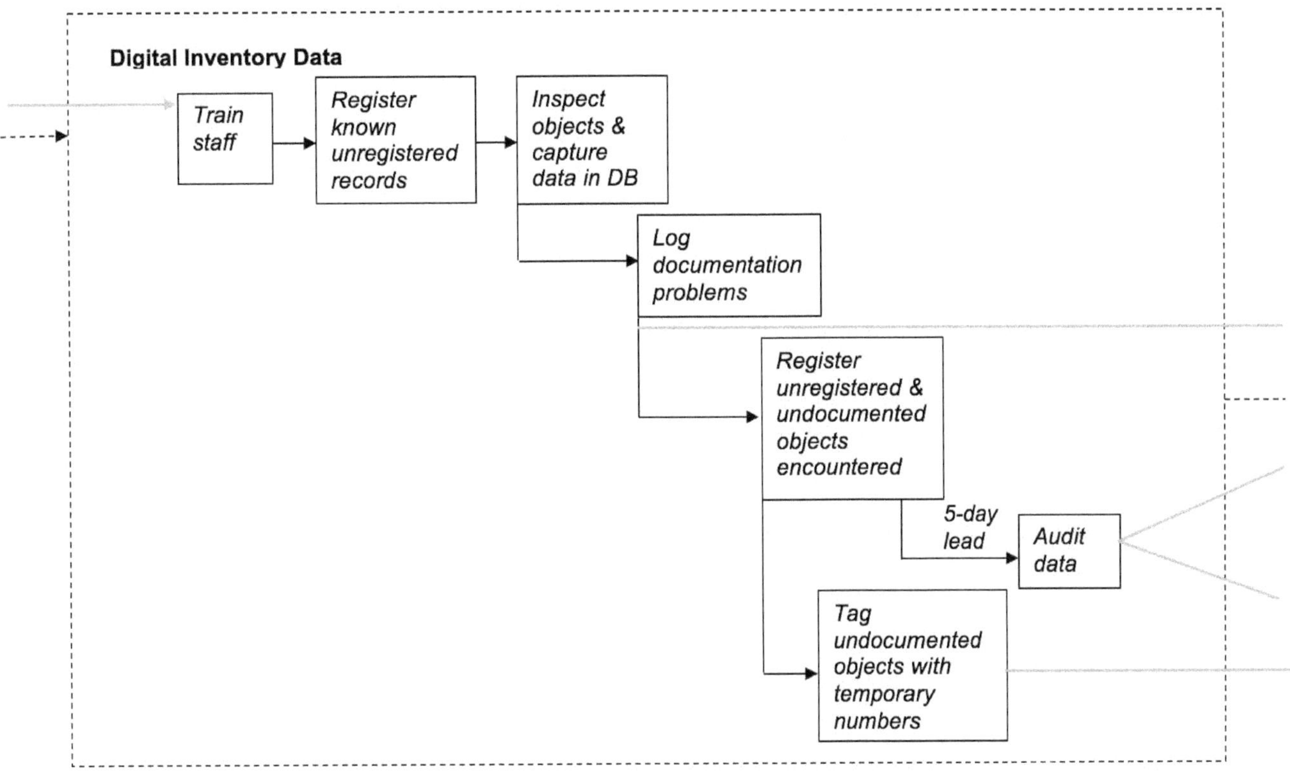
Digital Inventory Data
Train staff
Register known unregistered records
Inspect objects & capture data in DB
Log documentation problems
Register unregistered & undocumented objects encountered
5-day lead
Audit data
Tag undocumented objects with temporary numbers

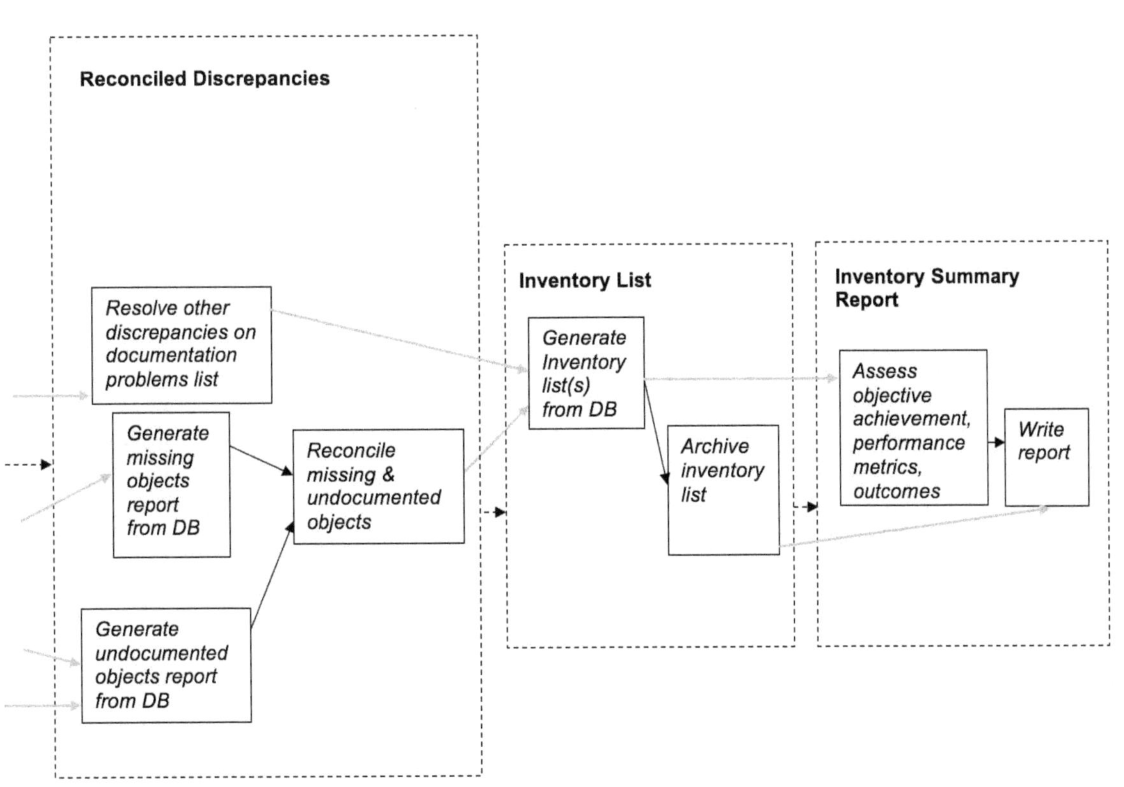
Reconciled Discrepancies
Resolve other discrepancies on documentation problems list
Generate missing objects report from DB
Reconcile missing & undocumented objects
Generate undocumented objects report from DB
Inventory List
Generate Inventory list(s) from DB
Archive inventory list
Inventory Summary Report
Assess objective achievement, performance metrics, outcomes
Write report

the project duration. However, durations assigned to fit activities into arbitrary, predetermined, or desirable timelines will prove to be unrealistic.[8] Another benefit of the activity network is that it allows planners to identify deliverables, activities, or quality standards that may need to be scaled back or cut in order to accomplish the inventory's objectives under a strict deadline.

Despite best attempts at estimating timelines, a realistic picture of the inventory's duration may emerge only once the project is underway due to unforeseen factors. It is not uncommon for inventory timelines to require adjustment during the life of the project, and the activity network is critical to the process.

At Museum A, because a comprehensive inventory is unprecedented, staff decided to invest some extra time developing their duration estimate for inspecting objects and capturing data in the database. The registrar and collections manager devoted a few full workdays to practicing inventorying objects in different parts of the collection. They found that on average, they inventoried fifty objects per day. During this trial run, they also kept track of how many hours each day were actually spent inspecting objects and collecting data. Notably, out of an eight-hour workday, they found that between breaks, meetings, and socializing with colleagues, they spent about five hours per day working on the inventory. Knowing that these workplace activities are unlikely to change, Museum A proceeded with the notion that capturing data for fifty objects will take one elapsed workday. Staff also decided that calculating durations in elapsed workdays rather than hours was more easily understood and readily translated to calendar time. With roughly 15,000 objects in the collection, Museum A therefore estimated it will need about fifteen months, or 300 elapsed workdays, to complete object inspection and data capture. To buffer the estimate somewhat, an additional ten days were added to the duration estimate to account for time that will be needed to register the last unregistered objects from the documentation problems list and capture inventory data for them. Table 7.5, Museum A's full activity network, shows duration estimates in the top center box above each activity.

Unconventionally, the duration assigned for "reconcile missing and undocumented objects" is not based on an estimate like the other activities in Museum's A's network. A fixed duration of twenty working days (roughly one calendar month) has been assigned. A fixed duration rather than an estimate is used for a couple of reasons. First, the full extent of records and objects needing reconciliation won't be known until object inspection and data capture are complete, which makes estimating the duration uncertain. Second, in any museum inventory, reconciliation can take more or less time. Reconciling some objects and records may require ongoing research well beyond the project timeline, and some may be unreconciled indefinitely. Although reconciliation may not be complete after twenty workdays, Museum A judged it essential to carve out time for this critical and often deprioritized activity.

Using the Activity Network to Estimate the Length of the Inventory Project

So far, the activity network has been useful for understanding the activities needed to produce each project deliverable, the order in which the activities will occur, and the relationships between them. But now, activity durations, estimated previously and converted to elapsed workdays, are integrated with the activity network to approximate how long it will take to execute the entire inventory.

To do so, three numbers are noted above each activity in the network, as shown in table 7.5: earliest start date (top left), duration in elapsed workdays (top center), and earliest finish date (top right). Starting with the first activity "identify dataset, queries, reports needed," the earliest start date of 0 (zero) is placed at top left. (If multiple independent activities initiate the project simultaneously, zero would be the earliest start date for each.) Based on Museum A's estimated duration in elapsed workdays, 20 is placed in the top center box. The third number, earliest finish date, is the sum of the earliest start date and duration. Thus, 20 appears in the top right box. The earliest finish date of an activity becomes the earliest start date for any finish-to-start dependent activities, which describes most of them. In this case, 20 becomes the earliest start date for "identify DB changes needed." For this activity, the sum of the earliest start date and duration are again calculated to determine the earliest finish date. These calculations are carried forward, always following the arrow pathways.

Where two dependent activities follow one activity, the earliest finish date is used as the earliest start date for both, as can be seen where the earliest finish date for "engage DB developer" is the earliest start date for both "implement DB backup plan" and "await changes." Where one activity depends on multiple preceding activities, the earliest start date is the latest earliest finish date among the deliverables it depends on. This can be seen with "test changes," which depends on "await changes" and "implement DB backup plan." The earliest finish date for "await changes" is 70, while the earliest finish date for "implement DB backup plan" is 60. Thus, the later of the two dates, 70, is the earliest start date for "test changes."

For start-to-start dependent activities, the earliest start date of the first activity is the same as the earliest start date for the dependent activity, as illustrated with the activities "inspect objects & capture data in DB" and "log documentation problems." Where there is a lead-time dependency, as between "register unregistered & undocumented objects encountered" and "audit data," the start date of the dependent activity is the earliest start date of the activity it depends on plus the lead time.

Completing the forward pass calculations to the end of the network yields an idea of how long the inventory will take. For Museum A's hypothetical case, the inventory will take about 482 elapsed workdays. The next sections demonstrate how inventory planners can use the network to adjust the project if needed, for example, to align with shorter timeline goals.

Identifying Slack

Slack refers to how much spare time there is to complete an activity without delaying the next activity or extending the length of the project.[9] Knowing where there is room for delay in a project is useful when the unexpected happens, which it inevitably will. Calculating slack can also help pinpoint how and where activities can be adjusted to meet timeline targets.

To begin identifying slack, two numbers are calculated and placed below the activity: latest start date (bottom left) and latest finish date (bottom right), as shown in table 7.5. These numbers refer to the latest an activity can start and finish without delaying succeeding dependent activities. Then the difference between the earliest and latest finish dates is calculated and placed at bottom center. This number represents slack.

Calculating Latest Start Date and Latest Finish Date

This process is a backward pass, which starts at the final activity at the end of the network and follows the arrow pathways backward to calculate latest finish date and latest start date for each activity. Beginning at "write report," the earliest finish date (top right) is copied down as the latest finish date (bottom right). Then the difference between the latest finish date and the duration, 10 (top center box), is calculated to arrive at the latest start date, which is placed in the lower left box. With any finish-to-start dependent activity, the latest start date is carried backward as the latest finish date for any predecessor activity. It follows, then, that 472 is the latest finish date for "assess objective achievement, performance metrics, outcomes." When a finish-to-start dependent activity has a double dependency, the latest start date is the latest finish date for both activities it depends on. In keeping with this, the latest start date for "write report" is the latest finish date for both "assess objective achievement, performance metrics, outcomes" and "archive inventory list."

When multiple activities depend on one activity but have different latest start dates, the earliest of the latest start dates (the lowest number) is used as the latest finish date for the predecessor activity. An example of this among finish-to-start dependent relationships can be seen with "generate inventory list(s) from DB"; its latest finish date is the latest start date of "assess objective achievement, performance metrics, outcomes" because it is earlier than the latest start date for "archive inventory list."

For start-to-start and lead-time dependent relationships, it is the latest start date of the dependent activity that drives the latest start date for any predecessor activity; this is calculated first, then added to the duration to calculate the latest finish date. For example, 125 is the latest start date for "audit data" because it has a five-day lead-time dependency on its predecessor, "register unregistered and undocumented objects encountered," which can't start any later than day 120 (latest start date of "audit data" less the lead time). Similarly, for start-to-start dependencies, the latest start date of a predecessor activity can't be later than the latest start date of a succeeding start-to-start dependent activity. That is to say, the latest start date for "register unregistered and undocumented objects encountered" can't be later than 130, the latest start date for the start-to-start dependent activity "tag undocumented objects with temporary numbers." In this scenario, "register unregistered and undocumented objects encountered" has multiple dependent activities. Again, on the backward pass, latest start date is driven by the earliest latest start date of its dependent activities—that of "audit data." Adding duration to the latest start date yields the latest finish date for activities preceding start-to-start or lead-time dependent activities.

If calculations are correct after completing the backward pass, zero will be the latest start date for the first activity in the network.

Calculating Slack

Slack derives from the latest finish date minus the earliest finish date. The result is placed in the center bottom box, as shown in table 7.5. Calculating slack is very useful because it reveals where there is or isn't spare time in the event of delays as well as how delays will impact the

Table 7.5. Museum A's Activity Network

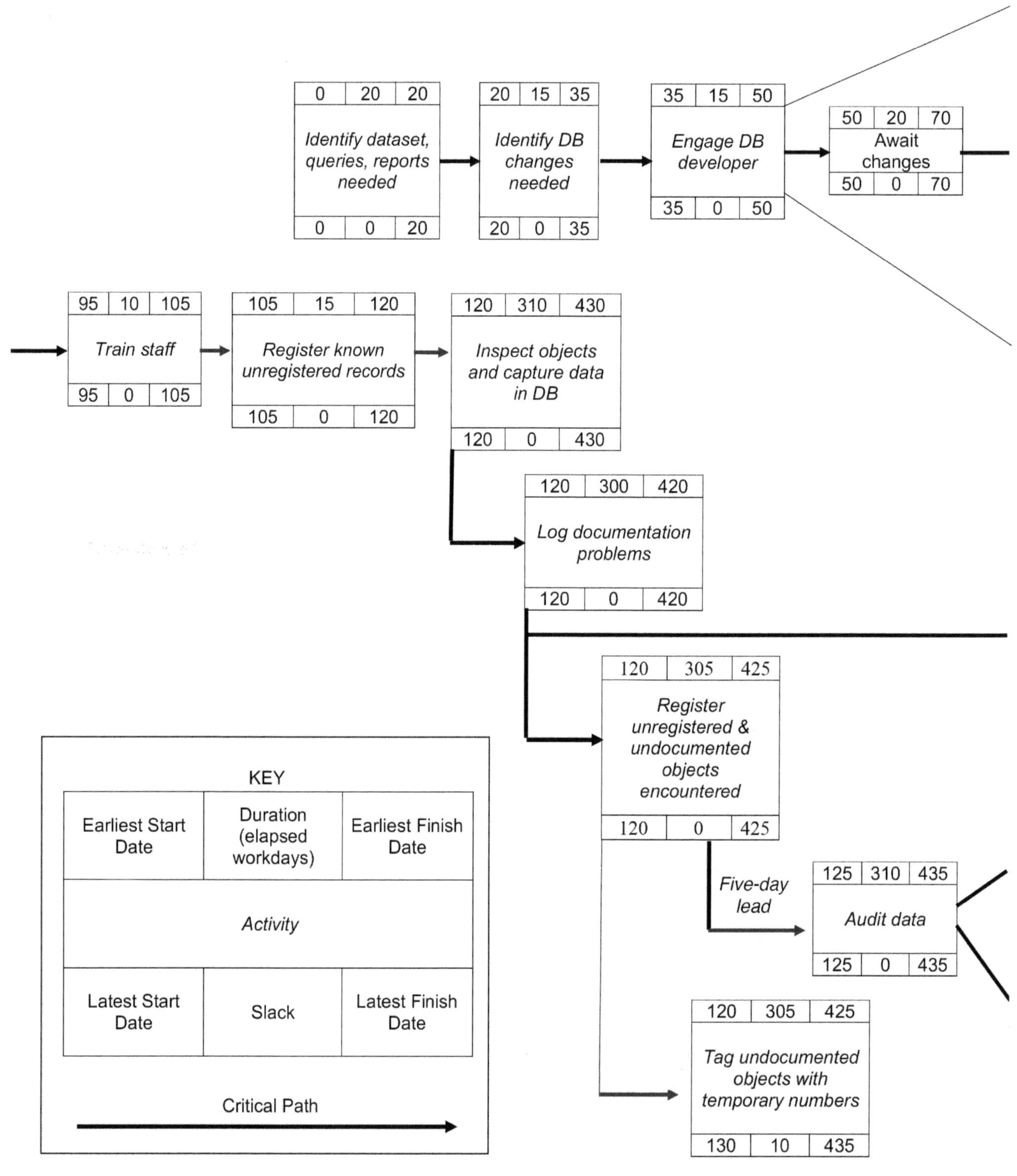

0 | 20 | 20
Identify dataset, queries, reports needed
0 | 0 | 20
20 | 15 | 35
Identify DB changes needed
20 | 0 | 35
35 | 15 | 50
Engage DB developer
35 | 0 | 50
50 | 20 | 70
Await changes
50 | 0 | 70
95 | 10 | 105
Train staff
95 | 0 | 105
105 | 15 | 120
Register known unregistered records
105 | 0 | 120
120 | 310 | 430
Inspect objects and capture data in DB
120 | 0 | 430
120 | 300 | 420
Log documentation problems
120 | 0 | 420
120 | 305 | 425
Register unregistered & undocumented objects encountered
120 | 0 | 425
Five-day lead
125 | 310 | 435
Audit data
125 | 0 | 435
120 | 305 | 425
Tag undocumented objects with temporary numbers
130 | 10 | 435
KEY
Earliest Start Date
Duration (elapsed workdays)
Earliest Finish Date
Activity
Latest Start Date
Slack
Latest Finish Date
Critical Path

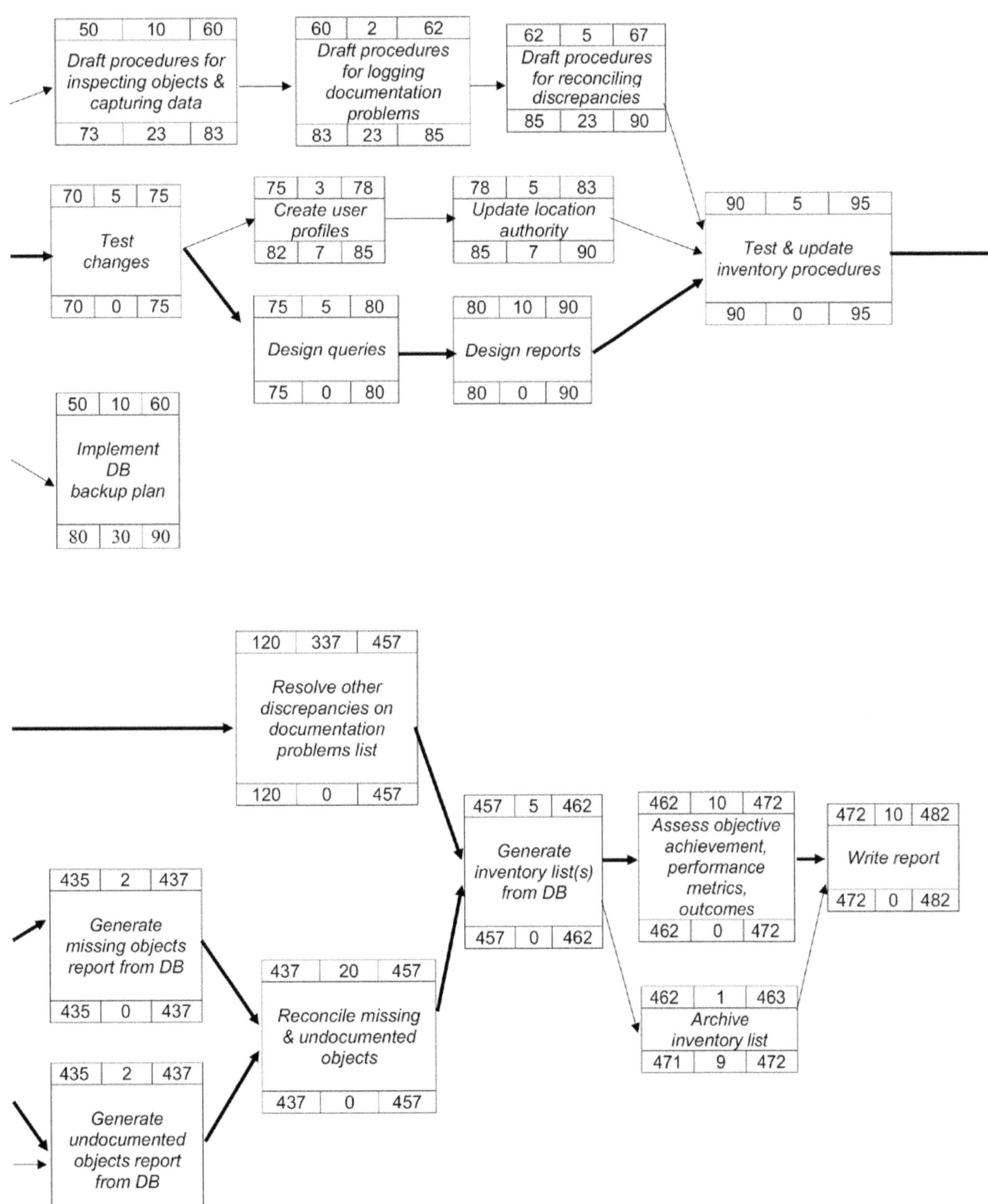
50 10 60
Draft procedures for inspecting objects & capturing data
73 23 83
60 2 62
Draft procedures for logging documentation problems
83 23 85
62 5 67
Draft procedures for reconciling discrepancies
85 23 90
70 5 75
Test changes
70 0 75
75 3 78
Create user profiles
82 7 85
78 5 83
Update location authority
85 7 90
90 5 95
Test & update inventory procedures
90 0 95
75 5 80
Design queries
75 0 80
80 10 90
Design reports
80 0 90
50 10 60
Implement DB backup plan
80 30 90
120 337 457
Resolve other discrepancies on documentation problems list
120 0 457
457 5 462
Generate inventory list(s) from DB
457 0 462
462 10 472
Assess objective achievement, performance metrics, outcomes
462 0 472
472 10 482
Write report
472 0 482
435 2 437
Generate missing objects report from DB
435 0 437
437 20 457
Reconcile missing & undocumented objects
437 0 457
462 1 463
Archive inventory list
471 9 472
435 2 437
Generate undocumented objects report from DB
435 0 437

rest of the project activities and timeline. For Museum A, most slack occurs early in the project. For example, the start of "implement DB backup plan" can be delayed up to thirty days without delaying the next dependent activity; the two numbers on either side show the latest start date and latest finish dates, then, with respect to the slack time. Slack also occurs with the sequence "draft procedures for inspecting objects and capturing data," "draft procedures for logging documentation problems," and "draft procedures for reconciling discrepancies." These occur as an uninterrupted chain. Slack will always be the same for two or more activities in an uninterrupted chain; but the number 23 represents slack time for the entire uninterrupted chain, not for each activity in it. This is also seen with the uninterrupted chain "create user profiles" and "update location authority." Thus, if "create user profiles" is delayed or extended by three days, there will be only four days of slack for "update location authority." That is, if one activity in the uninterrupted chain uses some slack, the time used must be subtracted from the slack in subsequent activities in the uninterrupted chain.

Finding the Critical Path of the Inventory

Another reason slack is so useful is that it helps identify the project's critical path. Critical path is "the longest chain of dependent activities going through the activity network."[10] Activities along the longest chain of dependent activities determine the duration of the entire project. They have zero slack and represent the longest activity durations along a chain of dependent activities.[11] Any delay in an activity along the critical path will delay the entire inventory project. In table 7.5, the critical path is indicated by bold activity dependency arrows. This chapter focuses on the utility of the critical path for inventory planning, while chapter 10 discusses how it can be utilized after the inventory is underway.

For up-front planning, scrutinizing the critical path can reveal where activity sequences may be tweaked to increase efficiency. The critical path also suggests where and how to scale down if, for example, the initial duration estimate exceeds the target timeline. Museum A's provisional project duration is 482 elapsed workdays. With about 261 workdays in a calendar year, the project will take just under two calendar years. Fortunately, this aligns with the maximum two-year timeline set by the grant Museum A is applying for to fund the inventory.

If the length of the project were too long, Museum A could scrutinize activities on the critical path to determine whether and how activities can be scaled down or eliminated. The museum can also discern where dedicating more human resources to an activity might meaningfully reduce the duration, as is the case with "register known unregistered records." The duration of a project cannot be shortened by arbitrarily reducing the estimated duration of an activity, for example, by reducing the duration for "await changes" for the database upgrades. While everyone may want the changes in ten days, that's an unreasonable expectation in many cases. Following Museum A's critical path, the only sound way to shave off time would seem to be reducing the discretionary fixed duration dedicated to "reconcile missing and undocumented objects." Because the amount of time needed for reconciliation is unknown without complete digital inventory data, reconciliation activities may exceed that duration and, as is often the case, may become part of ongoing daily work. To shorten the project timeline, planners would have to consider whether decreasing the duration of reconciling missing and undocumented objects would be effective and acceptable.

Alternatively, it may be necessary to reduce the scope of objects to be inventoried and accordingly, the duration of activities comprising the "digital inventory data" deliverable. The museum may also consider reducing the quality standards for some deliverables, such as custom database upgrades for "inventory-equipped database." If reasonable, the museum could opt to use its existing version and aim to initiate a separate project for database upgrades later.

On the other hand, following the critical path also enables planners to recognize where changes to activities would not meaningfully reduce the project duration. For example, someone may like to shave five days off "implement database backup plan," and that might be reasonable. But this activity is off the critical path, so shortening it would have no impact on the project duration.

As in Museum A's case, the critical path may split, as after "log documentation problems." At this juncture, one branch of the critical path leads to "resolve other discrepancies on documentation problems list," whose duration is somewhat discretionary. That is, Museum A applied a discretionary duration of 20 for the activity "reconcile missing and undocumented objects." Thus, this activity starts on day 437 and ends on 457, which is when all activities for the deliverable "reconciled discrepancies" must end. While "resolve other discrepancies on documentation problems list" may start as soon as "log documentation problems" starts, it must also end by day 457. Its duration, then, derives from the difference between the earliest start and finish dates. So, although in this case it is on the critical path, the numerous activities on the other branch of the split critical path merit closer scrutiny.

This chapter has shown that the activity network is a critical, time-saving planning tool for visualizing the activities required to achieve the inventory deliverables and how the activities must play out, and for approximating how long this will take. But it drives yet another element of the project scope: planning the resources required to execute the activities. The next chapter discusses how to use the activity network to estimate what resources will be needed, how much, and when. In doing so, planners may again find the need to modify the inventory scope and in turn, the activity network to align the master plan with needs and constraints beyond time.

Notes

1. Nick Graham, *Project Management for Dummies* (Chichester: John Wiley & Sons, 2015), 98.
2. Ibid., 101.
3. Ibid., 99.
4. Ibid., 101.
5. Ibid., 112–17.
6. Ibid., 104.
7. Willpower Information: Information Management Consultants, "Time Taken to Create Catalog Records for Museum Objects and Archives," modified February 16, 2010, http://www.willpowerinfo.co.uk/catrates.htm.
8. Graham, *Dummies*, 123.
9. Ibid., 107–11.
10. Ibid., 109.
11. Ibid.

CHAPTER EIGHT

Estimating Resource Needs

To get its inventory project up and running, Museum A needs the stamp of approval from influencer stakeholders who decide how the museum uses its resources. These stakeholders may agree that the inventory objectives are important, but the burning question from their perspective will likely be, how much is this going to cost? The answer to this question derives from the activity network, which maps out the activities needed to achieve the inventory objectives and how long they will take. Referencing Museum A's case, this chapter identifies the staff and nonstaff resources required for carrying out each inventory activity and how much of each resource will be needed. Costs for acquiring these resources are tallied to get an idea of how much it will cost to produce each deliverable and to execute the full project. This gives a sense of whether the project falls within a reasonable budget range or the requirements of the project—dictated by the objectives, deliverables, and activities in the scope—must be scaled back.

But the activity network is more than just a means of getting to the bottom line. It further guides the resource plan because it enables planners to determine not only what and how much they'll need but also when. Planners can again turn to the activity network's start/finish dates and durations to map the project and resource needs onto the calendar. This approach allows inventory planners to accurately cost out expenses, avoid resource conflicts, and develop a sound project budget proposal.

Staff Resources

Staff resources are people the museum employs or must employ to perform the inventory activities. These may be existing permanent staff or temporary staff hired for the project. This section uses Museum A's case to project which staff will be needed for each inventory activity, how much of their time will be required, and when. The resulting plan lays out staff costs for each deliverable and determines whether adjustments to the plan are needed. This exercise is also a key strategy for avoiding staff resource conflict when the inventory is underway.

Identifying the Inventory Staff You'll Need

Identifying the core staff needed to execute an inventory means returning to the activity network and determining the knowledge, skills, and experience required to carry out the activities in each deliverable. Inventories are executed by a range of museum professionals, including registrars, collections managers, curators, conservators, museum specialists, database managers, and information technology personnel. Although some of these professionals have distinct areas of expertise, there is frequently an overlap of knowledge, training, skills, and experience among them in areas that relate to carrying out inventories. These include collections and records management; describing collections; preventive conservation as it applies to object handling and storage; and the ability to input, extract, and manipulate data from a collections database.

Table 8.2 shows the core staff necessary for executing an inventory based on Museum A's activity network, discussed in chapter 7. Not surprisingly, the greatest demand is on the registrar, a staff resource required across every deliverable. Registrars are experts in administrative, legal, and ethical aspects of collections and records management systems. The registrar formulates and implements procedures for registering, numbering, and capturing data about objects in the database. During the inventory, they will also research collections records in various formats to resolve documentation discrepancies such as conflicting or missing object numbers and ownership status. When there is no perfect resolution, the registrar exercises sound judgment to determine how an object will be documented in records moving forward. Given their prominent role, the registrar is often also the default project manager. As such, they will document and communicate inventory progress, navigate setbacks, manage data quality control through audits, and resolve problems. The project manager may also be responsible for setting up contracts and purchase orders, paying invoices, and managing the budget to ensure timely resource availability.

Museum A's collections manager also features prominently across the inventory deliverables. They have in-depth knowledge of the collections database and the data deficiencies the inventory must remedy in order to store, manage, preserve, and access collections effectively and efficiently. Overall, they will assume a more hands-on role in the course of the physical inspection. Coordinating the inventory rollout from one storeroom to the next is a key responsibility. They will also oversee the movement of objects in and out of collections areas, implement object handling protocols, organize objects according to the museum's classification system, manage the museum specialist's mobile workstations, improve storage space efficiency, monitor storage environments, and coordinate housekeeping and pest management. The collections manager will also plan, order, and manage supplies and equipment that will be used to handle, transport, and stage objects during physical inspection. Identifying collections that pose health and safety issues and knowing when a conservator should be consulted before proceeding are also among the collections manager's responsibilities.

Information technology (IT) personnel are a third core staff resource requirement for Museum A. The IT systems administrator will collaborate with the registrar to engage the developer and implement and test collections database upgrades, install and update the database and other software, and enable network access for new hires. IT can also guide selections for new hardware and software procured for the inventory to ensure they are compatible with existing systems and facilitate installation and setup. During the physical inspection, IT will continue to maintain networks and troubleshoot when systems are not functioning as needed.

Consistent with recommended practice, a two-person inventory team will physically inspect objects, capture the requisite dataset, log documentation problems, tag objects with temporary numbers, and support reconciliation of discrepancies.[1] In addition, they'll keep track of the supplies inventory; report on what's most effective; alert the collections manager to any pest infestations or other emergencies; and organize workspaces, tools, and equipment. The museum knows it's unreasonable to add these tasks to the registrar's or collections manager's portfolio of responsibilities. Museum A therefore intends to hire two temporary museum specialists for the project. These staff typically possess broad knowledge and demonstrated experience in collections documentation, management, and preventive conservation. Ideally, their experience will also align closely with the collection profile, and they will have prior inventory experience. Because they usually work with each other in storerooms for long stretches of time, the ability to focus and strong interpersonal skills is critical. In geographic regions with small applicant pools, it can be challenging to recruit individuals to satisfy this inventory staff resource need. In many scenarios, artists, craftspeople, historians, archaeologists, and hobbyists make for exceptional inventory personnel. In keeping with this, finding the right museum specialists may involve announcing vacancies broadly through hobby and arts circles as well as the established museum job boards, such as American Alliance of Museums JobHQ; Association for Registrars and Collections Specialists OnContract Directory; American Association for State and Local History Career Center; and Preparation, Art Handling, Collections Care Information Network Job Listings Forum.

The registrar, collections manager, IT systems administrator, and two museum specialists form the core staff resource for Museum A's inventory. Other inventory scenarios may of course require different staffing, depending on the project scope and available resources. For example, a conservator on the team may inform appropriate terminology for describing and documenting object condition in the database, determine intervention and quarantine protocols if an active pest infestation or deterioration is encountered in collections, and guide rehousing and handling protocols. Curators may also be key participants in determining the inventory dataset and may provide discipline-specific terms or classification systems to document objects or provide administrative oversight. A preparator, exhibitions staff, or art handlers may also be called on to lead handling and moving objects during physical inspection, particularly those that are heavy, oversized, unwieldy, or difficult to access or store or require special equipment.

At some time or another, the core inventory staff will need additional staff support from across the institution.

Human resources, for example, will be needed for hiring and onboarding. Operations staff may need to run electricity to storage rooms, install adequate lighting, secure unstable shelving units, or otherwise make sure inventory workspaces are safe and functional. Security staff may be called on to guard an empty gallery used as a swing space while oversized objects are inventoried. While these resources are significant, they may be considered part of the cost of doing business, in which case they may be accounted for under indirect costs, a budget category discussed later in the chapter.

Projecting How Much Staff Resource You'll Need

In order to express staff resource needs in dollars, planners need to project how much of each person's time will be spent carrying out the activities. Once again, the activity network guides these projections. In chapter 7, Museum A was tasked with estimating work effort and durations for each inventory activity. Planners acknowledged that the museum's permanent staff—the registrar, collections manager, and IT systems administrator—would need to divide their time between inventory activities and their usual workload. In keeping with this, activity network durations are expressed in elapsed workdays rather than work effort: a task estimated to take sixteen hours of work effort may actually require five workdays. The rationale used to estimate elapsed workdays informs the percentage of time each person will devote to the activities.

Table 8.2 shows the estimated percentage of time each core staff member will dedicate to activities across deliverables. Museum A's registrar estimates that roughly 60 percent of their time will be spent on the inventory activities, while the collections manager shows a roughly 50 percent time commitment across most deliverables. Though involved in fewer activities, on average, the IT systems administrator estimates they will spend roughly 15 percent of their time on the project. More time will be required to produce the inventory-equipped database (25 percent); a lesser time commitment is anticipated for resolving technology issues while digital inventory data is being produced (10 percent). Finally, the two museum specialists will spend 100 percent of their time on inventory activities; the activity network already showed that they'll be needed for about 362 workdays by subtracting the "train staff" activity start date from the "reconciled discrepancies" finish date.

Once time projections are complete, the number of hours represented by the percentage of time budgeted can be multiplied by staff's hourly compensation rates to create a picture of staffing costs for each deliverable and the project as a whole. Depending on worker classification, staff resource costs may also include fringe benefits, such as health insurance, typically calculated as a percentage of the compensation. These can be added here or while preparing the overall project budget, discussed later in the chapter.

At this juncture, the compensation rate for the two temporary museum specialists may not yet be established. The Bureau of Labor Statistics' (BLS') Occupational Employment Statistics provides a sense of current compensation rates for staff who do inventory work. Relevant data can be found in two categories: "museum technicians and conservators" and "curators."[2,3] Compensation data is broken out by region and hourly wage. Salary surveys conducted by the American Alliance of Museums, Association of Art Museum Directors, and the American Institute for Conservation can further inform compensation research. However, some of these surveys are not free, the data can be difficult to apply to temporary workers who perform inventory work, and the data for several worker categories is often statistically unrepresentative. While the BLS survey data is certainly a starting point, it doesn't mean the compensation rates are fair; they overwhelmingly fail to reflect the financial investment required to attain the credentials for the job and underscore unjustified pay inequities. Querying equitable-minded colleagues and comparing proposed compensation rates to Massachusetts Institute of Technology's online living wage calculator can further inform decisions around pay. Fair pay is not only the right thing to do. It's also a primary strategy for avoiding staff resource conflict. Although the temporary basis of the museum specialists' work may increase the likelihood of turnover from the start, fair compensation and planned increases may persuade them to stay instead of taking another job in the middle of the inventory.

If the inventory budget projection as a whole is deemed too high, staff resources will likely be revisited, as they account for the bulk of expenses. Rejiggering temporary staff costs is often targeted. At this juncture, the worker classification of the museum specialists may also be undefined. Planners can consider whether museum specialist staffing must be full-time or could be fulfilled with part-time or independent contractor relationships. While engaging inventory workers as contractors may reduce the museum's bottom line by eliminating fringe benefits and lowering tax obligations, classifying the museum specialists this way may be unlawful. According to the Internal Revenue Service, the museum specialists could be classified as independent contractors if the museum controls only the result of their inventory activities and not what they'll do or how they'll do it.[4] This is rarely if ever the case with museum inventories. As well, the increased tax burden for contractors reduces their net compensation as compared to employees'. In the end, if planners decrease staff resource, they must also scale back the other elements of the project scope.

Determining When You'll Need Inventory Staff

In addition to who and how much, a resource plan must tell the museum when the resources are needed in terms of money and scheduling. This helps ensure that staff will be available and that the museum can effectively manage its cash flow and pay staff on time. The activity network is again the reference point for identifying when inventory staff services will be required.

Museum A's activity network calculates the length of the inventory project in workdays. Table 8.2 shows Museum A's provisional start date of January 3, 2022. By referencing this date and each activity's earliest start date, duration, and earliest finish date, planners can generate a timeline in calendar dates. Timeanddate.com's Working Days Calculator provides one of the easiest ways to convert workdays to calendar dates. The first activity's duration can be added to the calendar start date to arrive at the earliest finish date that automatically excludes weekends and/or holidays. As shown in table 8.2, these calculations can be carried forward to the end of the activity network.

By completing this exercise, the project staff can see exactly when staff resource expenditures will be incurred, which may illuminate additional resource needs. For example, the activity network has already shown that the museum specialists will be needed for about 362 workdays. They can now see that holidays will extend the timeline and add to their compensation projections.

Avoiding Staff Resource Conflicts

Mapping out staff resources not only projects how much the inventory will cost and when the costs will be incurred, but it's also one of the main ways to avoid resource conflict; it lays out who is needed when and for how long. For instance, table 8.2 makes it clear that May 19 to June 3, when Museum A's collections manager is training the museum specialists, is not a great time for the department head to schedule a collections storage show-and-tell. Staff can also point to the resource plan to validate time expenditure on inventory activities. Nevertheless, conflicts are inevitable: Staff assigned to more than one task scheduled around the same time, staff leave, and competing priorities between behind-the-scenes and public-facing work are common. Inventory planners have already attempted to mitigate these conflicts by adding some cushion to the activity durations or the project timeline. They can also mitigate staff resource conflicts by considering when and how to be flexible and communicating effectively with stakeholders whose work may be impacted by the inventory.

For permanent staff like Museum A's registrar, who will divide their time between inventory and other responsibilities, it's guaranteed that noninventory work will take priority from time to time, which will temporarily reduce their 60 percent time commitment. Although they will be in high demand throughout the project, the demand will ebb and flow as the inventory plays out. In the face of resource conflicts, it may be reasonable to use an informal time "banking" system. For instance, if the registrar is committed to inventory activities three days per week but can manage only two during a busy exhibition installation, they can add a one-day credit to their time bank. This means they can add an extra inventory workday to a week after the installation is complete. This flexibility may be effective after the physical inspection is well underway, for example, but perhaps not the first week of inspection or when database upgrades need to be tested in collaboration with IT and the database developer.

On the other hand, there are some instances that merit an unwavering commitment to the staff resource plan. Museum A's museum specialists, for instance, will be hired for the express purpose of inspecting objects, capturing the inventory dataset, and reconciling discrepancies. Obliging requests to assign them noninventory activities not only invites further redirection of this resource but will derail the inventory.

Inventories have the potential to create resource conflicts among stakeholders in other departments. These stakeholders may be noncore staff who provide resources needed to support the inventory from time to time. When these resource needs are anticipated, planners can avoid conflict by communicating exactly what the work will entail and when support will be needed so that managers can plan effectively to incorporate these additional responsibilities into workloads. Staff resource conflicts may also result if the inventory disrupts the work of other departments whose staff are not involved in the inventory. This can be sidestepped by determining whether any large-scale projects are on the horizon, such as a planned move out of a storage facility, a building renovation, or upcoming maintenance activities. Similarly, institutional calendars will alert planners to potential conflicts related to recurring activities or special events.

Planning Nonstaff Resources

The activity network comes into play again when Museum A begins planning nonstaff resources. As with project staff, making sure the right nonstaff resources, such as equipment, supplies, services, and infrastructure, are in place will help the project run smoothly and prevent delays. In the same way that practicing the inventory gives insight to activity durations, it also provides a sense of which nonstaff resources will be needed to carry out inventory activities and their quantity. Mapping the activity network onto the calendar again helps planners visualize when these resources will be needed. When planning nonstaff resources, the project manager will consider which ones are already available; what needs to be acquired; whether any supplies or equipment require a long lead time; and whether any specialized equipment must be rented, borrowed, or shared. Table 8.2 shows the nonstaff resources Museum A will need to acquire, which have been itemized below staff resources. Costs to procure these resources can be added to staff costs to anticipate spending across each deliverable and the project as a whole.

Mapping nonstaff resources on the resource plan shows that for Museum A, the most resource-intensive deliverables are the inventory-equipped database and digital inventory data. At the beginning of the project, Museum A will engage a database developer to make necessary system updates for recording inventory data. It will also renew database licenses for the head registrar and collections manager and pay database maintenance and cloud storage service fees to ensure inventory data is secure and preserved in the event of a technology failure.

Table 8.2 also shows that digital inventory data will be Museum A's most resource-intensive deliverable. During object inspection, Museum A will utilize object handling and transport equipment, such as tiered carts and ladders. While the museum already has some on hand, it will purchase a few more to be sure the inventory team won't be delayed by having to wait for shared equipment. Nitrile gloves, preservation-appropriate board, tissue, polyethylene foam, cotton muslin, and trays and bins will also be purchased for object handling and inspection. Finally, because the museum specialists will work in spaces that are infrequently accessed, dust will likely be disturbed, so masks and a HEPA vacuum will be purchased to protect them against dust and other airborne contaminants and to keep spaces clean.[5]

A number of other supplies and equipment will be needed for producing digital inventory data. Computers will be central to recording the inventory dataset and will include hardware, software, and the network on which they run.[6] The museum already has a suite of office software in place but will purchase two laptops, two additional database user licenses for the museum specialists, and Ethernet cables to enable network connectivity in storerooms that don't receive a Wi-Fi signal. Another museum might prefer desktop units or tablets for moving through galleries and storage rooms to document large objects, such as furniture. Printers and paper for creating shelf, inventory, and box contents lists are already on hand.

Worktables and standing desks will also be purchased, along with an object naming lexicon that supports capture of the inventory dataset. The supply list further includes rulers and measuring tapes, prestrung tags for labeling objects with temporary numbers, and labels and label holders for creating box and shelf labels. Object photography isn't in Museum A's project scope, but a digital camera will be purchased, for example, to share images for object identification or to alert staff to condition issues. If Museum A was undertaking professional photography, specialized lighting equipment, stands, and backdrops may be required.

In addition to these resources, Museum A will need to be sure that infrastructure servicing workspaces is sufficient for producing inventory data and consider whether any infrastructure items need to be arranged and/or included in the project budget. Adequate and clean space, for example, will be needed for inspecting objects and organizing and storing supplies. If Museum A's inventory scope included rehousing, reorganizing, or photographing the collection, additional space would be needed to accommodate these activities.

Electricity is required for adequate lighting in work areas; charging devices; and running computers, printers, and other equipment. Proper lighting is important for the safety of people and objects but also critical for detecting condition issues and discerning accession numbers. This conserves resources in the long run by eliminating the need to move objects to be inventoried or take handwritten notes that must later be deciphered and transcribed. Network access—internet and intranet—will also be needed to run collections management software, communicate with staff via email, and access digital resources.

Additionally, Museum A will check that ventilation in collections spaces is adequate since the museum specialists will spend the majority of their work hours there. Good ventilation is important for avoiding aggravated allergies, asthma, and other negative health effects. Because Museum A does have some collections stored off-site, the budget will include costs for transportation between workspaces. After object inspection is complete, the print job for the final inventory lists will be outsourced.

Assembling the Inventory Project Budget

The inventory budget is a detailed summary of all resource cost estimates for the entire project.[7] To produce Museum A's full budget, staff and nonstaff resource estimates are aggregated. A spreadsheet can be used to list costs and group expenses into categories to see how money will be spent. Because Museum A is requesting grant funding, it will follow the funder's budgeting template that categorizes expenditures as either direct or indirect costs and distributes expenses over two years, consistent with the projected timeline. Museum A will also be required to list any cost sharing, such as in-kind donations and matching funds they will contribute to the project. Table 8.1 shows Museum A's provisional budget, modeled after the National Endowment for the Humanities sample budgeting template.[8]

Five full-time staff comprise Museum A's project team: the registrar, who is acting as the project manager; the collections manager; two museum specialists; and the IT systems administrator. The registrar will devote 60 percent of their work time managing the inventory. Thus, 60 percent of their salary is the estimated cost of their project compensation in Year 1. A 2 percent cost of living increase will be given to all employees at the beginning of Year 2, so a dollar amount reflecting the head registrar's 2 percent salary increase will be entered in the column for Year 2. Salaries for other staff are calculated the same way. Staff salaries are followed by fringe benefits, which represent a percentage of project salaries and account for paid vacation, holidays, sick leave, retirement contributions, and other employee benefits. Fringe benefit rates are provided by Museum A's human resources staff and will be added to the project cost.

At the beginning of the project, a database developer will be contracted to update the collections management system. The project manager has budgeted twenty-five days for this work during Year 1 and will list this expense under consultant fees. For the project's duration, travel between Museum A and its off-site storage facility will be necessary, so annual transit passes for the registrar, collections manager, and museum specialists will be accounted for in the budget's travel line.

These expenses are followed by the necessary supplies, equipment, and software licenses for producing Museum A's deliverables. Some items, such as the laptops and digital camera, will be one-time purchases, while other supplies, such as gloves for object handling, will be budgeted for each year. Salaries, fringe benefits, consultant fees, travel, supplies and equipment, and licenses are direct costs, or expenses used to produce a specific item or service.[9] The sum of direct costs for Year 1 and Year 2 yields the project's total direct costs. In most inventory scenarios, compensation for the people who will carry out inventory activities will be the project's greatest direct cost. While not shown here, a reasonable reserve, or "cushion," is often added to direct cost estimates as a safety net; the original estimate is increased by a reasonable percentage to account for unforeseen expenditures.

Indirect or overhead costs include those that can't be tied directly to the inventory, as they are incurred jointly with other functions, making it difficult to assign them specific values.[10] Examples include costs for utilities; maintenance, such as ensuring that HVAC systems in storage rooms and workspaces are operational; general insurance; and administrative tasks. Because attempting to assign exact costs to these resources can be impractical, they are often omitted from in-house project budgets, depending on scope and institutional policy. Some granting agencies allow applicants to use a predetermined or negotiated indirect cost rate not to exceed a predetermined percentage of total direct costs.[11] Using a rate of 10 percent of modified total direct costs, indirect costs for Year 1 and Year 2 are totaled. The sum of direct and indirect costs yields the total project budget.

Museum A will ask the grantor to fund the salary and fringe benefits for the registrar and museum specialists as well as consultant fees, travel, supplies and equipment, database licenses and maintenance fees, and indirect costs for the duration of the project. Funding the salary of an existing employee, such as the registrar, increases the grant's appeal to project stakeholders, as it represents cost savings. Museum A will share the cost of the project by funding the salary and fringe benefits for the collections manager and IT systems administrator. A third-party monetary contribution secured by Museum A will also be added to the cost-sharing total. The sum of the requested amount and the cost share represents the project's total funding.

A carefully assembled resource plan allows project stakeholders to know what staff and nonstaff resources will be needed and when. Translating the plan to a project budget guides the cost of each deliverable and the project as a whole. If the budget projection is judged too high, the inventory scope, which defines the project requirements, will need to be scaled down to reduce costs. This may mean revisiting and adjusting the inventory objectives, deliverables, and activities. For example,

Table 8.1. Museum A's Inventory Project Budget Template

2022 Collection Inventory Budget	*Computational Details*	*Notes*	*Year 1*	*Notes*	*Year 2*	*Project Total*
1. Salaries & Wages			Jan–Dec 2022		Jan–Dec 2023	
Registrar (project manager)	Annual Salary yr. 1 Annual Salary yr. 2	60% of time	$	60% of time (+2% COLA increase)	$	
Collections manager	Annual Salary yr. 1 Annual Salary yr. 2	50% of time	$	50% of time (+2% COLA increase)	$	
Museum specialist 1	Annual Salary yr. 1 Annual Salary yr. 2	100% of time	$	100% of time (+2% COLA increase)	$	
Museum specialist 2	Annual Salary yr. 1 Annual Salary yr. 2	100% of time	$	100% of time (+2% COLA increase)	$	
IT systems administrator	Annual Salary yr. 1 Annual Salary yr. 2	15% of time	$	15% of time (+2% COLA increase)	$	
2. Fringe Benefits						
Project manager	%		$		$	
Project assistant	%		$		$	
Museum specialist 1	%		$		$	
Museum specialist 2	%		$		$	
IT systems administrator	%		$		$	
3. Consultant Fees						
Database developer	Daily Rate	25 days	$			
4. Travel						
Transit passes to off-site storage	Annual Pass 4 x		$	Annual Pass 4 x	$	
5. Supplies & Equipment						
Object naming lexicon	1 x		$			
Laptop computers	2 x		$			
Ethernet network cables	2 x		$			
Worktables	2 x		$			
Standing desks	2 x		$			
Digital camera	1 x		$			
Gloves, archival board, trays, bins	10 packs ea. x		$	10 packs ea. x	$	
Polyethylene foam, cotton muslin, acid-free tissue	10 packs ea. x		$	10 packs ea. x	$	
Rulers & measuring tapes	3 x		$			
Labels and label holders	10 packs x		$	10 packs x	$	
Prestrung object numbering tags	10 packs x		$	10 packs x	$	
HEPA vacuum	1 x		$			
Dust masks	10 packs x		$	10 packs x	$	
Ladders	2 x		$			
Object transport carts	4 x		$			

(continued)

Table 8.1. *Continued*

2022 Collection Inventory Budget	*Computational Details*	*Notes*	*Year 1*	*Notes*	*Year 2*	*Project Total*
6. Other						
Database user licenses	4 x		$			
Database maintenance fee	Annual fee		$			
Cloud storage service fee	Annual fee		$			
Printing service (final inventory lists)					$	
7. Total Direct Costs	**Per Year**		**$**		**$**	**$**
8. Total Indirect Costs	**Per Year (10% of modified total direct costs)**		**$**		**$**	**$**
9. Total Project Costs	**All Costs for Entire Project**					**$**
Project Funding						Requested from grantor: $ Cost Sharing Applicant's contributions: $ Third-party contributions: $ Total cost sharing: $ Total project funding: $

Museum A may scale back the database changes required, further delimit the objects that will be inventoried, or limit reconciliation activities to logging documentation problems and registering undocumented objects under temporary tracking numbers.

The last several chapters have focused on developing the elements of the project scope: objectives, deliverables, activities and time, and the resource plan. Completing this important groundwork culminates in a project road map that can be used to guide the project forward through the next phase: execution. The next chapter focuses on executing inventory activities to produce two key deliverables: digital inventory data and reconciled discrepancies.

Notes

1. Maureen McCormick, "Inventory," in *Museum Registration Methods*, 5th ed., ed. Rebecca A. Buck and Jean Allman Gilmore (Washington, DC: AAM Press, 2010), 303.

2. U.S. Bureau of Labor Statistics, "Occupational Employment and Wages, 25-4013 Museum Technicians and Conservators," June 10, 2021, https://www.bls.gov/oes/current/oes254013.htm.

3. U.S. Bureau of Labor Statistics, "Occupational Employment and Wages, 25-4012 Curators," June 10, 2021, https://www.bls.gov/oes/current/oes254012.htm#ind.

4. Internal Revenue Service, "Independent Contractor (Self-Employed) or Employee?," accessed June 10, 2021, https://www.irs.gov/businesses/small-businesses-self-employed/independent-contractor-self-employed-or-employee.

5. Kathryn A. Makos, Dennis C. Ertel Jr., and Michal McCann, "Occupational Hazard Control," in *Health & Safety for Museum Professionals* (New York, NY: Society for the Preservation of Natural History Collections, 2010), 154–55.

6. Suzanne Quigley and Christina Linclau, "Computer Systems and Data Management," in *Museum Registration Methods*, 6th ed., ed. John E. Simmons and Toni M. Kiser (Lanham, MD: Rowman & Littlefield, 2020), 174.

7. Nick Graham, *Project Management for Dummies* (Chichester: John Wiley & Sons, 2015), 154.

8. National Endowment for the Humanities, "Sample Budget," accessed June 16, 2021, https://www.neh.gov/sites/default/files/inline-files/sample-budget-september-2018_5.pdf.

9. Will Kenton, "Direct Cost," *Investopedia*, accessed June 16, 2021, https://www.investopedia.com/terms/d/directcost.asp.

10. Graham, *Dummies*, 155.

11. Institute of Museum and Library Services, "IMLS Office of Museum Services FY2018 IMLS Forms," accessed June 16, 2021, https://www.imls.gov/sites/default/files/webinar/transcripts/imlsomsfy2018imlsformstranscript.pdf.

Table 8.2. Museum A's Resource Projections

	YEAR 1 - Q1 - 2022														
	Jan 3 -7	Jan 10-14	Jan 17-21	Jan 24-28	Jan 31-Feb 4	Feb 7-Feb 11	Feb 14-Feb 18	Feb 21-Feb 25	Feb 28-Mar 4	Mar 7-Mar 11	Mar 14-Mar 18	Mar 21-Mar 25	Mar 28-Apr 1	Apr 4-Apr 8	Apr 11-Apr 15
DELIVERABLE	INVENTORY-EQUIPPED DATABASE (90 Days)														
ACTIVITY	**Identify Dataset, Queries, Reports Needed** Jan 3-Feb 1 (20 days)				**Identify DB Changes Needed** Feb 1-Feb 24 (15 days)				**Engage DB Developer** Feb 24-Mar 17 (15 days)			**A. Await Changes** Mar 17-Apr 14 (20 days) **B. Implement BD Backup Plan** Mar 17-Mar 31 (10 days)			
STAFF RESOURCES	Registrar - 60% of time 84 hrs				Registrar - 60% of time 63 hrs				Registrar - 60% of time 63 hrs			B. Registrar - 60% of time 42 hrs			
	Collections Manager - 50% of time 70 hrs				Collections Manager - 50% of time 52.5 hrs				- -			- -			
	- -				- -				IT - 25% of time 26.25 hrs			B. IT - 25% of time 17.5 hrs			
NON-STAFF RESOURCES	Database developer fee			Cost											INVEN
	Database user licenses (2)											**Draft Procedures for Inspecting Objects & Capturing Data** Mar 17-Mar 31 (10 days)		**Draft Procedures for Logging Documentation Problems** Mar 31 - Apr 4 (2 days)	**Draft Procedures for Reconciling Discrepancies** Apr 4-Apr 11 (5 days)
	Database maintenance fee											- -		Registrar - 60% of time 8.4 hrs	Registrar - 60% of time 21 hrs
	Cloud storage service fee											Collections Manager - 50% of time 35 hrs		- -	- -

YEAR 1 - Q2 - 2022												
Apr 18-Apr 22	Apr 25-Apr 29	May 2-May 6	May 9-May 13	May 16-May 20	May 23-May 27	May 30-Jun 3	Jun 6-Jun10	Jun 13-Jun 17	Jun 20-Jun 24	Jun 27, 2022-Sep 22, 2023	Sep 25-Sept 29

Test Changes Apr 14-Apr 21 (5 days)	A. Create User Profiles Apr 21-Apr 26 (3 days) B. Design Queries Apr 21-Apr 28 (5 days)	A. Update Location Authority Apr 26-May 3 (5 days) B. Design Reports Apr 28-May 12 (10 days)
Registrar - 60% of time 21 hrs	B. Registrar - 60% of time 21 hrs	A. Registrar - 60% of time 21 hrs
Collections Manager - 50% of time 17.5 hrs	A. Collections Manager - 50% of time 10.5 hrs	B. Collections Manager - 50% of time 17.5 hrs
IT - 25% of time 8.75 hrs	- -	- -

TORY PROCEDURES MANUAL (22 Days)

	Test & Update Inventory Procedures May 12-May 19 (5 days)
- -	Registrar - 50% of time 21 hrs
- -	Collections Manager - 50% of time 17.5 hrs

DIGITAL INVENTORY DATA (340 Days)

Train Staff May 19-June 3 (10 days)	Register Known Unregistered Records Jun 3-Jun 24 (15 days)	A. Inspect Objects & Capture Data in DB Jun 24-Sep 22, 2023 (310 days) B. Log Documentation Problems Jun 24-Sep 8, 2023 (300 days) C. Register Unregistered & Undocumented Objects Encountered Jun 24-Sep 15, 2023 (305 days) D. Tag Undocumented Objects with Temporary Numbers Jun 24-Sep 15, 2023 (305 days) E. Audit Data July 1-Sep 29, 2023 (310 days)
Registrar - 100% of time 70 hrs	Registrar - 60% of time 63 hrs	A., C., E. Registrar - 60% of time 1323 hrs
Collections Manager 100% of time 70 hrs	Collections Manager - 50% of time 52.5 hrs	A. Collections Manager - 50% of time 1085 hrs
Museum Specialist 1 100% of time 70 hrs	Museum Specialist 1 - 100% of time 105 hrs	A., D. Museum Specialist 1 - 100% of time 2170 hrs
Museum Specialist 2 100% of time 70 hrs	Museum Specialist 2 - 100% of time 105 hrs	A., D. Museum Specialist 2 - 100% of time 2170 hrs
IT - 10% of time 7 hrs	IT - 10% of time 10.5 hrs	IT - 10% of time 220.5 hrs

NON-STAFF RESOURCES	Dust masks	Cost
	HEPA vacuum	
	Ladders (x2)	
	Object carts (x4)	
	Gloves, archival board, trays, bins	
	Polyethylene foam, cotton muslin, acid-free tissue	
	Worktables (x2)	
	Standing desks (x2)	
	Object naming lexicon	
	Rulers and measuring tapes	
	Laptop computers (x2)	
	Ethernet network cables	
	Pre-strung object numbering tags	
	Labels and label holders	
	Digital camera	
	Transportation between storage sites	

RECONCILED DISCREPANCIES (

A. Resolve Other Discrepancies on Documer Jun 24-Nov 1, 2023 (337 da B. Generate Missing Objects Repo Sep 29, 2023-Oct 3 (2 day C. Generate Undocumented Objects R Sep 29, 2023-Oct 3 (2 day D. Reconcile Missing & Undocumen Oct 3-Nov 1 (20 days)
A.-D. Registrar - 60% of time (22 days) 92.4 hrs
A. Collections Manager - 50% of time (22 days) 77 hrs
A., D. Museum Specialist 1- 100% of time (27 days 189 hrs
A., D. Museum Specialist 2- 100% of time (27 days 189 hrs

(*continued*)

Table 8.2. *Continued*

YEAR 1 - Q2...YEAR 2 Q4 - 2023					
Oct 2-Nov 3	Nov 6-Nov 10	Nov 13-Nov 17	Nov 20-Nov 24	Nov 27-Dec 1	Dec 4-Dec 8

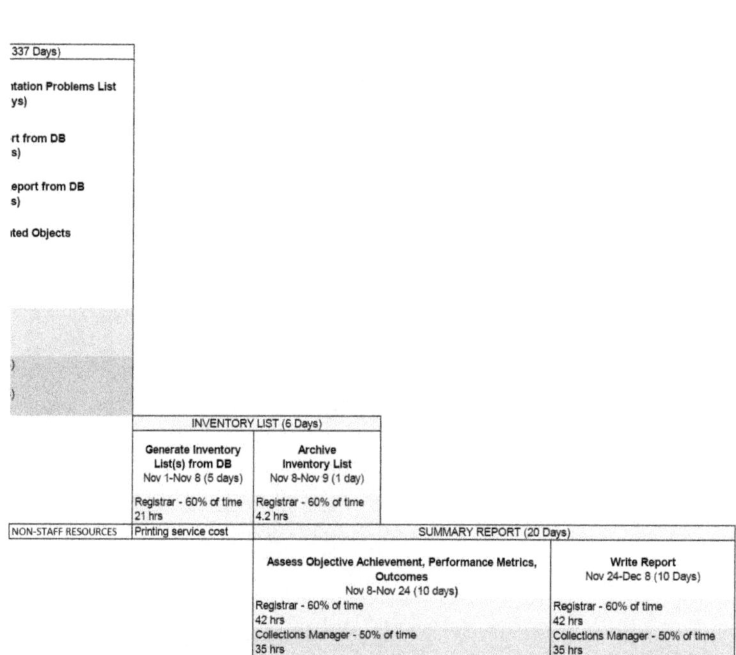

337 Days)			
ıtation Problems List ys)			
rt from DB s)			
eport from DB s)			
ıted Objects			
	INVENTORY LIST (6 Days)		
	Generate Inventory List(s) from DB Nov 1-Nov 8 (5 days)	**Archive Inventory List** Nov 8-Nov 9 (1 day)	
	Registrar - 60% of time 21 hrs	Registrar - 60% of time 4.2 hrs	
NON-STAFF RESOURCES	Printing service cost	SUMMARY REPORT (20 Days)	
		Assess Objective Achievement, Performance Metrics, Outcomes Nov 8-Nov 24 (10 days)	**Write Report** Nov 24-Dec 8 (10 Days)
		Registrar - 60% of time 42 hrs	Registrar - 60% of time 42 hrs
		Collections Manager - 50% of time 35 hrs	Collections Manager - 50% of time 35 hrs

CHAPTER NINE

~

Executing the Inventory

Earlier chapters dealt with Museum A's objectives and why they are needed, the deliverables that will achieve them, the activities that will produce the deliverables, and which resources will be needed and when. These answer the "why," "what," "who," and "when" of the inventory project. They further culminated in a project scope that serves as a road map for steering the museum to its collections stewardship goals. This chapter deals with the "how" of inventory execution, focusing on the activities for producing the "Digital Inventory Data" and "Reconciled Discrepancies" deliverables as mapped out on Museum A's activity network. Although the case studies in part II of this book illustrate that the same activities play out differently at a given museum, the chapter provides a jumping off point for answering and anticipating the "how" in many inventory scenarios.

Digital Inventory Data

In its objectives, Museum A determined it needs baseline descriptive data for 100 percent of the collection. For Museum A, this means physically inspecting objects and capturing a predetermined inventory dataset for every object in the collections database. Because it knows it has a large number of records that aren't registered in the database, Museum A will register these records before object inspection begins. Based on its collection documentation assessment, Museum A anticipates it will encounter some roadblocks to capturing the data; these problems will be tracked in a documentation problems log. These elements—registered records in the database, the inventory dataset for 100% of the collection, and the documentation problems log—comprise Museum A's primary deliverable: digital inventory data.

Registering Known Unregistered Records

To address known unregistered records, Museum A's registrar, collections manager, and two museum specialists hired for the project will collectively undertake retrospective registration before proceeding to the physical inspection. Retrospective registration refers to the creation of database records to ensure that paper records have a corresponding version in a centralized digital collection information system. By accomplishing this first, object record queries performed during physical inspection will return more records ready to receive inventory data. This reduces disruptions to the workflow: if retrospective registration occurred in tandem with the physical inspection, each time inventory takers encountered an unregistered object, they would have to stop and wait for it to be registered in the database before capturing the dataset.

In the regular course of business, the ability to create, edit, and delete object records is usually restricted to one or very few individuals—typically a registrar—as a quality control and security measure. The issue of who can create, edit, and delete records is of particular concern when those individuals will also access objects. This concern recurs throughout audit reports of inventory practices at several Smithsonian museums.[1,2,3] In these audits, the Smithsonian Office of the Inspector General (OIG) describes a worker having access to both objects and records as an "improper segregation of duties" since an individual could steal an object "and then mask the theft by altering or deleting the object's audit trail" or record.[4] Realistically, many museums may be incapable of fully segregating these roles and functions. The OIG offers a compromise by allowing "different levels of separation based on the value of the collections; while high-value collections may need full separation of duties, other collections may only need an audit trail to track changes" and "where separation of duties is not possible, other compensating controls should be implemented to minimize any risk."[5]

In Museum A's case, the museum specialists hired for the project will be authorized temporarily to create new records in the database in order to complete retrospective registration. Before proceeding to the physical inspection, the registrar will restrict database access to populating, editing, or deleting data in fields corresponding to the inventory dataset. During the physical inspection, the tasks of creating or deleting records will be funneled through the registrar, whose access to storerooms and objects is largely restricted. In addition to being more secure, this approach helps ensure data accuracy by providing another layer of review as requests for new records are cross-checked and approved. But this approach may also slow the inventory. To mitigate this, Museum A's registrar will extend some record creation privileges to inventory staff. Within a master or "parent" record representing an object made of multiple separate components, inventory takers will be permitted to create "child" records to account for each component.

Physical Inspection and Inventory Data Capture

After completing retrospective registration, Museum A's museum specialists will begin the physical inspection of objects, during which the inventory dataset will be confirmed, corrected, or recorded to reflect the museum's holdings. Museum A will deploy a team of two museum specialists to physically inspect objects. This comports with a favored approach that suggests that using a team of two (or more) people with no hierarchical relationship between them enhances the likelihood that security and preventive conservation protocols will be modeled. As well, Museum A's collections environments demand two sets of hands for safely ascending ladders and retrieving objects that are large, bulky, or out of the way.

During the physical inspection, Museum A's inventory takers will capture data directly in the database. One museum specialist may assume the role of "scribe," querying, capturing, and confirming data in the database, while the other acts as the handler, calling out objects' unique identifiers, locations, and other data. Typically, direct entry is the fastest and most accurate method for recording inventory data. Handwriting inventory data takes much longer than direct entry, and more inaccuracies and omissions stem from illegibility, transcription mistakes, data entry backlogs, and misplaced papers.

While direct entry is preferred, Museum A may occasionally opt to use printed reports generated from database location queries. Objects encountered will be checked against the list, which will be manually annotated with updates to the dataset. The data updates and an inventory episode will be entered in database records the same day. Although not ideal, this indirect approach may be reasonable in areas where a laptop workstation is difficult to maneuver, if the network is disrupted, or in parts of the collection that are reliably documented in the database and for which few changes are anticipated. A third alternative, should the database be inaccessible, is to capture the data in a spreadsheet and import it into the database as soon as possible.

When planning the rollout of the physical inspection, Museum A's registrar decided to start in the most poorly documented areas of the collection to reduce the risk that these areas will go unaddressed if the project faces delays. After targeting these areas, the team will proceed spatially through collections areas in a logical order. Moving systematically through storage helps prevent undocumented objects from being overlooked and promotes efficiency, as objects of similar type, size, and material are often stored together. Working through groups of similar objects rather than alternating between different types streamlines handling, data capture, and other activities such as photography. Objects on display present an exception to this approach; Museum A will inventory those collections on Tuesdays when the museum is closed to the public.

On a typical day, Museum A's museum specialists will set up a workstation with a computer or mobile device in the work area and ensure ample space is available to receive and inspect objects. They will begin by querying a discrete storage location in the database to return a list of objects that should be there according to the database, for instance, everything recorded as being in Storeroom 1, Shelf 10, which holds ceramic vessels. Museum A's team of two will systematically inspect each object on the shelf and compare them to the database's query results. If the shelf is high, the handler may climb a ladder, inspect the first vessel, and read off its number from that vantage point. With the query results sorted by number, the scribe can easily navigate to the record and confirm that the object and record match by comparing the object to the record's descriptive information and/or to photographs linked to the record. Then the dataset is verified or captured directly in the database. If the handler detects instability, they will alert the collections manager to prepare a foam wedge or ring to stabilize the base of the vessel. The team will proceed in a logical order inventorying all vessels on the shelf.

Comparing location query results with what they see on Shelf 10 will give the inventory takers a sense of how accurate the data is for objects in that location. If many vessels are on Shelf 10, but the database query returns only two records, the scribe can attempt to find pertinent records by querying numbers marked on objects, classification, object name, donor, or other distinguishing data. As a time-saving measure, the team may inspect all objects on Shelf 10, capturing part of the dataset on a record-by-record basis, and then record the location and inventory episode via a bulk transaction if the database supports it. If the inventory team encounters an unnumbered vessel on Shelf 10, the scribe may query the database for all vessels, then filter or scan the results to find the object's record. If successful, the handler will tag the object with its number and proceed with capturing inventory data.

Once inventory criteria are satisfied in a given location, the museum specialists may print inventory index sheets to attach to box fronts, cabinets, or shelving units; the lists can be exported from the database following data capture. They may also create "inventory complete" labels, which inventory takers may sign, date, and attach to storage units to indicate that the contents have been inventoried.

Logging Documentation Problems

Museum A anticipated that inventory takers would encounter additional unregistered objects during the physical inspection even though they registered a large number of known unregistered records in advance. To address this, the museum specialists will generate a log of documentation problems encountered during the physical inspection. The documentation problems log records problems or discrepancies that impede recording, confirming, or updating data in an object's database record. In addition to unregistered objects, objects with incorrect or conflicting numbers and undocumented objects with no apparent number typically end up on the list.

When problems are encountered, inventory personnel will research collection records to resolve the issue. If it can't be fixed quickly, the issue will be recorded on the log and funneled to Museum A's registrar for review. The log will be updated to reflect attempts to address the problems, and inventory takers will circle back to record the dataset for objects whose issues have been resolved.

From time to time, Museum A's inventory takers may encounter documentation problems that don't impede recording inventory data but are significant. For instance, the wrong object image may be linked to a record, or an object may not be marked with its number. The project scope will not be expanded to address these issues, but the museum specialists will track them in the log to be addressed post-inventory.

Reconciled Discrepancies

To satisfy the "Reconciled Discrepancies" deliverable, Museum A will need to resolve the issues on the documentation problems log, which mainly lists objects that are unregistered, undocumented because they can't be linked to a record, or numbered incorrectly. Collection records are the essential resource for researching and resolving discrepancies encountered throughout the inventory. Before commencing the physical inspection, Museum A's registrar identified collection documentation likely to be useful for reconciliation (textbox 9.1). Inventory takers and registrars will research this material to reconcile discrepancies and to reunite undocumented objects with their records. The team can start to reconcile issues as soon as the physical inspection kicks off. To avoid getting bogged down by difficult documentation problems, which can result in lost momentum and oversights, Museum A's registrar established methods for resolving these issues in advance and documented the protocol in the inventory procedures manual. After analyzing the full body of documentation problems captured during physical inspection, there will likely be two additional types of discrepancies to address: 1) undocumented objects that ultimately cannot be matched with legitimate records and 2) records for which no objects were found.

Objects Not Registered in the Database

When additional unregistered objects are encountered during inspection, inventory takers will double-check that the object isn't registered under a different record by querying the database for similar objects, for donations featuring similar objects, or by storage location. If unsuccessful, the inventory takers will record the issue on the documentation problems log. The registrar will reference accession documentation and register the object in the database. Typically, objects requiring records will be registered at the item level following existing registration protocols. But there may be times when it is more logical to assign one number to a large number of similar objects or object parts rather than creating individual records for each, a method known as lot registration or lot cataloging.[6] To strengthen accountability, Museum A will also need to address the registration of objects with multiple components.

Textbox 9.1

REFERENCE MATERIAL FOR RECONCILING DOCUMENTATION DISCREPANCIES

- Accession ledgers
- Deeds of gift, offers of gift, or transfers of title
- Handwritten catalog records
- Field collection notes
- Financial records
- Historic inventories/indexes
- Exhibition labels
- Loan agreements
- Annual reports and meeting minutes produced by the institution or by a former parent organization
- Deaccession records
- Donor files
- Correspondence
- Exhibition catalogs
- Journals, digitized newspaper archives or clippings, other publications
- Research notes
- Photographic slides or other image formats
- Previously used databases
- Staff memory

Source: Adapted from Collections Trust, "Spectrum 5.0 UK Collections Management Standard, Inventory—Suggested Procedure," accessed October 14, 2021, collectionstrust.org.uk/resource/inventory-suggested-procedure/.

Lot Registration

Lot registration can be used to account for a large number of objects (generally small ones) from the same source with similar or indistinguishable characteristics, such as potsherds in an archaeology collection or a set of nails in a history collection.[7] For lot registration to work effectively, a record used to track multiple objects or object components must include a unit of measure, such as item count or weight, that represents the entire lot. Typically, lot registration is unsuitable for documenting high-value objects, those that are significant as individual objects, or objects stored in different locations.

When large groups of unregistered objects or object components are discovered during an inventory, deciding which method is best—item or lot-level registration—depends on the significance of the objects, the likelihood of needing individual tracking in the future, and available resources. These decisions become easier with practice and will also be influenced by the amount of time required to inventory hundreds of similar items.

Multicomponent Object Registration

Inventory takers will also encounter objects that feature multiple components, which are separate parts that form a set or pair, or that otherwise complete an object. Methods for accounting for components rely heavily on database capabilities. Many collections management systems support the creation of records used to track object components or parts of sets that exist as subrecords ("child" records) to an object's master record ("parent" record). These subrecords can be assigned separate storage locations, ensuring that all parts are accounted for. Conversely, many databases lack dedicated features for documenting components, and creating unique records for each is unrealistic.

Museum A's legacy documentation systems have accounted for multicomponent objects inconsistently, so it will use the inventory as an opportunity to shore up protocols for tracking multicomponent objects, especially since they may have different storage or display locations than their "parent" objects. Newly documented components will reflect protocols set forth in the inventory procedures manual. Inventory personnel may consider whether components that were documented heterogeneously in the past should be renumbered. They may also evaluate whether components of the same object registered under unique records should be combined in a parent record if the database now supports it. For Museum A, the answer is no. Its goal is not to make legacy numbering systems match current formats. Changing previously assigned numbers or altering records for components that are otherwise adequately accounted for would not elevate achievement of its objectives but would divert resources away from them. Changing numbers also raises the possibility that numbers marked on objects will need removal, an unjustified risk of damage.

Undocumented Objects

During physical inspection, inventory takers may encounter objects that are dissociated from their records because the object's record number was never applied, the number was abraded, or the object tag fell off. To reunite these objects with their records, Museum A's inventory takers will seek clues to their identity by noting the objects' locations, features, or housings. For instance, if an unnumbered object is found among similar objects from the same acquisition, the museum specialists will check records to determine whether the object is part of it. Once identified, the object can be tagged with its number and inventoried. In other cases, the registrar or collections manager may know the source of an object with no number, but an accession number has not yet been assigned. The registrar will create the new record and route the object back to inventory takers for tagging and inventorying.

When an object can't be identified easily, the registrar may attempt other means of determining the object's legitimate record number, perhaps by examining the accession ledger or a binder of historic slides photographically documenting the collection. If a potential match is found, they will cross check it against other records. If confirmed, they will note the resolution and object number in the documentation problems log. The inventory team will then revisit the object to tag and capture the dataset for it.

Objects that have no clues connecting them to documentation and whose identity can't be determined within a reasonable period of time are known as undocumented objects.[8] These items may be assigned and tagged with temporary numbers to begin tracking them. Museum A will consistently apply a temporary tracking number format that is logical, immediately identifiable, and easily queried in the database. The formats will employ the unique prefix "NN" (for "no number"), followed by a binomial that indicates when the dissociated object was encountered. For example, the number NN2022.1 will be used to track the first undocumented object encountered in 2022.

In Museum A's case, some parts of the collection are poorly documented and have scant inventory history. It expects that numerous undocumented objects may require registration under temporary tracking numbers. Stopping to request temporary records one by one as these objects are encountered and noted on the documentation problems log will disrupt the inventory workflow. To mitigate this, Museum A's registrar will preregister batches of temporary tracking records in the database, which can be used as needed. For example, the registrar may preregister twenty-five shell records under the temporary tracking numbers NN2020.1 through NN2020.25. When inventory takers encounter an undocumented object, they can note the issue on the documentation problems log, query the database to see the next available temporary number, tag the object with the number, and proceed to capture the inventory data in the shell record. If the team splits up and works independently at some juncture, the registrar may assign distinct blocks of temporary records to each museum specialist. This avoids the scenario of staff assigning the same temporary number to two objects or attempting to enter data into the same record simultaneously. If unused temporary tracking records remain post-inventory, they will be deleted.

Objects with Incorrect Numbers

Often, incorrectly assigned identifiers can be corrected after a records review reveals the error. If two objects are assigned the same number, a general guideline is to preserve the more established relationship.[9] For example, Museum A's inventory takers observe the number 1985.10.4 on a painting and a drawing. The corresponding database record describes the painting and contains years of accumulated cataloging information as well as location, exhibition, and loan history. In this case, it makes sense to preserve the relationship between the painting and the number. If the drawing is from the same acquisition, it can be assigned the next sequential number in the accession. If the origin of the drawing is unknown, it may be assigned a temporary number. If two objects are marked with the same number and the record is scant, object condition may come into play when deciding which will retain the number. It may be more appropriate to preserve the numbering relationship with the more vulnerable object, rather than risk damage by attempting to remove the number and apply a new one.

Some databases don't prevent the registration of multiple records with the same number. In this scenario, a review of documentation will show which number was assigned erroneously. With the error identified, digital and paper records can be updated to note the correct number and to archive the old one. In some collections, the same number has been assigned to multiple objects intentionally. This may occur when museums collect mass-produced items or receive multiple examples of identical objects from one donor. For instance, Museum A's former registrar registered five indistinguishable posters as a lot under one record number and noted the object count. This may have been adequate if they were all in the same location. However, some of the posters have different locations and exhibition, loan, and conservation treatment histories. Because Museum A's registrar has sufficient time and resources, they will break up the lot by linking one poster to the original number and assigning the other posters the next sequential numbers in the acquisition, creating additional records accordingly.

Museum A's inventory team will also encounter objects marked with more than one number, a result of new numbering systems superseding legacy systems. Once Museum A's inventory takers confirm the current object number, they will record the legacy number as a former or alternate number in the database record and in the original records. They have opted to leave defunct numbers marked on objects in place after ensuring that the correct number is easily decipherable. This serves the interests of conservation and provenance documentation.

Reconciling Undocumented and Missing Object Records

After completing the physical inspection, Museum A ended up with digital inventory data that reflects three statuses: (a) inventoried objects matched with records, (b) undocumented objects assigned temporary tracking numbers, and (c) records for which no objects were found, which are currently considered missing. Museum A will compare undocumented objects to missing object records and attempt to match them.

Comparing Undocumented Objects to Missing Objects

Undocumented objects may correspond to records for which no objects were found. To identify any matches between these sets, Museum A's registrar will query the database for all undocumented objects that were registered under temporary tracking numbers. Query results will be sorted by object name or other logical criteria and then exported to produce a list of undocumented objects and components. The registrar will produce a list of objects believed to be missing by querying the database for all records lacking an inventory episode. If the lists are extensive, the team may subdivide them into groups based on typology or similar characteristics for easier comparison. If the number of undocumented objects is manageable, they may lay them out on a table organized by type for comparison against the records representing missing objects.

If matches between undocumented objects and missing object records are made, the objects will be tagged with the correct number. Records will then be updated by merging temporary records with correct records. This may involve transferring inventory data from the temporary record to the legitimate record and retiring the temporary number. Alternatively, temporary records may be annotated to indicate that the undocumented item was reunited with its legitimate record (e.g., "reconciled with 1984.10.3"). The matched record may likewise be annotated to cross-reference the temporary record (e.g., "previously tracked under NN2017.0.3") or by entering the temporary number in the field dedicated to alternate or previous numbers.

Unreconciled Undocumented Objects

The chances of a one-to-one match between undocumented objects and records for missing objects are slim. If a significant number of matches between undocumented objects and missing object records were made, Museum A will generate a refreshed list reflecting the remaining undocumented objects. Staff will research collection reference material in a final attempt to reunite undocumented objects with legitimate records. The process of researching undocumented objects, reuniting them with documentation, and deciding how to treat them moving forward can be a time-consuming and resource-intensive process that may extend well beyond the official inventory timeline. Nevertheless, the Smithsonian OIG emphasizes the critical nature of this inventory activity. For temporary tracking numbers to be an effective means of recording undocumented objects, time and resources must be dedicated to reconciliation. The OIG argues that this style of record keeping without an intentional reconciliation follow-up "creates the appearance that objects are missing when in fact objects may have actually been deaccessioned or assigned a temporary tracking number. The temporary tracking numbers create the potential for duplicate records . . . and increase the risk that objects could be lost or stolen without detection."[10]

Following a final review, some objects may remain undocumented. Buck's and Gilmore's well-known approach for addressing these objects is to classify them as "found in collection" (FIC), defined as "undocumented objects that remain without status after all attempts to reconcile them to existing records of permanent collection and loan objects fail."[11] They note that FIC objects are a common occurrence and aren't something staff should be admonished for. Rather, FICs can be attributed to deficiencies in past collecting or documentation practices and insufficient collections care resources.[12]

If Museum A opts to classify undocumented objects as FIC, it must decide how it will treat these objects moving forward. Given the objects' unknown provenance, staff may question the ownership status of FIC objects. Buck and Gilmore argue that FIC objects most likely belong to the museum. Unless state law dictates that FICs should be treated otherwise, protocols should reflect this likelihood if Museum A wishes to make the strongest possible ownership claim.[13,14] Operating under this policy, the museum may accession or deaccession FIC objects following protocols in its approved collections management policy. It may be required to first claim the objects under applicable state law and replace temporary tracking numbers with permanent accession numbers.

If undocumented objects will be assigned accession numbers, Buck and Gilmore recommend the following format: 2022.00.1.[15] This number indicates the first undocumented object assigned an accession number in 2022. Later, if an FIC object's original documentation is found, the object can be returned to its original status and accession number. The FIC number can be discontinued[16] and documented as a former number. If Museum A follows this approach, it will need to update its collections management policy and inventory protocols to specify how the institution distinguishes between undocumented and FIC objects, what must occur for an undocumented object to be considered FIC, and how the museum treats FIC objects.[17,18,19]

Especially for large collections, the time between assigning temporary tracking numbers, completing reconciliation research, and subsequently assigning FIC numbers can be long. For this reason, museums whose policy is to claim ownership of undocumented objects might consider assigning accession numbers to them from the start. This approach eliminates the need to retire temporary numbers but sidesteps reconciliation, as these undocumented objects may match uninventoried records at the end of physical inspection. Assigning an accession number suggests that some sort of review has occurred and that the objects may be used or removed from the collection in the same way as other accessioned collections.[20] However, reconciliation research is ultimately incomplete until a full records inventory has been performed. Assigning accession numbers to undocumented objects may therefore give collections personnel pause if they will be considered for deaccessioning, if outside claims of ownership could be made, or if reproducing the objects could be construed as copyright infringement. In short, assigning accession numbers without a documented rationale for doing so may increase risks of liability and lead to inconsistent practices.[21]

On the other hand, Museum A's registrar may regard replacing a temporary tracking number with yet another number following completion of reconciliation efforts as a time-consuming activity that increases potential for errors and confusion. Although FIC numbers are beneficial in that they can signal that reconciliation research efforts have been exhausted, Museum A may opt to retain the temporary tracking numbers, which presumably can be used to document unsuccessful reconciliation efforts.

Because the inventory could result in a large number of FIC objects being brought to light, these objects may be reported like other accessioned material so they can be considered when calculating collection size, which may factor into the allocation of collection care resources. Transparency with FICs can also strengthen the collection, as curators may assess their significance relative to the museum's mission and collecting scope.

Old Loans

Reconciliation research may reveal that some undocumented objects are old loans. These are loan objects whose owners have not claimed them and whose owners the museum is unable to locate after the expired or unspecified loan period.[22] Old loans are troublesome. In addition to being separated from their rightful owners, Museum A is unable to make full use of the objects. Without legal title, the museum can't ethically loan them, perform conservation treatments, dispose of them, or reproduce images of them if they are protected by copyright.[23] When a loan agreement is signed, a legal relationship known as bailment is established. In this arrangement, the museum (the bailee) is obligated to care for the borrowed object(s) until the lender (the bailor) claims them. This obligation can continue indefinitely unless the loan agreement states terms for concluding the loan or a state statute instructs how the loan can be terminated.[24] To resolve old loans, Museum A's registrar will attempt to contact the lender and plan to return the objects. If the lender is unknown or can't be located, the museum may eventually assert ownership of the objects. However, this means that the bailment relationship is broken. Processes for ending bailment—including relying on common law principles or following the guidelines of state-specific old loan statutes—have been covered extensively in museum literature.[25,26] Moving forward, Museum A's registrar will attempt to prevent old loans by avoiding long loan terms, which increase the chance of losing contact with the lender; clearly stating loan termination terms in loan agreements; and periodically inventorying loan records. Sharing inventory data about the missing object is a universal aspect of these reporting processes.

Unreconciled Missing Objects

As with unreconciled undocumented objects, further attempts must be made to research any remaining records for which no object was found before officially declaring objects lost or missing. To do so, Museum A will double-check the object's recorded location, scrutinize location histories and "object removed" slips or historic object transfer logs, check areas where similar objects are stored, review outgoing loan and deaccession records, check administrative spaces where collections might be used as office décor, and query veteran staff. Inventory personnel may also review the database record audit trails and check for oversights, such as duplicate records or records created in anticipation of pending gifts that never arrived. Many databases lack an adequate solution for merging duplicate records when one object has been tracked erroneously under two records in the database. To merge, the registrar may be required to choose which to retain, in which case some data, such as location history, may not transfer to the retained record. Manually copying data over to the selected record may therefore be necessary. Erroneous records can then be flagged or retired.

Objects that can't be found after reasonable attempts to locate them have failed may be considered "lost in inventory," a preferred term Buck and Gilmore use to describe objects "that have been previously located but not found when needed or during an inventory."[27] Missing objects may be a result of simple human error when objects were moved, theft, or an overlooked outgoing loan. It can be difficult to say when an object is truly lost, and objects lost in inventory often turn up eventually. However, recording objects as lost when they can't be found is a means of accounting for the objects Museum A believes it should have and is therefore an important part of reconciliation.

Museum A will record objects as lost in inventory rather than retire their database records or deaccession them from the collection because objects can't be considered deaccessioned without having dispersed them.[28] As well, maintaining database records for lost objects provides a means of identifying them, documenting the date the loss was noticed, and proving ownership should the objects resurface. To this end, Museum A's registrar will add the location "Lost in Inventory" in the database's location authority. They will query remaining unlocated objects and "move" them to this location in a bulk transaction, recording the date of the move and the recorder's name. Objects may also be recorded as lost in tandem with the physical inventory when they aren't found in their recorded locations. This immediately flags them as potentially lost. Searching for lost objects by their "location" quickly returns a complete list.

Museum A will bring the list of missing objects to the attention of the museum's governing body and security personnel and, in some instances, to external agencies. While it may make staff uneasy or anxious about potential allegations of mismanagement, officially reporting missing objects to external agencies may provide the only means of recovering them. For instance, Art Loss Register (ALR) enables museums to report lost or stolen artwork for registration in its database, which is checked against worldwide sales in the art market. The company claims that database queries regularly carried out by ALR; law enforcement officials; and private entities, such as auction houses, art fairs, galleries, and dealers, increase the chances of recovering cultural heritage that was possessed or sold unlawfully.[29] ALR's website celebrates its role in the recovery of a Roman marble head of Marcus Aurelius, which was stolen from a museum in Skikda, Algeria, in 1996. In June 2004, ALR found the bust during a review of an antiquities sale in New York City; it was repatriated in 2008.[30] In keeping with this, the U.S. Department of the Interior (DOI) advises museum personnel to exercise professional judgment in determining whether to notify law enforcement concerning the possibility of theft.[31] The DOI further highlights the potential to add missing objects to the Federal Bureau of Investigation's National Stolen Art File or to the International Criminal Police Organization's Stolen Works of Art Database. Sharing inventory data about the missing object is a universal aspect of these reporting processes.

If a museum declares an object lost in inventory and is reasonably certain it won't be found, it may wish to claim the loss with its insurance company if such a loss is covered. However, a claim could affect coverage renewal terms and premiums, and if a claim on a missing object is paid, the insurance company will own the object if it is ever found.[32]

Good inventory outcomes are predicated on sound planning, and smooth execution is served by an understanding of how the activities may play out. But no matter how well versed a team may be in the nuances and complexities of inventory activities, project execution almost always differs from the theoretical plan. The next chapter continues answering the "how" of an inventory project by exploring how to stay on track in the face of changes that will present throughout the inventory's execution.

Textbox 9.2

INVENTORY WORKFLOW AT THE NATIONAL SEPTEMBER 11 MEMORIAL & MUSEUM

Danielle Butterly, Inventory Technician

Museums that have an established inventory schedule and comprehensive documentation in their collections management system may opt to use collection data as the starting point to begin an inventory project. Inventory staff would verify the presence of objects and the accuracy of their records by physically locating and inspecting objects based on information queried from the database.

Not every museum will be in such a position, however, especially if they have never completed a full inventory or collection documentation is incomplete. Such was the case at the National September 11 Memorial & Museum. Known at the time as the World Trade Center Memorial Foundation, the Museum began collecting in 2006. Following a call for donations, its nascent staff responded to an overwhelming public response by receiving and processing thousands of gifts prior to opening its doors in 2014. The Museum had yet to conduct a comprehensive inventory, and spot-checks in 2015 revealed that item-level cataloging for early acquisitions was often inconsistent and incomplete. When recorded storage locations existed, they tended to be unreliable. Moreover, accession ledgers were not kept between 2008 and 2012, meaning the Museum's hard-copy and electronic acquisition files provided the most centralized resource for verifying collections. However, while object-level cataloging was often incomplete or in need of correction and collection documentation was somewhat decentralized, staff felt confident that acquisition or lot-level records existed in the database for all or nearly all acquisitions, as creating this record was considered a minimum requirement with the understanding that object-level cataloging could occur when resources permitted.

Though a significant portion of the collection would require item-level cataloging, staff decided to incorporate this process into the inventory rather than address retrospective cataloging separately. Staff also opted to begin with physical objects and verify collection documentation against them and vice versa. In other words, as objects were encountered in storage, their records were examined to create a picture of the contents of the acquisition that would need to be accounted for and documented. At the end of the project, acquisition lots reviewed by the inventory team (a list that can be generated by the collections management system) would be compared against the Museum's records to determine whether any had not been encountered by the inventory team. Though this approach made for a longer process, it allowed staff to begin the work of verifying storage locations while simultaneously dramatically improving the quality, standardization, and completeness of collection data. The following describes the workflow we followed in our first attempt to locate and document every object in the collection.

We generally began by selecting a container from a shelf and pulling an object from it. Fortunately, most of our objects were assigned and tagged with a number, so the first step was to locate the number. If we found a number on a tag, we queried the object's catalog record and examined the object to see whether it was physically numbered as well. Many of our objects had not yet been physically numbered, so after confirming that the object matched the catalog record, these objects were added to an Excel spreadsheet to be numbered later. Rather than stopping work to physically number objects, entire days would be devoted every few weeks to numbering objects that had been placed on the list in the preceding days or weeks.

Once objects were identified, they were checked against the database record for accuracy of information. We verified the object name and type, identified the medium(s), recorded the dimensions of the object, identified and documented any possible conservation concerns, and verified the presence of a photograph. In many cases, a photograph of the object had not yet been taken. To ensure the comprehensiveness of the data, we photographed these objects, titled the image files according to our institutional file-naming standards, and copied the files to their corresponding electronic donor folder. We then uploaded the files to the object record in our database to facilitate future object identification. If the object had additional parts, we created a component record (or multiple component records, depending on the number of pieces) and entered inventory data in those records as well. This was commonly required for objects that had fragments once belonging to the larger artifact. In cases where the object had a "parent/child" relationship, we created records to be linked back to the larger object.

Once the physical inspection of the object was complete, we proceeded to rehouse the object according to archival standards. We considered the object's medium, weight, and size before making any decisions. Upon choosing a container and storage method for an object, we updated the location in our database to reflect the new and correct container number and then updated the location of the container on its newly designated shelf. With all the steps completed, we marked the object's record in the database "inventoried" and annotated it with the date of the action. As an added measure against human error and inaccuracy, we created a checklist to document the actions taken during the inventory of an object. The spreadsheet served as a backup record of final location and date of inventory and could be easily reconciled with final inventory counts from the database at the end of each working day.

In some instances, objects did not have a catalog record and needed to have a number assigned and a record created. If the acquisition lot number could be identified, we assigned a number to the object following the last object number in the acquisition. We then photographed the object, titled the image file according to the number we assigned, copied the file to the electronic donor folder for the corresponding lot, and added the object to a spreadsheet for our head of cataloging and archives to create its record. Upon creation of that record, we then proceeded to inventory the object as usual.

If the acquisition number could not be identified through research or consulting with colleagues, we assigned an "NN," or "unknown," number to the object and entered inventory data for tracking purposes until it could hopefully be reconciled in the future.

Notes

1. U.S. House of Representatives Committee on House Administration, *Hearing: Collections Stewardship at the Smithsonian*, 113th Cong. (2013) (testimony of Mr. Scott S. Dahl, Inspector General, Smithsonian Institution), https://docs.house.gov/Committee/Calendar/ByEvent.aspx?EventID=101132, 5.

2. A. Sprightley Ryan, *Collections Stewardship at the Cooper-Hewitt, National Design Museum*, OIG-A-11-02 (Washington, DC: Office of the Inspector General, 2011), www.si.edu/oig/Audit_Reports, 12.

3. A. Sprightley Ryan, *Collections Stewardship of the National Collections at the National Museum of American History—Preservation and Physical Security*, OIG-A-10-03-2 (Washington, DC: Office of the Inspector General, 2011), www.si.edu/oig/Audit_Reports, 23–24.

4. Ryan, *Cooper-Hewitt*, 16.

5. Ibid., 12.

6. Department of the Interior, *Guidance for Cataloging Department of the Interior Museum Collections* (Washington, DC: Department of the Interior, 2016), https://www.doi.gov/sites/doi.gov/files/uploads/museum_cataloging_guidance_march_2016_fnl.pdf, 24-29.

7. Ibid.

8. Rebecca A. Buck and Jean Allman Gilmore, *Collection Conundrums: Solving Collections Management Mysteries* (Washington, DC: American Association of Museums, 2017), 38.

9. Ibid., 59.

10. Ryan, *Cooper-Hewitt*, 9.

11. Buck and Gilmore, *Collection Conundrums*, 38.

12. Ibid.

13. Ibid., 41.

14. Marie C. Malaro and Ildiko P. DeAngelis, *A Legal Primer on Managing Museum Collections*, 3rd ed. (Washington, DC: Smithsonian Books, 2012), 391.

15. Buck and Gilmore, *Collection Conundrums*, 45.

16. Ibid.

17. Ibid., 23.

18. Malaro and DeAngelis, *A Legal Primer on Managing Museum Collections*, 391.

19. Association of Registrars and Collections Specialists, "Museum Property Acts and Abandoned Loan Legislation," accessed March 1, 2020, https://www.arcsinfo.org/content/documents/arcsmuseumpropertyandoldloanlegislationjune2018.pdf.

20. Ibid., 43.

21. Ibid., 40.

22. Buck and Gilmore, *Collection Conundrums*, 32.

23. Malaro and DeAngelis, *A Legal Primer on Managing Museum Collections*, 319.

24. Sheppard Mullin, "Museum Loans," *Art Law Blog: News & Updates on Legal Issues Facing the Art World*, March 25, 2013, https://www.artlawgallery.com/2013/03/articles/art-collectors/museum-loans/.

25. Buck and Gilmore, *Collection Conundrums*, 32.

26. Malaro and DeAngelis, *A Legal Primer on Managing Museum Collections*, 319.

27. Buck and Gilmore, *Collection Conundrums*, 59.

28. Ibid., 60.

29. Art Loss Register, "Loss Registration," accessed March 1, 2020, http://www.artloss.com/services/loss-registration.

30. Neil Brodie, "Marcus Aurelius Head," *Trafficking Culture*, modified October 11, 2016, https://traffickingculture.org/encyclopedia/case-studies/marcus-aurelius-head/.

31. U.S. Department of the Interior, *Inventory of Museum Collections*, DOI Museum Property Directive 21 (Washington, DC: Office of Acquisition and Property Management, 2014), doi.gov/sites/doi.gov/files/migrated/museum/policy/upload/Dir-21-Collection-Inventory.pdf, 6-7; 14.

32. Buck and Gilmore, *Collection Conundrums*, 60.

CHAPTER TEN

~

Staying on Track

Staying on track means actively monitoring the inventory to ensure objectives are being achieved in line with the scope specifications, timeline, and cost projections. Regular progress assessments highlight achievements, and communicating these to stakeholders sustains morale, builds confidence, and promotes engagement with the project. But staying on track also involves identifying and communicating the need for adjustments. An effective inventory hinges on a sound project plan, but in practice, the execution usually diverges somewhat from the theoretical plan, as is the case with all projects. Additionally, inventory projects carry an inherent degree of uncertainty and risk. For one, they are often longer projects that rely heavily on temporary staff. They also differ from everyday collections work, which is more familiar and predictable. As such, some details that will impact the project will come to light only after the inventory is underway. Since planners can't predict the future, staying on track is about navigating the project forward in spite of inevitable changes.

While generating the initial inventory plan, stakeholders devoted attention to developing the project scope, which identified the requirements—deliverables and activities—needed to produce the objectives. As they developed the resource plan, available time and the budget were scrutinized to strike a balance between the project scope, costs, and time; ultimately, this exercise produced a plan that seemed feasible. This approach describes the so-called project management triangle. Also known as the triple constraint, it refers to the dependent and dynamic relationship between the project scope (the requirements of the project), time, and cost.[1] It holds that if one of these constraints change, one or both of the other two must also change: if the scope grows, so must time and/or budget; if time is reduced, the budget must grow or the scope must be reduced; if the budget is reduced, the scope must also be reduced. This chapter explores keeping an inventory on track through the lens of the triple constraint triangle by demonstrating how scope, time, and cost continue to be balanced throughout the inventory's execution.

Time

During execution, the activity network, developed in chapter 5, becomes a valuable resource for monitoring time and progress. The network displays activity start dates, estimated durations, and finish dates, all of which determined the approximate length of the project (table 7.5). These dates were mapped onto a calendar to determine calendrical start and finish dates and the entire inventory timeline (chapter 8). To track progress, Museum A's registrar can annotate the activity network to show actual start and finish dates, durations, and the use of slack time to determine whether activities will be completed by the target dates and to recalculate new target dates. By watching the critical path, Museum A can see how changes to start and finish dates will impact the overall schedule. Because activities on the critical path determine the entire project duration, any delay on the critical path will extend the project duration. Activities off the critical path can change the path itself if "off-path" activities are delayed. Thus, the activity network affirms that activities are moving along as projected or provides an early signal that the project is falling behind schedule.

While inventory activities serve as natural progress markers, in Museum A's case, physical object inspection and related activities for producing digital inventory data occur in tandem over more than a year. It makes sense, then, for Museum A's registrar to set milestones across the duration of these activities to keep tabs on progress. While estimating activity durations, Museum A projected that the museum specialists would inventory about 1,000 objects per month. The registrar can refer to this estimate to set monthly, weekly, or daily milestones. To assess performance relative to the target, the registrar will use one of the database queries developed while setting up the "inventory-equipped database" to see how many records were inventoried within a date range. Unless the collection is homogeneous or already well documented, it's unrealistic to expect that the same number of objects can be inventoried each month, week, or day. Work rates will ebb and flow organically as staff work through a collection that varies by media, form, housing status, and documentation state. A few months of data will give a realistic picture of whether the projected timeline is reasonable or off base.

Museum A attempted to project a realistic timeline by prototyping physical inspection activities. It also added a "cushion" to the estimated project duration to mitigate delays caused by staff turnover (a risk inherent to many inventory projects), extended staff leave, and other hiccups. To "solve" any significant timeline changes, however, Museum A must trade against the other two project constraints: scope and cost. For example, if Museum A's developer takes longer than expected to make database updates, the activities "design queries" and "design reports" will also be delayed. These activities are on the critical path, so the entire project may be held up. While assembling the activity network, the dependent relationships in the "inventory-equipped database" deliverable were logical and preferable. But as a response to the developer delay, the registrar may propose to stakeholders that "design queries" and "design reports" be taken up after physical inspection is underway since queries and reports will be used primarily for monitoring progress during object inspection and records reconciliation. However, this will impact when and how staff resources are spent: stakeholders will need to approve the cost of the registrar's increased time commitment to the project while they simultaneously develop queries and reports and participate in object inspection.

In another scenario, monitoring progress against monthly targets may reveal that the duration of physically inspecting and documenting objects will be much longer than projected. While most inventory projects carry a degree of uncertainty, the likelihood of underestimating inspection durations increases when substantial portions of the collection are undocumented, when collections are poorly represented in the database, or when planners had low awareness of the extent or profile of the collection. Physical inspection of objects may proceed more fluidly for some collections, for example, matted drawings or items neatly housed and stored on open shelving. Other collections may require more effort and time to access objects, such as furniture that must be moved to access other pieces or large textiles that require unrolling. In other cases, a project manager may be brought on to oversee an inventory whose timeline has been set arbitrarily, in which case the scope may be unrealistic relative to time and cost allocated to the project. In these instances, monitoring work rates for a few months will show that the projected timeline is off base, which is better to know sooner than later. In response, the project manager and other stakeholders may consider extending the inventory timeline, which will also increase staff resource costs. Alternatively, Museum A may opt to concentrate all available resources on physical inspection and data capture or bring in additional staff to expedite those activities. Another option is to reduce the scope: Museum A may reduce the inventory dataset, delimit the objects that will be inventoried, or limit reconciliation activities to logging documentation problems and registering undocumented objects.

Scope

Staying on scope means monitoring the project to ensure activities are consistent with the requirements spelled out in the project scope, as dictated by the deliverables and activities required to achieve the objectives. Changes to the scope often occur via "scope creep," which refers to unauthorized expansion of the agreed-on project scope—what it will produce and what is required to produce it—after the project is underway.[2] Scope creep may stem from decisions made independently by core project staff or from other stakeholders who feel an expanded scope would benefit their work. When every object in the collection will be inspected, it can be tempting to add on unplanned activities, such as rehousing, or to add more features to the database than what were originally agreed. While unplanned activities may be worthwhile endeavors, a key benefit of an inventory is that it enables stakeholders to identify gaps in stewardship to be addressed post-project. Scope creep can be avoided by reaching consensus with stakeholders on the project scope, sticking to it, and reserving task delegation for the inventory project manager. That said, instances of scope creep might reflect important objectives or deliverables that were overlooked during the planning stage. Stakeholders may agree that an expanded scope is justified but must adjust time and costs accordingly.

While some activities are easily recognizable as scope creep, others may be less so. At Museum A, scope creep has the potential to occur while the museum specialists are producing digital inventory data. To maintain focus on the inventory dataset, the registrar may restrict access to the corresponding fields in the database. Still, the museum specialists are detail oriented, and there is a possibility that the agreed-on brief object descriptions will expand into full catalog entries. This risks lengthening the project or underachieving the objectives. To address this, Museum A's registrar can audit, or spot-check, the inventory data to rein in lengthy descriptions and to otherwise assess the data. To perform spot-checks, the registrar may periodically review a subset of object records and check the data against the objects and scope specifications. If chosen randomly via spreadsheet functions or the database's random sample query, this subset of records enables the registrar to draw conclusions about the quality of data being captured in all the records. The U.S. Department of the Interior provides guidance on how to determine a statistically representative random sample size relative to the number of records in the sample population.[3]

Given the nature of inventories, other changes to the scope may occur as a result of incidents project planners could not have prevented. For instance, during inventories, staff sometimes work with infrequently accessed collections that may be stored in spaces with varying levels of maintenance and housekeeping. In such areas, inventory personnel are more likely to encounter things like active pest infestations and inherently hazardous collections. Hazards may also be a result of environmental conditions, such as airborne particulates, mothball fumes, or the aftereffects of leaks and floods. Some of these issues may have been identified during the planning phase, but there is always the possibility for surprises. Personal protective equipment, prepared object quarantine protocols and supplies, and a list of professional contacts (i.e., an integrated pest management vendor and an industrial hygienist) can expedite responses to such discoveries. When issues surface, the project manager must assess whether they can simply close the door and redirect work to other parts of the collection until the problem can be dealt with. Situations that could imperil the health and safety of staff, however, need to be addressed immediately, as do active pest infestations. If the project falls behind due to weeks of unplanned pest remediation activities, the project manager may seek stakeholder approval to extend the project timeline and resources or propose reducing the scope. In situations where less is known about the collection's environment, it may be wise to build a percentage of contingency into the resource plan.

Cost

While planning the project scope, Museum A attempted to ensure sufficient resource availability by estimating resources needed to carry out each inventory activity. This culminated in a resource plan that showed which resources would be needed, how much, and when. Once the inventory execution is underway, budgeting is an active process; the project manager will regularly track and report actual expenditures and compare them against the projected budget. This informs spending projections for the duration of the project. If the exact nature or extent of inventory work becomes clear only after work has begun, the project manager may propose amendments to increase the project duration and subsequently, the budget. If the budget is firm, stakeholders will be required to determine what is reasonable and most useful to achieve given the allotted time and scale back the project scope accordingly.

Redirection of resources may also occur during an inventory, especially when additional staff are brought on board to execute it. Because inventories can sometimes feel less deadline driven than public-facing initiatives, such as opening a new exhibition or debuting the museum's online catalog, it can be tempting for colleagues to call on inventory staff to help with unrelated activities. While inventory personnel may be willing to oblige these requests, these diversions draw down on the inventory's staff resource budget and risk underachieving the objectives. Furthermore, once a precedent of redirecting staff resources away from the inventory has been set, it will be difficult for colleagues to abstain from relying on inventory staff as a supplemental workforce. To steer clear of this, the project manager must stick to the project scope, which clarifies what work inventory personnel may perform and who may delegate work to them.

In other scenarios, redirection of resources may occur due to circumstances beyond the project manager's control. For example, in environments marked by financial and administrative instability, a core inventory staff member may leave the museum for a new employment opportunity after the project has been approved but before execution. If stakeholders in charge of allocating resources opt to leave the outgoing staff member's position vacant, the project team will be short a member.

In the case of Museum A where grant funding has been requested, the grant award may also be less than initially requested to reflect the museum's reduced cost share. As a result, more time will be needed to fulfill the project requirements, but the projected timeline is already near the maximum length allowed by the funding body. In response, Museum A's stakeholders must determine whether the inventory can absorb this change and if so, how the scope will be adjusted. Similarly, a museum may not receive project funding at the requested level. Reaching consensus among stakeholders around the inventory scope in these scenarios may prove especially challenging. There is no easy solution to a significant budget cut. To prepare for this, the project manager may wish to consider which areas of the collection are most in need of attention or how the inventory scope can be scaled back if necessary.

Admittedly, balancing the constraints of the project management triangle can't solve every issue that influences how the inventory plays out, and it certainly can't predict the future. In addition to a poorly planned scope, a non-collegial workplace culture, financial or administrative instability, or strained interpersonal dynamics can also influence the end result of an inventory project. These issues may contribute to underachievement or increase the cost of achieving the inventory objectives. Still, the impact of these issues will be exacerbated by the absence of effective strategies for keeping the inventory on track. To this end, the project management triangle offers a framework for steering the inventory through change during execution and achieving an end result that satisfies stakeholders' expectations. Eventually, after perhaps rebalancing the triple constraints a time or two, the work of inspecting objects, recording inventory data, and reconciling discrepancies will be complete. But the inventory isn't quite over yet. The next chapter discusses the last phase of the project: closing the inventory.

Notes

1. C. J. Van Wyngaard, J. H. C. Pretorius, and L. Pretorius, "Theory of the Triple Constraint, a Conceptual Review," in *IEEE International Conference on Industrial Engineering and Engineering Management*, Hong Kong, December 10–13, 2012, https://ieeexplore.ieee.org/document/6838095.
2. R. Larson and E. Larson, "Top Five Causes of Scope Creep . . . and What to Do about Them," paper presented at PMI® Global Congress, Orlando, Florida, 2009—North America, https://www.pmi.org/learning/library/top-five-causes-scope-creep-6675.
3. U.S. Department of the Interior, *Inventory of Museum Collections*, DOI Museum Property Directive 21 (Washington, DC: Office of Acquisition and Property Management, 2014), doi.gov/sites/doi.gov/files/migrated/museum/policy/upload/Dir-21-Collection-Inventory.pdf.

CHAPTER ELEVEN

~

Closing the Inventory

As inventory activities wind down, it may be hard to resist returning to business as usual, but a period of closure is a critical phase of the project. During this phase, the final inventory deliverables are completed and transferred to stakeholders. Closing an inventory project also leads to a discussion of how to maintain good collections data over the long term. To this end, an examination of cyclical inventories may encourage some museums to reframe their inventory practice and other collections management protocols. Finally, closing the inventory invites collections practitioners to consider what's next for the collection. The data produced during the inventory or the inventory process itself can inspire and support future collections management, access, and preservation initiatives.

Transferring the Final Inventory Deliverables

At this juncture, Museum A's inventory personnel will have completed most of the deliverables described in chapter 5, including the inventory-equipped database, procedures manual, digital inventory data, and reconciled discrepancies. The inventory list and inventory summary report are the last deliverables to check off.

Inventory List

The inventory list is the authoritative snapshot of the collection's contents (or objects in the inventory scope). For Museum A, the inventory list is extensive; the registrar will export it as a database report and outsource the print job. Reports may be formatted in a number of ways to include the minimum inventory dataset, a thumbnail image, and the date of the report; internal and external stakeholders may also dictate a format that best suits their needs.

The inventory list may merit printing in more than one sort order, for example, by location, accession number, or object name or classification, based on how it will be used by various stakeholders. It's also common to generate sublists for object groups, such as high-value collections, incoming and outgoing loans, the final list of undocumented objects, and the final missing objects list.

Ideally, these reports exist in identical paper and digital versions, with three copies of each stored in different locations. While the database is backed up regularly, digital copies of the inventory list may live on the institutional network, on a mobile storage device, and in the cloud. Paper copies may live in the registrar's office, the institutional archive, and/or an additional off-site location. This ensures the data will remain accessible, whether for day-to-day collections work, in the event of a disaster, or during a network failure.

Inventory Summary Report

The inventory summary report evaluates the inventory's outcomes by assessing whether the objectives were achieved and by comparing the actual deliverables, costs, and timeline against the original plan.[1] It also assesses the inventory's methodologies and processes to determine how they influenced objective achievement. Often assembled as a final communication to stakeholders, the report may also serve as the central repository for the nuts-and-bolts information that flowed from planning and executing the inventory. This may culminate in a project archive, which will be an invaluable reference for documenting work performed, planning future inventories, drafting project proposals for the next collections care project, and streamlining day-to-day activities.

Evaluating the inventory outcomes is primarily a task of synthesizing and distilling data from periodic progress and budget reports to demonstrate that the project produced the intended deliverables and whether it completed them in alignment with the projected timeframe and budget. The total number of objects inventoried, the number of missing objects found, the number of undocumented objects reconciled, and the percentage by which the documented collection increased are statistics that will impress the extent of work accomplished. If object photography was an inventory activity, stakeholders will no doubt be interested to learn the number of images now available to bolster the online catalog, education programs, virtual exhibitions, research requests, and museum merchandise. Likewise, if collection rehousing and/or reorganization occurred, before and after images will testify to dramatic improvements in collection care. It's also important to note where the inventory fell shy of its targets, for instance, by summarizing objects that were not inventoried or other activities that weren't quite completed as intended. Conveying how the inventory solved problems outlined in the project scope justification can amplify metrics used to evaluate the inventory outcomes.

After determining how the inventory outcomes align with stakeholder expectations, the next question to consider is, why or why not? This can be determined by reflecting on the relationship between the inventory's activities and processes and the project outcomes. The following are effective prompts for identifying what worked well and what could be improved the next time around:[2]

- What worked well, and what didn't?
- Could anything have been done better, faster, easier, or more cost effectively?
- When problems arose, how well were they handled? Could any have been anticipated?

Perhaps work was impeded or delayed due to a redirection of resources, a pandemic, staff turnover, or a buggy collections management system. The project manager may also document how the inventory scope, cost, and time constraints were rebalanced in response to changes throughout the course of the project. Input from inventory personnel can further shed light on how inventory processes could be tweaked for optimal results. For example, inventory takers may observe that digitizing historic paper accession records and annual accession reports would significantly expedite reconciliation.

For future reference, the summary report may also centralize other key documents generated throughout the inventory. The original project scope document, budget, personnel roster, vendors, supply lists, progress reports, and grant applications may all be of use. In addition, any protocols produced during the inventory may be included, such as the final inventory procedures manual, the documentation problems log, and protocols for rehousing and photographing objects. Research related to activities or deliverables that did not come to fruition, such as selecting and developing a new database or barcode system, may also be useful references even if they were tabled this time around.

Maintaining Good Collections Data

As remarkable as they are, inventory project outcomes are fleeting unless they are followed by a plan for maintaining good collections data. This is of particular importance since project-style inventories are often invoked exceptionally as a means of reining in administrative and physical control of a collection after a period marked by stewardship practices that were not as effective as they could be. This section discusses tactics for encouraging accurate collections data all the time: implementing a cyclical inventory policy, updating the collections management policy, and creating a work culture that values and prioritizes good collections data.

Implement a Cyclical Inventory Policy

Cyclical inventories are a primary means of maintaining good collections data and collections accountability. Cyclical inventories take place on a regular, predetermined schedule. They may be full inventories or partial inventories that target a "specific percentage or sampling of the entire collection."[3] In the context of commercial inventory management, Muller argues that "cycle counting" is the best way to maintain accurate inventory data in the long term.[4] He argues that regular cycle counting activates a continuous process of improvement whereby staff more quickly discover and correct errors and procedural dysfunctions. There are several cycle counting methods, including the A-B-C categorization, random selection, diminishing population, and product categories methods.[5] While cycle counting techniques are rooted in commercial practice, some museums have developed cyclical inventory policies that derive from them. To get a sense of how cyclical inventories play out in museums, three institutional approaches are discussed. A case is then made for a dynamic application of cyclical inventory methods to respond to an institution's unique circumstances.

Cyclical Inventory Methods in Museums

According to its Interior Museum Program website, the U.S. Department of the Interior (DOI) manages one of the world's largest museum collections—over 200 million artifacts and scientific specimens. The DOI's *Inventory of Museum Collections* directive describes procedures for maintaining inventory data accuracy and accountability for a collection of such magnitude.[6] The DOI classifies museum property into three groups: controlled property, cataloged objects, and accessioned objects that are not cataloged. Controlled property is material that is of high intrinsic or scientific value, especially vulnerable to theft or loss; a museum firearm; or an incoming loan. The directive indicates that 100 percent of controlled property be inventoried annually. For the other two categories, a random sample of objects, generated by the database, is inventoried every two years. Perceived deficiencies in a collecting unit's system may require subsequent 100 percent inventories. The National Park Service, a child agency of the DOI, further directs park collections with fewer than 250 catalog records to complete a 100 percent inventory annually.[7]

In a second example, the collections management policy of the Metropolitan Museum of Art (MMA) directs curatorial departments to inventory collections at least once during every calendar year.[8] An exception is made for departments with "large collections," which may organize inventories around cycles ranging from one to five years. In addition, every calendar year, the registrar is expected to inventory a limited number of works in each curatorial department as well as 100 percent of all works in off-site storage. For outgoing loans, borrowers are expected to furnish an inventory report every two years.

The Smithsonian Office of the Inspector General's (OIG's) audit report of inventory practices at the Smithsonian National Museum of African American History and Culture (NMAAHC) provides a third example:

> NMAAHC's new inventory plan calls for cyclical inventories to be conducted during the third quarter (April to June) of alternating fiscal years. These inventories will use a random list of collection objects and incoming loan objects representing 1 percent of the collection. The plan calls for a complete inventory of high-value or historically significant objects every other year. The plan requires the registrar to prepare a report that outlines the findings of the inventory and to identify any errors in the records.[9]

These three inventory policy examples feature expressions of the A-B-C categorization cycle counting method.[10] In this method, objects are not treated equally but rather are classified into groups based on value or significance. Objects in group A are the most valuable and are inventoried more frequently than those in group B and so on. In addition to value, characteristics connected to risk, such as storage or display location, incoming loan status, and objects that are firearms, may factor into an object's classification. While the MMA policy is silent on the characteristics and numerical threshold of works from each curatorial department that must be inventoried each calendar year, the policy outlines an A-B-C–style process in which a selection of objects is inventoried every year, complemented by 100 percent inventories conducted annually or at least every five years. In the DOI and NMAAHC policies, group A objects are inventoried annually and biannually, respectively. Other groups are inventoried via random selection. This integrates an expression of the random selection cycle counting method, in which a random sample representing a statistically significant cross section of the collection is inventoried.[11] Random selection inventories are thought to produce a reliable snapshot of collection records accuracy.

When crafting a cyclical inventory policy, collections practitioners may like to consider how the A-B-C approach is applied. This is particularly so since assigned value or significance often reflects collecting, preservation, and access practices that stem from systems of inequality, such as patriarchy and white supremacy. In these value systems, objects made or used by groups who control access to essential resources are often deemed most valuable or significant. Moreover, as the influence of provenance research evidences, the very act of inventorying an object—or the presence of a historic inventory episode—can increase its perceived value or significance. Certainly, a diamond is more likely to be stolen than a bullet casing. However, cyclical inventory policies based on value classifications also mean that objects outside of group A may go decades without inspection. Because inventory inspection is a function of preservation, it is important to consider that objects in group A may not reflect a cross section of the collection or its vulnerabilities.

A stronger implementation of cyclical inventory practice would perhaps combine the random selection and diminishing population methods with (or without) the A-B-C method. In the diminishing population method, each object in a defined population is inventoried before being inventoried again, ensuring that all objects are inspected within a given cycle.[12] In a combined approach, objects in group A are still inventoried most frequently, as in the above examples. For the other groups, a random selection of objects is inventoried during the cycle. However, each subsequent random sample draws from the object population that has not been inventoried until 100 percent of the collection has been inventoried. One disadvantage of the diminishing population method is that subsequent random samples may not be a truly representative cross section of the entire collection. Moreover, because random sample inventories lead staff to various corners of the collection, the diminishing population method may be less effective for detecting theft, pest infestation, or other issues.

Combining the diminishing population and random selection methods, however, relies on a database with the ability to generate random sample queries and exclude objects from a sample population. For museums that organize collections by classification, implementing cyclical inventory policy based on collection category may be an alternative option. Planning inventories based on collection classification correlates with the so-called product categories cycle counting method.[13] In this scenario, the inventory cycle proceeds by object classification; staff decide the sequence in which the classifications will be inventoried, and the diminishing population technique is used until each object in the classification has been inventoried. While in some ways the categories method is more straightforward, the benefits of random sampling are absent. An example of putting a cyclical inventory into place using this method can be seen in the case study "I've Seen It All—Inventory at The Children's Museum of Indianapolis" in part II of this book.

How long should an inventory cycle be? When should work occur during the cycle? In the DOI, MMA, and NMAAHC examples, the cycle frequency ranges from one to five years. Only the NMAAHC details when work takes place during the cycle (April, May, and June of alternating fiscal years). Although Muller addresses inventory in the commercial context, he argues reasonably that such lengthy audit trails make it difficult to realistically determine the nature of errors and why they occurred.[14] By the time discrepancies are discovered, the process of untangling them may be too long and complicated. This is to say, restricting inventory activity to a short period of time within the cycle may be less effective than inventorying a smaller number of objects more frequently, perhaps monthly, throughout the cycle. Thus, cycle duration is probably less significant than the frequency of inventory activity within the cycle. With this in mind, rather than replicating an institution's cyclical inventory policy, effective approaches reflect unique circumstances, such as collection size, workload, and resources. Testing and adjusting schedules and cycle durations will reveal what works best.

The Case for a Dynamic Cyclical Inventory Policy

Cyclical inventory theory provides a solid framework for developing a policy. But practitioners may benefit from viewing the policy as dynamic rather than immutable, as something that can be adjusted to respond to institutional needs, goals, and resources. There are several scenarios where a dynamic policy might work well.

By recalling the three prongs of inventory methodology discussed in chapter 3—a survey of objects, a survey of records, and the reconciliation of discrepancies between the two—a disadvantage of many of the cyclical inventory approaches discussed thus far is recognized. That is, they seem to privilege the records-to-objects inventory approach and assume all records are registered in the database. By more or less relying on database queries, objects that would be encountered during an objects-to-records survey may be overlooked and discrepancies missed. Thus, institutions might consider alternating cyclical inventories between records-to-objects and objects-to-records approaches.

On the other hand, if a museum has privileged the objects-to-records approach, it may wish to prioritize a deep-dive records inventory. This would allow for a systematic review of accession records to ensure that a corresponding database record exists. Unregistered records encountered during this review may ultimately be matched with undocumented objects located during a previous round of inventory. A comprehensive record review that includes deaccessioned objects may resolve missing object statuses or reconcile undocumented objects with those that were recorded as deaccessioned but never dispersed.

Other scenarios support a dynamic cyclical inventory approach. For example, if objects within the scope of a 100 percent inventory couldn't be inspected or an element was dropped from the inventory dataset mid project, the subsequent cyclical inventory could go "off script" to address these objects first. Likewise, a new piece of data may be added to the dataset in a subsequent cycle to expand the depth of documentation or prepare for a future project. In especially underresourced settings, a cyclical inventory practice can be initiated with any number of objects that seems reasonable, however small. As record accuracy increases, staff will be able to increase inventory targets.[15]

But perhaps the strongest argument for a dynamic approach to inventory policy is that museums are not infallible. Systems degenerate, museums are in a state of flux, resource allocation fluctuates, and collections are stewarded by people who make choices. Records representing decades or centuries of collecting almost always reveal that documentation systems broke down at least once during an institution's history. The DOI's policy seems to allude to this reality with the caveat that inadequate inventory results may justify a 100 percent inventory. Indeed, inventories are a tool for measuring the effectiveness of registration and documentation practices. But by what criteria do museums decide that practices are effective or in need of tweaking? In a commercial context, Muller indicates that few organizations accept anything lower than 95 percent inventory record accuracy (i.e., no more than 5 percent error rate) in any category.[16] The museum field, however, lacks clear guidelines for what is being measured through inventory as well as what is considered a reasonable percentage of error. The Smithsonian OIG provides some insight, but performance quality criteria remain ambiguous. In a 2011 audit, the OIG seemed to emphasize objects being located as the principal criterion: at the Cooper Hewitt, a 4 percent error rate (objects not located) was deemed "reasonable."[17] In the OIG's 2020 NMAAHC audit, 99 percent of object records in the random sample featured accurate location data. But the OIG placed greater emphasis on the level of minimum dataset completion.[18] In lieu of a standard, setting objective parameters may help guide a museum's assessment of how its systems are working. In any case, museums that continuously assess the effectiveness of their systems through a cyclical inventory practice are positioned to determine whether and how their systems need to change.

Although there are limitations to cyclical inventory techniques, the approach presents perhaps the most viable means of sustaining collections data accuracy and completeness. This strategy diminishes the need for resource-intensive, project-style, 100 percent inventories. In addition to catching problems more quickly, regular partial inventories break inventory work into smaller, more manageable chunks. While some museums already model the technique, others may like to reframe their inventory practice as an ongoing collections care function rather than intermittent projects alternating with protracted periods of inactivity.

Update the Collections Management Policy

In addition to correcting errors, inventories illuminate deficient processes that lead to those errors. Before and during the inventory, staff will have devised ways to prevent these errors from recurring—principally through a refined cyclical inventory policy, consistent and timely location tracking, and registration protocols that include capturing the minimum inventory dataset. Revising the collections management policy (CMP) to reflect updated methods is another tactic for sustaining collection data integrity. Formalizing these developments in the CMP guides current and future staff, brings these aspects of collections care to the attention of the museum's governing authority, and creates accountability for carrying out the work to a self-determined standard.

Foster a Work Culture That Values Good Collections Data

Fostering a culture that values the goals and impact of accurate collections data is a logical way to sustain it. While spelling out inventory expectations and procedures in the CMP is critical, the power to maintain inventory data lies primarily with the people who work with the collection on a daily basis and with those authorized to allocate resources to collections management. Increasingly, conscientious museums are specifying inventory and location control as responsibilities in job descriptions and integrating these expectations into performance reviews. Prioritizing these responsibilities means that senior leadership dedicates adequate time and resources to accomplishing the work and to professional development trainings. It also means modeling sound practices, such as meeting the inventory schedule and recording location changes when objects are moved, 100 percent of the time.[19]

Putting Inventory Data to Work

Collections staff will benefit from accurate collection data most immediately through increased efficiencies in their day-to-day work. Looking beyond this important benefit, this section examines how inventories can be a springboard for a number of collections management, access, and preservation initiatives.

The institution's strategic plan is a good place to start when considering how data from a recent inventory can be put to work across the museum. Applying for accreditation with the American Alliance of Museums, digitizing collections to expand online accessibility, a facility expansion or collection relocation, and developing an exhibition are classic examples of initiatives for which inventory data is a critical planning tool.

Curatorial personnel also benefit from complete and accurate data, which enables them to identify material that is potentially out of scope or redundant with respect to the museum's collecting plan and to review those items for deaccession. Good data also means staff can more clearly analyze collection strengths and gaps to target areas for growth.

Another application of inventory data is to use it to prioritize and secure funding for preservation projects, such as conservation surveys, examinations, and treatment. Funders look favorably on applicants who have invested time and resources to clarify needs and define the scope of such projects. For example, if object medium was captured during inventory, staff can easily quantify objects made from chemically unstable plastics and estimate resource needs for implementing a mitigation strategy. Likewise, dimensions captured during an inventory will streamline storage reorganization and housing upgrades.

Accurate collection data also positions staff to hone disaster preparedness and response plans. Sound data quickly allows staff to determine which objects may have been impacted by a disaster based on their location, underpins the development and review of high-value or priority object lists, and clarifies insurance coverage needs.

Lastly, planning and executing the inventory may have clarified the need for development in the digital realm. For instance, workflows may be adjusted to ensure digital catalog records are an outcome of accessioning, retrospective registration may be prioritized, or historic accession records may be digitized to expedite future reconciliation and provenance research. Staff may also have observed that database development is needed to streamline documentation activities. Clunky systems that discourage location tracking may be reconfigured to move objects with fewer clicks or to perform location transactions and record retrieval in bulk. Staff might conclude that a barcode system would significantly expedite location tracking and inventory recording. The inventory also may have uncovered the need to develop the database to adequately document certain types of collections, such as digital objects.

The final chapters of this book zero in on these latter two aspects of inventory in the digital sphere. Chapter 12 foregrounds barcoding as a valuable, underutilized element of the inventory toolkit. Then chapter 13 brings digital collections into the lexicon of inventory practice. While barcoding and digital collections aren't new, there is a lot more room for discussion in the context of inventories.

Notes

1. Nick Graham and Stan Portney, *Project Management for Dummies*, 2nd ed. (Chichester: John Wiley & Sons, 2015), 307.
2. Ibid., 308.
3. Smithsonian Institution, *Smithsonian Directive 600* (Washington, DC: Smithsonian Institution, 2001), https://www.si.edu/content/pdf/about/sd/SD600andAppendix.pdf, 19.
4. Max Muller, *Essentials of Inventory Management* (New York, NY: AMACOM, 2003), 176.
5. Ibid., 177–78.
6. U.S. Department of the Interior, *Inventory of Museum Collections*, DOI Museum Property Directive 21 (Washington, DC: Office of Acquisition and Property Management, 2014), doi.gov/sites/doi.gov/files/migrated/museum/policy/upload/Dir-21-Collection-Inventory.pdf.
7. National Park Service, *Museum Handbook Part II: Museum Records* (Washington, DC: National Center for Cultural Resources, 2000), nps.gov/orgs/1345/cr-publications.htm, 4:1.
8. Metropolitan Museum of Art, "Collections Management Policy," September 8, 2020, https://www.metmuseum.org/-/media/files/about-the-met/policies-and-documents/collections-management-policy/collections-management-policy-9_8_2020.pdf?la=en&hash=5512B67EE5A7B552E4D98C8225393C65, 13; 15.
9. Cathy L. Helm, *Collections Management: The National Museum of African American History and Culture Needs to Enhance Inventory Controls Over Its Collections*, OIG-A-20-05 (Washington, DC: Office of the Inspector General, 2020), si.edu/oig/Audit_Reports, 8.
10. Muller, *Essentials*, 188.
11. Ibid., 184.
12. Ibid., 184–85.
13. Ibid., 185–88.
14. Ibid., 176–77.
15. Ibid., 178.
16. Ibid., 166–68.
17. A. Sprightley Ryan, *Collections Stewardship at the Cooper-Hewitt, National Design Museum*, OIG-A-11-02 (Washington, DC: Office of the Inspector General, 2011), www.si.edu/oig/Audit_Reports, 9; A-1; B-2.
18. Helm, *Collections Management*, 8.
19. Maureen McCormick, "Inventory," in *Museum Registration Methods*, 5th ed., ed. Jean Allman Gilmore and Rebecca A. Buck (Washington, DC: AAM Press, 2010), 305.

CHAPTER TWELVE

Barcoding to Enhance Inventory Performance

The familiar skinny black and white bars and squares are a way of expressing letters, numbers, or symbols so that a machine can read them. When someone scans a barcode into a text field on the computer, it's "translated" back to letters, numbers, and symbols that humans can read. This is significant because barcodes can be used to replace inventory data entry that someone would otherwise do using the computer keyboard. The Smithsonian National Museum of American History's collection holds one of the first scanners that heralded the widespread commercial success of barcodes in 1974 at a supermarket in Ohio.[1] The first item scanned was a ten-pack of Wrigley's Juicy Fruit gum. Before, a cashier had to use the computerized cash register keyboard to manually key in the product number on the package to pull up a record that showed the gum's price and other information. Instead, the product code was barcoded so that a machine could read it. This enabled cashiers to enter the product number by swiping the gum's barcoded product number across a scanner, which acts as a virtual keyboard. Scanning product numbers instead of manually keying them into the cash register substantially accelerated the process of ringing up shoppers and getting them out the door.

Although barcoding is now a vintage technology, its utility remains valid. Museums started using barcodes around 1990, but it seems like relatively few have taken advantage of them.[2,3] This is despite the fact that many museums that barcode enjoy not only increased accuracy in data capture but also expedited inventory durations amounting to one-half to one-quarter of the time it took to execute the same activities before barcoding. Museums that do intend to barcode find few resources in the museum literature to guide and facilitate the process. In connection with this, questions about what a museum wants barcoding to do, whether barcoding can do it, and how to do it are not answered as easily as they could be.

This chapter aims to contribute to museum practitioners' understanding of what barcodes do in inventory and how they can be optimized. Although the technology has evolved since the 1970s, the application is the same: barcodes replace manual input of some elements of the inventory dataset, such as object number and location. As emphasized in the chapter opening, the function of stand-alone barcodes is basic. Furthermore, off-the-shelf barcode equipment can be used on top of any database in any field that receives text. That is, barcodes don't need to live in the database. But they also do not replace a computer, and they do not add features to a database. Just how effective stand-alone barcodes can be is tied directly to how the database works. If a museum wants barcoding to do something other than what it can currently do in the database using a keyboard and mouse, a supplementary technology application that talks to the database or one that extends its capabilities is required. As highlighted in the chapter's case studies, these applications, which are bespoke or provided by the database developer, are more costly but can substantially extend the benefits of barcoding. However, both stand-alone and fancy barcode applications can expedite inventories and free up collections practitioners to do work that only people can do. For those that decide to incorporate barcoding into their inventory practice, the chapter provides a rough guide for initiating the process.

How Stand-Alone Barcodes Work during Inventory

Generally, museums use barcodes the same way they're used in supermarkets—to retrieve information about items more quickly by scanning the object number into the collections database search field instead of using the keyboard to enter it. In addition, location names and other elements of the inventory dataset are often barcoded to speed up data entry. Actions such as hitting "enter" or "tab" can also be added to barcodes to further streamline data capture. The barcodes don't carry any other information or powers. But they can result in substantial time savings when facing inventory projects that involve querying thousands of object records or logging hundreds of location transactions.

At the same time, barcodes can't be applied blindly to any inventory situation and yield transformative results. There are some scenarios where barcoding may be a low-impact use of resources. Fishman-Armstrong and Van Horn noted that barcoding may not promise worthwhile benefits for collections that are smaller, rarely accessed or moved, not expected to grow, and/or not registered (or not going to be registered) in a database.[4] They further encourage museums to answer the question, what do you want barcoding to do? To formulate a valid response, inventory stakeholders need to understand what a barcode system can or can't achieve. This section contributes to this dialogue by demonstrating how a stand-alone barcode system can be applied to inventory work.

Object Number Is Barcoded

At the most basic level, the object number, which is a unique identifier, is barcoded. The number is used most frequently to retrieve the object record in the database, which enables workers to capture or confirm other information from the inventory dataset. The number is also used in other inventory tasks, such as file naming or creating lists. Instead of typing the number into the collections database search field, the user scans it. The transaction looks something like this:

> Navigate cursor to object record query field in database → scan barcoded object number into query field (instead of typing it) → select "enter" → object record is retrieved → capture inventory data using keyboard and mouse.

As basic as it is, barcoding the object number alone can yield meaningful time savings. In recent years, the Cooper Hewitt Smithsonian Design Museum barcoded the collection preliminary to a mass digitization project.[5] Scanning the barcoded unique object identifiers instead of manually entering them into the digital file names shaved off about 103 workdays from the project timeline.

The benefits of barcoding the object number increase significantly if the database offers bulk transaction features, which allow an action to be applied to multiple object records at once. For example, a user may perform uninterrupted scans of a random group of object numbers to retrieve their records, to record a location transaction, or to record an inventory episode for all the records simultaneously, instead of one by one.

Locations Are Barcoded

Although any element of the inventory dataset can be barcoded, location names or identifiers are the other most common barcoded element. Once a location hierarchy has been created in the database, each discrete location (i.e., hierarchy level) or the full or partial string can be barcoded. The location transaction looks something like this:

> Scan barcoded object number into database query field to retrieve record → navigate cursor to first discrete location field using keyboard or mouse → scan barcoded location name "Building 1" → navigate cursor to next field → scan barcoded name "Storeroom 2" → tab or navigate cursor to next field → scan barcoded name "Cabinet 3, Shelf 4."

As basic as it is, barcoding object numbers and location names reduced a collection inventory duration to six months from two years at the National Museum of Mongolia following a project sponsored by the U.S. Ambassador's Fund for Cultural Preservation in 2017.[6] Stand-alone barcoded locations and object numbers (or container barcodes) may also be useful for tracking collection moves. Scanned data can be stored in the scanner memory and uploaded to a spreadsheet; the spreadsheet data can then be imported to the database to log the day's location transactions. This may be particularly useful if a collection move occurs as an emergency response.

Control Characters Are Barcoded

Input such as hitting "enter" (called a carriage return) and "tab" can be integrated with barcodes to further increase the speed of data capture. These actions are represented by control characters. Barcoded control character codes do not result in printed characters when they're scanned; instead, the codes tell the computer to carry out the action. Common control characters can be added to existing barcodes by configuring the scanner to add them as a suffix after every scan, which is usually achieved by scanning a configuration barcode in the scanner manual. Barcode generation software also provides options for embedding control characters in barcodes.

Adding control characters can further streamline data entry. To retrieve an object record, instead of scanning

Textbox 12.1

NOMAD SCIENCE: USING A STAND-ALONE BARCODE SYSTEM TO DOCUMENT ARCHAEOLOGICAL FINDS IN THE FIELD

In 2017, the cultural heritage nonprofit organization NOMAD Science (NS) piloted a no-frills barcode system to enhance protocols for documenting archaeological finds in the field. The team applied the system at a habitation site located in northern Mongolia within a mountain and steppe landscape that includes material ranging from the Paleolithic to present day.

Due to its remote, off-grid location, all barcoding of data occurred before traveling to the field. Based on previous field seasons, the types and volume of objects likely to be encountered were known. The classification system for the finds was based on the medium (i.e., lithic, ceramic, metal, bone). For each medium, there was a corresponding dataset captured from a fixed menu of descriptive terms. These factors enabled the team to barcode most elements of the inventory dataset in advance: preassigned unique identifier, medium and fixed menu of descriptive data, storage container number, collection date, and cataloger name. While unique identifying numbers were barcoded and printed on barcode labels, the other elements of the barcoded dataset were printed on reference sheets to expedite data capture. For example, a set of sheets was organized by medium with the corresponding menus of fixed descriptive terms (figures 12.1 and 12.2). Daily, the finds were registered in a spreadsheet by scanning the unique identifier and descriptive data barcodes. This occurred in tandem with object photography, and the unique identifier barcodes were again used to expedite image file naming. The data was later uploaded from the spreadsheet to other applications for storage and visualization.

Artifacts were collected from an area divided into units. Each unit was assigned a prebarcoded unique identifier, and all objects collected from that unit were registered under that identifier. Thus, the identifier documented a single object or an object lot. Each unit's finds were stored together in a zippered plastic bag, and a barcode label was adhered to the bag interior along with a handwritten label with location coordinates, collector name, and date. One hiccup with the preassigned unique identifier registration system was that if a unit yielded objects of different mediums (e.g., ceramics and bone), the unique identifier required manual extension (e.g., from 344 to 344a and 344b) to account for the respective medium lots while retaining their common provenience. Extensions were marked on the artifact bags and keyed into the spreadsheet. Still, the stand-alone barcode system eliminated daily documentation backlogs and made objects and their documentation accessible sooner for research.

Figure 12.1. Ceramic finds such as these thin-walled, incised Early Bronze Age (3400 BCE–1600 BCE) sherds were documented using the Ceramics barcoded inventory dataset featured in figure 12.2. COURTESY OF NOMAD SCIENCE

Figure 12.2. Part of the barcoded inventory dataset used to inventory ceramic finds. COURTESY OF NOMAD SCIENCE

the barcoded object number and manually pressing the "enter" key, a user can activate the scanner's carriage return suffix. The user then scans the object number into the query field, the scanner tells the computer to hit "enter," and the object record is retrieved. Similarly, using a "tab" barcode suffix can streamline multilevel location data capture. If an inventory taker activates the "tab" suffix, they scan the first discrete location level barcode for "Building 1," the field populates accordingly, and the cursor automatically tabs to the next location field, and so on. Barcode generation applications can also link together, or concatenate, each barcode comprising a multilevel location entry. By integrating the appropriate control character codes, a three-scan location data capture task can be executed in a single scan. Clearly, how navigating across location level fields is accomplished using the keyboard drives which control character will be barcoded. Once inventory stakeholders decide what they want barcoding to do, they can scrutinize the keyboard sequences for performing inventory data capture tasks and consider how barcoding may or may not perform those tasks more efficiently.

Implementing a Barcode System

If inventory stakeholders decide to move forward with a barcode idea, it will add to the inventory activity network, a project planning element discussed in chapter 7. In particular, barcoding will impact the activities and quality standards for producing an inventory-equipped database, which is the first deliverable in the hypothetical inventory project plan described in earlier chapters. The first two activities for producing the inventory-equipped database are to identify the inventory dataset to be captured and to assess the database for any changes needed to effectively capture that data. Because barcode systems are inextricably linked to the type of data stakeholders want to capture and the database's functionality, how to implement a barcode system is best considered early in the inventory project planning stage. This section overviews considerations for implementing a barcode system, including what type of barcode to choose, how barcodes are generated, and how barcode labels are created. While a comprehensive discussion of supplemental technology applications used to amplify the benefits of barcoding is needed, it's outside the scope of this chapter. Nevertheless, two case studies from the American Museum of Natural History and the Yale University Art Gallery demonstrate the potential for scaling up a barcode system with supplemental integrated technology applications.

Choosing a Barcode Symbology

There are many types of barcodes, called symbologies or barcode fonts. For collections practitioners, one of the main differences between symbologies is the character set—or the types of numbers, letters, punctuation marks, and symbols—they can encode (table 12.1). They also differ in their density, which can impact how big or small the printed barcode will be. A symbology's potential for technical obsolescence is a third consideration discussed in this section.

Character Set

Collections practitioners need a symbology that encodes the type of collections data they want to barcode. Thus, it is critical to compare the type of inventory data that needs barcoding to a potential symbology's character set. Typically, museums barcode unique identifiers that are used to retrieve object records in the database. The unique identifier may be a user-assigned object number, which may contain a variety of letters, numbers, punctuation marks, and symbols. This number may change at some point as a result of a reconciled discrepancy or correction. The unique identifier may also be a permanent database-assigned unique record number, which is usually letters and numbers. This number remains linked to the user-assigned identifier even if it changes, and both can be used to query the object record. For this reason, some museums opt to barcode the database-assigned identifier while also showing the more familiar human-readable user-assigned object number on the barcode tag. Similarly, object location names or identifiers may also be user- or database-assigned. Deciding what will be barcoded and collecting representative examples of that data will give an accurate idea of the type of characters a symbology needs to support.

Table 12.1 compares character sets of four symbologies commonly encountered in museum collections management applications: Code 39, Code 128, QR (quick response) code, and Interleaved 2 of 5. While the 1D symbologies may suffice for most applications, the relatively recent widespread adoption of the QR code makes barcoding more accessible for museums whose collections are documented with writing systems based on something other than Latin script and Arabic numerals or that are logographic (e.g., kanji or certain letters in the Mongolian Cyrillic alphabet). The character set for Code 128 makes it a versatile symbology that supports some so-called international characters found within the ASCII character set encoding system. Other writing systems, or multilanguage data, however, may rely solely on the QR code because it's one of the few symbologies

Table 12.1. Comparison of Limitations Among Barcode Symbologies Commonly Used in Museum Inventory Applications

Symbology		Characters to Encode				
		117	F2023	77-2-3	2017.22.75a/e,g	1981.22.14Ѳ
1D	Interleaved 2 of 5		Unsupported: letters, symbols, Unicode Cyrillic character Ѳ			
	Code 39				Unsupported: minuscule, comma, Unicode Cyrillic character Ѳ	
	Code 128					Unsupported: Unicode Cyrillic character Ѳ
2D	QR code					

that can be configured to encode characters based on the Unicode encoding standard, which supports most of the world's writing systems.

Data Density

Density refers to the number of characters a symbology can encode per unit of space. Ultimately, this influences the minimum size at which a barcode can be printed while still being easily read by the scanner. In this sense, a collection's object sizes and housings may impact the symbology choice. Broadly, barcode symbologies are classified as one dimensional (1D) and two dimensional (2D). One-dimensional barcodes are vertical parallel black and white bars that contain information in one dimension, horizontally across the bars. Two-dimensional barcodes are black and white squares or other geometric shapes arranged in a matrix that contain data both vertically and horizontally. As a result, 2D symbologies, like the QR code, are more space efficient (table 12.1). This makes it easier to tag small objects or to affix barcodes to existing object tags. Prior to the widespread awareness and accessibility of QR codes, the space inefficiency of 1D symbologies deterred some museums from barcoding.

Technical Obsolescence

Many symbologies may meet collections needs, but choosing a less prevalent symbology may risk obsolescence, which can impede future efforts to acquire technology for reading and generating the barcodes.[7] While the QR code is now well established, 1D symbologies have been around the longest, and the technology for applying them is more budget friendly than that for 2D symbologies. These factors inclined some collections practitioners to shy away from 2D symbologies well into the 2000s even though others foresaw their potential for collections use back in the 1990s given their efficient performance features.[8,9]

Generating Barcodes

In recent years, mobile device pop culture has contributed to misconceptions that barcodes are free and easy to implement. There are myriad "free" barcode generators available online that enable users to type data into a field and download the barcode as an image file. These are useful for an introductory investigation of barcodes, but they do not meet the needs of inventory applications. In inventories, staff need to autogenerate large batches of barcodes and print them to specifications without manually keying in the data they need to barcode. For inventories, there are a variety of methods, and they generate barcodes via a two-step or integrated process.

Two-Step Process

In a two-step process, users generate barcodes by importing or linking data to a barcode generation software program such as Seagull Scientific's BarTender. For example, users export data they need to barcode from a database into a spreadsheet, then import it into the barcode program. Some applications also allow users to import data directly from database fields. These applications offer a robust menu of symbologies, configurations, advanced barcoding functions, and label templates in a user-friendly interface.

The process for generating barcodes is similar to the mail merge feature in standard office software. In the barcode application user interface, users design a label template and insert fields for each piece of data they want to appear on the label, such as object number and object name. They then apply the desired formatting for each field. For the object number field, which will be barcoded, users apply the font corresponding to the chosen symbology. They link each label field to the field in the spreadsheet (or data source) containing the data that will be imported to populate the label fields. The barcode program imports the data and populates the corresponding label fields to create the labels, which can be printed or saved for later. To get a sense of whether a barcode program is a good match for an inventory application, the software can be demonstrated on the vendor's website. Some desktop label printers also include label-making software with suitable barcode generation features.

Barcodes can also be generated via a two-step process using Microsoft Word's mail merge feature.[10] The most common 1D symbologies as well as QR codes are inherent to the program. Although the options are limited and the process is less intuitive, this might be an option for some inventory scenarios.

Integrated System

With an integrated system, the barcodes "live" in the collections database and can be generated in a single step. No import or export of data to barcode generation software is required. Integration, which may be inherent to an application or a custom feature, enables the user to generate and print barcodes while working within the database's user interface. If barcodes aren't inherent to an application, basic custom integration may involve purchasing and importing a barcode symbology font into the database. Barcodes can then be generated and printed using the database's inherent reporting software by applying the barcode font to the desired data field in the report/barcode tag template.

Some databases, such as PastPerfect, The Museum System, and FileMaker Pro, offer inherent integrated barcode features as optional add-ons. In terms of barcoding data and generating barcodes, the inherent features (e.g., symbology options) are more limited than those offered by dedicated barcode generation software, but many museums may find them adequate (textboxes 12.2 and 12.3). In some instances, activating the database's barcode feature extends the database capabilities to include bulk transactions. Noted earlier, this enables users to perform multiple uninterrupted scans of random objects to a location or record inventory for them in one transaction.

In museums, earlier generations of integrated barcode systems emphasized a multiscan function specific to inventory. The protocol involved saving a "found set" of records representing all objects that needed to be inventoried.[11,12,13] When barcodes were scanned, their corresponding records were eliminated from the found set. Objects remaining in the found set were unaccounted for. As concepts of museum inventories have expanded to include capturing and confirming object locations and additional data, this system has fallen out of museum use.

Although integrated barcode features can be convenient and long lived for some museums, there are potential downsides that can prevent sustainable enjoyment of the technology. Fishman-Armstrong highlighted some of these caveats.[14] In one case, custom barcode features she integrated were invalidated when a database update was released by the developer. In another case, the barcode features became invalid when a museum migrated to a new database.[15] In addition to these considerations, some databases don't support the desired symbology, and the optional enhanced database features activated with the barcode functions may provide a clunky workflow. Finally, while a customized integrated system may add features that meet a museum's specific needs, these technology solutions may be out of reach for many institutions.

Scanning Barcodes

Several devices are used to read barcodes in museum inventory applications. These include specialized handheld barcode scanners and multipurpose mobile devices. Museums mainly use barcode scanners with stand-alone barcode systems. These devices can be thought of as virtual keyboards that replace manually keyed data entry at a computer workstation. These devices are relatively moderately priced and require minimal maintenance over time. Scanners are also used with supplemental technology applications that extend database functions, such as optional bulk location transaction features offered by the database developer, but the function is the same. Overall, mobile devices used in museum collections barcode applications function differently in that they usually do not replace keyed entries for an inventory taker working at a desktop computer. They are used with systems featuring a supplemental technology application paired with an application programming interface that enables the application to talk to the database. This allows users to perform some inventory data capture tasks remotely, using methods beyond what the database provides, or with applications that extend the database. These typically require network connectivity. They also tend to be more costly than specialized barcode scanners—up front and in the long term due to planned obsolescence.

Barcode Scanners

Barcode scanners are specially designed for reading barcodes, and they replace manually keyed input in the computer via device-to-device communication, that is, from the scanner directly to the computer the inventory taker is working at or near. Symbology is a main factor influencing scanner choice. One-dimensional scanners decode 1D symbologies, while 2D scanners decode both. However, even if staff identify a symbology that encodes the characters represented by the inventory data, it doesn't mean that any scanner can decode it. This is mainly an issue with QR codes that are employed to barcode characters that require Unicode encoding to be expressed digitally (e.g., kanji). Few scanners can read Unicode encoded characters—Honeywell Voyager 1452G 2D is one of them. This factor may become more significant as cultural groups increasingly revive the use of traditional scripts in documenting cultural heritage collections.

A main difference between 1D and 2D scanners is the technology employed to read the barcodes. One-dimensional scanners use lasers, while 2D scanners employ digital camera technology. While both are effective, this difference affects their performance features and price point. One-dimensional scanners—which are more budget friendly—typically read from only one direction, while 2D scanners scan omnidirectionally, and do so more quickly. This can make a noticeable difference in the inventory workflow if workers must repeatedly reorient barcodes or the scanner. The collections environment may also influence scanner choice. One-dimensional scanners perform better in lower light levels and when scanning from a longer distance. While both can scan through glass, only 2D scanners scan barcodes from a computer screen. Both types have excellent error rates, but QR codes are widely promoted for their ability to be read correctly even if they are somewhat damaged, smudged, or distorted.

Another factor to consider is whether the inventory setting requires a corded or cordless scanner. Corded models connect to a computer with a USB cord. Although they work well and are less expensive than cordless models, cords tend to get in the way of objects and workspaces during inventory. As well, corded scanners limit the work range and may require overhandling to transport objects to the inventory workstation. Cordless scanners feature a cordless handheld scanner component and a cradle, which connects to the computer with a USB cord. Cordless scanners are also sometimes referred to as wireless because they use radio waves (i.e., Bluetooth) to communicate to the computer. This enables device-to-device communication without a cord; they do not use or connect to the internet to transmit data.

Depending on the barcode system and database features used for the inventory, the scanner's memory performance features may merit scrutiny. For example, if inventory takers use a cordless scanner to scan a group of object barcodes while out of wireless range, the scanner will store the data until they return within range of the computer. Then they may use the mouse to navigate the cursor to the database's bulk location transaction window, where the data will be uploaded when they place the scanner in its cradle. If the scanner model deletes data after a single transmission, this may result in data loss if users unintentionally transmit the data, for example, to an open email window.

Mobile Devices

Mobile devices, such as smartphones, tablets, portable media devices, and handheld computers, can read barcodes, but only some are effective for inventory applications. To date, smartphones and tablets have proved unsuitable. These devices do not provide device-to-device communication. Barcodes can be decoded via the device's digital camera, but the data isn't transmitted to a field in the database (or anywhere in the computer). At best, some smartphone applications export scanned codes to a spreadsheet that users can download. Furthermore, phones and tablets provide a clunky scanning experience. It requires both hands to manipulate, the camera takes too long to focus on and read the barcode, and users often perform several scans before getting an accurate read.[16]

The iPod Touch is a portable media device that has been used as a scanner in inventory settings. At American Museum of Natural History, the device was used in conjunction with inherent integrated FileMaker Pro barcode features with acceptable results (textbox 12.2). However, the device sometimes decoded the barcode inaccurately and retrieved the wrong object record. University of Alberta Museum and Collections Services sidestepped this issue by purchasing a scanning sleeve that fits over the device and provides scanning functionality comparable to a barcode scanner.[17] Yale University Art Gallery highlights the use of a handheld

Zebra Touch Computer that features integrated barcode scanner technology (textbox 12.3).

The mobile devices in these examples differ from barcode scanners because they do not offer device-to-device communication. That is, users can't scan random barcoded data into database fields on the computer where they are entering data. Instead, they replace a computer temporarily and enable workers to capture part of the inventory dataset on the go, without carrying a laptop around and without needing to return to the computer to transmit the scanned data. The systems accept object barcodes or location barcodes since the primary purpose is to expedite location transactions. The systems also rely on network connectivity and supplemental integrated technology applications. Users scan a barcode and use the scanning device's screen to tell the application what they want to do; the application sends the transaction data through the network to the database. These systems are effective for location tracking and recording inventory episodes in bulk, but they do not replace the full scope of inventory activity and do not allow users to change, capture, or store any other inventory data.

Textbox 12.2

AMERICAN MUSEUM OF NATURAL HISTORY: INHERENT INTEGRATED SYSTEM WITH FILEMAKER PRO AND IPOD TOUCH SCANNER

The American Museum of Natural History employed an iPod Touch as a barcode scanner to track frequent object location changes that occurred in tandem with the museum's new Mignone Halls of Gems and Minerals. Inherent FileMaker barcode features and FileMaker Pro Advanced were used to create an inventory barcode application integrated with the FileMaker database. The application, which relied on internet connectivity, enabled technicians to scan and transmit data remotely, without being at a computer workstation. When users scanned a mineral object number, the device screen displayed an image and other limited data pulled from the object's database record. The application then provided options to scan a location to record a move transaction or to add an image to the record using the device's camera. Users scanned an object or container barcode to change its location or scanned multiple objects to a location in uninterrupted succession (figures 12.3 and 12.4). Barcodes were printed from object records within the database user interface.

On the downside, the device sometimes scanned codes incorrectly and retrieved the wrong mineral record. In one case, substantial scanned data was lost due to a technology glitch, so locations failed to update. While imperfect, the system was critical to efficiently tracking hundreds of objects moving in and out of storage to temporary staging areas, exhibition halls, and conservation labs.

Figure 12.3. While preparing the new gem and mineral halls, the American Museum of Natural History employed a barcode system to track specimens traveling between permanent storage, staging areas, and the exhibition hall.
COURTESY OF SANDRA VANDERWARF

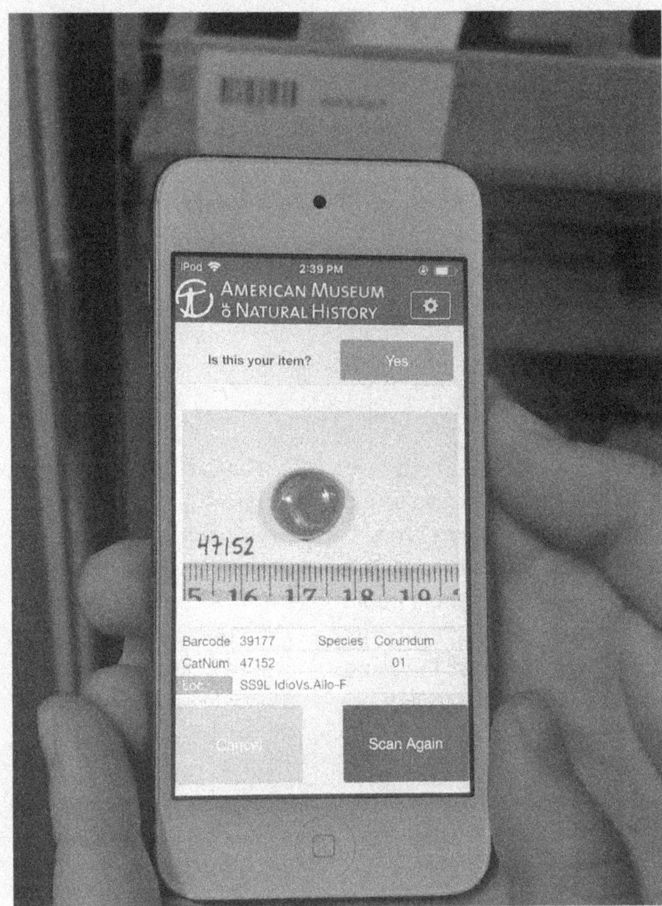

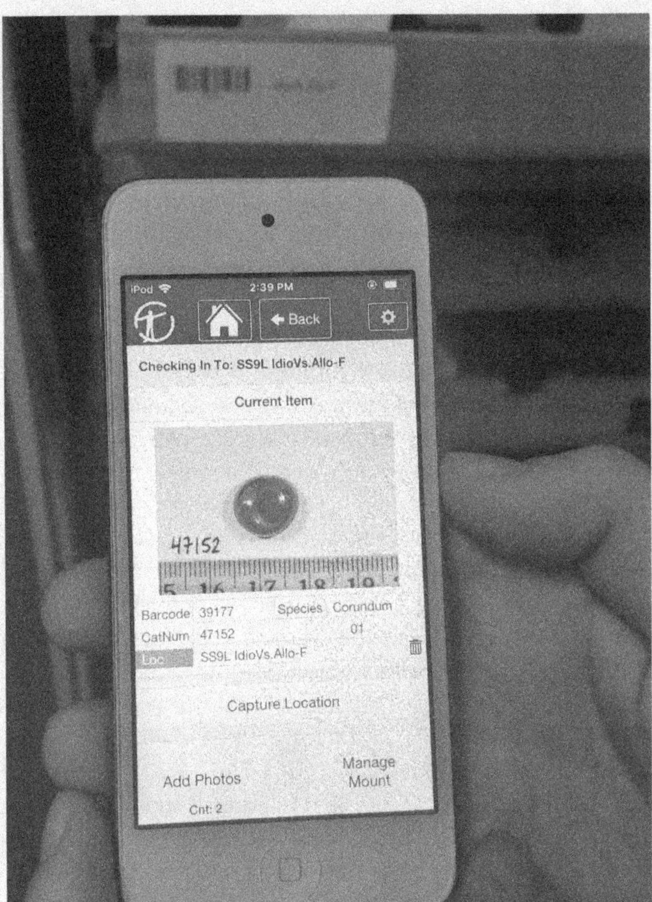

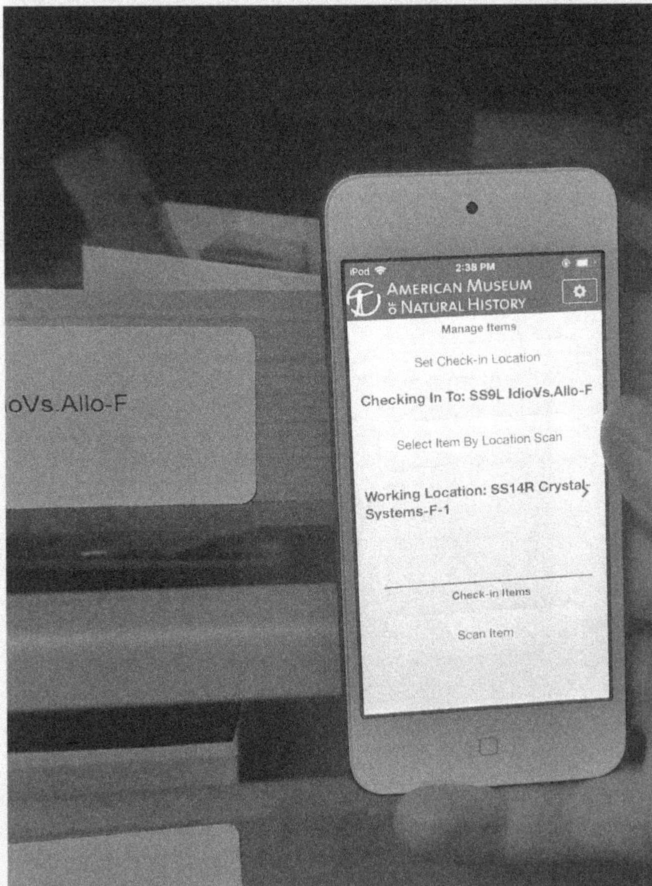

Figure 12.4. Clockwise from top left: Scanning the specimen barcode with the iPod Touch displays this ruby's image and other basic data pulled from its FileMaker Pro record. Users logged bulk location transactions by "checking-in" and scanning multiple random objects or containers to the scanned location.

COURTESY OF SANDRA VANDERWARF

Textbox 12.3

YALE UNIVERSITY ART GALLERY: INTEGRATED BESPOKE AND INHERENT SYSTEM WITH THE MUSEUM SYSTEM AND HANDHELD ZEBRA TOUCH COMPUTER SCANNER

In 2015, Yale University Art Gallery deployed a barcode system that married bespoke and inherent features integrated with The Museum System database. The institution implemented barcoding to expedite a collection move to a new research facility, Wurtele Study Center, which also displays visible collections storage.

In this system, when a record or location is registered under a user-assigned number or name, the database inherently assigns a separate permanent, unique identifier to each component documented in an object record and to each location. The database autogenerates a 1D barcode for these database-assigned identifiers. To account for all components of an object documented within a record, the unique identifiers were barcoded by pulling the data from each component identifier field rather than barcoding the master object record unique identifier.

The bespoke aspect of the system is an integrated application that enables users to retrieve a subset of data from an object record and to perform bulk location transactions and inventory episodes remotely in near real time. The scanning device is a handheld Zebra Touch Computer fitted on a pistol grip. When users scan an object barcode, the device screen displays the object's image and other basic information, which are pulled directly from the database record. In addition, the application provides options to log a move transaction or to view the object's move activity. Scanning a location barcode shows a summary of object and container counts within that location and offers uninterrupted scanning of multiple random objects to a location. Users may record inventory episodes for objects in bulk by selecting "inventory" as the purpose for the location transaction (figures 12.5 and 12.6). Barcodes are placed next to objects housed in visible storage vitrines. Authorized gallery personnel may use the scanner to perform information scans by scanning the barcode through the vitrine, which accounts for a substantial portion of scanning activity.

This type of integrated system requires a supplemental technology system, an application program interface that enables it to talk to the database, and network connectivity. If the network is interrupted, scanning functions halt; no scans are stored for future upload when the connection resumes. Data that can be entered is also limited to usernames, object identifiers, and locations. That is, the scanning device doesn't store or transmit random scans, nor does the scanner replace manually keyed entry of other inventory data in the stand-alone barcode sense.

While this "champagne" barcode system is an effective and elegant solution for logging location transactions and inventory episodes on the go, such a resource-intensive system is out of reach for many institutions. On the other hand, open-source code was used to create the bespoke aspects of the system so it could be applied to many other databases. This opens the door for more museums to benefit from it. Collaborations to troubleshoot integration paired with technical tutorials would propel the field forward in its quest for accessible collections inventory technology solutions.

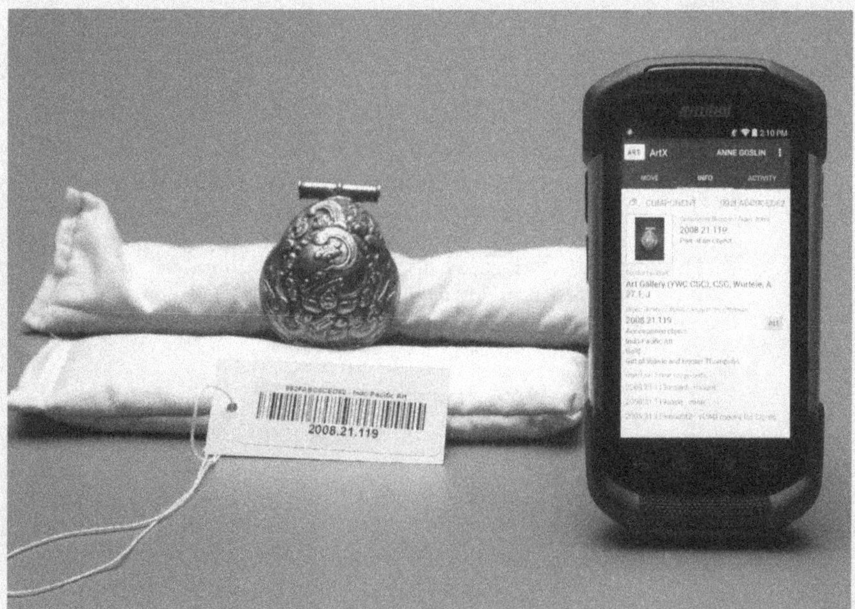

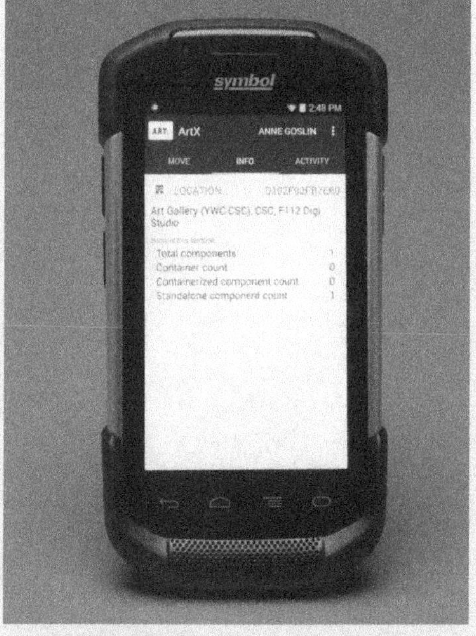

Figure 12.5. An "info" scan of this 13th-century Javanese gold rattle pendant barcode displays an image and other elements of a limited dataset pulled from the object's database record (left), while an "info" scan of a location barcode displays a summary of contents (right).
YALE UNIVERSITY ART GALLERY

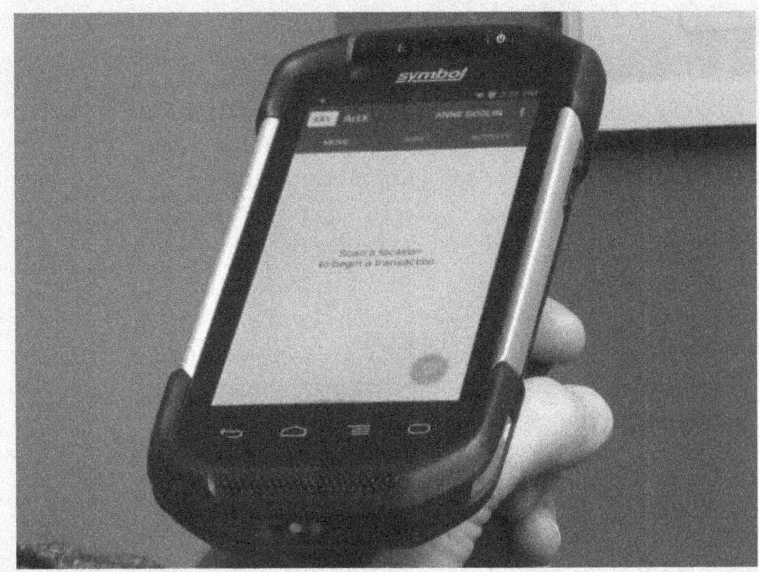

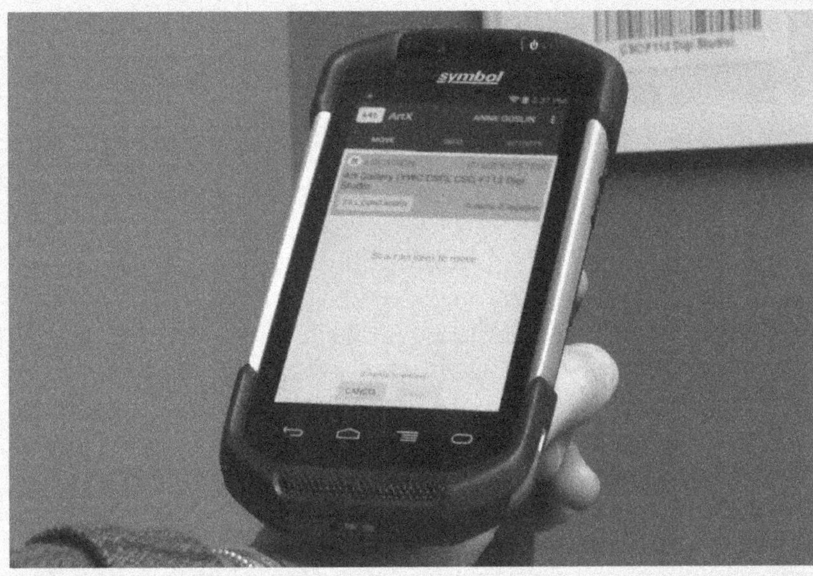

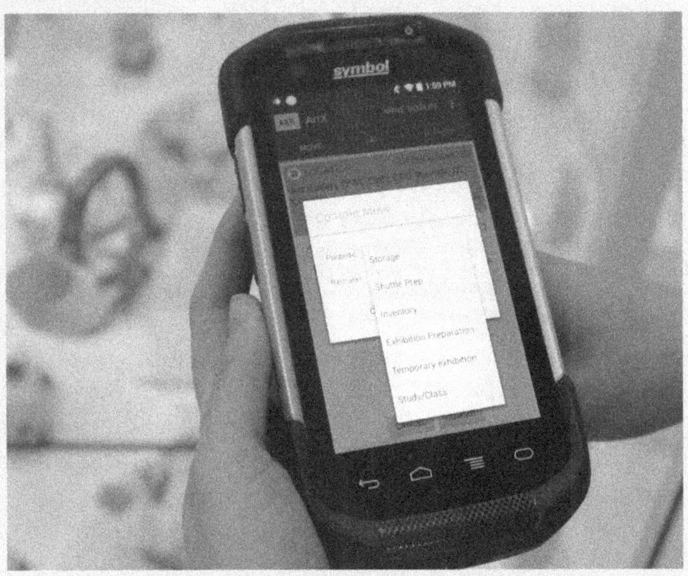

Figure 12.6. From top: The "move" feature prompts users to "scan a location to begin a transaction." The user may then "scan an item to move" or "fill a container" with uninterrupted scans of multiple objects. To "commit" the location transaction, the user must select a purpose—to log an "inventory" episode or reason for moving the object—from a menu pulled directly from the database. YALE UNIVERSITY ART GALLERY

Barcode Labels

Considerations for labeling objects with barcodes are similar to those that guide general object-labeling protocols for cultural heritage collections: barcode labels and printing media need to be chemically stable and durable, and the label, its application, or removal shouldn't change the condition of the object. The Society for the Preservation of Natural History Collections provides a comprehensive resource to guide practitioners in developing general object-labeling protocols, and much of it can inform barcoding label decisions for cultural heritage collections.[18] Echoing the guide, a label consists of three parts: the substrate, printed data on it, and an attachment method. The objects' condition, composition, size, housing, environment, and current labeling method are additional factors to keep in mind when developing the barcode-labeling protocol.

Label Substrate

For cultural heritage collections, suitable barcode label substrates are chemically stable and durable. This diminishes the risk of damage to objects and ensures the label will last in the given collection environment. Pressure-sensitive adhesive labels are the most common barcode label type. These feature a laminated structure with two or more layers: a facestock, which is the printing substrate, and an adhesive, which is the attachment method. Facestocks used in museum barcoding are typically paper or synthetic plastic films.

Chemically stable ("archival") paper facestocks are made of 100 percent cellulose cotton or linen rag, both of which are pH neutral (7.0), or of wood pulp that's been processed to remove most of the lignin and buffered to maintain a nonacidic pH (7.5–10).[19] Many heritage institutions use PermaPlus and Perma/Seal labels, which sandwich a foil layer between the paper facestock and adhesive. Although barcode labels are not affixed directly to objects, the foil prevents ink from migrating through to the back, where it could change the condition of the barcode carrier material beneath. The label features an acrylic resin adhesive, which has been shown to be the most stable and permanent.[20] The label format is provided on A4 sheets for standard office laser and inkjet printers but not in rolls for desktop label printers. For synthetic plastic film facestocks, polyester and polypropylene are chemically inert, durable printing substrates used widely in museum barcoding. 3M is one manufacturer that produces labels featuring a polyester facestock and liner, with an acrylic adhesive. These labels are formatted for desktop label printers.

Unfortunately, nonadhesive printable label substrates are scarce. This means that barcode labeling is often a two-step process that involves the adhesive barcode label and a carrier substrate for the label, such as a strung hangtag or a tombstone label. DuPont Tyvek (spun and bonded high-density polyethylene fibers) may have potential as a nonadhesive barcode label substrate formatted for label printers. However, it is associated with printing challenges in terms of ink penetration and drying time and may require a custom order. In addition, many standard Tyvek products are finished with an acidic antistatic coating and corona treatment. "Archival" Tyvek, which is uncoated, is readily available in other formats used in collections preservation applications, but it has not been encountered in printing label formats. Although not ideal, nonadhesive thermal transfer tags used by labs to track tube specimens may carry more potential as a one-step barcode label substrate.[21]

The manufacturer's product specification sheet can be referenced to confirm the label substrate and adhesive materials and to identify the environmental performance properties. Once a label is sourced, samples may be acquired to test their suitability. While many labels have a long service life once they're printed and attached, they may have only a one-year shelf life (unused in storage) before performance properties decrease.

Printing Barcodes

Desktop label printers and standard office printers can be used to print barcodes. The choice depends on resources and whether the desired label substrate, format, and other specifications are compatible with the printer.

Desktop label printers are typically classified by the printing technology they employ: thermal transfer or direct thermal. Direct thermal printers are unsuitable for collections barcoding because they do not produce durable, stable impressions. Thermal transfer printers penetrate the label substrate, which results in permanent impressions on paper and synthetic plastic labels. The method requires a printer ribbon and labels formatted on rolls wrapped around a tube core. Thermal transfer printing is more efficient and durable than office inkjet and laser printers and more budget friendly per label, and the printing ribbon costs less than liquid toners and inks required by office printers. Since thermal transfer label printers enable users to print a single label or hundreds at a time, there is potentially less waste created than when using sheet labels required by office printers. The label printers are also compact and often offer label-making software that includes barcode features that may be sufficient for an inventory project.

Ribbons for thermal transfer printers are resin, resin wax, and wax. Wax ribbon impressions are unsuitable for collections labeling. They contain the highest percentage of wax, and the impression is easily abraded with a fingernail. Resin ribbons are the most durable; they contain carbon pigment and the highest percentage of resin. As a result, they create lifelong impressions that withstand almost any environmental condition encountered in collections contexts. In keeping with this, they're the most expensive ribbon type. While they're not used with paper label substrates, chemically stable plastic label rolls are an option. Many collections use resin-wax ribbons, which contain a lower percentage of resin than full resin types. Resin-wax ribbons are durable in a wide range of environments, less costly than resin ribbons, and print on both paper and synthetic substrates.

In terms of chemical stability, there is little in the way of manufacturer specification sheets or other literature that identifies the composition of the resin or wax used in label printer ribbons. One manufacturer reports that thermal transfer ribbon resin can be "natural or synthetic, like urethane, synthetic rubber, silicone, polyester, and polyolefin."[22] Even resin ribbons contain some wax, which may be "natural or synthetic, like paraffin, beeswax, and carnauba."[23] Although museums already use these ribbons, materials testing and assessment has not been encountered in the conservation literature.

Office inkjet and laser printers are used in collections barcode applications that utilize labels formatted on sheets. Inkjet printers produce high-resolution impressions, but they leave a majority of the ink on the label surface rather than penetrating it.[24] This renders the impression vulnerable to abrasion. If this method is used, it's advised to use ink that is carbon pigmented, and not dye based, so that the impression won't fade or dissolve in water.

Laser printers are faster than inkjet printers and are already available in many office settings. They typically print on paper label substrates. However, these impressions have the potential to abrade and may be weakly fused to the label substrate due to variations in toner recipes. Using carbon-pigmented toner produced by the same company that makes the printer is a strategy for producing a more durable impression.[25]

Attaching Barcodes

In earlier generations of museum barcoding, the lack of a perfect way to attach barcodes to objects and keep them attached disinclined museums to implement the technology or inclined them to abandon it. Some practitioners aspired to replace conventional number marking methods with barcodes and experimented with interesting direct application methods based on what they perceived to be sound conservation materials and techniques.[26,27,28] Not only did it take forever to barcode the collection, but the barcodes fell off or abraded. Today, museums are more accepting of the reality that there is no perfect way to attach barcodes to every object and that for cultural collections, direct application will likely result in unwanted changes to the object's condition. Because barcode labels are largely adhesive types, cultural institutions attach barcode labels indirectly by adhering the barcode to a tag or object housing or by placing a barcode near an object.

A simple way to attach barcodes is to adhere them to the object's existing hangtag or label. If the objects lack labels or the labels are historically significant and intended to be preserved, the financial burden of barcoding increases, as it amounts to double tagging. Label expenditures can be minimized by cutting labels from preservation appropriate paper stock or Tyvek, for example. Even if barcodes can be affixed to existing tags, barcoding may still increase expenditures if traditional marking procedures remain part of the object-labeling protocol. While not ideal, some museums utilizing barcodes have discontinued traditional object marking.

Depending on the collection's housing status, barcodes may be easily affixed to an object's enclosure, mat, handling support, tube, protective sleeve, or tray (figures 12.7 and 12.8). There are usually some objects that aren't good candidates for the aforementioned attachment methods, whether due to their condition, housing status, form, or size. In these scenarios, the barcode can remain on its silicone release paper or be affixed to a carrier tag that will be placed near the object. Alternatively, barcodes can be affixed to or printed directly on coversheets that index the contents of a container, drawer, or shelf (figure 12.9).

Barcode labels can't solve the problems of unregistered or dissociated objects during inventory. But the technology can increase inventory staff resource availability to tackle those issues by speeding up other inventory work. While RFID and other new technologies have been applied to museum inventory applications, so far, they have failed to prove as useful as barcoding. For museums that intend to enhance their inventory practice, barcodes are still worth a look.

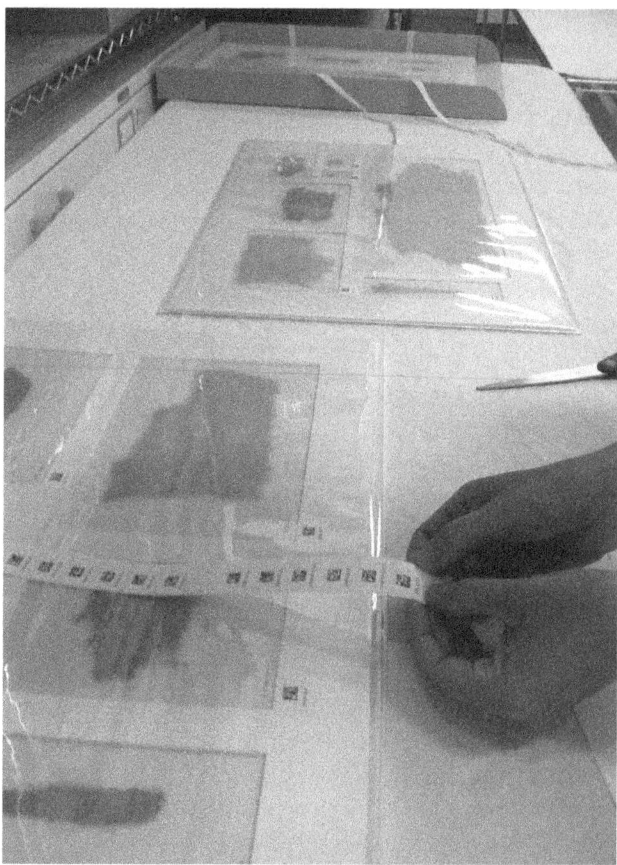

Figure 12.7. At Cooper Hewitt, QR code tags are adhered to mats housing textile fragments. COOPER HEWITT, SMITHSONIAN DESIGN MUSEUM

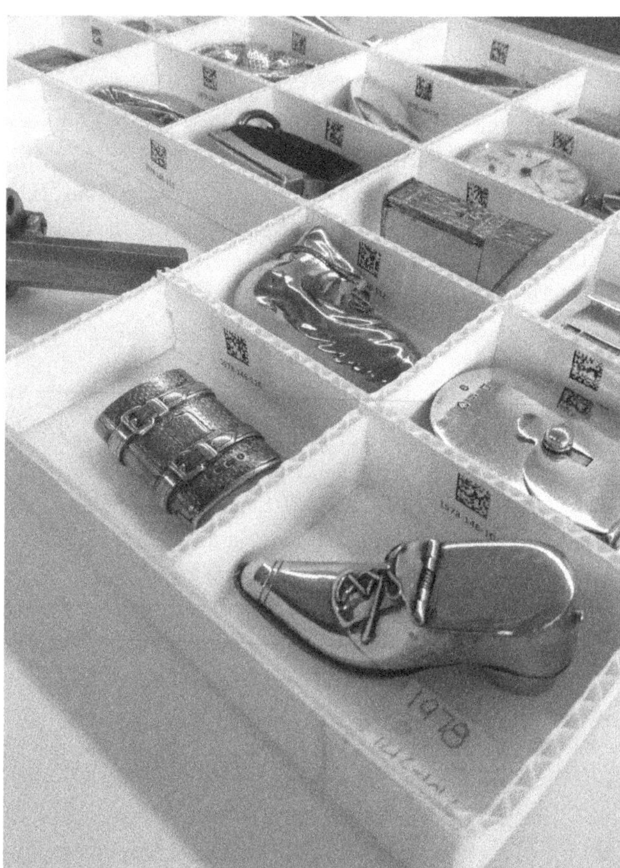

Figure 12.8. The high density of QR codes makes it easy to incorporate them into each compartment of this tray that houses small match safes. COOPER HEWITT, SMITHSONIAN DESIGN MUSEUM

Figure 12.9. Barcodes are adhered to a coversheet that indexes the contents of a box of unmatted works on paper. COOPER HEWITT, SMITHSONIAN DESIGN MUSEUM

Acknowledgments

Anne Goslin
Beata Gruszka
Bianca L. Ruthven
Boldbayar Lkhagvasuren
Bumaa Dashdendev
Darby Reiners
Heath J. Garner
Jamie Newman
Julia Clark
Kendra Dean-Wallace
Kyle Dayton
Lori M. Garst
Munkhtogoo Dulamjav
Susan Fishman-Armstrong
Thomas Raich
Terri L. Carnes
Wendy Rogers

Notes

1. National Museum of American History, "Supermarket Scanner," accessed July 31, 2020, https://americanhistory.si.edu/collections/search/object/nmah_892778.

2. Susan Ward, "Bar Codes for Identification: Object Cataloguing at Biltmore," *History News* 46, no. 4 (1991): 12–14.

3. Lori D. Meeks, "Barcoding the Archival Way," *Registrar's Quarterly: A Publication of the Registrar's Committee—Western Region* (Spring 1993): 7.

4. Susan E. Fishman-Armstrong and Deborah Rose Van Horn, "Considerations for Implementing a Bar Code System in a Museum," *Collections: A Journal for Museum and Archives Professionals* 4, no. 4 (Fall 2008).

5. Allison Hale, "Mass Digitization: Workflows and Barcodes," *Cooper Hewitt Labs* blog, June 30, 2016, https://labs.cooperhewitt.org/2016/mass-digitization-workflows-and-barcodes/.

6. American Center for Mongolian Studies, "ACMS National Museum Barcoding Project," July 19, 2019, YouTube video, 5:10, https://www.youtube.com/watch?v=KKtrfdfTAeQ.

7. iDigBio, "Barcoding Protocols, July 2012," accessed January 12, 2020, idigbio.org/wiki/images/7/77/R_6nz08vO41gyMFUN_barcode_equipment.pdf.

8. Gabor R. Racz and William L. Gannon, "Improving Collection Maintenance Through Innovation: Bar-Code Labeling to Track Specimens in the Processing Stream," *Collections: A Journal for Museum and Archives Professionals* 1, no. 3 (February 2005): 229.

9. William Albert Manning, "Automated Systems in Museums: The Use of Bar Code Technology in Collections Management," *Museum Management and Curatorship* 18, no. 1 (1999): 3–18.

10. Clearly Inventory, "How to Print Barcodes with Excel and Word," accessed November 1, 2019, https://clearlyinventory.com/resources/how-to-print-barcodes-with-excel-and-word/.

11. Susan E. Fishman-Armstrong, "Incorporation of Barcode Capabilities to Existing Museum Databases," master's thesis (Texas Tech University, 2000), accessed February 2, 2020, https://ttu-ir.tdl.org/bitstream/handle/2346/13041/31295015930455.pdf?sequence=1.

12. Ward, "Bar Codes for Identification."

13. Meeks, "Barcoding the Archival Way," 7.

14. Fishman-Armstrong, "Incorporation of Barcode Capabilities."

15. Darby Reiners, collection manager, Panhandle-Plains Historical Museum, email message to author, January 27, 2020.

16. Maria Consuelo Sendino, "Use of QR Code Labels in Museum Collection Management," *Collections: A Journal for Museum and Archives Professionals* 9, no. 3 (Summer 2013): 239–54.

17. University of Alberta Museums Blog, "Post #1—An Introduction to the Location Tracking Project" through "Post #13—Location Barcodes," December 5, 2016, to April 28, 2017, http://ws.macs.ualberta.ca/wordpress/index.php/2017/02/23/post-9-barcoding-the-meteorite-collection/.

18. Society for the Preservation of Natural History Collections, "Labeling Natural History Collections," accessed June 14, 2021, https://spnhc.biowikifarm.net/wiki/Labeling_Natural_History_Collections.

19. Ibid.

20. Ibid.

21. GA International, "PCR-TagTrax®: Non-Adhesive Thermal-Transfer Tags for High Profile PCR Tubes, Strips, and Plates," accessed July 31, 2020, https://www.labtag.com/brands/pcr-tagtrax/.

22. DNP Imagingcomm America Corporation, "Thermal Transfer Ribbon Ingredients," accessed July 31, 2020, https://am.dnpribbons.com/assets/Uploads/RibbonIngredients.pdf.

23. Ibid.

24. Society for the Preservation of Natural History Collections, "Labeling Natural History Collections."

25. Ibid.

26. Manning, "Automated Systems in Museums."

27. Ward, "Bar Codes for Identification."

28. Meeks, "Barcoding the Archival Way."

CHAPTER THIRTEEN

~

Inventorying Digital Collections

The world's heritage is becoming increasingly digital. More cultural and scientific content is created in digital formats than ever before, and analog formats are being digitized for long-term preservation as degrading physical media and obsolete playback equipment threaten their longevity. People use digital technologies to create and share information, ideas, and knowledge and to express themselves artistically. Though created with and read by computers, digital objects are created by people to communicate and document what is important to them and their communities. Digital heritage may take the form of artwork, music, oral histories, sound recordings, websites, software, scientific studies, documentary film and photography, primary documents, and interviews, just to name a few. In the same way that natural and cultural heritage is passed from one generation to the next because it is valued, digital resources are now recognized as a heritage that should be preserved for current and future generations.[1]

Digital heritage requires skillful care and management for long-term preservation. The safekeeping of these materials for future generations is largely possible due to the communities and institutions that have committed to their caretaking. The propagation of digital heritage collections is a purely human endeavor that requires both the creators of digital materials and the institutions, policies, resources, and people committed to carrying out the work of preserving them.

In museums, collections inventories support the documentation, accessibility, and long-term preservation of collections. Regular inventories confirm the location and condition of collections and help managers identify and prioritize work to strengthen the collections' documentation, management, and care. With collections becoming increasingly digital, uneven institutional support for inventories combined with perhaps a natural disposition to focus limited resources on tangible collections has led to insufficient resources being devoted to the management and preservation of digital collections.

The deprioritization of digital collections at many institutions is compounded by a lack of knowledge among museum professionals about how to document, manage, and preserve digital objects. The dearth of expertise in this area may stem partly from the fact that while there is now abundant scholarship and information available for implementing digital preservation at museums, developments in this area have emerged from well-funded cultural and government institutions largely focused on preserving vast digital archives and collections of often complex time-based media artworks. Often presented in a highly technical framework that can be intimidating to novices, these advancements appear to have left out consideration of professionals at smaller museums and historical societies collecting digital materials of a different scope, leaving them unsure how to implement documentation and conservation practices that may not feel relevant to their collections.

But while proficiency among these individuals may be stymied, the growth of digital collections is not, representing a shift in collecting that has led to backlogs at many museums of unprocessed and undocumented digital materials. Collections practitioners charged with addressing these backlogs know the most effective way to establish control over any collection is through inventory; however, available digital preservation literature also tends to focus on the acquisition and ingest of digital materials rather than processes for addressing the needs of digital objects already in museum collections.

This chapter will therefore attempt to examine the preservation of digital collections through the lens of inventory by exploring the inextricable link between the two functions. It will describe the basic tenets of digital preservation, explore methods for documenting digital objects, and review how digital object documentation and preservation actions can be applied through the process of inventory. The hope is that readers will feel empowered to begin surveying their digital collections and use the results of their work to advocate for the establishment of digital collecting and preservation policies, training, and ongoing financial support for preserving digital collections at their institutions.

Recommendations for implementing digital preservation often begin with the task of assessing what digital content an organization produces in order to determine what should be preserved. While museum-produced content may very well be worthy of long-term preservation, this chapter will focus on accessioned digital objects managed by the professionals responsible for the long-term care of the museum's collection.

It is also important to note that the field of time-based media artwork conservation has established practices for documenting the life of time-based digital artworks that are rather specific to this medium and include condition, identity, and iteration reports; artist interview templates; and conservation plans with the goal of attaining a full understanding of the technical and creative aspects of the artwork as well as the artist's intentions. This chapter's review of documenting digital objects will omit this aspect of documentation in order to focus on baseline information that is critical to establishing physical and intellectual control of undocumented or underdocumented digital collections.

Finally, while digital collection inventories require specialized systems and tools, this chapter will not include a review of nor recommend specific software or digital preservation tools, as there are multiple options available for every digital preservation function. These tools are also always evolving, and others have taken on the monumental task of compiling and organizing these resources for prospective users.[2]

What Are Digital Collections?

For decades, and increasingly so in the past twenty years, museums and other collecting institutions have been adding digital objects to their collections. Libraries and archives have been managing these materials since at least the 1980s[3] while art museums have been stewarding them even longer—since the 1960s.[4] As museum collections grow, especially those born in the digital era, they are becoming substantially and sometimes majority digital, even at institutions such as history museums, where one might assume that traditional collections remain primary.[5]

Digital objects can be defined as pieces of binary code that must be read by a computer to make them viewable or audible by people.[6] Digital objects found in museum collections may include photographs, moving images, web-based content, and text documents, among others, and may be fine art or documentary in nature. Increasingly so, artwork in museum collections is composed of both physical and digital components. Time-based media art, which is characterized as having both physical and temporal dimensions, often requires computer hardware and other tangible items in addition to software and digital files to be displayed.

A digital object can either be born digital, meaning it was created in a digital format, such as a photograph taken with a digital camera, or digitized from an analog format, for instance, a print photograph that has been scanned and saved as a digital file. Digitized objects may be surrogates for and exist alongside physical items in the collection, for example, a digitally photographed version of a parchment manuscript, or be the only version the museum possesses, for instance, when a museum receives and accessions the digitized contents of a VHS tape.

Accessioned-born digital and digitized objects may be treated as discrete items, for example, a museum may choose to individually catalog and track a group of photographs with unique accession numbers. Alternatively, digital archives composed of large volumes of digital objects in the form of historical documents or other materials may be assigned a collection record and made discoverable with a finding aid. Museums may develop policies that specifically guide their collecting of digital materials or simply align what they collect digitally with existing physical collection development policies.

For the purposes of this chapter, analog media will be considered alongside digital media with the assumption that analog formats will eventually need to be digitized to ensure long-term preservation. Analog media will refer to any nondigital item that requires technology to view it.

Standard of Care for Digital Collections

The idea that museums bear the responsibility of documenting and effectively caring for their collections has been discussed at length. We know that good stewardship means striving to know what you have and where it is or, more specifically, having systems in place for describing each object in the collection and its current location and condition.[7] To that end, inventories serve as a means to help ensure that minimum standards for documentation, preservation, and retrievability are being met and are often taken as an opportunity to perform baseline condition assessments. However, while digital objects are at risk from traditional threats, such as extremes of light, temperature, and humidity, they must also be assessed for and guarded against risks unique to their composition, such as technological obsolescence and media degradation. Storage for digital collections must ensure redundancy of files in different locations to ward off accidental loss, and the capture of metadata unique to digital objects is necessary to document their fixity, authenticity, and actions taken to keep them operative over time. In other words, in addition to knowing where digital objects are located, information gathered during an inventory of digital materials supports their preservation by "creating metadata that allows the verification of the integrity of content . . . and signaling when preservation actions such as a format migration or an integrity check should be undertaken."[8] In fact, the very act of mounting a digital object to describe and account for it is itself an act of preservation and presents the opportunity for additional preservation actions.[9] Thus, when speaking about digital collections, the concepts of inventory and digital preservation are very much intertwined.

Unfortunately for many museums, the acquisition of digital collections has outpaced a comprehensive understanding among collections practitioners of what is required to preserve them.[10] Now, well into the twenty-first century, documenting and caring for these materials still poses challenges to registrars, conservators, and curators who remain accustomed to caring primarily for physical objects.[11] Uncertainty around how to describe, number, track, and store digital files and associated physical media (compact disks, thumb drives, etc.) remains commonplace. Likewise, the systems these professionals work within often lack the capacity or technologies required to adequately document and preserve digital materials. Commonly used collections management systems, for instance, are often ill equipped for describing and tracking multiple versions of digital objects or objects composed of both physical and digital elements, resulting in workarounds for this purpose. A lack of institutional policies and workflows for acquiring, documenting, and storing digital materials exacerbates the problem. As a result, standards developed for tangible materials have in some instances been applied wholesale to digital collections in a way that ultimately does not serve their long-term preservation. For example, while carefully storing compact disks in acid-free boxes has undoubtedly been done with the best of intentions in mind, this effort falls short of ensuring the content stored on those disks will remain accessible to future generations.

For these reasons, many museums face a backlog of digital materials stored on physical media that have yet to be copied to a storage system, fully described, or assessed for long-term preservation.[12] Other institutions may be grappling with digital collections that have been handled inconsistently over the years. Establishing physical control of digital materials can be especially challenging, for instance, if there is uncertainty as to what analog media has been digitized or whether files have been consistently copied from physical media and saved in a centralized location. Gauging this can be even more tricky when accessioned digital objects lack corresponding physical media.

There is work to be done, then, for museums to be able to describe the current location and condition of digital collections and ensure their long-term accessibility. As knowledge of best practices for documenting and caring for digital collections develops, the need to address the backlog of digital objects already in museum collections through the process of inventory has come into focus as a fundamental step toward achieving digital preservation but also accountability.[13] Because a rigorous discussion about inventorying digital collections can't be had without first considering the principles of digital preservation, the next section will explore exactly what is meant by this term.

Digital Preservation

Digital preservation can be defined as a set of activities carried out to ensure continued access to authenticated digital materials over time, beyond inevitable media failure and technological and organizational change.[14]

In the heritage sector, libraries, archives, and art museums have been on the forefront of developing digital preservation concepts and their real-world application to digital and time-based media collections. Pioneers in this area include the National Digital Stewardship Alliance (NDSA) (https://ndsa.org/), the Matters in Media Art project (http://mattersinmediaart.org/), the Guggenheim (https://www.guggenheim.org/conservation/time-based-media), and the Smithsonian Time-Based Media and Digital Art Working Group (https://www.si.edu/TBMA). As some of the first cultural heritage organizations to engage in the caretaking and conservation of digital materials, their contributions have coalesced into a body of knowledge that is now being put into practice by the wider museum community.

Preserving digital materials encompasses several concepts and activities, which taken as a whole, can be intimidating to beginners. In an effort to delineate the fundamentals of digital preservation and make them more approachable, the NDSA created the Levels of Digital Preservation as a "tiered set of recommendations for how organizations should begin to build or enhance their digital preservation activities."[15] The Levels of Digital Preservation, now in its second iteration, is a useful tool for becoming familiar with the overarching concepts of digital preservation and their application, which most authorities in the field recommend implementing incrementally and iteratively, focusing on easier-to-achieve steps first to create a foundation that can be built upon over time. The Levels of Digital Preservation are organized around five key areas that encompass digital preservation: storage, integrity, control, metadata, and content.

Storage

Storage refers to the baseline objective of documenting storage media where digital collections are stored; copying digital content off physical media (optical disks, thumb drives, etc.) as it is received and saving the files in some sort of storage system; and having at least two complete copies of digital objects backed up in different geographic locations. This is to protect digital objects against inadvertent loss, which may be caused by human error or natural and man-made disasters. As an institution's systems develop, more robust storage methods may be implemented, and the number of copies and storage locations may be expanded to further protect against these threats. A multitude of options exist for storing digital materials, each with advantages and disadvantages.[16] Museums may, for example, opt to store their digital collections on designated hard drives or servers; use a cloud service that delivers files stored on servers to users via the internet; or utilize flash memory devices, such as thumb drives, depending on the size of their collection and available resources.

Integrity

One of the most essential components of digital preservation is integrity, or the idea of maintaining the authenticity of digital objects. When museums add tangible objects to their collection, they work to maintain them as truthful representations of what was originally received and are careful not to alter them beyond taking actions to preserve them. The same is true for digital objects. Authenticity in a digital context means ensuring digital objects don't change over time, either through degradation or inadvertent changes made by software or people. Managers of digital materials take steps to ensure files aren't modified upon or after entering the museum's collection, are maintained as they were created by the producer, and remain free from tampering and corruption.[17] One important exception to this is the practice of migrating digital objects to newer formats, which may be required to combat obsolescence and keep digital objects accessible into the future.

To ensure digital objects don't change over time, museums must first have a record of their checksums. Checksums are unique values typically expressed as a string of letters and numbers generated by a computer algorithm that express the exact contents of a file (figure 13.1).[18] In some instances, digital acquisitions will arrive with checksums already recorded and included in the information sent along with the files. Other acquisitions may arrive without this information, in which case the museum must record the objects' checksums upon receipt. With the recording of a digital object's checksum, or unique signature, its fixity is established and can be confirmed by using software to periodically compare the checksum recorded upon receipt with the one generated at the time of the check, indicating the "unchangedness" of the file.[19] A number of tools exist for recording the checksums of digital objects. Bagger, a free tool developed by the Library of Congress, allows users to generate checksums for a single file or group of files that are "bagged" with their checksums and other object information for storage or transfer to another institution.[20] Checksums can also be recorded through the creation of disk images, which are exact copies of the entire contents of a storage device, such as a hard drive or thumb drive, including all data on the device and its organizational arrangement.

Assuring the integrity of digital objects is further aided through the use of write blockers, which prevent staff from accidentally changing or deleting files while working with them, and antivirus software, which prevents files from being corrupted. Thus, applying the concept of integrity involves several considerations and requires specialized hardware, software, and knowledge.

MD5 signature:84ef0baf03bfe1f7e273bd63d5af8ca9

Figure 13.1. Example of a checksum generated using the MD5 algorithm, a widely used checksum algorithm. Checksums result from running an algorithm on a piece of data to generate a unique sequence of numbers and letters. BETHANY ROMANOWSKI

Control

Control means being aware of what people and software currently have access to digital object files; establishing which people and software should have the ability to read, write, move, and delete them; and restricting access accordingly. Documenting these decisions and the rationale behind them leaves a helpful record for future staff, who can use the written policy to guide future security reviews.

Metadata

Another critical aspect of digital preservation is metadata. Metadata refers to structured information associated with an object for the purposes of description, discovery, retrievability, management, and preservation.[21] As was discussed in chapter 6, museums record information about objects through the process of cataloging, which generally takes place as items enter the museum's collection. For tangible objects, information recorded at the time of acceptance often focuses on descriptive information, such as an item's title, maker, physical description, and use, which is built upon over time as curators learn more about items in the collection. In addition to information about an object itself, an item's accession number and data about its donor, acquisition status, usage permissions, and storage location is also likely to be recorded during cataloging. Over time, information added to an object's record documents its life as a museum object and may reflect its movements in and out of storage, inclusion in exhibitions and loans, inventory status, and steps taken by conservators to extend its life. All this information is metadata.

Metadata can be broken down into three overarching categories: descriptive metadata, structural metadata, and administrative metadata.[22] Descriptive metadata is information about an object that helps people to discover and understand it, such as an object's name, title, description, and use. Curators generally rely on descriptive metadata to interpret collections and explain their historical significance to museum visitors. Structural metadata is information that describes relationships between objects and their parts, for example, an object numbering system that indicates the relationship between the items comprising a tea set. Administrative metadata refers to information necessary for facilitating the management, use, and preservation of objects in the collection and can include information such as an object's acquisition status, storage location, conservation treatment history, or copyright status.

It has become the practice of most museums to record these types of metadata about their collections centrally in some type of computerized database. To organize all the information, museums adopt data structure standards or metadata schemas.[23] In chapter 6, it was explained that metadata schemas define the "categories" or "containers" of data[24] that make up an object record. These schemas typically manifest in collections management systems as a set of database fields used to capture information important to the institution, such as an object's accession number or creator. Because particular needs for describing collections can vary greatly from one museum to another, it is not uncommon for institutions to use more than one, or a combination of, metadata schemas to capture all the relevant information associated with their collections.

The metadata described thus far reflects information routinely gathered by museums for physical collections, using metadata schemas that are well established in most collections management systems. With the advent of digital collecting, however, two more categories of metadata become critical for museums to capture to understand and preserve digital objects over time. These categories, which were developed under the umbrella of administrative metadata, are technical and preservation metadata. Technical metadata describes the attributes of a digital object and includes information such as the equipment that was used to create it, its file type, format, and size. Technical metadata is important to capture because it provides information about how to render a digital file and may be used to assess the continued usability of a file or reconstruct it if it is damaged. Preservation metadata supports the long-term use of digital objects and includes information about the processes and actions taken to preserve them over time. Examples of preservation metadata include an object's checksum, fixity check outcomes, and documentation around the migration of a digital object to a new format, done to ensure its continued accessibility.

Museums with a history of collecting digital materials may have established metadata schemas that accommodate technical and preservation metadata long ago. Others that have only recently begun collecting digital objects or those with a backlog of unprocessed digital materials may be in a position of needing to modify their metadata schemas to include fields for recording information relevant to digital preservation, perhaps combining schemas in a way that allows for the documentation of both physical and digital objects using a single schema.

For collections practitioners just beginning to learn about metadata and digital collections management, two publications by the National Information Standards Organization, Understanding Metadata: What Is Metadata, and What Is It For?[25] and *A Framework of Guidance for Building Good Digital Collections*,[26] provide a thorough overview of metadata as well as a review of metadata schemas used in the cultural heritage sector for documenting digital objects. Concerning the preservation of digital materials, the NDSA recommends at minimum producing an inventory of the contents of the digital collection and recording the collection's storage location. Relying primarily on descriptive and some administrative metadata at this stage, the notion is that this inventory will provide a foundation of information on which to build as an institution's documentation standards are expanded to include technical and preservation metadata for digital materials.

Content

The final aspect of digital preservation specified by the NDSA is content. To maintain a collection's accessibility, the NDSA recommends documenting digital object file formats (which may be stored as technical metadata in object records), monitoring these formats for obsolescence, and acting as needed to keep the files accessible. Mentioned previously, one method for keeping files operable over time is migrating them to new formats as older formats near obsolescence. Another option is emulation, or the practice of using a different computer platform or software to imitate the original platform or software used to create a digital object with the goal of rendering the object in a way that recreates its authentic look, feel, and functionality.[27]

Museums may wish to institute the use of open or sustainable file formats for storing digital data as much as possible. Open file formats are nonproprietary, free, can be used by anyone, and are often supported by user communities.[28] They are generally considered less vulnerable to obsolescence because they don't belong to a particular software company and aren't restricted by any copyright, patent, or trademark. This is in contrast to proprietary formats, which are developed and owned by software companies. Proprietary format files can pose problems for accessibility over time if they are compatible only with the software used to create them, for instance, being required to use Microsoft Word software to open a document created using Microsoft Word. Proprietary format files are also at risk of becoming obsolete if newer versions of the software used to create them render them unreadable or the software company goes out of business and the software becomes unavailable.

Open file formats may also be vulnerable, however, if the communities that develop and support them dissolve or decide certain formats are no longer needed.[29] Others argue that because certain proprietary formats are so ubiquitous, the chances of their suddenly becoming unavailable are remote; if a particular format were to be phased out, there would be ample time to migrate files to a new format. To rein in the number of different file formats being managed, museums may also identify a limited number of acceptable formats that all incoming digital objects will be migrated to if they differ from this standard, a process known as normalization. Every museum will need to assess its own risk of file format obsolescence and decide on a strategy most appropriate for its collection.

When devising a digital preservation strategy, it is important to understand that for each area of preservation identified by the NDSA, myriad tools exist for carrying them out. Many of these are stand-alone hardware and software that can be used with existing systems to piece together the necessary elements of digital preservation. For instance, while collection metadata has traditionally been captured in collections management systems (CMSs), it is unusual to find a CMS that can facilitate both collections management and digital preservation activities. It is therefore often the case that a CMS is combined with other tools to achieve these functions.[30] A museum may, for instance, rely on its CMS for digital collections cataloging and management; an integrated digital preservation system, such as Archivematica, for performing and automating digital preservation functions, such as identifying file formats and generating and storing checksums; and a secure museum server for storing collections. For large digital collections, tools that automate digital preservation functions can be advantageous in terms of saving time and accurately recording technical and preservation metadata. For smaller collections, it may work well enough to manually incorporate information necessary for digital preservation into a system designed for collections management.[31] For example, a museum might continue to rely on its CMS for collections cataloging and management but add additional database fields for recording technical and preservation metadata, such as checksums and file formats, which are generated using separate stand-alone software. Notably, as the need for all-in-one systems is becoming more apparent, developers of CMSs traditionally used to manage physical collections are beginning to incorporate digital preservation functionalities into their software.[32] The takeaway is that there isn't a one-size-fits-all approach to preserving digital objects and an institution's practices will ultimately depend on existing systems, available resources, and staff skill set. It is also important to understand that experts recommend implementing digital preservation practices gradually as resources become available and staff expertise is developed. This allows for a gradual and achievable strengthening of practices and lessens the chances of digital preservation activities being abandoned due to a lack of knowledge or resources.

How Are Digital Collections Documented?

With a basic understanding of the concepts of digital preservation established, the next section will explore how museums have adapted their documentation practices to be accountable for the digital collections in their care.

To anyone tasked with managing digital collections, it becomes quickly apparent that documenting and tracking digital objects is a very different animal than accounting for traditional collections. For instance, when a physical object is received, it is generally thought of as a singular, authentic object, with a singular catalog record created to hold information about it and track it. In other words, there is a one-to-one relationship between the physical object and its record. If an object is composed of multiple parts, component records may be created to account for each individual piece. In the digital realm, while it is possible that a museum will acquire a singular digital object that can be tracked with a singular record, it is unlikely when one considers the easily replicable nature of digital objects. It is more likely that the intake of any one digital object will involve multiple elements, which may be tangible, intangible, or both. For instance, accepting one digital photograph for the museum's collection could very well mean receiving a negative that was digitized and modified to create the digital photograph, a USB flash drive containing the digital photograph, and a custom-made box holding a "presentation" version of the flash drive that has been decorated and signed by the photographer. In such a scenario, the registrar may ask herself, what is the object? What is the "thing" we are acquiring? If the object is an intangible digital file, how can that as well as the physical elements of the accession (i.e., the thumb drives, negative, and custom presentation box) be registered and accounted for? Furthermore, how can metadata unique to each item be captured?

Luckily, institutions with years of experience considering practices for managing time-based media art and digital archives have developed strategies that allow practitioners to account for the full scope of tangible and intangible items that could comprise just one digital object or archive. These methods build on practices collections practitioners already use to document and describe their physical collections.

One strategy for tracking digital objects mirrors a method used to track physical objects composed of separable but integral parts. It differs, however, in that rather than following a one-to-one relationship between objects and their records, digital objects are assigned a record that serves to represent the object in the abstract, with subrecords utilized to track the intangible or tangible media that comprise the object. Using the earlier digital photograph example, figure 13.2 illustrates the direct relationship between a physical object and its catalog record, contrasted with the representative relationship between a digital object and its catalog record.

Importantly, the use of subrecords linked to the representative object record allows registrars to capture metadata unique to each item comprising a digital object for the purposes of management and preservation. In addition to allowing metadata capture for all object elements received upon acquisition, this method is beneficial in that it is expandable and allows for the documentation of subsequent versions of digital objects created by the museum over time. Similar methodologies are used by practitioners to document and track unique and general equipment required for the presentation of digital objects.[33]

In addition to accounting for each part or aspect of a digital object, experts in the field have established another layer of documentation that addresses how museums can care for digital objects while still providing meaningful access to them. Recall from NDSA's Levels of Digital Preservation that an integral part of preserving digital objects is maintaining their authenticity by protecting them from tampering, corruption, and accidental change. For staff charged with this task, this means organizing the elements of a digital object into different categories based around concepts of preservation and access. Referred to by the Smithsonian American Art Museum as *content formats*,[34] these categories allow practitioners to distinguish "authentic" digital objects from other content formats so they can be kept secure and operable. With the authentic version of a digital object secure, other formats can be made available for use by curators, researchers, or other museums seeking to borrow the digital object for exhibition.

The Smithsonian American Art Museum has established four categories of content formats that may be applied to any given digital object. These content formats may be tangible or intangible. *Preservation formats* can be defined as versions of a digital object that are used for preservation purposes. These versions often represent the "best" or "highest-quality" content received by the museum with the greatest amount of metadata detail. Preservation formats, also referred to as masters, are typically infrequently accessed, and access is restricted to individuals who require it to perform their

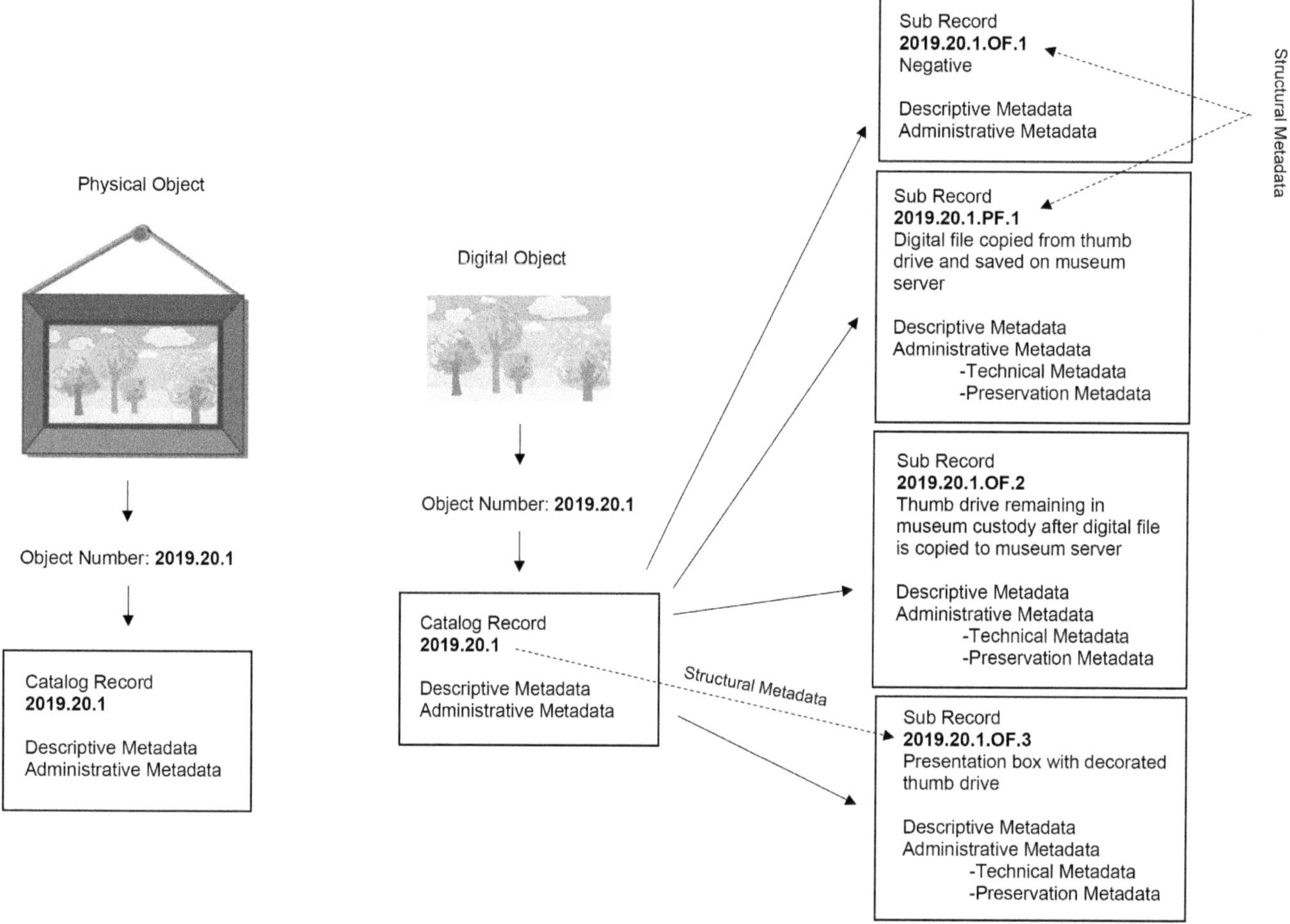

Figure 13.2. Example of the direct relationship between a physical object and its catalog record as compared to the representative relationship between a digital object and its catalog record. BETHANY ROMANOWSKI

job duties. Referring back to NDSA's Levels of Digital Preservation, institutions strive to keep two complete copies of preservation formats stored in at least two different geographic locations. *Access formats*, which may be created from preservation formats, are versions of the digital object that can be made available to curators or researchers for viewing while the preservation format is being kept secure. Access formats, also known as viewing copies, may be kept on physical media, such as CDs or flash drives, or on a hard drive or be downloadable from a museum's collections management system. If an institution will exhibit or lend a digital object, an *exhibition format*, or a version of the work created to be played in a gallery or sent out on loan, can be tracked by the registrar until the object (often shipped on physical media) is returned or destroyed. Finally, a miscellaneous or *other format* category may be used to track content formats that don't fit into the first three categories. This may include items such as physical media customized by an artist; a version of the object that is slightly different from the "authentic" version, such as a draft or working copy; or the physical media the digital object arrived on and has since been copied from, which may be kept for historical purposes or discarded by the museum if it is determined to be irrelevant or nonfunctional. In the digital photograph example (see figure 13.2), the unique identifiers assigned to the various content formats identify them as an *other format* (OF) or a *preservation format* (PF). The content format numbering structure also links the formats to each other and to the representative object record in human readable terms and through standardized database relationships (an example of structural metadata). Note that digital objects may be composed of multiple content formats in each category. For instance, if a museum digitizes an original analog film, it will likely wish to retain both the original film and the digitized version as preservation formats. The museum may also be tracking multiple access and exhibition formats, depending on the level of need.

This method of accounting for digital objects works well for documenting and tracking relatively simple objects, such as films and digital photographs, at the object level. As Trevor Owens points out in his book, *The Theory and Craft of Digital Preservation*,[35] however, some digital objects can be so complex that the various elements that comprise them are challenging to characterize and the boundaries between them difficult to distinguish. An archived website, for instance, may simultaneously be viewed as an item and a collection of items. Advocating for a More Product, Less Process[36] approach to arranging and describing digital collections in the interest of expediting access, Owens advocates for documenting these types of objects with a single record where possible to represent the digital item in the aggregate, rather than attempting to describe each individual item or sub-element. According to Owens, attempting to do so may not be a worthy endeavor given that complex digital objects are largely self-describing, referring to their built-in structures, ordering, and metadata, and suggests that one record for the aggregate object may be sufficient for describing complex digital objects and collections, at least in the short term. Further down the road, an institution can always extract and further describe sub-elements of the object if it desires.

To illustrate this idea, consider pioneering internet artist Wolfgang Staehle's time-based media artwork *2001* in the collection of the National September 11 Memorial & Museum. *2001* is an excerpt of an untitled artwork first shown at Postmasters Gallery in New York City composed of three dual-channel projection-based works featuring views of iconic architectural sites—a television tower in Berlin, the Comburg monastery outside of Stuttgart, and New York City's Lower Manhattan skyline.[37] At each location, stationary webcams captured still images every four seconds, which were transmitted live to the gallery over several days. Intended to be a meditative study of place, the New York cameras inadvertently captured Flight 11 striking the World Trade Center at 8:46 a.m. on September 11, 2001. In 2015, the 9/11 Memorial Museum acquired the New York City "footage" and has shown excerpts of it on the anniversary of the 9/11 attacks. Custom software "plays" the images back in real time, mimicking their original projection.

In acquiring the New York City excerpt, the museum received thousands of JPEG files organized in a file directory titled "Manhattan." Within this folder, a series of subfolders represent a sequence of days in 2001, spanning from September 9 to October 3. Within each of these, there are two additional subfolders, one for each channel of the Manhattan projection. Within the folders for each channel, there is yet another series of subfolders for each hour of the day. The hundreds of individual JPEG files within these folders are named to indicate the hour, minute, and second the image was captured.

In this example, the files acquired by the museum could be considered part of an object (an excerpt of the untitled work that includes projections from two other locations), an object (the Manhattan projection), or a group of objects (thousands of individual files that comprise the Manhattan projection). While the JPEG files that comprise the Manhattan projection could certainly be individually described, as stand-alone items they are not the *artwork* but rather an element of the artwork when they are shown in sequence in four-second intervals synced with real time. Additionally, while the files could be considered components of the Manhattan excerpt, creating individual records for each image may not be an especially useful exercise given that the structure of the file directory provides a wealth of information about what each image depicts, not to mention what can be gleaned from the metadata embedded in each file. For this type of complex object, Owens suggests that assigning one record to represent it may be a reasonable approach to accounting for it. Fortunately, the abstract representation model discussed earlier can be used for this approach as well; a single catalog record created to represent the artwork as a conceptual whole can include descriptive and administrative information about the artwork. Subrecords linked to the representative record can be created to manage different content formats of the aggregate work, such as the preservation format received from the artist and a copy of the work created for exhibition, with fields in each subrecord for storing technical and preservation metadata, such as file counts and checksums.

Through these examples, we see that strategies for accounting for digital objects can vary from object to object, and as Owens suggests, methods for arranging and describing digital objects may emerge naturally from their inherent structures and metadata as well as the level of description desired by end users.[38] Working together, these documentation strategies and variations of them allow registrars to be accountable for the digital objects in their care, that is, to know what they have and where it is; collect metadata for each element of a digital object that supports its management and long-term preservation; and provide appropriate access to digital content to curators, researchers, and the public.

How Can Digital Collections Be Inventoried?

With an understanding of how digital objects can be preserved as well as tracked and accounted for, the next section will take a look at how collections practitioners can use the process of inventory to rein in physical and intellectual control of digital collections while simultaneously carrying out critical digital preservation activities.

Collection- or Group-Level Digital Inventories

Recall that in the area of metadata, the NDSA's Levels of Digital Preservation recommends having at minimum an inventory of the contents of the digital collection that includes storage locations. As was described earlier, however, many institutions face a backlog of unprocessed digital and to-be-digitized analog materials, preventing them from having a full grasp of their digital holdings. In fact, the Institute of Museum and Library Services' Heritage Health Information Survey released in 2019 points out that among the 41 percent of U.S. collecting institutions involved in preserving born-digital content, 73 percent had no digital preservation plan and had not completed a digital condition assessment, suggesting that their holdings have not been comprehensively surveyed.[39] At these institutions, digital objects residing on physical media (and perhaps not yet copied from them) may be mixed in and stored with regular collection materials, while files that have been copied may be stored and documented inconsistently. Furthermore, both digital and analog media may be physically deteriorating or nearing obsolescence; that is, the hardware, software, or equipment needed to access the content may no longer be readily available.

Gauging the type, quantity, and storage location of digital materials can be especially challenging given that one piece of physical media may contain 1 or 100 discrete digital objects. Additionally, files comprising the digital collection may exist on physical media as well as a museum server or other computerized storage location, resulting in collection totals that are muddied or simply unknown.

To address this type of scenario, especially when dealing with large collections, experts suggest carrying out a "high-level" inventory as a first approach to taking stock of existing digital holdings. A thoughtfully planned high-level review, which examines materials at a group level, can result in a much greater understanding of the breadth and scope of the collection and subsequently the collection's digital preservation needs. As described earlier, fully implementing digital preservation practices will require some specialized tools, knowledge, and potentially staffing. Inevitably, funds will need to be allocated to support staff training and preservation processes over the long term. If funding for digital preservation will be new to the museum's budget, information gathered during a high-level inventory can be a helpful tool for explaining and quantifying need. Additionally, for those just getting started with digital preservation, high-level inventories offer an easy first step in that they can generally be undertaken without special knowledge or equipment.

Specifically, high-level inventories can bring into focus the significance, quantity, format, condition, storage needs, and location of digital collections, thus helping to identify items at risk due to loss, damage, or obsolescence and plan for adequate storage.[40] High-level inventories can also be used to flesh out the scope and plan resources for an item-level inventory where processes may include standardizing descriptive metadata, digitizing analog materials, recording checksums, or systematically moving files to a designated and secure storage location. While it may seem desirable in some instances to try to gain control of digital holdings by diving into an item-level review, unless methodologies for the preservation and documentation of digital objects have been established and the appropriate tools procured, high-level inventories represent an important step in an iterative and achievable approach to implementing digital preservation that allows for better long-term planning, especially when dealing with large or diverse collections.

High-level inventories can take a few different forms. Their structure will be unique to each institution and depend largely on the way digital materials are already organized as well as their level of documentation. For instance, the inventory document may take the form of a questionnaire[41] or be structured to analyze digital materials by group, such as photographs, text documents, and audiovisual materials, or by collection or acquisition lot. The inventory document, often in spreadsheet form, can be structured to facilitate a review of collections via a list generated from a CMS and/or accommodate the entry of information as items are encountered in storage. For example, if the collection is fairly well documented, inventory takers may get started by exporting a list of acquisition lots that include digital materials from the CMS and build out the list by cross-referencing it with what is encountered in storage rooms and computerized storage locations. Structuring the template to ensure a review of all locations where digital content might be stored, whether on a museum server, on physical media, or as analog formats, helps to clarify whether digital objects are stored in more than one location. Whether content exists in both analog and digitized formats can also be noted. Following this exercise, the museum's acquisition records may be compared to information captured thus far to identify any additional holdings.

As with physical collections, inventorying digital and to-be-digitized analog collections should be limited to capturing or confirming a set of information previously set out in a scope document. While information captured during the inventory will be tailored to an institution's specific needs, during a high-level inventory it will be beneficial to record at minimum the following:

- The lot or collection number associated with the media
- A brief description of the collection contents
- The type and quantity of each piece of physical media
- The maximum storage capacity of each piece of physical media
- Their storage location(s)
- An object count and description of digital file formats if possible

Institutions concerned about media degradation may also wish to survey the physical condition of their analog and physical media or note of what type of environment the materials are stored in (i.e., whether materials are stored in climate-controlled spaces).

Table 13.1 shows an example of a high-level inventory template structured to survey a collection that is fairly well documented in that the majority of digital objects have been copied from their physical media, saved on the museum's server, and cataloged at the object level in the museum's collections management system. The museum's collections manager knows, however, that some objects haven't been copied to the museum's server and exist only on physical media, some are saved on the museum server but not cataloged in the database, and others are represented by a collection-level record only in the CMS. Further, it's unclear which of the museum's analog materials have been digitized, though there is an awareness that all analog materials will need to be digitized eventually for long-term preservation. Thus, in addition to gathering information about the types and quantity of physical media present and their maximum storage capacity, staff plan to record the digital collection's level of documentation and survey whether content exists in analog format, on physical media, on the museum server, or all three. Organized by acquisition lot, each format type within a collection will receive its own line in the template to facilitate tallying formats. For example, the Paulina Smith Collection contains both audio and video format types, so a line is allocated in the spreadsheet for each. Completing the template reveals that the short film in the Paulina Smith Collection was received on VHS; was digitized; and now exists as a digital file saved on the museum's server, on physical media, and in analog format.

During high-level inventories, physical media is generally not mounted on the computer and viewed; rather, work is focused on reviewing physical and analog media as well as locations where files copied from media may be stored. This is because the objective of a high-level inventory is to determine the overall type and quantity of digital items in order to plan for the next phase of work, which may include performing preservation actions, such as running virus scans, recording checksums, creating disk images, and migrating objects from physical media to a long-term storage solution. Performing these actions, however, requires planning for appropriate tools, systems, and resources, the need for which will be informed by the results of the high-level inventory.

For real-world examples of high-level inventory templates and outcomes, see the case study A Pan-Institutional Approach to Audiovisual Collection Inventories in part II of this book, which describes an inventory undertaken by the Smithsonian Institution Archives to "document the breadth and scope of audiovisual collections by gathering group-level data on formats, condition, and storage environments"[42] as well as the Canadian Heritage Information Network's (CHIN) sample Digital Preservation Inventory Template for Museums. Along with a template that can be downloaded and customized, CHIN's website offers case studies examining the template's application at three Canadian museums.[43]

Item-Level Digital Inventories

With the completion of a high-level inventory, staff will have a clearer sense of what materials comprise the museum's digital holdings. In addition to perhaps a better understanding of the material's cultural and historical significance, staff will have a sense of how many objects comprise the digital collection, their format and condition, whether any materials are nearing obsolescence, the collection's storage space requirements, and where materials are stored. Management and preservation practices revealed by the inventory can also be compared to current standards to determine what needs to be done to bring the collection's stewardship in line with best practice. For instance, the inventory may have identified digital objects that are undocumented in the museum's CMS, uncovered a set of VHS tapes for which the museum has no playback equipment, or clarified a pattern of object files being saved inconsistently in unsecure locations.

To formulate a plan for the item-level inventory, the same strategies discussed in chapters 2 through 8 for

Table 13.1. High-level inventory template example.

Inventory Date	*Collection/ Lot Number*	*Collection/ Lot Title*	*Collection/ Digital Content Description*	*Collection/ Lot Registered in CMS*	*Item Level Cataloged*	*Approximate Digital Object Count*	*Aggregate Record Candidate*	*Analog or Digital Media*	*Physical Media Type*
1/4/2019	2018.15	P. Smith Collection	Short Film by P. Smith	Y	Y	1	N	Digital	USB flash drive
1/4/2019	2018.15	P. Smith Collection	P. Smith Oral Histories	Y	N	100	N	Analog	N/A
1/5/2019	2012.5	Susan Chui PowerPoint Collection	Susan Chui PowerPoint Presentations	N	N	3	N	Digital	USB flash drive
1/5/2019	2013.54	Jane Weinstein Photograph Collection	Digital Photographs by Jane Weinstein	Y	Y	34	N	Digital	N/A
1/5/2019	2008.23	Robert Ramirez Photograph Collection	Digital Photographs by Robert Ramirez	Y	Partially cataloged	400	N	Digital	N/A

Physical Media Quantity	*Physical Media Storage Capacity (GB)*	*Analog Media Type*	*Analog Media Quantity*	*Analog Media Estimated Duration (min)*	*Analog/ Physical Media Storage Location*	*File Format Type*	*File Format*	*Files Uploaded to Server*	*Server Name/ Location*	*Notes*
1	256	VHS	1	6	Box 30, 25	Video	MPEG-4	Y	Digital collection storage drive	Digitized from VHS in 2018
N/A	N/A	Compact audio cassette	50	3,000	Box 23	Audio	n/a	N	N/A	Requires digitization
1	16	N/A	N/A	N/A	Box 30	Presn.	PPT	N	N/A	
N/A	N/A	N/A	N/A	N/A	N/A	Still image	JPEG	Y	Digital collection storage drive	Received from donor via FTP in 2013
N/A	N/A	N/A	N/A	N/A	N/A	Still image	JPEG	Y	Collection dept. drive	Print photographs scanned & returned to donor

planning a physical inventory's objectives, deliverables, activities, and resources may be applied. In addition to capturing or confirming item-level information, the project may include strengthening the institution's digital preservation infrastructure. For instance, are security controls for accessing the digital collection adequate? Is the museum equipped to store at least two complete copies of the digital collection in different locations? Will digitizing analog materials be part of the item-level inventory? If yes, can this be done in house, or must it be outsourced? Planning the capture of item-level information for each digital object will raise additional points to consider, such as what metadata will be captured, whether the museum's cataloging schema needs to be adjusted to accommodate it, what digital preservation activities will be carried out during the inventory, and to what extent those activities can be automated. A review of NDSA's areas of digital preservation can help to ensure the project scope is hitting critical marks related to both digital preservation infrastructure and object-level information capture.

Though specific digital preservation tools won't be discussed here,[44] once the project's scope is established, it will be important to consider what tools will be used for the inventory in conjunction with a review of what processes can be performed by existing systems. For example, a CMS that can generate and store checksums or extract technical metadata from files uploaded to the system may preclude the need to source other software for this purpose.

Workflows for item-level inventorying digital collections will be unique to each institution and will be dictated by the project's scope and tools. As with any workflow, steps taken to capture item-level information will need to be drafted, tested, and likely adjusted to ensure the workflow functions smoothly and produces the desired deliverables. The entry point to the inventory may be informed by the structure or methodology of the preceding high-level inventory. For instance, completing a preliminary inventory that established an authoritative list of digital acquisitions would allow inventory staff to systematically work through that list, recording inventory data and performing digital preservation activities for each acquisition. Other institutions may approach the collection by media or format type to streamline work with a particular type of media.

To establish processes for inventorying digital objects, it will be helpful to examine the workflows authorities in the field have established for ingesting digital materials. Much work has been done in this area to establish practices for documenting digital objects' chain of custody, that is, ensuring that objects are acquired without being altered and being able to demonstrate it. Two examples include the Online Computer Library Center's (OCLC) guide, "Walk This Way: Detailed Steps for Transferring Born-Digital Content from Media You Can Read In-House,"[45] which outlines step-by-step practices for transferring digital content from physical media to storage. In addition, Matters in Media Art identifies critical information to capture about digital objects upon acquisition in order to detect whether files have changed over time, take actions to keep them accessible, and protect them from uncertain provenance.[46] By reviewing established ingest processes, project managers can devise an inventory workflow that will allow these processes to be applied retroactively, thereby achieving an inventory of the collection while simultaneously performing critical digital preservation activities. Generally, workflows for ingesting digital objects include the following steps:

- Establish a designated computer workstation that is regularly scanned for viruses and equipped with write blockers for transferring digital content off physical media. Virus scanning protects files from being corrupted. Write blockers prevent people working with files on physical media from accidentally altering or deleting them.
- Connect the physical media to the computer.
- Establish the digital object's fixity by generating its checksum.
- Check the digital object for viruses.
- Record the object's core descriptive and administrative metadata, including technical and preservation metadata.
- Move the digital object to a designated, secure storage location.

Within this framework, current standards suggest that project planners will maximize the benefit of an item-level inventory by capturing or confirming the following minimum dataset, laid out in table 13.2.

To capture this information, it is common for core descriptive and administrative data to be entered into a catalog record in the museum's CMS. To list storage locations, the CMS may be configured to point to a storage location, such as a particular museum server or a complete file path. An object's checksum, file format, and size may be extracted by the CMS from uploaded files, generated using stand-alone software, then imported or entered into the CMS or recorded and stored in a digital preservation system used in conjunction with the CMS. Moving digital objects will entail electronically transferring the files to an established secure storage location and may include tagging, rehousing, and storing physical media. It is important to note that the more technical

Table 13.2. Digital Object Minimum Inventory Data Capture

Descriptive and Administrative Metadata	*Preservation Metadata*	*Technical Metadata*
• Object's unique identifier, which is often an accession number or incorporates an accession number • The object's name • A brief description of what is viewable and/or audible • Content format (i.e., preservation or access copy?) • Storage location • Inventory record (recorder, date, whether object was located)	• Checksum	• File format • File size

metadata that is recorded, for example, metadata that is specific to different file format types, the less likely manual entry will be a feasible option, unless the collection is very small and isn't expected to grow. Computers can do this work faster and more accurately and consistently and can scale to handle large quantities.[47]

Utilizing similar workflows, recent surveys undertaken to evaluate the condition of digital collections has demonstrated the successful implementation of digital preservation through the process of inventory, and vice versa. For example, in 2016, the Denver Art Museum began an electronic media conservation project with the goal of documenting all collection material stored on videotapes, optical disks, and external hard drives in the museum's CMS and migrating these items to the museum's digital repository.[48] During the survey, physical media was disk imaged to establish fixity and packaged with metadata created during the disk imaging process. These packages were then ingested into the museum's digital preservation system, Archivematica, and transferred to storage. At the same time, existing catalog records were updated, and new records were created to document the migration of analog materials to digital media. The pilot project that established the framework for this comprehensive survey is described in part II of this book in the case study Venturing into New Territory: Inventorying Born-Digital Objects in the AIGA Design Archives at the Denver Art Museum.

Similarly, in 2012, Smithsonian Institution Archives began a survey of existing born-digital collections at several units to inventory and assess the condition of their holdings. The goals of the project were to uncover undocumented collections, establish physical and intellectual control of the collection, and perform a baseline preservation assessment. As digital objects were identified and described, they were scanned for viruses, checksums were generated, and objects were moved into secure storage environments. Notably, 6,613 new pieces of physical media containing 651,629 files were identified during the Smithsonian survey.[49]

These examples demonstrate the inherent interconnection between the processes of inventorying and preserving digital materials. As digital heritage proliferates, it is more likely than not that digital materials will eventually comprise a significant portion of any museum's collection. It goes without saying that an institution's efforts to document and preserve its holdings extend to collections in digital formats. However, to successfully manage and make digital resources accessible for future generations, practitioners must first understand the vulnerabilities of digital objects, know what is required to preserve them, and feel comfortable navigating their documentation—a function that is the cornerstone of digital preservation efforts. Establishing a framework for examining digital objects within the context of inventories to record baseline information, especially for institutions just beginning to implement digital preservation, is vital. With fundamental documentation and preservation methodologies in place, digital objects already in museum collections can be retroactively documented, and preservation actions can be simultaneously performed. The establishment of successful ingest and inventory processes means that future inventories of digital collections may rely heavily on confirming the presence of files and elements of digital objects, performing fixity checks and recording outcomes, evaluating file formats for obsolescence, and migrating objects to new formats as necessary.

Indeed, the notion that digital preservation is not a one-time process but rather a continuous activity performed by people is reinforced by the practice of inventory, which has traditionally been a mechanism for facilitating a checkup for every object in the museum's collection. With the advent of digital materials, the need for regular inventories is not diminished but rather strengthened, as they are a means of facilitating the ongoing preservation actions required by digital objects due to their distinct vulnerabilities.

Notes

1. United Nations Educational, Scientific and Cultural Organization (UNESCO), "Concept of Digital Heritage," accessed October 15, 2021, https://en.unesco.org/themes/information-preservation/digital-heritage/concept-digital-heritage.
2. Andy Jackson, Andy Tester, and Paul Wheatley, "Community Owned Digital Preservation Tool Registry (COPTR)," COPTR, modified April 26, 2021, https://coptr.digipres.org/Main_Page. See this website for a comprehensive listing of digital preservation tools organized by preservation function and media content type.
3. Erin O'Meara and Kate Stratton, "Preserving Digital Objects," in *Digital Preservation Essentials*, ed. Christopher J. Prom (Chicago, IL: Society of American Archivists, 2016), 9.
4. Frances Lloyd-Baynes, "When 'Digital' Meets Collection: How Do 'Traditional' Museums Manage?," MuseumNext, published March 6, 2019, https://www.museumnext.com/article/when-digital-meets-collection-how-do-traditional-museums-manage/.
5. The National September 11 Memorial & Museum, which began collecting in 2006, counts 70 percent of its collection as digital.

6. O'Meara and Stratton, "Preserving Digital Objects," 8.

7. Elizabeth E. Merritt, *National Standards and Best Practices for U.S. Museums* (Washington, DC: American Association of Museums, 2008).

8. Jenn Riley, "Understanding Metadata: What Is Metadata and What Is It For?," National Information Standards Organization, accessed October 15, 2021, https://groups.niso.org/apps/group_public/download.php/17446/Understanding%20Metadata.

9. Eddy Colloton and Kate Moomaw, "Rewind, Pause, Playback: Addressing a Media Conservation Backlog at the Denver Art Museum," Electronic Media Review, accessed October 15, 2021, http://resources.conservation-us.org/emg-review/volume-5-2017-2018/colloton/.

10. Ibid.

11. Smithsonian Institution, "Pan-Institutional Audiovisual Collections Survey: Final Project Report," published March 28, 2017, https://siarchives.si.edu/sites/default/files/pdfs/SI_AVSurvey_FinalReport_03282017.pdf.

12. Ricky Erway, "You've Got to Walk Before You Can Run: First Steps for Managing Born-Digital Content Received on Physical Media," published August 2012, accessed October 15, 2021, https://www.oclc.org/content/dam/research/publications/library/2012/2012-06.pdf.

13. Colloton and Moomaw, "Rewind, Pause, Playback."

14. Association for Library Collections and Technical Services Preservation and Reformatting Section, "Definitions of Digital Preservation," published June 24, 2007, accessed October 15, 2021, http://www.ala.org/alcts/resources/preserv/defdigpres0408.

15. National Digital Stewardship Alliance, "Levels of Digital Preservation," accessed October 15, 2021, https://ndsa.org/activities/levels-of-digital-preservation/.

16. Elizabeth R. Leggett, *Digitization and Digital Archiving: A Practical Guide for Librarians* (Lanham, MD: Rowman & Littlefield, 2014). This guide offers a comprehensive description of computerized storage solutions, how they work, and the pros and cons of each, for those starting out with digital preservation.

17. InterPARES 2 Project, "The InterPARES 2 Project Glossary," modified October 15, 2021, http://www.interpares.org/ip2/display_file.cfm?doc=ip2_glossary.pdf&CFID=19420182&CFTOKEN=91479646.

18. O'Meara and Stratton, "Digital Preservation Storage," 124.

19. Ibid.

20. World Digital Library, "Bagger," accessed October 15, 2021, https://project.wdl.org/arab_peninsula/workshop2012/en/doha_workshop_2012_bagger_en.pdf. "Bags" are a means of packaging digital files of any type with metadata for transfer and digital preservation.

21. NISO Framework Working Group, *A Framework of Guidance for Building Good Digital Collections*, 3rd ed. (Baltimore, MD: National Information Standards Organization, 2007), https://www.niso.org/sites/default/files/2017-08/framework3.pdf.

22. Riley, "Understanding Metadata."

23. Anne J. Gilliland, "Setting the Stage," in *Introduction to Metadata*, 3rd ed., ed. Murtha Baca (Los Angeles: Getty Publications, 2016), http://www.getty.edu/publications/intrometadata/setting-the-stage/.

24. Ibid.

25. Riley, "Understanding Metadata."

26. NISO Framework Working Group, *A Framework of Guidance for Building Good Digital Collections*.

27. National Library of the Netherlands, "What Is Emulation?," accessed November 30, 2020, https://www.kb.nl/en/organisation/research-expertise/research-on-digitisation-and-digital-preservation/emulation/what-is-emulation.

28. The Linux Information Project, "Free File Format Definition," published February 11, 2007, http://www.linfo.org/free_file_format.html.

29. Digital Preservation Coalition, "Digital Preservation Handbook: File Formats and Standards," accessed October 15, 2021, https://www.dpconline.org/handbook/technical-solutions-and-tools/file-formats-and-standards.

30. Matters in Media Art, "Sustaining Media Art," accessed October 15, 2021, http://mattersinmediaart.org/sustaining-your-collection.html.

31. Ibid.

32. Collective Access, "FAQs: Digital Preservation + Collective Access," accessed November 30, 2020, https://collectiveaccess.org/preservation.

33. Smithsonian American Art Museum, "Equipment Categorization and TMS Entry for Artwork Equipment," accessed December 1, 2020, https://www.si.edu/content/tbma/documents/SAAM_TBMA_Equipment_Categories_and_TMS_entry.pdf.

34. Smithsonian American Art Museum, "Content Formats Categorization and TMS Entry for Content Formats," accessed November 30, 2020, https://www.si.edu/content/tbma/documents/SAAM_TBMA_Content_Formats_Categories_and_TMS_entry.pdf.

35. Trevor Owens, *The Theory and Craft of Digital Preservation* (Baltimore, MD: Johns Hopkins University Press, 2018).

36. Mark A. Greene and Dennis Meissner, "More Product, Less Process: Revamping Traditional Archival Processing," *American Archivist*, Fall/Winter 2005, http://www.archivists.org/prof-education/pre-readings/IMPLP/AA68.2.MeissnerGreene.pdf. See this article for an introduction to the More Product, Less Process archives processing ideology.

37. Rhizome, "Net Art Anthology: Untitled, Wolfgang Staehle, 2001," accessed November 30, 2020, https://anthology.rhizome.org/untitled.

38. Owens, *The Theory and Craft of Digital Preservation*.

39. Institute of Museum and Library Services, "Protecting America's Collections: Results from the Heritage Health Information Survey," published February 2019, accessed October 15, 2021, https://imls.gov/sites/default/files/publications/documents/imls-hhis-report.pdf.

40. Erway, "You've Got to Walk Before You Can Run."

41. Matters in Media Art, "Survey: Scoping Your Digital Collection," accessed November 30, 2020, http://mattersinmediaart.org/downloads/Survey_Scoping-your-collection.pdf.

42. Smithsonian Institution, "Smithsonian Pan-Institutional Survey of Audiovisual Collections," accessed October 15, 2021, https://siarchives.si.edu/about/smithsonian-pan-institutional-survey-audiovisual-collections.

43. Canadian Heritage Information Network, "Digital Preservation Toolkit," modified November 22, 2020, https://www.canada.ca/en/heritage-information-network/services/digital-preservation/toolkit.html.

44. Jackson et al., "Community Owned Digital Preservation Tool Registry (COPTR)."

45. Julianna Barrera-Gomez and Ricky Erway, "Walk This Way: Detailed Steps for Transferring Born-Digital Content from Media You Can Read In-House," accessed October 15, 2021, https://www.oclc.org/research/publications/2013/oclcresearch-transferring-born-digital.html.

46. Matters in Media Art, "Sustaining Media Art."

47. Michael Chui, associate cataloger for the 9/11 Memorial Museum, personal communication, December 7, 2019.

48. Colloton and Moomaw, "Rewind, Pause, Playback."

49. Smithsonian Institution Archives, "Born Digital Collections Holdings Survey," accessed November 30, 2020, https://siarchives.si.edu/what-we-do/digital-curation/born-digital-collections-holdings-survey.

PART II

INVENTORIES IN ACTION

~

Case A

A Pan-Institutional Approach to Audiovisual Collection Inventories

Alison Reppert Gerber, Preservation Coordinator,
Smithsonian Institution Archives

As the world's largest museum complex, the Smithsonian Institution encompasses nineteen museums, multiple research entities, and the National Zoo. Currently, the Smithsonian is the steward for 155.1 million objects and specimens, 2.1 million library volumes, and 162.3 thousand cubic feet of archival collections. Within these collections, you can find dozens of audiovisual formats containing a vast variety of content—from African American home movies to animal studies conducted by Devra G. Kleiman to original recordings of folk music legend Woody Guthrie—that represents our world's rich heritage. Unfortunately, many of these assets are at a high risk for loss due to the degradation of the physical carriers and obsolescence of the playback equipment used to digitize the content for long-term preservation. In 2014, to support future planning for audiovisual preservation initiatives, the Smithsonian-led Audiovisual Archivist Interest Lunch (AVAIL) group proposed a pan-institutional audiovisual inventory and condition survey of eight archival unit collections.[1] The primary goals of the survey were to document the scope and breadth of audiovisual collections by gathering group-level data on formats, condition, and storage environments and to report on areas of greatest strengths and needs in preservation practices gleaned from staff interviews.

Internal funding for this project was secured from the Smithsonian Institution's National Collections Program (NCP) Collections Care and Preservation Fund (CCPF). CCPF provides strategic funding, dispersed through a competitive proposal process, for projects that improve the preservation of collections, mitigate deterioration, and address priority collections management needs throughout the Smithsonian. The Pan-Institutional Audiovisual Survey received CCPF funding in May 2015, and a contracted audiovisual archivist was brought on later that year to begin the inventory.

Prior to this survey, the Smithsonian had undertaken two other pan-institutional inventory-based projects—one for photographic collections and one for born-digital content. Both of these projects were conducted using the Messier Tool,[2] a Microsoft Access–based system that was originally developed by Paul Messier for photographic collections. Due to the complexity of audiovisual collections and the extensive modifications that would be required for the Messier Tool, the decision was made to forgo the use of this tool and, instead, use widely available systems, such as Microsoft Word and Excel, to document information about these collections.

There were four components to the audiovisual survey: group-level inventory, multiple-choice questionnaire, on-site staff interview, and condition assessment. Each activity added to the preservation narrative regarding Smithsonian audiovisual collections. As previously stated, the primary goal of the inventory was to create an estimate of what formats and quantities of audiovisual media were in each participating unit's collection. All inventory data was recorded using a Microsoft Excel spreadsheet that contained predetermined fields. On account of the anticipated volume of collections, the inventory was conducted at a group level, meaning that each format type in a selected collection was given a line item in the spreadsheet. Due to the amount of data gathered during the inventory and to maintain the functionality and manageability of the data, separate spreadsheets were maintained for each unit, and larger units had multiple spreadsheets. The following fields were included in the inventory: unit, building, date inventoried/

	A	B	C	D	E	F	G	H	I	J	K	L	M	N	O	P	Q	R	S
1	SI Unit	Building	Room	Date Inventoried / Imported	Box #	Collection / Accession Number	shelf number	Title / Description	Item Count	Medium	Format	Base Substrate / Material Type	Diameter (inches)	Playback Speed	Estimated Footage (each)	Estimated Footage (Total)	Estimated Duration Each (minutes)	Estimated Duration Total (minute	Media Condition
47	SIA	Iron Mountain		2/22/2016	001	454		National Museum of American Art (U.S.). $b Office of Public Affairs.	1	audio	1/4 inch audio tape								2 - minor visible dam
48	SIA	Iron Mountain		7/18/2016	005	455		Smithsonian Institution Archives; various content	9	video	¾ inch videotape: U-matic	polyester				30	270		2 - minor visible dam
49	SIA	Iron Mountain		7/18/2016	006	455		Smithsonian Institution Archives; various content	12	video	¾ inch videotape: U-matic	polyester				30	360		2 - minor visible dam
50	SIA	Iron Mountain		7/18/2016	007	455		Smithsonian Institution Archives	5	video	¾ inch videotape: U-matic	polyester				60	300		2 - minor visible dam
51	SIA	Iron Mountain		7/18/2016	007	455		Smithsonian Institution Archives	3	video	¾ inch videotape: U-matic	polyester				30	90		2 - minor visible dam
52	SIA	Iron Mountain		7/18/2016	008	455		Smithsonian Institution Archives	3	video	¾ inch videotape: U-matic	polyester				30	90		2 - minor visible dam
53	SIA	Iron Mountain		7/18/2016	009	455		Smithsonian Institution Archives	11	video	¾ inch videotape: U-matic	polyester				60	660		3 - moderate visible d
54	SIA	Iron Mountain		7/18/2016	002	455		Smithsonian Institution Archives; various content	18	video	¾ inch videotape: U-matic S	polyester						20	2 - minor visible dam
55	SIA	Iron Mountain		7/18/2016	003	455		Smithsonian Institution Archives; various content	19	video	¾ inch videotape: U-matic S	polyester						20	2 - minor visible dam
56	SIA	Iron Mountain		7/18/2016	004	455		Smithsonian Institution Archives; various content	17	video	¾ inch videotape: U-matic S	polyester				20	340		2 - minor visible dam
57	SIA	Iron Mountain		7/18/2016	006	455		Smithsonian Institution Archives; various content	1	video	¾ inch videotape: U-matic S	polyester				20	20		2 - minor visible dam
58	SIA	Iron Mountain		7/18/2016	007	455		Smithsonian Institution Archives	5	video	¾ inch videotape: U-matic S	polyester				20	100		2 - minor visible dam
59	SIA	Iron Mountain		7/18/2016	008	455		Smithsonian Institution Archives	12	video	¾ inch videotape: U-matic S	polyester				20	240		2 - minor visible dam
60	SIA	Iron Mountain		7/18/2016	001	455		Smithsonian Institution Archives	19	video	¾ inch videotape: U-matic S	polyester				20	380		2 - minor visible dam
61	SIA	Iron Mountain		7/18/2016	010	455		SIA Smithsonian Institution Credit Roll 1985	1	video	1 inch videotape open reel	polyester	6.5						2 - minor visible dam
62	SIA	Iron Mountain		7/18/2016	010	455		SIA	5	audio	1/4 inch audio tape	polyester	7					7 1/2 IPS	2 - minor visible dam
63	SIA	Iron Mountain		7/18/2016	010	455		SIA	2	audio	1/4 inch audio tape	polyester	5						2 - minor visible dam
64	SIA	Iron Mountain		7/18/2016	011	455		Smithsonian Institution Archives; Nakian-Abelson Narration	1	audio	1/4 inch audio tape	polyester	10					15 IPS	2 - minor visible dam
65	SIA	Iron Mountain		7/18/2016	011	455		Smithsonian Institution Archives; Nakian	4	audio	1/4 inch audio tape	polyester	7					15 IPS	2 - minor visible dam
66	SIA	Iron Mountain		7/18/2016	011	455		Smithsonian Institution Archives; Nakian	2	audio	1/4 inch audio tape	polyester	5					15 IPS	2 - minor visible dam
67	SIA	Iron Mountain		7/18/2016	012	455		Smithsonian Institution Archives; Voice of America interview with Dr. Harry Rand 1982	1	audio	1/4 inch audio tape	polyester	7						3 - moderate visible d
68	SIA	Iron Mountain		7/18/2016	007	455		Smithsonian Institution Archives	3	video	Betacam	polyester				60	180		2 - minor visible dam
69	SIA	Iron Mountain		7/18/2016	012	455		Smithsonian Institution Archives; Archives of American Art; Patrick Ireland	1	audio	Compact audio cassette	polyester		90	90				2 - minor visible dam
70	SIA	Iron Mountain		7/18/2016	007	455		Smithsonian Institution Archives	2	film	Film: 16mm	acetate		800	1600				2 - minor visible dam

Figure A.1. Example of a completed inventory worksheet. ALISON REPPERT GERBER

imported, collection number, box number, shelf number, title/description, estimated item count, medium, format, base substrate/material type, diameter (inches), playback speed, estimated footage each, estimated footage total, estimated duration each (minutes), estimated duration total (minutes), visible media condition, fungus evident, storage temperature (°F), storage relative humidity (%), A-D strip test date, A-D strip test level, notes. A combination of direct (hand counting) and indirect (importing of existing collections data) entry was used to populate the inventory spreadsheets.

Due to the variety of ways the participating units maintained cataloging data within their collection management systems, many of the fields were deemed optional or were slightly modified to capture unit-specific data. The *Notes* field was primarily used by units to capture additional data, such as item-level asset numbers, barcode information, or notable format data. For example, the Human Studies Film Archive used the *Notes* field to document sync pulse in specific audio formats. The Smithsonian Institution Archives used this field to note whether the existing finding aids contained item-level information for cases where survey hand counts and finding aids required comparison and data reconciliation.

The second component of the survey, a multiple-choice questionnaire, was developed by AVAIL, based on questions from previous collections surveys that employed the Messier Tool. Stakeholders revised the questions in order to address the nuances of storing, preserving, and accessing audiovisual collections. Using Google Forms, the questionnaires were distributed to the appropriate staff at each unit. Responses to the majority of the questions were based on the observances and experiences of unit representatives regarding audiovisual preservation practices, rather than numerical data.

On-site interviews were also conducted with unit staff tasked with managing and preserving audiovisual collections. These interviews, typically conducted on the first day of each unit's inventory, served to familiarize the contracted audiovisual archivist with the unit's history, collection, and storage spaces. The interview questions focused on the cultural value of the collection, storage facilities, rehousing and digitization practices, intellectual control and access, and unit roles and responsibilities.

Lastly, group-level condition assessments were completed for the majority of inventoried assets. Using a five-point scale, each hand-counted group was visually assessed for evidence of mold, popped strands, visible dirt, warping, odor, and broken carriers or cartridges. For acetate-based assets, acid-detecting (A-D)[3] strips were used to test for acetic acid vapor (in ppm). Each one of these factors adversely affected condition scores, which were as follows: 1—no visible damage, 2—minor visible damage, 3—moderate visible damage, 4—significant visible damage, and 5—severe visible damage (likely to require specialist intervention). In cases in which collections could not be physically accessed, institutional knowledge was utilized to estimate the condition.

This survey had several deliverables—unit inventory spreadsheets, multiple-choice questionnaire responses, interview responses, unit reports (eight), and a final project report. Each participating unit was provided with its compiled inventory spreadsheets, multiple-choice responses, unit-edited interview responses, and individual unit report. The unit reports contained unit-specific information about total assets, general condition, collection breakdowns by format, project methodologies, storage spaces, and general observations. The final project report contained similar information to the unit reports but at an institutional level and was made publicly available on the Smithsonian Institution Archives' website[4] to promote transparency and increase access to data and recommendations.

While the inventory was originally intended to provide a starting point for understanding the scope of the collection and as a tool for cross-unit comparison, the Smithsonian has been able to use the gathered information for much larger efforts. By including eight units, we were able to create a stronger and more comprehensive narrative about audiovisual collections within the Smithsonian and thus create a powerful argument for increased preservation capacity at an institutional level. Concurrently, each unit has also been able to use the inventory data to increase awareness and capacity to preserve its individual collections. In accomplishing the first comprehensive audiovisual survey in the recent history of Smithsonian collections, we have been able to advocate for these materials in ways not previously possible.

As an example, in 2018, the Smithsonian Institution Archives spearheaded an audiovisual preservation readiness assessment in direct response to the success of the audiovisual survey. Harnessing the expertise of three contracted audiovisual archivists, this assessment aims to expand on the survey data by inventorying three additional unit collections, identifying preservation priorities based on format and cultural value, conducting equipment and digitization workflow analyses, and reporting on the risk for loss given four future scenarios. This assessment will build on the momentum of the survey and provide critical information for continued audiovisual preservation efforts at the Smithsonian.

Notes

1. While audiovisual materials exist in other units, the eight participating archival units encompass the majority of audiovisual collections within the Smithsonian.

2. In 2010, Paul Messier created a survey methodology for assessing large decentralized photographic collections, which was first implemented at Yale University. The final report for that project can be found at https://ipch.yale.edu/sites/default/files/files/Mellon%20final%20photo%20rptmabHvD%20_2_.pdf.

3. A-D strips are manufactured by the Image Permanence Institute. They are dye-coated paper strips that detect and measure the severity of cellulose acetate film deterioration. The parts per million measurement provides an indication of where the asset currently falls in the deterioration process.

4. https://siarchives.si.edu/about/smithsonian-pan-institutional-survey-audiovisual-collections.

~

Case B

Inventory and Cataloging Project at the Museum of Danish America

Angela Stanford, Registrar and Curator of Collections

Introduction

In the fall of 2017, the Museum of Danish America (MoDA) finished an intensive inventory of its object collection. At the close of this eleven-year project, more than 15,000 objects have complete catalog records, current condition reports, accurate home locations, and new digital images. Each object now has a corresponding record in PastPerfect, the collections management system MoDA uses, and the electronic records also include all known provenance information pulled from the accession files and learned through staff research. The project also included rehousing objects when necessary and deaccessioning many pieces. The inventory involved objects of various types—housewares, agricultural equipment, furniture, tools, paintings, textiles, and more.

MoDA's total collections number around 30,000, including objects, photographs, archival materials, and some books. The collections document Danish immigrants and their descendants as well as the continuing relationship between the United States and Denmark. As the only national museum telling the Danish–American story, the collection covers a broad range of topics, periods in history, and places in both countries—people, businesses, social groups, sports, and military history being a few. Included in the collection is the very first piano Danish immigrant and world-renowned comedian Victor Borge ever bought and a sculpture by Gutzon Borglum, the son of Danish immigrants and creator of Mount Rushmore.

Officially created in 1983, the museum began collecting two years later, and with the exception of less than two dozen purchases over the years, all pieces have been donated. The museum has four vaults in which collections are stored. Depending on size and type, objects are stored either on open shelving or in boxes in one of two vaults. Paintings are located on hanging racks in a third vault. Finally, more than 8,500 of the 15,000 objects in the collection are stored on open shelving in Visual Storage, a large room with glass on three sides. Until 2014, objects were also stored at three off-site locations.

The Need and Process

As with many museums, the early push was to simply grow a collection. Many pieces arrived with recorded histories and significance, but many others did not. While almost the entire collection was documented on paper through deeds of gift and assigned standard three-part identification numbers, further cataloging was spotty. A few limited inventories that confirmed only identification numbers and home locations had been done in the mid- to late 1990s, but those were now out of date and inaccurate. In the late 1990s, the museum transitioned from an Access database to the PastPerfect collections management system, but the majority of records from that migration remained skeletal and did not include images or condition reports. In addition, a backlog of more than 630 donation lots developed between 1997 and 2003.

Museum staff simply did not have a good idea of what was in the collection already and therefore what new artifacts would strengthen it. The lack of complete database records meant that identifying artifacts for exhibition involved physically looking in multiple storage spaces rather than doing a quick digital search. Locating pieces to fulfill requests from museum stakeholders was next to impossible because of sporadic home locations. Access and artifact safety were also issues due to a lack of early storage planning.

Figure B.1. The museum's painting storage vault. ANGELA STANFORD

Figure B.2. The museum's Visual Storage. ANGELA STANFORD

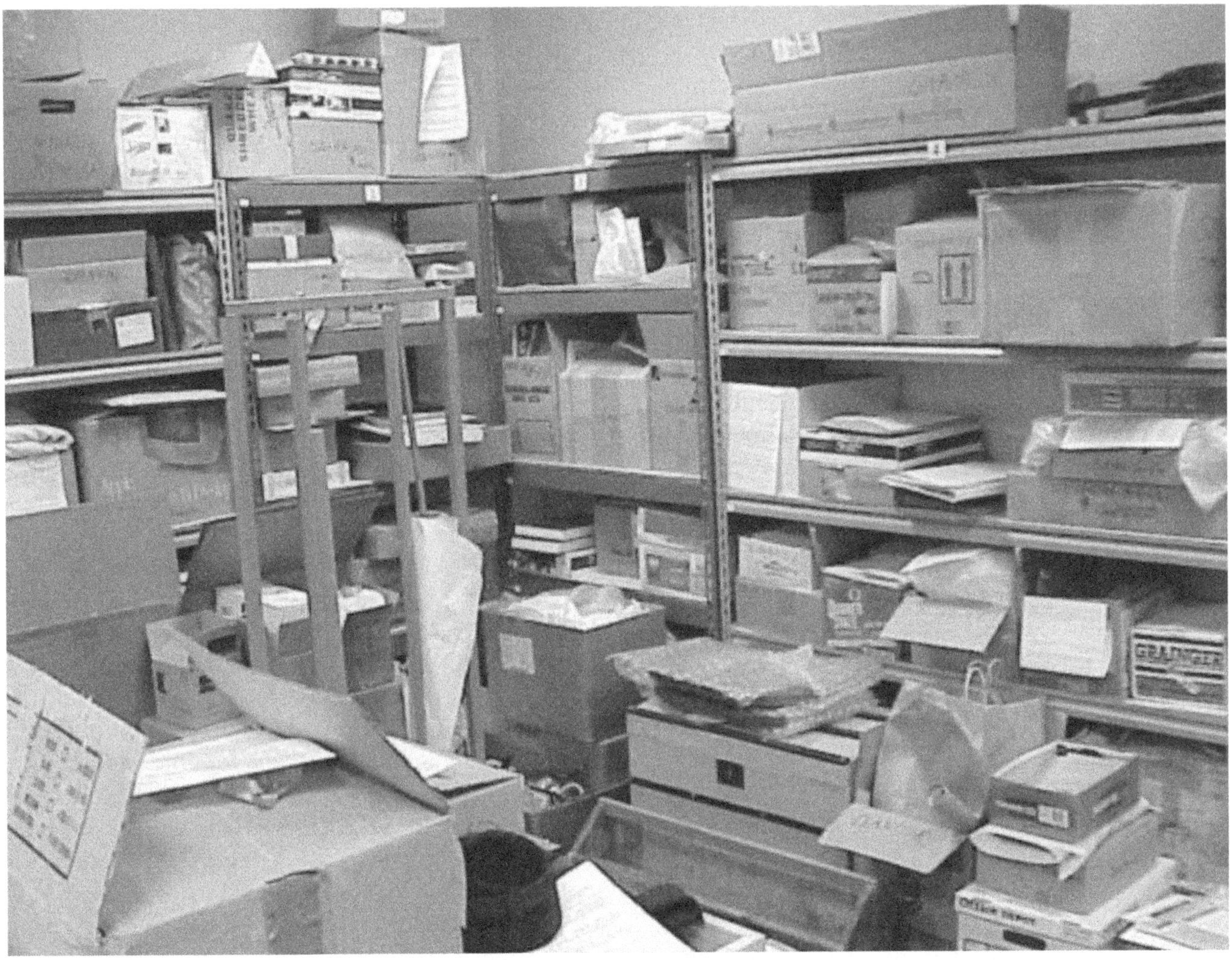

Figure B.3. The museum's unprocessed donations, prior to completion of the inventory. ANGELA STANFORD

Figure B.4. Large object storage area prior to inventory and rehousing. ANGELA STANFORD

In 2004, staff began to look at the collection, along with existing paper and digital records. Clear needs emerged, and an inventory plan was developed. In addition to recording identification numbers and home locations, the planned process would include the following:

- Cataloging details such as place of origin, color and shape, inscriptions and maker's marks, dimensions, etc.
- Creating condition reports documenting all damage and wear
- Taking photographs from all angles of each artifact before returning it to its home location
- Rehousing objects as needed (e.g., mounting a fragile artifact to a backing board for support or providing padding for textiles to alleviate stress caused by hard folds)
- Perusing paper accession files to make sure identification numbers on objects match deeds of gift and finding all known historical information about each object (As time allowed, additional research was also conducted.)
- Data entry of all information and images into PastPerfect
- Adding the identification number, object name, and home location to an Excel inventory list for each storage room (While PastPerfect reports could have been used, these lists were easy to create in Excel and mirrored the format of earlier inventory lists.)
- Labeling each completed shelf with an "inventory complete" tag

Figure B.5. Shelf tagged with an "Inventory Complete" sign.
ANGELA STANFORD

These steps were the same for most artifacts, with some modifications depending on size, location, or condition.

Conducting the Inventory

For the first four years, the registrar, interns, and volunteers worked on the inventory between other projects. Because network access was either limited or not available in collection storage areas, direct entry of data into PastPerfect was not really possible. Instead, they recorded information manually using pencil and paper and took photographs using a digital camera. Once they reached the end of a shelf or cabinet, they returned to their desks to begin data entry.

Searching paper records revealed a notable lack of provenance for many pieces, and overcrowded shelves made removing artifacts challenging. As pieces were returned to storage, they were arranged in more space-effective ways as much as possible.

Beginning in 2010, inventory became the primary project for interns and volunteers, with the registrar supervising all aspects of the project and participating to a large degree. While direct entry of data into PastPerfect was still limited, it increased as the project continued. At this point, identifying objects for deaccession consideration was added to the process. Those pieces that lacked strong provenance, were not mission based, were heavily redundant, or whose condition was poor were first recommended for deaccessioning to the staff-level Collections Review Committee. If approved, those recommendations were then sent to the board of directors for final approval. From 2010 through the end of the inventory project, over 5,500 objects were deaccessioned from the collection.

During the inventory project, about 400 objects were found with no visible identification number or a number that did not match the description on the associated deed of gift. These pieces were relocated to a designated shelving unit and listed on an Excel spreadsheet that included the date they were found. In the future, any found-in-collection objects remaining after trying to match them with old paper or digital records will be considered for the collection or handled in a similar manner as deaccessions.

Outcomes

While the inventory took much longer than one more limited in scope, it reduced the number of times an object needed to be handled, thereby lessening the risk of damage. The unit-by-unit process also ensured that all steps were completed for each artifact, rather than need-

Figure B.6. Large object storage area after inventory, in newly expanded storage. ANGELA STANFORD

ing to return to objects multiple times. Once done, workers moved on to the next unit and repeated the steps.

Now that the inventory is finished, both the paper and digital records are complete and accurate. Objects can be searched within the database by numerous fields and search terms. Through deaccessioning, the museum knows the collections that remain support its mission and are well documented, properly stored, and have accurate location information. The inventory also allowed the museum to identify the gaps in the collection—time periods, events, and types of objects—and to be more vigilant and intentional with new acquisitions.

Notably, because of information provided by the inventory, the museum's board decided to expand the building. This addition contains enough storage space to allow the full collection to be consolidated under one roof, eliminating the need for off-site storage.

The Excel inventory list created alongside PastPerfect records will be especially helpful as staff and interns conduct spot inventories on a rolling basis and a complete inventory every ten years, as these lists can be printed and taken to storage areas. As objects are confirmed to be on their shelves, identification numbers will be checked off. Any location changes will be noted in PastPerfect immediately following.

Conclusion

Because of the inventory, the museum can now collect in a more focused and strategic way because gaps have been clearly identified. Artifacts can be easily identified for exhibit or research use because of accurate home locations. Thousands more catalog records and related photos exist in the collections management database, which is available not only to in-house staff but also to students, researchers, and museum members via an online catalog.

Throughout the project, one full-time staff member, sixteen interns, and at least nine volunteers participated in its successful execution. It was a massive project but one that provided for better storage conditions and stronger record keeping and set the stage for long-range care and planning for the collection.

~

Case C

Gazing into the Abyss and Demystifying the First Comprehensive Inventory

Britta Keller Arendt, Senior Collection Manager, Chicago History Museum

The Chicago History Museum (CHM) boasts a collection of approximately 100,000 artifacts (separate from its research holdings) divided into four distinct categories: Architecture (models and fragments), Costume and Textiles, Decorative and Industrial Arts, and Painting and Sculpture.[1] The Decorative and Industrial Arts (DIA) collection is the most diverse category, consisting of an estimated 40,000 objects, ranging from furniture, toys, and household products to agricultural, industrial, and military equipment. The DIA holdings document the rich history and evolution of the city of Chicago from its period as a fur-trading outpost to a modern metropolis. This collection also includes material documenting broader aspects of American domestic and political history, ranging from the Colonial Period through the Civil War. Highlights from this collection include Abraham Lincoln's moccasins, Abel Faidy–designed Art Deco furniture, and a variety of relics burned during the Great Chicago Fire of 1871.

While CHM began collecting three-dimensional artifacts in the 1870s (then the Chicago Historical Society), it is unclear how object locations were tracked during the first ninety years. Beyond listing acquisitions in the accession ledger, no consistent object numbering system was developed until the 1920s and 1930s. In some cases, materials acquired were not accessioned or assigned unique identifiers at all. Collection registration standards improved over time, but the size of legacy holdings and shifting institutional priorities prevented museum staff from fully cataloging or inventorying the collection. Until 1985, all DIA holdings were stored on-site. However, in preparation for a museum renovation in 1986, this collection was packed up and relocated to off-site storage. Because many of these objects were new acquisitions in the midst of being processed or recently removed from exhibition, they were not necessarily accessioned or cataloged, compounding the inherited problems of inventory control. Inventory records created during the move became the basis for the first electronic catalog, but due to the speed at which objects were packed, incomplete and incorrect records resulted. What complicated matters even more was the loss of a significant amount of designated storage space on-site following the museum renovation. The new, smaller DIA storage space could accommodate only a fraction of the 40,000 objects, so off-site storage became a permanent solution.[2] Material that returned to the museum in 1987 included a portion of the furniture, ceramics, metalwork, glass, toys, and other small artifacts. Unfortunately, location control had not yet been established for this new storage space when the objects returned. While efforts to improve organization of the space have been made in recent years, including a partial inventory of one section of the space in 2002, shifting institutional resources have made it difficult to complete these initiatives.

In 2015, CHM purchased the collections management system TMS to improve intellectual integrity and inventory control over the four museum collection categories. While plans had been developing for years to conduct the first comprehensive inventory of the DIA collection stored on-site, the implementation of TMS made collections management staff realize just how urgent the project would become. Data conversion from the previous system, STAR, was a messy task, revealing how problematic the data had become over the years—locations weren't always recorded correctly, accession numbers were incorrect or duplicated, and object names didn't necessarily align.

With a new senior collection manager recently hired to spearhead the inventory project with limited knowledge of the collection and its challenges, a step-by-step plan was developed prior to the actual inventory work:

1. Rationalize location code system and relabel all shelving units.
2. Using a laptop, develop a "documentation strategy" in the form of an inventory worksheet to record basic catalog information that could easily be transferred to TMS when Wi-Fi coverage in collections storage becomes spotty (a problem that occurs more often than not).[3]
3. Develop basic inventory procedures for collections staff and interns to follow.

The next step was implementing a new internship program that would focus exclusively on the inventory project. Each summer, two students would be hired to assist collections management staff and be trained on TMS data entry. The goal was to develop partnerships with local universities that would benefit both the museum and the participating students, enabling them to earn course credit while also getting practical hands-on experience in collections management best practices. Every week, students and staff would work alternate shifts between physical inventorying in storage and researching accession files, ledgers, deeds of gift, and other documentation in the office. Throughout the remainder of the year, staff would clean up any data issues discovered in TMS, such as deleting duplicate records or correcting accession numbers, that student interns were unable to execute themselves due to established database security protocols.

Once launched, collections management staff learned a lot about the challenges they would face as the project proceeded. Problems discovered during the first year of the inventory included the following:

- Object has not been labeled with an accession number, and it cannot be found after researching existing documentation.
- Object has been labeled with an accession number, but it is incorrect and does not match existing documentation.
- Multiple objects have been labeled with the same accession number.
- Object has been labeled with an unknown identifier other than an accession number, such as "Box 152" or a seemingly random name such as "Pamela" or "Iceland."

When accession numbers matched the documentation, the TMS record was updated or created if it did not already exist. The inventory worksheet was completed when technical issues arose in the storage space and then updated in TMS within the week. As locations were updated in TMS, "inventory" would always be selected as the "purpose" in the location authority so future staff would be able to track the date of the inventory. However, when problems such as those indicated above were found, they were documented on the reconciliation worksheet.

Figure C.1. A selection of Abel Faidy–designed chairs, stored on a rolling cart system and covered with unbleached muslin. BRITTA KELLER ARENDT

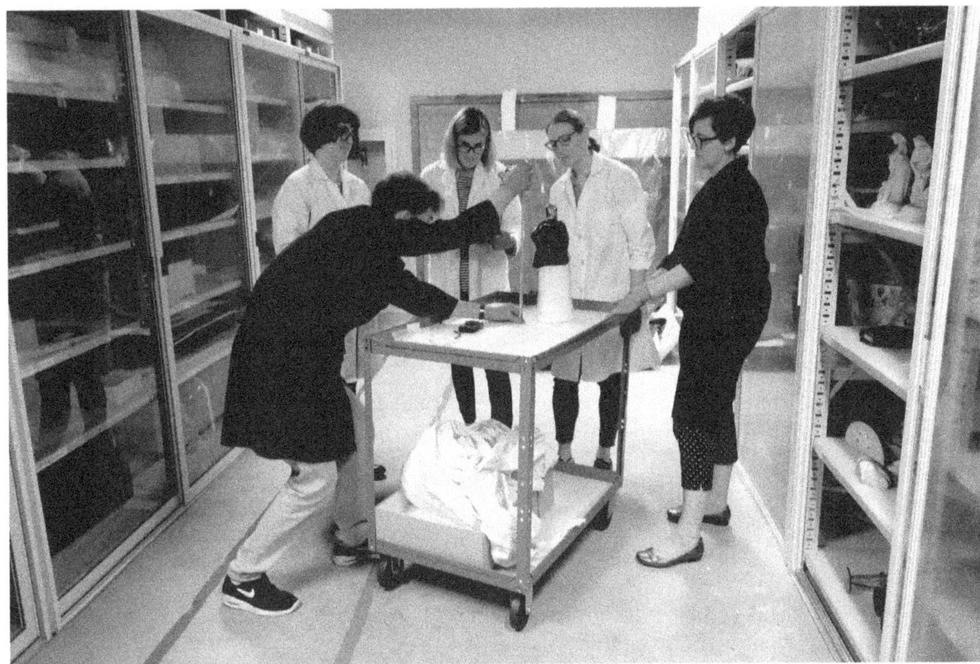

Figure C.2. A team of Collections Department interns are trained on proper object handling, documentation, and inventory procedures. BRITTA KELLER ARENDT

The purpose of the reconciliation worksheet is to document the research process and resolution of problematic accession numbers or lack of accession numbers. After the first year of inventory, as patterns were beginning to form, collections management staff were able to streamline this process into one of two reconciliation paths:

1. Assign a temporary inventory number (TIN): If after reviewing documentation (e.g., deeds of gift and ledgers), no accession number can be found, the object is assigned a TIN (e.g., TIN.001, TIN.002). Objects assigned TIN numbers are entered into TMS like any other object, but they are also flagged in the reconciliation worksheet to be assigned a permanent found-in-collection number by registration staff at a later date.
2. Complete a notice of number reconciliation form: If after reviewing documentation, it has been confirmed that the existing accession number on the object is incorrect, a notice of number reconciliation form is completed for the registrar. After the registrar has corrected the accession number in the ledger and deed of gift, it is then up to collections management staff to relabel the object, update the TMS record, and update any of the other hard-copy research files.

The implementation of the two reconciliation paths improved the inventory process drastically between the first and second years of the project. Inventory work has been accomplished each summer by two interns supervised by the senior collection manager for approximately twenty hours a week. While approximately 1,000 artifacts were physically inventoried during the

Figure C.3. A mobile work station allows for easy documentation as objects are removed from storage and inspected during the inventory process. BRITTA KELLER ARENDT

first summer of the project, over one-third of them required extensive research and reconciliation. Without the reconciliation paths fully developed at the time, collections management staff would spend numerous additional hours attempting to resolve documentation issues. The first year was a test run, which left a backlog of reconciliation problems to solve. Slowing the process down and improving the workflow resulted in a more complete inventory as the project progressed. The new streamlined reconciliation approach allowed staff to resolve issues quickly and move forward in a more efficient manner, leaving data cleanup to a minimum. Another improvement occurred halfway through the second year of the project, when the museum's IT department was able to make adjustments to improve Wi-Fi connectivity in the storage space, rendering the inventory worksheet obsolete.

At publication date, the CHM has proved that the established inventory workflows are highly efficient. Experimentation is currently underway to transform the reconciliation worksheet to an even more streamlined process via Airtable, a cloud-based platform for creating spreadsheets. Unlike Excel, this tool is much more intuitive and collaborative so that multiple users can edit and create their own views based on individual workflows. The next goal is to collect metrics that will inform upcoming grant initiatives. The comprehensive DIA inventory project will remain an institutional priority, as it has been written into the annual departmental operating plan as well as the institutional preservation plan as a high-priority initiative.

With institutional support, some resources have been identified to complete the process in a timelier manner, such as applying for funding to hire full-time assistance for the duration of the project and dedicating additional laptops to the workspace in order to capture data directly onto Airtable and TMS. While still in progress, the inventory has already greatly improved staffs' ability to assist scholarly research requests. Eventually, records will be enriched and finalized for sharing with the public through the museum's web-based collections portal. While the process has been slow, realistic expectations and refinement of workflows have been the key to assuring a positive outcome throughout the inventory project.

Notes

1. Chicago History Museum, "Museum Collections," accessed May 16, 2018, https://www.chicagohistory.org/collections/museum-collections/.

2. Chicago History Museum, "2006 Decorative and Industrial Arts Report," modified January 15, 2010.

3. Angela Kipp, *Managing Previously Unmanaged Collections: A Practical Guide for Museums* (Lanham, MD: Rowman & Littlefield, 2016), 86.

~

Case D

Migrating an Archaeological Collection Catalog to CollectiveAccess

Destiny Crider, Luther College Anthropology Lab and Collections Manager

Luther College Anthropology Archaeological and Ethnographic Collections reside at a small liberal arts college in Decorah, Iowa. The archaeological material is the largest collection of Native American tools, ceramics, and other artifacts for Northeast Iowa, spanning the archaic to the historic periods, especially Woodland-affiliated settlements. The collection began with a large donation in 1969 by a local resident and amateur archaeologist Gavin Sampson, who had been collecting and documenting sites since the 1950s. Many of his surface finds reflect the only sampling of archaeological sites in the area prior to site destruction through mechanical farming, quarry mining, or other development. The archaeological collection also includes contract archaeology projects conducted by Luther College anthropology staff in the 1970s and 1980s and includes artifacts, project reports, field notes, and photos from archaeological investigations throughout Iowa. New collections acquired intermittently are from the Luther College Archaeological Field School. At current estimation, there are over one million artifacts in over 300 boxes in permanent storage.

In 2012, Luther College Anthropology Collections initiated a project to migrate its entire archaeological catalog to the online platform CollectiveAccess. This ongoing procedure requires phased levels of implementation to ensure that collections are easily searchable and provide accurate documentation to the public and researchers but also protects the integrity of archaeological resources.

Management of cataloging and inventory of the collections are under the collections manager, with the day-to-day workforce composed of undergraduate work-study students in anthropology, museum studies, and history. Inventory creates "bag"-level catalog records, in which objects are recorded with descriptive information and the associated archaeological locational information. Each bag includes only objects of the same category (e.g., rim sherds or projectile points of the same type), and each bag must represent only one locus, from one site, in a particular excavation location. For example, if we encounter a bag of artifacts from an archaeological dig, we first record site, excavation unit, excavation level, and any special feature association (13WH01, Unit L150, Level 2: 10–20 centimeters below the surface, Feature 2: a hearth). Within that set of objects collected from a single excavation locus, the objects are separated and classified by material (e.g., lithic, ceramic, metal, bone), then further categorized by object type (e.g., tool, lithic debris, vessel rim, nail). Each bag of items is given a catalog number, the object count is recorded, and each catalog number associated to its excavation documentation. Therefore, there are multiple bags from a single archaeological locus, but each bag contains a unique class of artifact.

Over the decades, implementation of differing strategies in the catalog numbering systems, descriptive categories, methods of reporting archaeological location information, and visual documentation resulted in inconsistent records. In addition, the transfer of associated information moved across multiple platforms: first from the archaeological field notes and handwritten bag labels to paper catalog forms, small catalog information labels, and then into an Excel file and/or Microsoft Access database; these procedures introduced numerous opportunities for errors and inconsistent terminology.

Over time into the 2000s, the large quantity of bag-level catalog records began to exceed the storage capacity for Microsoft Access, and the archaeology data was divided into different databases organized by Iowa region. This created the inefficient and inconvenient process of having to search multiple databases when extracting needed inventory lists and queries. In addition, access to the original database was limited to one computer (therefore one user) at a time because of software limitations. Weekly manual backups required a person to copy files to a portable hard drive, further limiting access. Photo files in the catalog contained a hyperlink, requiring maintenance of a file structure external to the database and an extra step of inventory control.

In 2012, Luther College Anthropology Lab received a Resource Enhancement and Protection (REAP) Historical Resource Development Program (HRDP) grant from the State Historical Society of Iowa to implement a new open-source online catalog system for the archaeology collections. Whirl-i-Gig, which specializes in product development for museums and other cultural institutions, was contracted to build the database structure and coordinate the data migration into CollectiveAccess.

There were initial challenges in completing this project. My predecessor, who had written much of the grant proposal and initiated the project, moved on from the position shortly after the grant was awarded. As the newly appointed collection manager, I spent my first months analyzing the diversity of information recorded across archaeological and anthropological projects in the collections. This analysis indicated that there was a need to revise the database structure to make clear the relationships between hierarchical levels of information and resolve the issue of multiple database models within the archaeological dataset. This required modification to some data fields, tables, and relational structures within the catalog structure (table D.1). After coordination

Table D.1. This table, an expression of the modified CollectiveAccess database structure, shows the tables and their fixed list of data fields, which comprise a catalog record. The new structure enabled migration and centralization of decades of data documenting the archeological collections.

Archaeology Lot Table Accession status ***Project control number*** Project name Description Collector Acquisition date Acquisition type Contract information Collection owner Notes Report number Public access setting **Archaeology Context/Lot Table** Title ***Project control number*** (link archaeology lot table) ***Context control number*** Site number (link hierarchical site table) state → county → site number Excavation unit Level Level type Feature Feature type ***Excavator/collector*** (link entity table) Collection date Remarks **Individual/Organization Entity Table** **(named individuals and agencies)** Prefix, forename, middle name, surname/organization, suffix, other forenames, display name Biosketch (open comment field)	**Archaeology Site Table** ***Location in hierarchy (state → county → site → number [site name]*** Site ID Site name Occupational period & type (preset variable list) Description Comments Quadrangle/township/range/section/quadrant 1/4s UTM coordinates (UTM-E, UTM-N) Latitude and longitude Record access status for display to public **Archaeology Object/Bag Table** Title ***Bag control number*** (uses project control number as base) Storage box number Storage location (link hierarchical storage location table) storage space → unit number → shelf number → box number ***Project control number*** (link archaeology lot table) ***Context control number*** (link archaeology context/lot table) Object status (in box, missing, NAGPRA, deaccession, on loan) Previous catalog number Gavin Sampson catalog number Prenumbers (field identification numbers or previous cat#) Quantity Bag weight (g) Material class (preset variable list: e.g., chipped stone, ceramic, metal) Object type (preset variable list: e.g., rim sherd, body sherd, projectile point) Full artifact description (open comment) Object color (Munsell color code) Dimensions (recorded only when single object in bag) Length (mm) Width (mm) Height (mm) Thickness (mm) Measurement notes Research/style notes Cultural association notes

with the production team, the fully functional CollectiveAccess database was delivered around April 2014.

Integration of the archaeological collections into this management system allows multiuser access through a single online portal. Object descriptions, digital assets, and information relating to cultural and archaeological contexts are maintained for all sets of objects. The relational database allows for numerous associations to the catalog record, such as collector, donor, contractor, agency, project investigator, crew member, and researcher. Also associated are photos, project reports, and other significant records. This collections management database is a significant improvement over previous practices and allows access to records all through one management portal with open search terms.

With over a million archaeological objects, different recording practices over the last decades, and a new set of data fields in CollectiveAccess, I initiated a full inventory of the materials in order to provide the most transparent and accurate record of our collection. One of the most troublesome components was the construction of catalog numbers to assign to the bags of artifacts. I revised the system for accession numbers and catalog numbers to follow the more standard "Year.Collection.Object" numbering system. However, I needed to retain all previously recorded identifiers, so to clearly distinguish legacy information from the newly assigned numbers, I created new nomenclature for our tracking system. For example, in the previous system the accession number included only a year and archaeological site number (1969.13AM01). Unfortunately, there could have been (and were) more than one archaeological project in the same year at the same site, and as a result (on at least one occasion) two distinct projects were cataloged as though they were just one project. This sort of error immediately separates the associated documentation of the archaeological project from its artifacts. For archaeological work, the documentation is just as important as the objects themselves. By tracking accession as "year.site," the emphasis is on the archaeology site number 13AM01, which is already a coded set of information. This introduces unintended consequences for cataloging, record keeping, and organizing of higher-level documentation of larger seasonal (and multiyear) archaeological projects that can include more than one site.

To address this problem, I created a new unique identifier "project control number," which serves a similar function to the accession number but also reflects a contracted project, a single donor (who may have donated over several years), or a full archaeological field school season that may have moved to multiple excavation areas. The project control number (e.g., 2018.001 is the first archaeological project acquired in 2018) reflects the first year of the gift/acquisition of the archaeological materials into our collection combined with a unique identifier. This new tracking number serves as the base number applied to all artifact bags, reports, archives, and correspondence relating to the project. For instance, instead of the more complicated catalog number of 1969.13AM01.5.6.3B from the previous system, this bag number becomes 1969.001.00053 (bag 53 in the project from 1969.001). We retain any previously recorded tracking information assigned during fieldwork and previous catalog numbers. A simple label is created with the bag number and storage box location so each time a bag is removed for study, it can be easily returned to its permanent storage location. The bag number is easier to see and record as compared to the legacy catalog system of this collection. If objects from a bag are split, you simply generate a new unique bag number and update the associated records for counts, weights, and descriptions.

The project control number allows for quick reference regardless of what site number(s) is included. So instead of tracking objects only at the archaeological site level, they are tracked by the field season, the contracted project, or donor, regardless of what archaeological sites are assessed. Our first application of this system was to a large and historically significant donor that documented his collections across more than fifty sites and two counties in Iowa. Because all the contextual information is tracked to each object, they can receive the same project number, in this case 1969.001—the first collection/donation by one donor in 1969. All these project and bag numbers are assigned after the fieldwork is completed in preparation for curation. Any information or numbers applied during the course of the fieldwork are also recorded as "previous numbers" so no primary information is lost.

The real-world consequence of applying a new tracking system is that the collections staff are required to inventory and attach these tracking numbers to every artifact bag in the collection. This is time-consuming work. It will take many more years to complete the backlog of our forty years of archaeological collection, but there are numerous benefits to this strategy. As a liberal arts college, students learn transferable skills in working with detailed information, database relationships, photography, problem solving, and other complex management concerns. Many of our students choose to go on to the museum profession or collections-related work in archaeology. We have identified areas in our archaeological collection for deaccession that have limited research use, which resolves space issues for more

Figure D.1. This projectile point shows a former accession number format 13AM23 -5/14, signifying it is one of fourteen points from this site collection. The previously assigned catalog number—1969.13AM23.1.6—indicates that the collection was acquired in 1969, the object is from site 13AM23, and its object entry is 1.6 within the accession. The new tracking system assigns the number 1969.001.03557—the chronological and sequential project number followed by the object number, regardless of which archaeological site it is associated with. DESTINY CRIDER

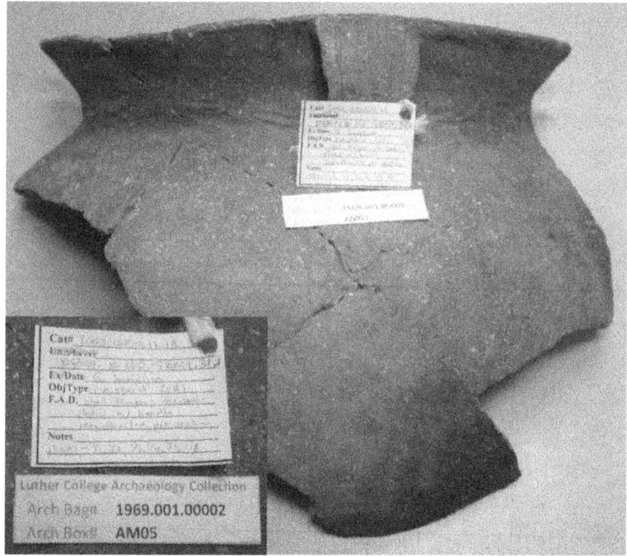

Figure D.2. Three previous numbering systems are associated with this shell temper vessel. One number identified each sherd separately prior to consolidation (i.e., 13AM1 – 1/1, 13AM1 –1/2, etc.). A second number 100.13AM1.31.1 was assigned at some point when the vessel was disassociated from the donor. A third number was assigned in 2003 when the object was re-associated with the donor collection. The new tracking system preserves all of these previous numbers, but tracks it with the "Archaeology Bag Number" 1969.001.00002 (the second bag in the donation. DESTINY CRIDER

relevant collections. For every new project control number assigned, we resolve a host of inconsistencies, typos, or misplaced and missing objects. And every project has a new and completely different set of problems, of course, which keeps things interesting.

The final production step for the grant included the development of the web portal to share collections to the public through a controlled interface. Luther College Information Technology Services provides server space, technical support, and programming and development for user interfaces. Whirl-i-Gig provided training and protocols for uploading large archaeological datasets from Excel files as we move through our full inventory of the archaeological collection. This enhances our autonomy in updating records in a systematic way and allows us to verify and correct our catalog before making material accessible to the public. We now have a fully functional product that is easy to use and has the capacity and flexibility to create additional public web portals with precrafted queries to define favored searches and numerous other flexible protocols that we have only begun to explore. We currently provide predesigned queries based on (a) project or donor, (b) object type and material class, and (c) specific archaeological sites organized by state and county. Queries can also use open keyword search, such as Woodland or Oneota cultural affiliations or projectile point types. The search acts quickly, providing a bag-level response with a photo, brief description, and associated archaeological context. For security and preservation of archaeological sites, GIS and location coordinates are not available to the public.

The Luther College Anthropology Lab is committed to providing the best accounting of our collections for professional, educational, and public use. It is our top priority to process the entire archaeological material holdings for inclusion in this collections management system and to vet and verify the quality of information prior to public posting. We hope that this project can serve as a useful model to other heritage organizations that seek to protect the integrity of their information while also providing access to the rich history and heritage of their community.

~

Case E

Bringing It Together: First Institution-Wide Special Collections Inventory at the New York Public Library Research Libraries

Rebecca Fifield

Inventories of large collections present both logistical challenges and incredible opportunities. In 2018, the New York Public Library (NYPL) began its first institution-wide special collection inventory and preservation survey. The challenges are obvious: develop an inventory and preservation assessment model for collections filling approximately 65,000 shelves in fifty-two storage areas at three campuses in Manhattan. By lobbying administration and colleagues to invest in and support the inventory project, collection stewardship has established greater visibility within the institution.

The NYPL first opened its doors in 1911 and has grown to include three research centers and eighty-eight branch libraries. The special collections grew dynamically under the leadership of fifteen curatorial divisions at the Humanities and Social Sciences Research Divisions at the Stephen A. Schwarzman Building, the Library for the Performing Arts, and the Schomburg Center for Research in Black Culture. The collection includes a copy of the Declaration of Independence, the archive of the Gay Men's Health Crisis, African American painting and sculpture of the Harlem Renaissance, set designs by Rouben Ter-Arutunian, Jack Kerouac's crutches, and the Sonny Rollins archive. The collections speak to the history and endeavors of New York and New Yorkers. The organic and enthusiastic growth of the collections combined with diverse departmental collection management practices over time hindered NYPL's ability to secure and create processing plans for backlog, storage renovation projects, and improved security.

NYPL hired the first head of collection management within the Special Collections and Preservation Services Division (SCPS) in 2016. Reaching beyond a traditional library preservation administration approach, this position uses an all-hazards approach to manage physical, legal, and collection ownership risks.[1] A key project for this position was to design and implement a full inventory of the special collections as well as establish the collection management program.

During the development phase, inventory project leaders gained buy-in from library administrators by illustrating how the data from the inventory and survey would support prioritized decision making around the collections. The inventory will establish baseline collection units upon which subsequent risk assessment will be performed, using the Cultural Property Risk Analysis Model.[2] Risk assessment is required to cut through preconceived notions of what threatens collection preservation to reveal those hazards that are most likely to occur with the greatest harm. For example, staff may fear water leaks but may not realize, without analysis, that collection loss from pest infestation is a greater risk due to the lack of an integrated pest management strategy. When the greatest risks are revealed through analysis, limited preservation dollars can then be strategically spent to lower the overall collection risk profile.

In early 2018, three permanent collection management staff were hired to perform the inventory and survey four days a week. On the remaining weekday, the staff provide support in building out the new collection management program. A complement of skills was sought when hiring the collection manager and two assistant collection managers. The structure of the project allows the staff to exercise their professional talents in developing integrated pest management, environmental management, and emergency preparedness functions at the library.

The lack of a unified collection management database required that a new system be created for the inventory and survey. The library catalog is the system of record, but traditionally, its structure and purpose create gaps in special collection information management. Many libraries have pressed empty MARC fields into imperfect service for the storage of preservation data.[3] In the absence of a central system, the curatorial departments kept collection information in an array of systems, including The Museum System and Microsoft Word and Excel documents.

To prepare a repository for the creation of unified collection data, a cross-disciplinary group representing physical, audio/moving image, and digital special collections developed a data model that accommodated library, archive, and museum approaches to collection information management (table E.1). Staff also developed a model for documenting collection storage locations in all research library buildings and a controlled vocabulary of preservation risks and hazards. The survey tool combines all these elements. Extant datasets in Word, Excel, and other systems from other divisions and the library's catalog are used to prepopulate the tool where possible to save typing time and establish a baseline inventory for surveyors to confirm.

Table E.1. Object Model Specification
The Object Model was developed by a variety of personnel from Special Collections and Preservation Services. It both accommodates library, archival, and museum approaches to cataloging and integrates the Getty's Art & Architecture Thesaurus (AAT). The Object Model was integrated into the survey tool so that new collection data will be staged for migration to a new platform.

Space	*Physical or Digital*
Class	Shape of the object, such as volume or cassette
Content	Type of intellectual content in the object, such as audio or graphic
Medium	Material from which the object is made
Format	Identification of the collection material within Getty's AAT
Extent	Dimensions of the object
Identifier	Such as box numbers, but not the UUID for the collection record
UUID	Autogenerated unique identifier
Relationship	Specifies relations between objects, such as "contained in"
Status	Indicates whether an object is active, deaccessioned, or missing
Restriction	Indicating whether the collection is restricted from service
Handling	Indicating specialized handling instructions

The Manuscript, Archives, and Rare Books Division established a FileMaker Pro database to track the acquisition, location, and circulation of its collections in 1997. This system grew into a suite of interconnected functions aimed at managing collections and information about them. Given the ability to quickly and inexpensively customize this robust system, the survey tool was integrated within the FileMaker Pro database (figure E.1). Collection data within this system will also be populated through other workflows carried out by the Preservation and Collections Processing divisions, including archival processing, outgoing loans, digitization, and conservation.

When first entering a room for survey, the survey team labels all shelves with barcodes and human-readable shelf labels, assigning locations within an overall NYPL location hierarchy. Each location has a four-part number, incorporating room number, row, unit, and shelf (e.g., 320.001.045.2 is Room 320, Row 1, Unit 45, Shelf 2). Inventory of a single item takes between two and five minutes. This process consists of linking an existing record preloaded from disparate datasets (or creating a record where no information exists); identifying the object by collection title, description, any identifying numbers, and materials; measuring materials not stored in standard-sized containers; and assigning them a location depending on where they were found. Records are annotated to document the protective enclosure in which the material is stored.

While other methods of random sampling could be used to understand preservation needs at a collection level, the inventory project allows the surveyor to review each collection at the container level. This is important for identifying when materials pose health and safety issues, have become unstable, or may require rehousing. The surveyor selects from drop-down lists condition issues, rehousing needs, inherent vices, and any suspected health hazards that would require special management.

While important for planning for the care of the overall collection, this assessment can also better document and quantify deferred preservation activities in archival collections created by a "More Product, Less Process" (MPLP) processing model.[4] This model favors minimal processing by reducing item-level preservation activities in order to make collections more quickly available to users. Ideal, if mythical, storage environments were suggested as a check against the damage left by not removing rubber bands or paper clips from manuscripts, for example. The NYPL inventory project provides an opportunity to identify MPLP-processed collections in need of preservation review. For example, the survey identifies what materials have damaging attachments.

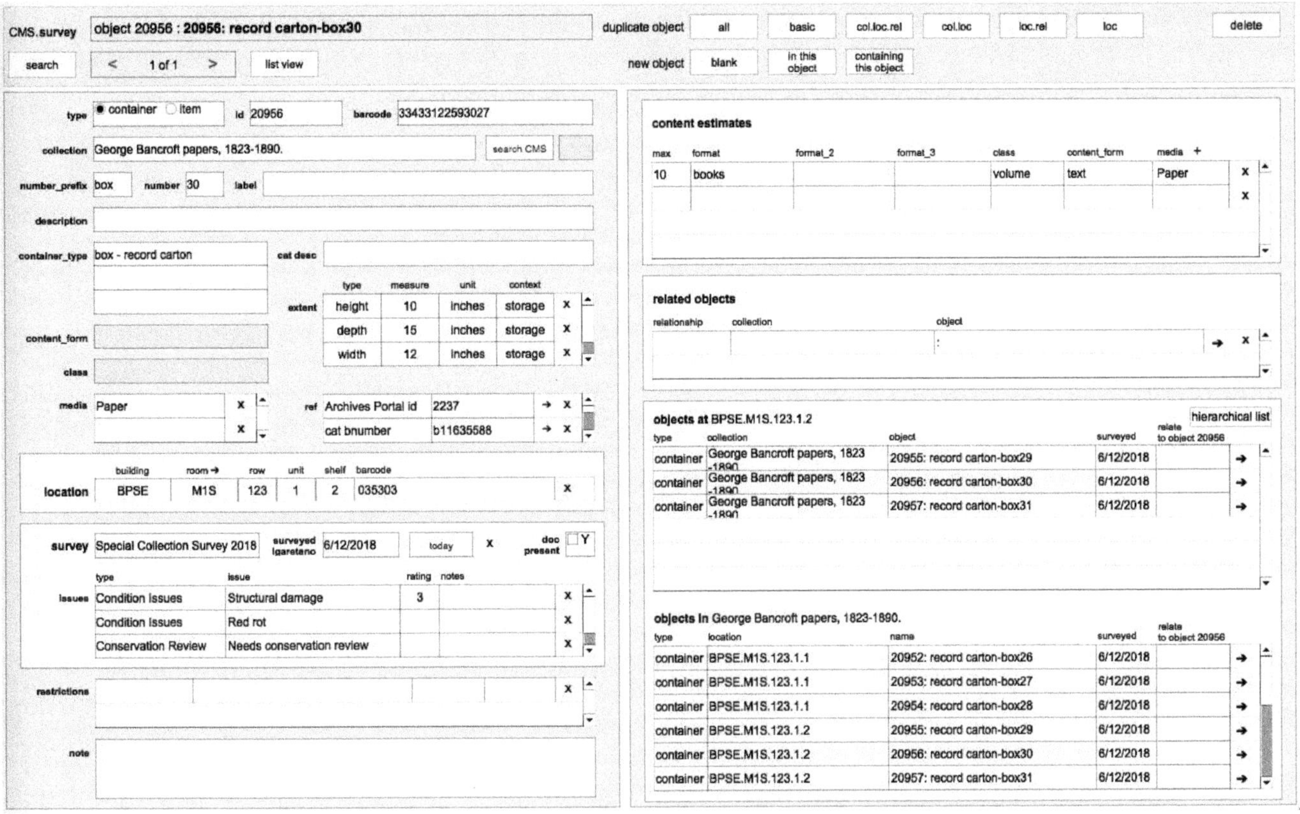

Figure E.1. The Survey Tool in FileMaker Pro both creates unified item or container records across the collections, records location, and records preservation needs (on the left), while building relationships across the collections (on the right). REBECCA FIFIELD

The selection could be limited by visual works, which are the most impacted by staining from paper clips and rubber bands, and these works prioritized for conservation. Foundations for future collection risk assessment work are being laid through the identification of collection units on which an assessment will be performed. Preparation for risk assessment will take place after a significant accumulation of data, around year three of the project.

To both demonstrate NYPL stewardship activities and provide access to the collection in new ways, the survey team created a new Instagram account to share the experience of the collection-wide inventory. Greater visibility of inventory and other collection management functions provides another conduit for sharing stories about our collections, our institutions, and our challenges in preserving culture for the future.

Notes

1. See the following references that established the Agents of Deterioration, which melds physical and stewardship risks. Stefan Michalski, "An Overall Framework for Preventive Conservation and Remedial Conservation," in *ICOM Committee for Conservation 9th Triennial Meeting*, Dresden, Germany, August 26–31, 1990, https://www.icom-cc-publications-online.org/2673/An-Overall-Framework-for-Preventive-Conservation-and-Remedial-Conservation; Robert Waller, "Conservation Risk Assessment: A Strategy for Managing Resources for Preventive Conservation," in *IIC Congress Preprints* (1994): 121–60, http://citeseerx.ist.psu.edu/viewdoc/download?doi=10.1.1.558.5358&rep=rep1&type=pdf.

2. Robert Waller, "Cultural Property Risk Analysis Model: Development and Application to Preventive Conservation at the Canadian Museum of Nature," *Göteborg Studies in Conservation* 13 (Göteborg: Göteborg Acta Universitatis, 2003), 107.

3. Library of Congress, "Preservation & Digitization Actions: Terminology for MARC 21 Field 583," December 2004, https://www.loc.gov/marc/bibliographic/pda.pdf.

4. Mark A. Greene and Dennis Meissner, "More Product, Less Process: Revamping Traditional Archival Processing," *American Archivist* 68 (Fall/Winter 2005): 208–63, http://www.archivists.org/prof-education/pre-readings/IMPLP/AA68.2.MeissnerGreene.pdf.

Case F

Recapturing Collections: Inventory at the Chicago Academy of Sciences-Peggy Notebaert Nature Museum

Dawn R. Roberts

The Chicago Academy of Sciences/Peggy Notebaert Nature Museum (CAS/PNNM) is a regional natural history museum founded in 1857. Its collections include the disciplines of zoology, botany, and earth science as well as history, anthropology, art, audiovisual materials, and archives, all of which strongly represent environments in the Midwest/Western Great Lakes region. Temporal and geographic data associated with scientific specimens provide valuable comparative data for biodiversity research, and CAS/PNNM's collection provides historic baseline data with specimens dating back to the 1830s. Ensuring the long-term preservation of the original specimens for future reference and making their data accessible are important facets of stewardship of scientific collections.

Utilization of the collections in the mid-2000s, however, was difficult for both internal and external groups. The collections were disorganized and suffered physical damage from prior moves. Collections records existed in a multitude of historic formats, none of which were comprehensive or organized. To regain physical and intellectual control of the collection and facilitate use of the materials, CAS/PNNM determined that an inventory of the collection was necessary. Over the course of five years, from 2008 to 2012, CAS/PNNM conducted a comprehensive inventory of its object-based collections—verifying and cataloging 280,000 specimens and artifacts in fourteen different collections. This was the first full inventory CAS/PNNM had ever carried out in its history, and embarking on such a major project required the full commitment of the administration, internal and external funding support, and significant staff time. Completion of the inventory facilitated preservation improvements, an increase in collections use, and the implementation of a new digital collections management system.

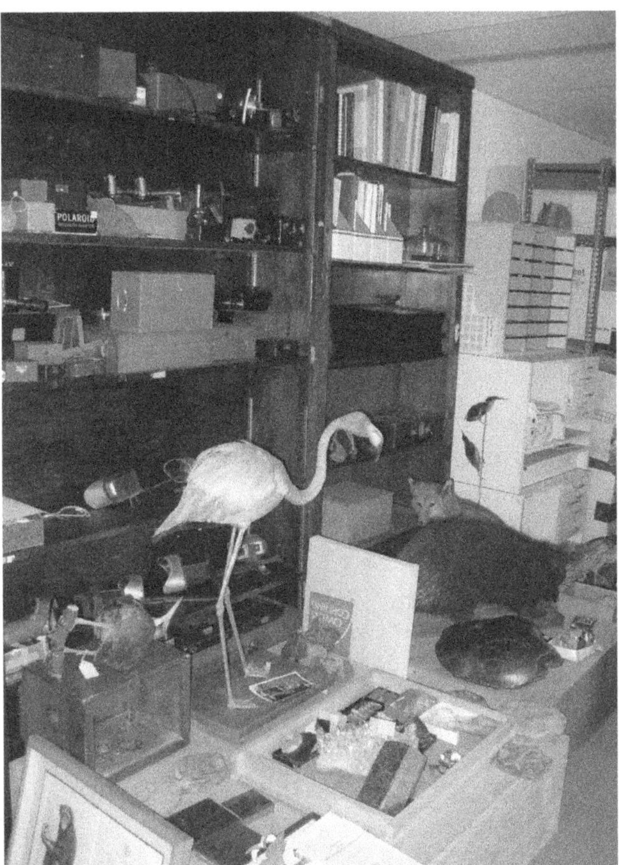

Figure F.1. Storage areas were disorganized, presenting obstacles to the care and use of the collection. DAWN R. ROBERTS

Project Team

CAS/PNNM had one staff member responsible for its collections prior to the project. With grant funds and additional operational support, four new staff were hired for the collections team. Grant-funded internships provided opportunities for students, and volunteers from the community enlisted to aid the project. Incorporating volunteers enabled the project to progress more quickly and strengthened CAS/PNNM's relationship with the community. In total, more than 14,400 hours of paid staff and intern time and 5,860 hours of volunteer time contributed to the inventory project.

Regular communication with the entire team was crucial. Project staff were assigned to specific collection disciplines and worked closely with interns and volunteers. Meetings ensured we maintained open communication and gave opportunities to address challenges that surfaced and adjust our methods. It was also important to acknowledge our achievements—when we reached a milestone, we made sure to celebrate!

Data Capture

Gathering information directly from specimen and artifact labels was determined to provide the most accurate account of what was currently in CAS/PNNM's holdings. Because we did not have an existing database, we elected to use Microsoft Excel for the inventory and designed a template to capture data. Excel has several benefits: it is relatively easy to use and train volunteers with varied levels of technological proficiency, it can be easily customized, and data in Excel could be migrated into a relational database afterward.

Maintaining data consistency was important; this streamlined processes for quality control and for when we began migrating data into a new digital collection management system. The inventory template included as many shared fields as possible across the scientific and cultural collections, while accommodating the addition of fields specific to certain disciplines, such as stratigraphic information for geology and paleontology or type of medium for art. We were able to match these later to Darwin Core standards with relative ease.

Team members were trained on data capture protocols and specimen handling, and project staff ensured data quality for their assigned collections. Moving systematically from cabinet to cabinet, our team physically handled and verified each specimen in the collection. Specimen label information was transcribed into the inventory spreadsheet, capturing taxonomic nomenclature and common names, names of collectors and donors,

Textbox F.1

STANDARD INVENTORY FIELDS

Catalog number
Accession number
Old CHAS #
Other institution #
Unknown #
Number of specimens/items verified
Parts—select from list (e.g., study skin)
Preparation style—select from list (e.g., in alcohol)
Discipline—select from list (e.g., ornithology)
Common name/item name
Taxonomy (e.g., order, family, genus, species)
Identification by, date
Old taxonomy
Age (select from list)
Sex (select from list)
Description
Verbatim measurements
Verbatim locality (also parse out into habitat, city, county/district, state/province, country)
Collector 1, verbatim name
Collector 2, verbatim name
Field/collector #
Verbatim date collected (also parse out into month, day, year)
Prepared by
Date prepared
Preparator number
Verbatim received from/presented by
Verbatim date received (also parse out into month, day, year)
Method obtained (select from list)
Permit information
Type status
Project/research notations
Remarks
Condition (select from list)
Description of damage
Preservation treatment notes
Storage location
Verified/cataloged by
Date verified/cataloged
Record updated by
Date record updated

Figure F.2. Inventorying ornithology specimens
DAWN R. ROBERTS

dates collected or created, locality information, and catalog and accession numbers as well as other identifiers.

Cabinet, shelf, and drawer numbers were assigned, and storage location information for each specimen was recorded. In addition, each specimen and artifact was evaluated for condition and issued a condition status, to provide a baseline by which to measure future changes. We used a system with four categories: Excellent—the item is in prime condition with virtually no damage; Good—the item is overall stable, with minor damage or deterioration; Fair—the item has more moderate damage or deterioration and may require repairs or further preservation; and Poor—the item has considerable damage or deterioration and may not be salvageable. Team members received training on the common types of damage and preservation issues they might come across and types of damage that could be repairable. Where appropriate, more specific condition issues were also recorded in the dataset, for example, "head of bird specimen is detached."

Managing temporal data proved to be an issue with Excel. Collecting dates were written in many formats on the labels (e.g., 17 July '75 or 17 VII 1875) and needed to be captured verbatim as well as be transferred into a usable format. Excel did not recognize years prior to 1900 and would automatically change them or would convert dates to five-digit numbers. To resolve this issue, we designated a verbatim date field where data was treated as a string and contained in quotes to prevent it from changing format (e.g., "17 VII 1875"). Month, day, and year data were parsed into separate fields that could be sorted.

Challenges

Physical storage issues discovered during the project presented some major hurdles that needed to be addressed before specimens could be inventoried. Specimens were found separated from their data labels, poorly stored and physically damaged, or in a deteriorated condition. Some specimens were covered in coal dust—a remnant of being stored next to the coal-fired furnace in the old building—and had to be cleaned. These situations resulted in significant delays, as curation and rehousing wasn't part of the initial grant-funded inventory. In the end, however, the extra effort resulted in improvements to specimen storage and opportunities for sharing the importance of preservation in a collection.

The degree of completeness of digital records generated by the inventory varied. For instance, in the malacology collection, important locality data tended to be omitted from specimen labels and recorded only in ancillary records, such as catalog books and field notes. Notations transcribed from labels or the specimens had to be deciphered, and the inventory revealed issues with catalog numbers, such as different numbering schemes across collections, duplications, or lack of identifiers. Continued research proved beneficial and often resulted in additional information found in historic ledgers or documents that were then added to the specimen record. For instance, we have been able to connect specimens to original photographs from publications and field studies and connected specimens in the collections to two ecological surveys done in the Chicago area in the early 1900s.

Support

For a project of this magnitude, support from CAS/PNNM's administration, staff, funders, and the community was imperative for its success. The project team

Figure F.3a. Malacology specimens were in disarray prior to the inventory. DAWN R. ROBERTS

Figure F.3b. Malacology storage after inventory. DAWN R. ROBERTS

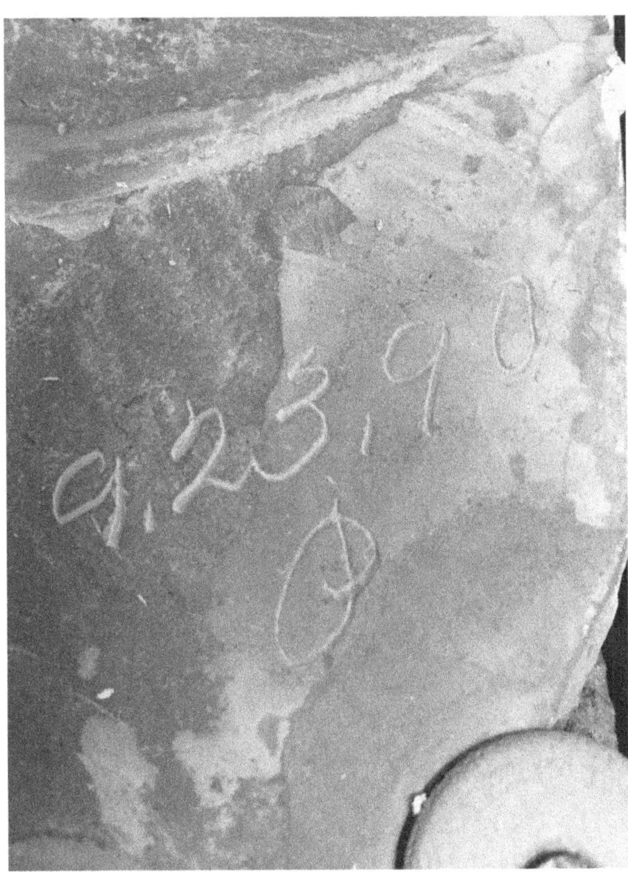

Figure F.4. Notations had to be deciphered. This inscription on a fossil specimen gives the date collected, September 23, 1890, and the mark of the collector, Jonathan Britts. DAWN R. ROBERTS

maintained three core staff, who provided continuity and aided in the effectiveness of the group. The veritable army of volunteers and interns working with project staff ensured that CAS/PNNM achieved its project goals. Commitment from the board and senior staff enabled the team to stay focused on the inventory, and funding from the Institute of Museum and Library Services and the Gaylord and Dorothy Donnelley Foundation helped to support project activities. Increased research interest in the collection and letters of support echoed the value of the scientific collections for research. All of this helped propel the project forward without a loss of momentum.

Next Steps

Carrying out a comprehensive inventory of CAS/PNNM's object-based collections was an ambitious project, but its completion enabled terrific changes: it established physical control of the collection; enabled staff to make information about the collection more readily available, which facilitated internal and external use of the materials; and helped highlight the institution's history and scientific legacy. Making specimen data generated from the inventory available online greatly expanded our institutional profile among active researchers. CAS/PNNM has assisted scientists with research on how climate change affects egg size of duck species in North America by providing historic egg specimens to obtain measurements from, contributed to planning efforts for ecological restoration in Louisiana by providing bird species data and historic images from the 1930s, and provided data for thousands of botanical specimens collected around the Chicago regions dating from the 1800s and 1900s to help establish changes in plant biodiversity over time.

Specimen data for many of CAS/PNNM's collections is now accessible online through several biodiversity data aggregators as well as our cloud-based digital collections management system, Arctos. We continue to expand the information provided about the scientific collections through integration of other records, digital imaging, and georeferencing and endeavor to provide broad accessibility to the scientific collections for a wide range of audiences.

~

Case G

From Hobbyists to Professionals: A Case Study at the National Museum of Toys and Miniatures

Calleen Carver and Geoff Woodcox

The National Museum of Toys and Miniatures (T/m), originally the Miniature Museum of Kansas City, was founded by two Kansas City friends in 1982. Mary Harris Francis, a collector of antique children's toys, and Barbara Marshall, a patron of the contemporary fine-scale miniature art movement, joined their collections to create a museum in the historic Tureman Mansion, owned by the University of Missouri-Kansas City. The university was bequeathed the home in 1966 and used it as office and classroom space. The avid collectors continued to add to their displays and quickly outgrew the space. They eventually struck a deal with the university to expand the building twice.

The museum was run by a handful of informal museum staff and volunteers and the founders themselves. They continued to collect enthusiastically and were passionate about sharing their collections with the public. Objects were often put on display immediately after acquisition, leaving little opportunity for the staff to create adequate records. Objects that had been assigned a number were marked with an adhesive sticker. The museum used an infinity numbering system starting with one, and this continued until the standard three-part numbering system was introduced in 2007.

Record keeping in the early days consisted of handwritten paper ledgers. When a Microsoft Access database was introduced in 1998, staff and volunteers entered the information from paper object worksheets. Each column in the Access database corresponded to a question on the object worksheet. This presented a number of issues. Because so many different people were entering information, the information was not consistent and did not conform to standard nomenclature. Additionally, it was common for information to be entered into the wrong cells (figures G.1–G.3).

Shortly before Mary Harris Francis's passing in 2005, the two founders and the museum board began a strategic plan to professionalize the museum, create an administrative infrastructure, and build an endowment to ensure permanency. Museum professionals were hired to begin

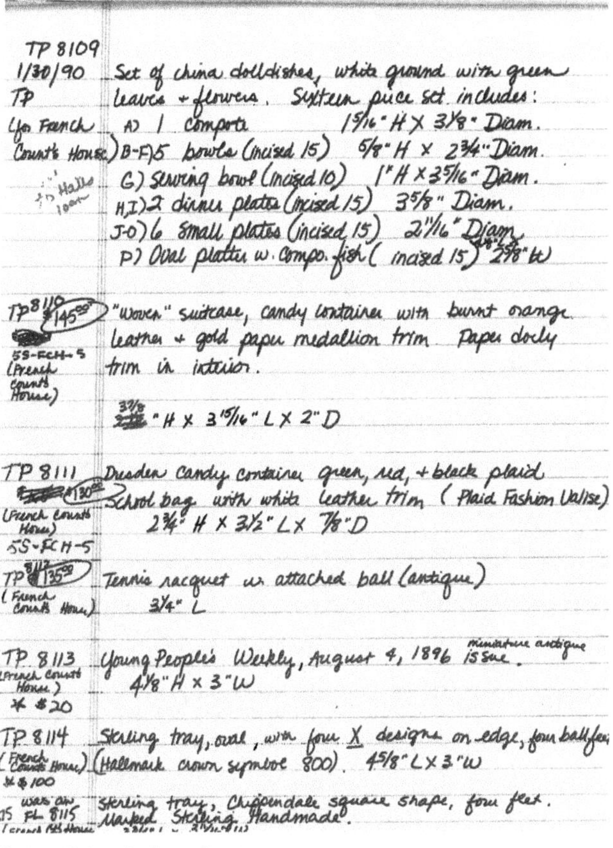

TP 8109 1/30/90 TP (for French Count's House)	Set of china dolldishes, white ground with green leaves + flowers. Sixteen piece set includes: A) 1 compote 1 5/16" H X 3 1/8" Diam. B-F) 5 bowls (incised 15) 5/8" H X 2 3/4" Diam. G) serving bowl (incised 10) 1" H X 3 5/16" Diam. H,I) 2 dinner plates (incised 15) 3 5/8" Diam. J-O) 6 small plates (incised 15) 2 11/16" Diam. P) Oval platter w. compo. fish (incised 15) 2 7/8" W
TP 8110 $145.00 5S-FCH-5 (French Counts House)	"Woven" suitcase, candy container with burnt orange leather + gold paper medallion trim. Paper doily trim in interior. 3 7/8" H X 3 15/16" L X 2" D
TP 8111 $130.00 (French Counts House) 5S-FCH-5	Dresden candy container green, red, + black plaid School bag with white leather trim (Plaid Fashion Valise) 2 3/4" H X 3 1/2" L X 7/8" D
TP 8112 $135.00 (French Counts House)	Tennis racquet w. attached ball (antique) 3 1/4" L
TP 8113 (French Counts House) * $20	Young People's Weekly, August 4, 1896 miniature antique issue. 4 1/8" H x 3" W
TP 8114 (French Counts House) * $100	Sterling tray, oval, with four X designs on edge, four ball feet (Hallmark crown symbol 800). 4 5/8" L X 3" W
TP 8115	Sterling tray, Chippendale square shape, four feet. Marked Sterling Handmade.

Figure G.1. **Ledger sheet.** CALLEEN CARVER AND GEOFF WOODCOX

object table 6/8/2018

designator	number	Entry Date	initials	class	object	date_acquired
TG	1017	4/13/1999	LB/AA		crock	3/10/1989
TG	1018	4/13/1999	LB/AA		bowl	3/10/1989
TG	1019	4/13/1999	LB/AA		mortar and pestle	3/10/1989
TF	102	8/25/1998	AA/LB		tea set	3/10/1989
TG	1020	4/13/1999	LB/AA		teapot	3/10/1989
TG	1021	4/13/1999	LB/AA		cigarette lighter	3/10/1989
TG	1022	4/13/1999	LB/AA		tray	3/10/1989
TG	1023	4/13/1999	LB/AA		box	3/10/1989
TG	1024	4/13/1999	LB/AA		cards	3/10/1989
TG	1025	4/13/1999	LB/AA		salt and pepper shakers	3/10/1989
TG	1026	4/13/1999	LB/AA		bowl	3/10/1989
TG	1027	4/13/1999	LB/AA		bowl	3/10/1989
TG	1028a	4/13/1999	LB/AA		book	3/10/1989
TG	1028b	4/13/1999	LB/AA		book	3/10/1989
TG	1028c	4/13/1999	LB/AA		book	3/10/1989
TG	1029	4/13/1999	LB/AA		bookends	3/10/1989
TF	103	8/25/1998	AA/LB		tea set	3/10/1989
TG	1030	4/13/1999	LB/AA		dishes	3/10/1989
TG	1031	4/13/1999	LB/AA		book	3/10/1989
TG	1032a	4/13/1999	LB/AA		wall mirror	3/10/1989
TG	1032b	4/13/1999	LB/AA		wall mirror	3/10/1989
TG	1033	4/13/1999	LB/AA		wall mirror	3/10/1989
TG	1034	4/13/1999	LB/AA		framed print	3/10/1989
TG	1035	4/13/1999	LB/AA		framed sketch	3/10/1989
TG	1036	4/13/1999	LB/AA		framed sketch	3/10/1989
TG	1037	4/13/1999	LB/AA		framed watercolor	3/10/1989
TG	1038	4/13/1999	LB/AA		wall mirror	3/10/1989
TG	1039a	4/13/1999	LB/AA		bed linens	3/10/1989

Figure G.2. Access page. CALLEEN CARVER AND GEOFF WOODCOX

Insurance/Inventory No: TG 109 80
Insurance Value $10

Toy and Miniature Museum–Inventory Date 8/26/92 Initials MW

Object Clothesline Kit
Location 19 - Nursery
Date Acquired 8/26/92
Gift ✓ Purchase Founder/Loan Check No. Amt.
Source Sue Thomson
Street 5930 Brookside Blvd City KC
State MO Zip 64113 Phone 523-2225

Materials case - leather, silk
clothespins - ivory
line - cording
line holder - celluloid

Maker Unknown
Origin

Description Travelling clothesline kit -- black leather folding case with snap closure, interior lined in peacock blue silk. Includes 6 ivory clothespins (2 3/8" L) and a cord clothesline wrapped around a celluloid holder (2 5/8" L x 1 1/16" W)

Identifying Marks None

Condition (9)

Circa date 19 teens ....
Dimensions Case folded H 4" W 3" D DIAM
References

Comments Belonged to Sue Thomson's grandmother, Cordelia Gibson. (born in MO + lived her married life in CO.

Figure G.3. Worksheet. CALLEEN CARVER AND GEOFF WOODCOX

the process of bringing the museum into the twenty-first century. It was clear that the institution could not advance until there was a better understanding of the scope of its holdings.

The T/m contracted with the university for IT support and was added to the university's network. In 2007, the museum migrated the contents of the Access database into a PastPerfect collections database. This presented many challenges, as information entered into the wrong cells was either lost or appeared in the wrong place. Boxes of paper records were reviewed against the digital records. As the museum started going in this new professional direction, it was clear the collection needed to be fully documented, and in 2007 the inventory project began.

There were many issues that needed to be addressed by the inventory project in both the database and with the objects physically. As a result of the inconsistencies, the staff did not have a solid grasp of the size or the true scope of the collection. There had been little to no tracking information entered in; even if objects had been documented, the locations were largely unknown. The use of the PastPerfect database was hit or miss, especially with the earliest objects because so many fields were empty or contained random information that should have been recorded in a different field. This made searching the database difficult to match a number with the correct object without the aid of an image. The description field was the most dependably used, but the text was often a single word and too vague to make object identification possible. Attempts were made to find the original number, but when that was unsuccessful, a found-in-collection number was assigned. Each object, both in storage and in galleries, was given its own trinomial number with the prefix FC. That allowed objects to have a database record created even though the source was unknown, and the project was able to keep moving forward. The inventory was being worked on by staff but was hampered somewhat by their day-to-day duties. As well, the museum had identified environmental concerns with the building and began planning a renovation. The museum also identified accreditation as one of its strategic goals, and the project transformed from an ongoing long-term target to an active project with dedicated resources.

The significance of the museum was recognized and valued for its two distinct collections. The miniatures collection, with its fine-scale decorative art pieces, provides historically perfect miniature examples of full-scale pieces and highlights the individual artists' skills. By contrast, the toy collection captures the personal histories and memories of children through the toys they held most dear. The importance of preserving those two collections was the driving force behind the decision to renovate, but before that was possible, the unknown of the collection first had to be addressed.

In the summer and fall of 2011, the museum hired four catalogers and one project manager who were divided into two teams: one for the toys collection and one for the miniatures collection. Two catalogers were assigned to each, with the project manager supervising the miniatures team and the museum's collection manager supervising the toys team. Finding space for four additional team members in a cramped building was a challenge. Two offices were divided; a basement storage room cleared; and best of all, a previous exhibit space converted. A child's nursery complete with viewing windows was packed up and placed in storage, allowing one of the catalogers to work in full view of the public with signs detailing the cataloging project. This allowed visitors to witness the work being done and understand the reasons behind some of the cases around the museum being empty.

The project began in October 2011, with the first two months spent primarily on preparatory tasks: standardization of location codes and the fields to be used in PastPerfect, the writing of cataloging procedures, creation of gallery maps, and creation of a timeline based on a two-year funding commitment.

Both teams started with objects located in storage and then moved through the galleries case by case.

Figure G.4. Public workspace. CALLEEN CARVER AND GEOFF WOODCOX

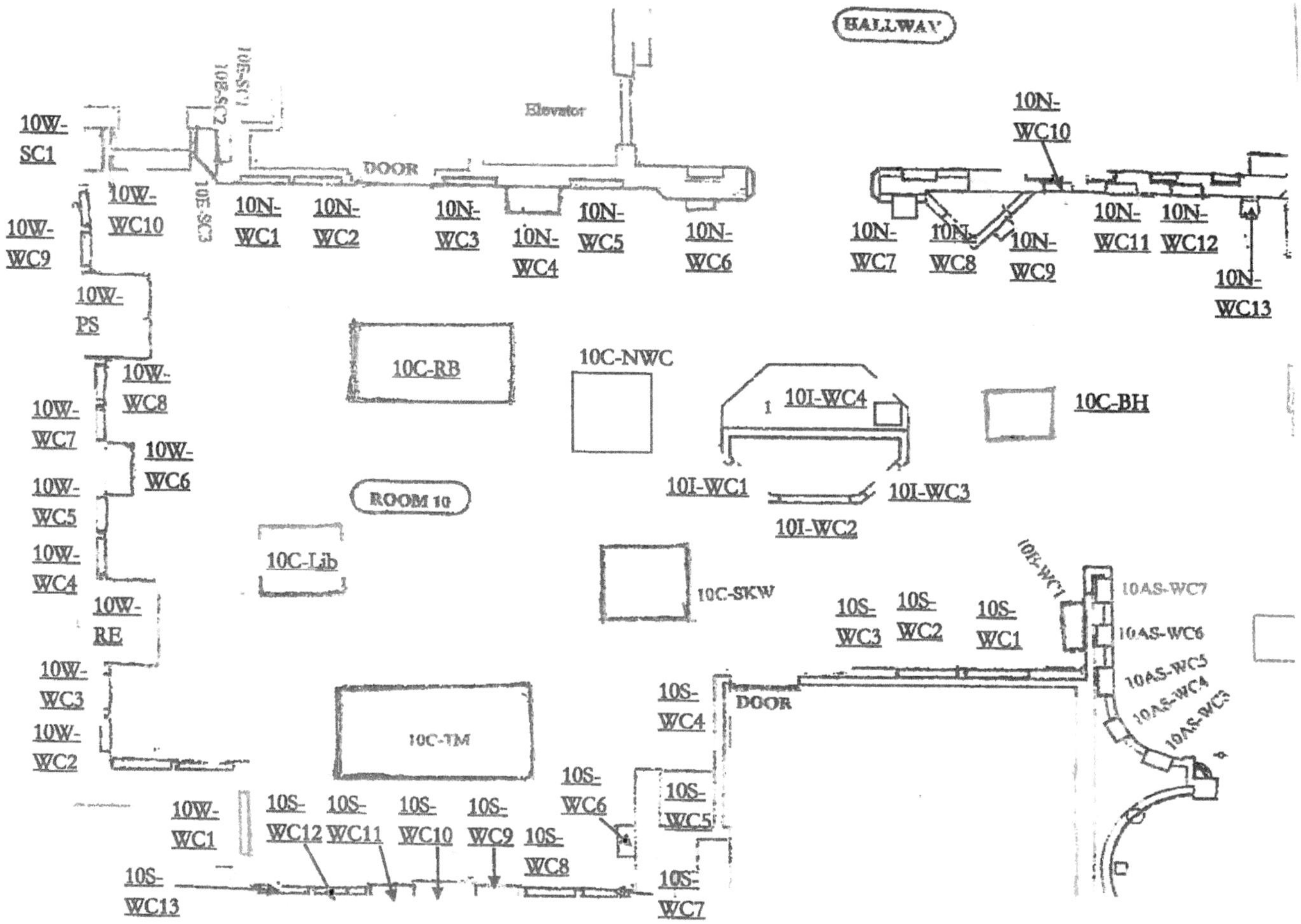

HALLWAY

10W-SC1 10E-SC2 10E-SC1 Elevator

DOOR

10W-WC9 10W-WC10 10E-SC3 10N-WC1 10N-WC2 10N-WC3 10N-WC4 10N-WC5 10N-WC6

10N-WC7 10N-WC8 10N-WC9 10N-WC10 10N-WC11 10N-WC12 10N-WC13

10W-PS 10C-RB 10C-NWC 10I-WC4 10C-BH

10W-WC7 10W-WC8 10W-WC5 10W-WC6 ROOM 10 10I-WC1 10I-WC2 10I-WC3

10W-WC4 10C-Lib 10W-RE 10C-SKW 10E-WC1 10S-WC3 10S-WC2 10S-WC1 10AS-WC7 10AS-WC6 10AS-WC5 10AS-WC4 10AS-WC3

10W-WC3 10W-WC2 10C-TM 10S-WC4 DOOR

10W-WC1 10S-WC12 10S-WC11 10S-WC10 10S-WC9 10S-WC8 10S-WC6 10S-WC5 10S-WC7 10S-WC13

Figure G.5. Room 10 Map. CALLEEN CARVER AND GEOFF WOODCOX

Figure G.6. Storage before (left) and after (right) the inventory. CALLEEN CARVER AND GEOFF WOODCOX

As items were inventoried, they were fully cataloged, with measurements, complete descriptions, condition reports, photographs, and other data input into PastPerfect. All previously applied adhesive numbers were removed when possible.

One challenge with the miniatures collection in particular is in marking the artifacts with object ID numbers. Due to their small size, it is often impossible to do, and it was the wish of museum founder Barbara Marshall that they remain unmarked. The solution for items on display was to create a location book, which consisted of photos of each shelf, case, or miniature room, with object numbers labeled on the photo. The book allowed staff to easily identify objects in exhibit cases and also acted as a reference for the miniature team while replacing artifacts that had been removed for cataloging and inventory. The book continues to be a reference for cleaning and future inventories. Sections of the book are updated as changes to the galleries are made. Photographs of each exhibit case were taken prior to the start of the project.

To aid in the planning process, the project manager of the miniatures cataloging team used a Gantt chart, a visual representation of tasks and the time periods allotted for their completion. Because locations were missing

10W-WC5-2 Object List

1. 19630	8. 15810	15. 19917	22. 15595
2. 16155	9. FC2012.14.369	16. 16156	23. 9064
3. 9065	10. 15809	17. FC2012.14.370	24. 17008
4. 15812	11. 15497	18. 9066	25. 9460
5. 19997.1	12. 15499	19. 17370	26. 15811
6. 19997.3	13. 15808	20. 20157	27. 15496
7. 19997.2	14. 20109	21. 20156	28. 15498

Figure G.7. Location book. CALLEEN CARVER AND GEOFF WOODCOX or inconsistent, the number of artifacts in each gallery had to be estimated. Cataloging speed was figured at twenty artifacts per day, and that information was used to set the time periods listed on the chart. As the project began, progress proved to be much faster than initially projected. In one example, the initial schedule for one gallery allowed for twenty-five workdays while in the end, it required only sixteen. The cataloging pace for most galleries moved faster than anticipated, with an average ranging anywhere from seventeen to thirty-six artifacts per person, per day, depending on the complexity of issues encountered in the gallery, and an overall project average of twenty-six objects cataloged per person, per day.

The initial guess of object numbers per gallery was also inaccurate. The miniatures collection consisted largely of individual pieces with minimal parts, making the overall number of objects smaller than anticipated. With the toys collection, the opposite was found. Single object numbers had been assigned to countless toys that ranged from dozens to hundreds of pieces that had to be individually broken out and cataloged. The individual exhibit aesthetic for each of the founders also accounted for the initial inaccurate guess of objects. Barbara Marshall, who collected the miniatures, favored a simple, more linear display of her objects, allowing all of the pieces to be viewed clearly. Mary Harris Francis, who collected the toys, favored a busier display aesthetic. Her exhibits had a playroom or childlike feel with layers upon layers of toys, some not even visible behind other pieces.

Monthly reports were generated by the collections manager to keep track of each cataloger's progress and to ensure that the project would be completed by the target date and adjustments made. Monthly numbers were pulled for each cataloger along with year-to-date totals. By early June, six months into the project, it was apparent that the miniatures team would complete the project far ahead of schedule. The initial completion date was estimated as October 2013, but the team finished with the initial phase of the project in October 2012, and they were reallocated to the toys team. The toys collection ended up being much larger, and the objects were able to be physically marked, which slowed the process.

The physical inventory was completed June 2013. For the next two months, the staff worked on database cleanup: rectifying found-in-collection and missing objects, verifying all records had images and locations, and finishing a room-by-room collection assessment. At the completion of the project, 51,344 objects were added to the database, which included 9,550 FC numbers. Many items were discovered during the inventory that did not match the museum's scope of collection or were found in poor condition. Catalogers prepared deaccession proposals for each item they felt should be removed, and each went through the museum's collection committee, resulting in 2,848 objects being deaccessioned.

The database contained 70,370 objects at the completion of the project, and of that number, 4,620 were uncataloged due to loss or the record being too vague to make identification possible. Of that number, 21,509 were from the miniatures collection, 43,620 from the toys collection, and 5,471 listed as other.

The entire collection was packed and moved off-site in the spring of 2014, and the museum underwent a fourteen-month renovation. The completed inventory allowed the collection to be relocated and tracked to an off-site storage location. The packing of objects on exhibit was tackled by gallery, which typically housed like items and materials. As each box was packed, it was assigned a box number that corresponded with the exhibit gallery and an inventory list of the contents was created. The list was then used to track the contents by entering the assigned box number into the Temporary Container field in PastPerfect. Adding the Temporary Container information had to be done one object at a time to ensure accuracy, but once the entire contents were updated, this made gathering group data and changes possible. This allowed the value to be calculated for each box to stay within the allowable insurance value for transport and a quick way to globally change the new location at the off-site storage for the entire box. The off-site storage space was tracked by row, unit, and shelf. Information was entered into the Temporary Location field in PastPerfect. Objects that were already boxed in existing on-site storage were treated similarly, but since the inventory list already existed and contents were tracked to an already numbered box, only the Temporary Location field needed to be updated once they were relocated.

At the completion of the renovation, the staff were able to create new exhibits with a full understanding of the collection, and objects were able to be pulled easily to be reinstalled in newly designed exhibits. The new exhibits have provided much needed interpretation for the collection and have allowed us to connect more with our audience. The behind-the-scenes work upon the conclusion of the renovation, though, is still very much ongoing. The number of objects on exhibit dropped significantly from approximately 70 percent before the renovation to approximately 30 percent today, allowing us to rotate and exhibit new acquisitions. Rehousing of the objects previously on exhibit is a current priority of the collections department. Objects that were pulled for new exhibits left boxes partially full, and staff are working to rehouse and incorporate them into our permanent storage system.

~

Case H

Running from the Wrecking Ball: Inventory in Response to Disaster

Gina Irish, Registrar

The February 2011 Canterbury earthquake caused widespread devastation across Christchurch, New Zealand's second largest city. This event resulted in the evacuation of Christchurch Art Gallery Te Puna o Waiwhetū and a government directive authorizing the occupation of the facility by emergency services, whose own headquarters were damaged in the earthquake. Emergency services commandeered back-of-house offices and front-of-house spaces, including exhibition galleries cleared by gallery staff, who relocated works to unoccupied back-of-house storage areas. With gallery operations suspended, the collection was static for a significant period of time.

The occupation ended several months later when a damaged fourteen-story apartment building on the gallery's neighboring eastern boundary forced the evacuation of emergency services and gallery staff, who at the time were sharing back-of-house office space with government authorities. The gallery apartments were structurally compromised in the February earthquake, and over time, developed a visible lean, resulting in the Canterbury Earthquake Recovery Authority (CERA) demanding immediate demolition. Demolition presented a significant risk to the collection, which at the time included some six thousand plus items housed in seven storage areas, across three floors on the neighboring boundary. The entire collection would need to be either left in situ at risk or relocated to a safe zone, identified by engineers as the gallery's ground-floor exhibition galleries farthest away from demolition activity. The gallery team opted to relocate the collection knowing that CERA's position was nonnegotiable. The deadline was looming, leaving just over a month for a relocation, which if it were business as usual, would be well planned and resourced and paced over years, not weeks.

The previous relocation had occurred in 2003 when the collection was moved from the old site, the Robert McDougall Art Gallery, to the new Christchurch Art Gallery. The collection was relocated and stored on the new site by media or type, and all works were assigned a permanent location, defined in the Vernon CMS as *usual location*. The following year, the entire collection was inventoried with the assistance of a contractor, who utilized Vernon's bulk inventory function to manage the assigned task. According to location history notes, this was the first inventory to be documented in Vernon. Documentation suggests it was a straightforward inventory with typical anomalies that for the better part were resolved. Thereafter, inventory in part or whole was not repeated, and funding to resource inventory projects of this scale was reassigned to support other collections management tasks.

In response to CERA's directive, registration staff planned to inventory the collection ahead of relocation. This decision was informed by an awareness that the last inventory was several years prior to the earthquake and works, while noted as being in their usual location in Vernon, could inevitably be elsewhere in storage. Location integrity was paramount.

Adding to our woes, hundreds of works were for very valid reasons temporarily not in their usual locations prior to relocation. Works were temporarily in conservation and photography, and several works evacuated from the galleries to make way for the occupation remained on trollies in storage areas that were already running at full capacity. These works were identified using the Vernon query tool and, in most instances, were returned to their usual locations. Registrars then inventoried store by store, running location reports that were exported from Vernon into spreadsheets. At this stage, and given looming deadlines, location was the only data captured and scrutinized.

When works were sighted, they were noted on the spreadsheet as checked. Vernon's bulk inventory function was used to confirm the works were sighted in that location, and thereafter these were flagged as ready for relocation. There were anomalies that were simple to resolve: often, by the time an entire store of like media or type had been inventoried, any works not found in earlier checks had been accounted for.

Inventory was straightforward in stores where works were visible, such as paintings hanging on racks, which we could categorically confirm as sighted. The same cannot be said of stores where works could not be sighted without time-consuming inspection, with the most problematic packing units being solander boxes holding thousands of high-use works on paper. In most instances, it was assumed that if a crate could not be opened and checked, the contents were within. Works that fell into this category were typically sculptures and small objects and textiles or unstretched canvases on rolls. These works, including those within solander boxes, were updated in Vernon as inventoried but with a note in Vernon's inventory notes field that the assigned status related only to the packing unit. While not ideal, these archived notes capture the circumstances relating to that particular location change and can easily be recalled should the location of a particular work be queried at some point in the future.

On relocation, the same Vernon list used for inventory was retrieved, and a bulk location change was actioned reflecting the relocation of works from their usual locations in storage to the new temporary location in the exhibition galleries. When the collection was returned to storage, the same list could be used again but, in this instance, changing the location from the temporary location back to the usual location. This was a fast and reliable method through which we avoided location processing backlogs. In addition, having earlier returned all works previously set to temporary locations to usual locations proved sensible. It ensured these works were captured in bulk location changes, eliminating or at least reducing the number of exceptions or incidental location changes we'd otherwise be making.

When relocation concluded, reconciliation reports were run to ensure all works had been moved, supported by physical inspections of storage. Given our underwriters were concerned the entire collection had been consolidated into one physical location, thereby increasing their exposure to loss or damage, all priority works were inventoried in their new temporary locations with supplementary reports supplied to insurers. Every attempt was made to scatter priority works throughout the space so that if there were a spot fire, a leak, or another earthquake resulting in damage to surroundings, exposure to loss would be limited to the area or zone affected. Works and their locations were illustrated in maps submitted to underwriters as well as being included in disaster plans for assessment, salvage, and evacuation purposes.

The location of a collection at risk was of concern not only to underwriters but also to lenders, our governing council, and the community. After all, in a city that had lost so much, the stakes were high. Having done all we could in response to an exceptional set of circumstances, we switched off the lights and closed the door. The demolition of the gallery apartments occurred without incident, and the collection remained in the exhibition galleries for several years while the facility underwent repair.

The gallery reopened in 2015, and inventory is now an annual activity. Rather than expect inventory to occur collection-wide over a short period of time as it

Figure H.1. Demolition of gallery apartments on the gallery's eastern boundary. GINA IRISH

Figure H.2. Collection relocated to exhibition galleries. GINA IRISH

Figure H.3. Collection relocated to exhibition galleries. GINA IRISH

did in 2004, the gallery has a revolving inventory program. Consequently, objectives are clearly established and achievable, and the workload is better balanced. In setting priorities, collections that are high use, as opposed to those that are seldom accessed and utilized, are identified as obvious contenders for inventory, as are collections that could not be sighted before the relocation. Where possible, other tasks are dovetailed into inventory projects; vice versa, a project relating to digitization, conservation, or storage might be an ideal time to confirm the location of works subject to those activities.

This revised inventory methodology was piloted with a 2018 textile inventory. Very few staff had sighted the gallery's textiles, with many works on rolls not inven-

Figure H.4. **Collection relocated to exhibition galleries.** GINA IRISH

Figure H.5. **Collection relocated to exhibition galleries.** GINA IRISH

toried since 2004. Because records were missing critical information relating to size, media, and condition and many had never been digitized, we were unclear as to what our holdings were. Consequently, we were unable to service reproduction requests or easily assist researchers. Early on, it was evident we'd aim to check not just the location record but also to fill in gaps in documentation, condition report, and where possible treat works, photograph the collection, and eventually rehouse textiles before returning them to their usual locations, marking the end of the process.

The project was a success, as clear objectives were identified at the outset. The exercise was scheduled and planned to occur over a blocked-out three-week period without interruption, ensuring deadlines were met. Workstations were established in storage, conservation, and photography labs. The textiles were mostly stored by size and inventoried accordingly, which proved sensible, especially because larger works requiring the support of the limited oversized tables or installation and photography in empty exhibition spaces could be batched to ease pressure on the team. This approach helped registration coordinate personnel, engaging additional technicians when required. At all times, a nominated curator was on hand to sight the works. As necessary, the nominated curator, sometimes accompanied by a conservator, interviewed a number of artists and their estates and other experts.

A collaborative approach will be applied to the time-based art survey set for 2019, set to be an exhaustive review covering multiple departmental objectives. In response to future obsolescence, the inventory of this collection is on a repeat inventory cycle. Likewise, the survey of works with electrical components that are at risk of obsolescence and require maintenance, replacement, or spare parts is inventoried using the same methodology involving the wider team.

In other instances, registrars are working independently of others, conducting inventories where location checks are the primary and sometimes sole objective. For instance, the annual works-on-paper inventory targets a select number of works housed in a high-use store, with works moving almost daily between usual locations, conservation, matting and framing, photography, exhibition, outward loan, or out for viewings and research visits. The likelihood of human error and location oversights is high, making this the only reason contents of solander boxes and plan drawers are audited.

That said, during these inventories, registration personnel check and report on storage capacity, which informs how the capital budget is spent. The inventory process ensures the bigger picture is considered. Proposals relating to long-term redevelopment or preservation projects and needs are strengthened when supported by compelling evidence, including inventory findings.

A collection that undergoes regular inventory will be easier to account for in a disaster when location integrity matters, time is short, and accountability is high. And while even the best-laid plans have the potential to unravel in a disaster, conventional inventory practice provides a framework for response that in part or whole might offer direction in times of crisis. In recovery, inventory offers focus and structure, and in collaboration with others, beneficial and far-reaching collection initiatives are realized.

~

Case I

Your History, Your Museum: Bringing Meaning to Chaos at Hennepin History Museum

Heather Hoagland

Introduction

Hennepin History Museum, a small museum in downtown Minneapolis, has been actively collecting for eighty years. The museum maintains an extensive collection of historic artifacts and archival materials, ranging from a lion skin rug to a Victorian hair wreath and everything in between. A full top-to-bottom inventory of the collection had never been done. Accessioning was spotty throughout the museum's history, rendering objects mystery items that have no identification number or donation record. Compounding the issue, at least three different inventory attempts were started but never finished, and one of those inventories removed original numbers from artifacts, dissociating the object from its original accession record!

An inventory of the object collection, about 25,000 objects, was initiated in 2017. Before, every closet, corner, and hallway and even public spaces overflowed with objects that were inadequately tagged or were complete mysteries. Rooms that once held a discrete subcollection—the hat room, for example—overflowed with unrelated objects. Garment racks overflowed with dresses; dolls; and even large radio cabinets, exhibit cases, and mannequins. As objects continued to accumulate with no space to adequately store them, they remained unaccessioned, often in cardboard boxes, piled on top of other objects, and eventually separated from their deed of gift.

Figure I.1. Hennepin History Museum is located in the historic Christian Mansion constructed in 1919. HEATHER HOAGLAND

Founded in 1938 as the Hennepin County Historical Society, Hennepin History Museum is dedicated to bringing the diverse history of Hennepin County and its residents to life through exhibitions, a library, collections, and educational programs. The museum needed to regain intellectual control of its buried gems in order to fulfill its mission—to serve as an approachable and representative historical society for over a million people, accurately reflecting the stories of one of the most diverse populations in the Midwest.

Involving Stakeholders

The decision was made to rely on volunteer power to complete the hard work of the inventory. Over fifty volunteers work to catalog the artifacts. That includes two to six interns, depending on the time of year, as well as twenty to twenty-five regular weekday volunteers, many of whom have worked on the project since the beginning. The volunteer corps also includes fifteen to twenty individuals who join us for "inventory blitzes" on the last Saturday of every month, when we gather as many individuals as possible to catalog and photograph as many objects as possible.

The volunteers were recruited at two orientations in December 2016. A mass email was sent to the museum mailing list inviting them to attend an orientation that promised to introduce a new way to volunteer with a hands-on object-oriented inventory project starting in January 2017. About half of the more than eighty individuals who attended the orientation became regular volunteers.

We believe that this great response is the result of two primary motivating factors. First, our existing stakeholders saw that an inventory was a critical need for the museum. Second, we offered a unique, hands-on volunteer opportunity. History-minded community members leap at the chance to go behind-the-scenes, especially if it involves collections work.

Our volunteers have become a highlight of this project. They have brought energy, enthusiasm, and fresh perspectives. They are an army of community spokespeople and advocates for the museum. Our primary photographer, for example, walked into the museum as a new volunteer in January 2016 and was elected board president a year later.

Almost a year into the project, after eleven months of setting up folding tables and carrying fifty-pound boxes up and down stairs daily, the project took a huge leap forward when one of the museum's three gallery spaces

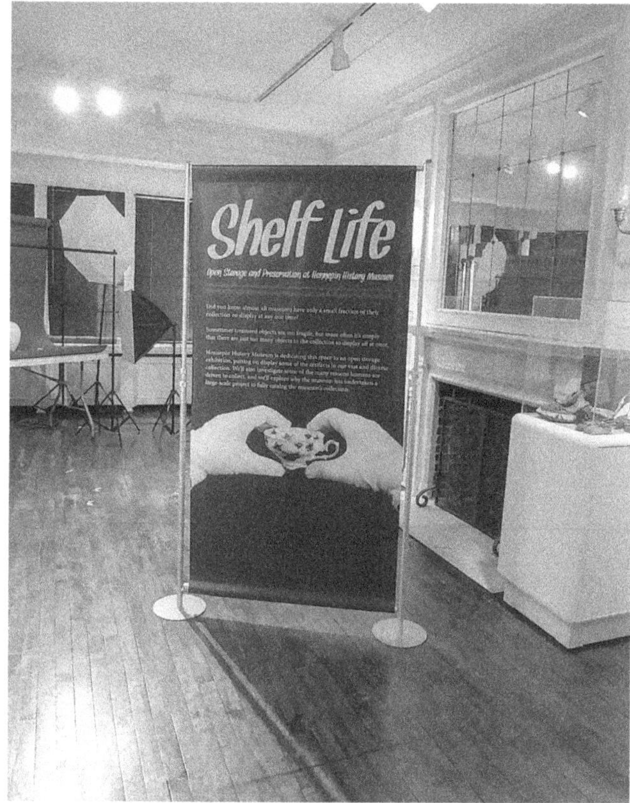

Figure I.2. The exhibition *Shelf Life* has changed the way the inventory progresses; it combines an open storage concept with a permanent photo studio. HEATHER HOAGLAND

Figure I.3. In addition to bringing visitors behind the scenes of the inventory process, *Shelf Life* provides a permanent cataloging workspace. HEATHER HOAGLAND

was dedicated to an open storage exhibit and cataloging workspace that brought visitors inside the inventory project. *Shelf Life* quite literally put our volunteers on display, with visitors able to observe the volunteers at work and ask questions about the inventory project.

Although we have lost a third of our gallery space, we have benefited in three important ways. First, we have created a space that educates the public, our members, and our stakeholders on the important work of the inventory process. Second, we have created a way to highlight the diversity and importance of the collection with rotating displays and open storage spaces that house the objects we are currently cataloging and pieces from seven subcollections, such as fashion or tools and technology. We have also carved out a physical space in our overcrowded facility where we can rehouse, catalog, and photograph, which will ultimately make the inventory project more successful and more efficient.

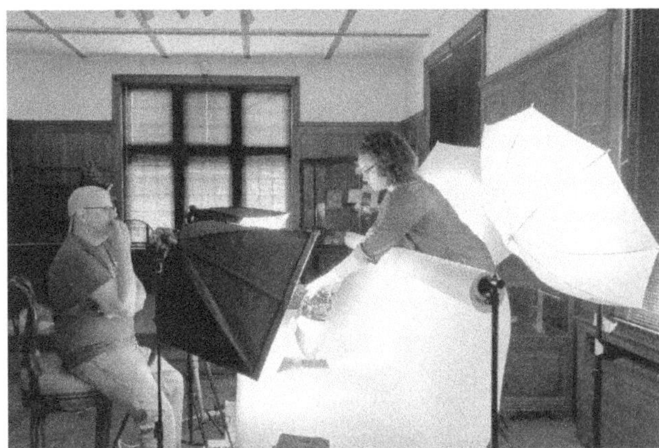

Figure I.4. The simple, relatively inexpensive photography studio set has allowed us to take professional quality photographs of objects, be it a small hat or a life size statue. HEATHER HOAGLAND

Worth a Thousand Words

Early on, we decided to incorporate a comprehensive photography effort. Since we were systematically evaluating each object in the collection, it made sense to digitize the collection at the same time. We purchased a simple mobile photography studio, one of the single most useful investments in the project. After more than a year and a half of weekly use, the simple, inexpensive Neewer brand system is still providing all the equipment we need to take archival-quality photographs of objects as cumbersome as a plow and as small as a campaign pin.

Photography has become a pillar of the inventory project, allowing us to use our collection in new and inventive ways even before we have a fully cataloged collection and a completed database. Beautiful photos of our art collection allowed us to create postcards and framed prints that have become great sellers in our gift shop. Photos accompany blog posts and exhibit didac-

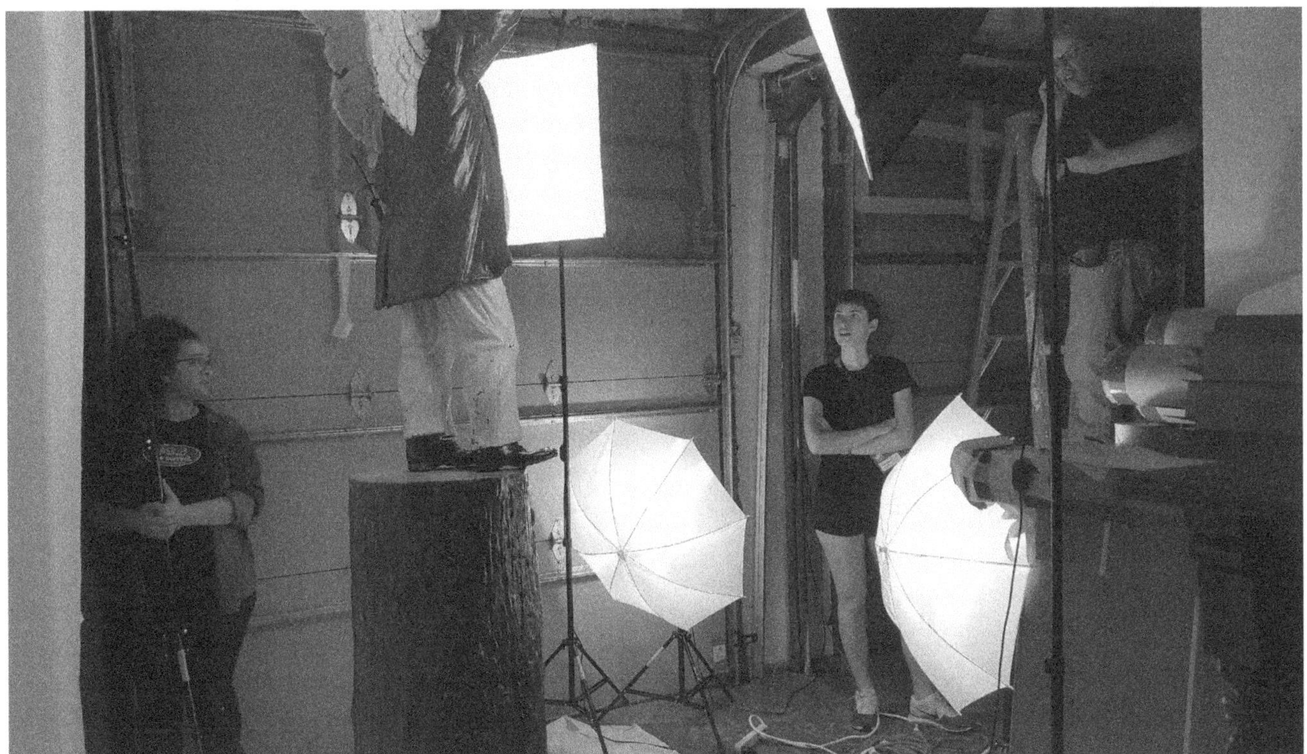

Figure I.5. The simple, relatively inexpensive photography studio set has allowed us to take professional quality photographs of objects, be it a small hat or a life size statue. HEATHER HOAGLAND

Figure I.6. This untitled watercolor by Bettye Olson was featured in a landscape exhibition in 2017. Photographs of select pieces are used to create prints, magnets, and notecards. HEATHER HOAGLAND

tics. Every PastPerfect record has a high-quality photograph that amplifies verbal descriptions. Photography has lent an air of authority and utility to this inventory project. Unlike the other inventory attempts where the description stopped at "wooden chair" and now can't be matched to the artifact, we are confident that this inventory is creating a useful foundation that can be built on in the future.

Building a Database

Another pillar of our inventory project has been creating a PastPerfect database from the ground up. The museum has used PastPerfect for over a decade to document the archival collection, but fewer than fifty object records have been created. As we catalog, we evaluate each object in light of the accession records and provenance we are able to find and any other Hennepin County stories it is able to tell. For example, a fascinator might stay in the permanent collection if the maker's mark identifies it as a creation from a local milliner even if it has no associated donor or information on when or where it was used.

If an object will remain part of the permanent collection, it is entered into PastPerfect. Objects in limbo—we're waiting to find all similar objects, for example, or we know there are more missing objects

Figure I.7. This gown was worn by Mahala Fisk Pillsbury, wife of John Sargent Pillsbury, the first governor of Minnesota. Our photography now allows researchers to examine it virtually at life size. HEATHER HOAGLAND

from that donor—are entered into a Microsoft Excel spreadsheet with only the most important critical information: catalog number, physical location, and inventory form location.

The museum is taking a "more is more" approach to the database. All research done on objects is published in 500 to 800 words on the museum's blog or written into an exhibit label length narrative blurb (70–100 words). These detailed descriptions are entered into the PastPerfect description field on the object record whole cloth and live with the object. The blurbs and blog posts usually focus on one or two main stories that the object tells—a section of wrought iron railing, for example, tells the story of the building the railing was salvaged from and the ironwork company that manufactured the piece.

There are two primary advantages of our approach to the object description field. First, having our research on the object allows us to eventually publish the record in an online database that has maximum value for off-site researchers and audiences. Second, it allows us to do keyword searches on the description of the object rather than try to accurately create a comprehensive and intuitive tagging system that encompasses all the possible ways future researchers might search for that object.

What's Next

The inventory project is still at least three years from completion. We estimate that we have cataloged and photographed less than a quarter of the collection in the first year—although we regularly remind ourselves that the first year was also about developing the process.

Already, though, the information we have collected and photographs we have taken are adding exponential value to what we are able to offer our community. Having accurate provenance and background information is raising the quality of the interpretation in our exhibits and our programming. Knowing what objects we have is allowing us to punctuate the stories we tell in a more impactful way, and having high-quality photographs is opening new avenues for sharing those stories with a more diverse audience.

Ultimately, the inventory project will allow us to take the next step forward as an institution. When we know what we have in the collection, we can make an educated decision about the future needs of the museum, for example, filling gaps in the collection with thoughtful, intentional collecting and deciding whether to stay in our current space and build or move to a new facility.

~

Case J

Blood, Sweat, and Tears: A Collections Inventory Story at the American Swedish Institute

Inga Theissen

Overview

The American Swedish Institute (ASI) is a vibrant arts and culture organization in Minneapolis, Minnesota. ASI's material collection includes more than 7,000 museum artifacts that focus on artwork and objects reflecting the daily lives of Swedish Americans as well as works by Swedish American or leading Swedish artists. The collection is strong in Swedish glass, wooden figure carvings, and woven textiles.

In October 2015, ASI was awarded a grant from the Anne Ray Charitable Trust, which allowed the institution to conduct the first full-scale collections inventory of its eighty-six-year history. Until this point, the handling and processing of collection objects had largely been performed by volunteers working with a PastPerfect database, with few standardized procedures in place. The project was scheduled to begin on January 1, 2016, and conclude by August 31 of the same year, allowing only eight months to complete the project. It was determined that the following staff were needed for the project: one full-time project manager, one part-time assistant project manager, six part-time cataloging assistants, and one part-time project aid. The project manager began working on the project in February, while the eight project staff members did not start until March. This shortened the project timeline to six months. To make things more challenging, all project staff were unfamiliar with ASI's collection and the PastPerfect database.

Figure J.1. Coffee Party, 1938, Herman Rosell (Swedish, 1893–1969), ASI Collection 54.01.01. INGA THEISSEN

Inventory Process

The initial days of the project were spent on orientation, procuring, and setting up photographic equipment; evaluating collection material; and preparing workspaces. Staff worked on establishing cataloging and database standards that would provide the foundation for all future cataloging. Digitization standards were set with reference to *Technical Guidelines for Digitizing Cultural Heritage Materials*, and it was decided that an external hard drive would be used in order to properly store collection images.

Data was standardized, and authority files were created, as cataloging information had previously been entered in a variety of ways. The largest and most disorganized of the fields was the collection names. This field was used as a catch-all of descriptors to expedite the search process due to the volunteers' diminished technical abilities when it came to utilizing the query function in PastPerfect. Collection names ranged from straightforward and simple (e.g., *Textiles*) to overly descriptive (e.g., *Glass/Kosta* or *Carving/Emil Janel*). The project manager and project librarian/archivist sat down with an overview of the collections and created eighteen new and logical collection names.

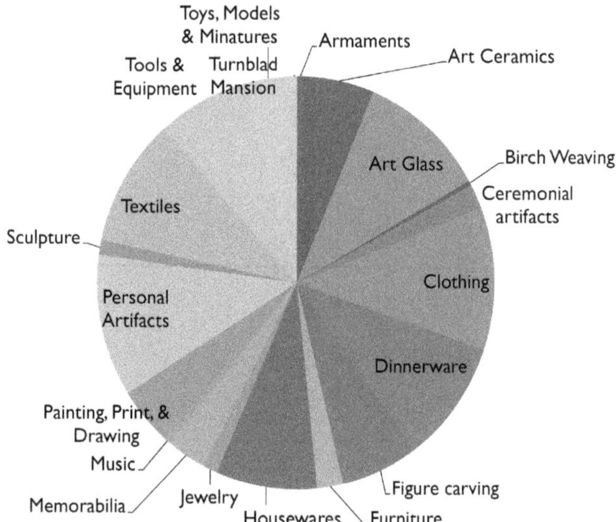

Figure J.2. ASI collecting areas. INGA THEISSEN

Using the collection groupings as a framework to process the collection, a list was made of every item on a particular shelf as the objects were pulled to be photographed. Once the items were photographed, a photographer cropped and renamed the photos, while a cataloger cleaned up the record entry—updating the item description, name, and location as well as making sure that all the information in the record was correct. The last step of the process was to link the photograph to the object record and return the object to its shelf.

While the team used this method to process each collection area, the project manager and project librarian/archivist broadly cataloged the collections being inventoried. This would include keyword and terminology cataloging as well as ensuring that all cataloging was consistent and each piece was discoverable. Records were pushed to the web at the completion of each collection area.

Many aspects of the project relied on ingenuity and improvisation. For example, large wall hangings proved difficult to photograph, as ASI did not have the space or equipment necessary to photograph them without distortion. The team improvised a large-scale copy stand in one of ASI's meeting rooms, using a chair to prop up a large piece of fabric-wrapped cardboard. Two team members would hold the cardboard in place while the photographer stood on a chair to capture the photograph. This teamwork not only helped the team advance their project goals, but it also fostered collegiality and created levity to balance the overwhelming nature of the project.

Challenges

As the inventory progressed, it was discovered that large amounts of unaccessioned objects were scattered throughout the collection. These found-in-collection (FIC) objects, common in most institutions, had no documentation or related information. These objects were accessioned into the collection with the hope that more information about them would be discovered as the project progressed. While this information was never found, the inventory process revealed another issue. It was discovered that approximately 10 percent of the collection was missing (approximately 668 objects of 7,081 total objects). These objects had a catalog record within PastPerfect but were not found during the inventory process. Unfortunately, the missing objects and the FIC objects did not correlate.

Figure J.3a. Tapestry, ca. 1791. ASI Collection 62.05.01. INGA THEISSEN

Figure J.3b. Staff improvised a copy stand to photograph tapestries and other large wall hangings. INGA THEISSEN

Figuring out the discrepancies of the missing and FIC objects was hampered by the fact that little to no accession or donor documentation existed within PastPerfect. The decision was made to go through the paper accessioning folders and capture all accession information within the database, linking each object to its donor, a task that in retrospect should have been completed at the start of the project. Instead of providing information on the missing or FIC objects, an additional problem was soon discovered: there were a number of objects that had paper accession records but were not cataloged within PastPerfect and were also missing from the collection.

In summary, out of the 7,081 objects currently in ASI's collection, there are 570 FIC objects with no documentation, 607 objects that have records in PastPerfect but are not physically in the collection, and approximately 600 objects that have a paper record but no record in PastPerfect and are also physically missing from the collection. That means there are approximately 1,200 objects missing from ASI's collection. Documentation was found from a 1980s collection survey listing approximately 500 objects missing at that time. It was determined that the conundrum of these missing objects should be solved in a future collections project.

Another problem encountered during the project was the inconsistency with which pieces were accessioned. For example, each cup in a set of twelve is given a different accession number, while a different grouping of similar cups is given the same accession number with an identifying component suffix (e.g., 2015.23.12-2015.23.24 vs. 2015.23.12A-2015.23.12L). Furthermore, FIC objects would be given either a 00.XX.XX accession number or an accession number based on the year they were entered into the collection, such as 2015.XX.XX. In addition, objects that had been given as an extended loan in the 1970s but were now the legal property of ASI were given an identifier before their accession number, such as EL70.XX.XX. All these inconsistencies made it difficult to find objects within the database. Unfortunately, because the accession numbers were written on the objects themselves and the catalog record already existed, the effort to make the records consistent was too great to attempt as part of this project.

Lessons Learned

At the end of this project, over 7,000 objects were inventoried, photographed, and cataloged. All these records were made available on ASI's collection website, making them widely available to the public for the first time in ASI's history. This project could not have been completed without the hard work and dedication of the project staff. The team worked together to finish an insurmountable task in an all-too-short period of time. The benefits of this project were quickly realized when a month shy of the project's end, ASI was contacted by a publisher who had discovered ASI's collections website and asked permission to include some objects in the design book *Red Thread—Nordic Design*.

Because projects such as this are often at the mercy of funding sources, in relation to both monetary support and timeframes, it makes the planning process all the more important. In retrospect, it would have been extremely helpful not only to have a project lead that was familiar with ASI's collections but also to have a qualified collections specialist involved in the planning process. A project such as this will often take more time than initially anticipated, and it is therefore advisable to increase a time estimate when planning for a collections inventory.

In addition, the problems encountered with the missing and FIC objects highlight the importance of having a trained collections professional overseeing collections management. The American Swedish Institute leadership recognized the monumental effort of this project and approved funding for a permanent, full-time collections manager. ASI continues to seek funds to further the cataloging and digitization work needed to showcase its unique collections.

~

Case K

From Storage Boxes to Research Options: Cataloging Ancient Mural Fragments at ASU's Research Lab in Teotihuacan, Mexico

Kristine F. Clark, Arizona State University, Collections Management Intern

Collections of archaeological materials have significant research potential across multiple fields of study. An art historian may think about how a mural painting's symbolic imagery contributes to the understanding of a religion during a certain time period. An archaeologist may think about how a mural's physical composition can reveal information about the conditions of its creation—from identifying regional pigments to providing evidence of trade economy. For the stewards of these mural fragments, the question is: How do we create a catalog to accommodate these varied research needs?

About the Lab

At the UNESCO World Heritage site in Teotihuacan, Mexico, researchers engage in a wide variety of projects to understand the largest Mesoamerican city of its time.[1] The Arizona State University (ASU) Teotihuacan Research Laboratory in San Juan Teotihuacan, Mexico, is a hub for international academic projects as well as a storage facility for artifacts. Close to the archaeological site and the pyramids, ASU's lab currently stores archaeological collections from projects directed by researchers from more than thirteen universities and five countries.[2]

The collections at the ASU lab provide numerous opportunities for research—research that does not require further digging or destruction. The challenge has been to catalog the decades' worth of accumulated material stored in an estimated 25,000 boxes. To increase access and facilitate collaboration, staff are working toward completing an inventory of their holdings and establishing a database that can be accessed online by researchers. Because it is an active research site, the more details we can provide about the nature and extent of the ASU Teotihuacan Research Lab's collections, the wider the scope becomes for new questions to be asked of existing materials.

The Story Behind the Collection of Mural Fragments from Amanalco

In 1976, antiquities collector Harald Wagner bequeathed a set of wall-size, fresco-painted murals from Teotihuacan to the M. H. de Young Memorial Museum in San Francisco, California. Due to "the size and importance of the collection, the questionable circumstances about its removal from Mexico, and the ethical issues regarding cultural patrimony," Wagner's gift launched an international collaboration among a collective of California museums and Mexico's Instituto Nacional de Antropología e Historia (INAH).[3] It took some years to negotiate which murals would remain in the United States and which would return to Mexico, how best to preserve the murals, and how to determine their provenience.[4]

The Mexican government authorized René Millon to complete an excavation to investigate the provenience of the Wagner murals (using his original work on the Teotihuacan Mapping Project as a guide). In 1984, using fragments from an area of Teotihuacan called Amanalco, Millon was able to successfully corroborate the murals' initial context.[5]

After Millon contributed his expertise and solved the mystery of the Wagner murals' provenience, the mural fragments from the 1984 excavations were stored at the ASU lab without further analysis.

Status of the Collection

The Wagner murals have been preserved and displayed in Mexico and the United States.[6] Meanwhile, mural fragments from the same context have been stored in the ASU Teotihuacan Research Lab. There is still more we can learn from them, but first, they need to be cataloged.

In the summer of 2018, Tia Ahlquist and I, graduate students in ASU's Museum Studies MA program, spent four weeks at the ASU Teotihuacan Research Lab. Knowing from the start we would not have enough time to complete the project, we created a chart of our work that others could continue. Remaining open to researchers' potential interests, we asked, what would be the most useful information to provide? Our answer: descriptions and photographs.

Inventorying the Fragments

Unpacking, Cleaning, and Measuring

As we unpacked the mural fragments, we carefully dusted them with paintbrushes to better expose their color and pattern for identification. Fragments ranged in size from specks requiring a tweezer to extract from surrounding pebbles to pieces larger than twenty centimeters. Pieces over three centimeters in size were individually bagged and assigned unique catalog numbers, while smaller pieces were collectively bagged for each box. Some fragments were a solid color, and others clearly contained portions of well-known iconographic motifs.

Descriptions

In addition to recording and counting items, we visually described each fragment. We created a protocol that provides a consistent description with categories and nomenclature that can be applied to all fragments. The guiding categories for a fragment's description are as follows:

1. Pattern vs. solid
2. Colors, in order of predominance
3. Condition

Following this system, an example of a description for a mural fragment could be "geometric pattern; rose red and specular hematite red; scratched, chipped, and eroded; partially obscured by soil."

Figure K.1. Range of fragment sizes. KRISTINE F. CLARK

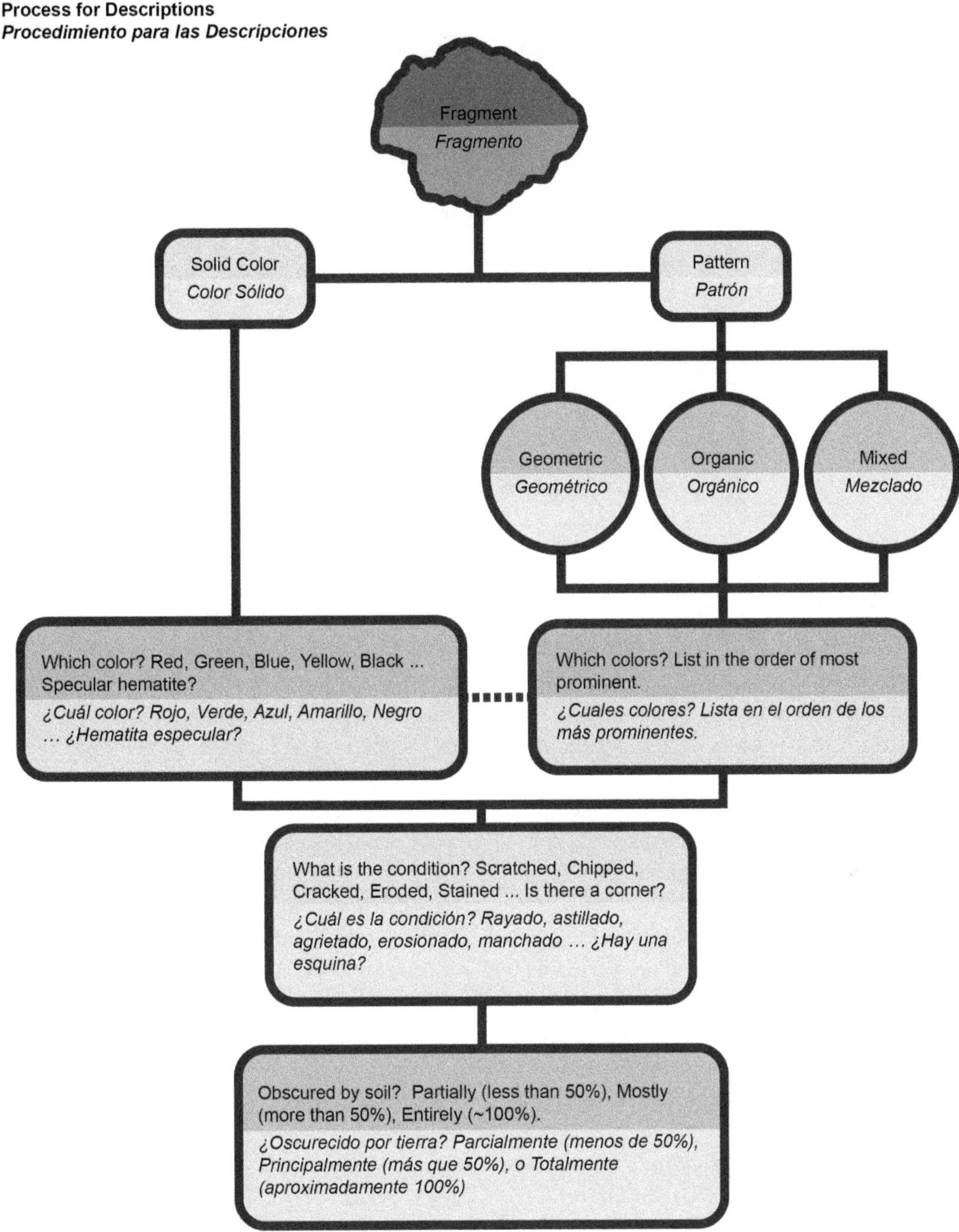
Process for Descriptions
Procedimiento para las Descripciones
Fragment
Fragmento
Solid Color
Color Sólido
Pattern
Patrón
Geometric
Geométrico
Organic
Orgánico
Mixed
Mezclado
Which color? Red, Green, Blue, Yellow, Black ... Specular hematite?
¿Cuál color? Rojo, Verde, Azul, Amarillo, Negro ... ¿Hematita especular?
Which colors? List in the order of most prominent.
¿Cuales colores? Lista en el orden de los más prominentes.
What is the condition? Scratched, Chipped, Cracked, Eroded, Stained ... Is there a corner?
¿Cuál es la condición? Rayado, astillado, agrietado, erosionado, manchado ... ¿Hay una esquina?
Obscured by soil? Partially (less than 50%), Mostly (more than 50%), Entirely (~100%).
¿Oscurecido por tierra? Parcialmente (menos de 50%), Principalmente (más que 50%), o Totalmente (aproximadamente 100%)

Figure K.2. Process for descriptions. KRISTINE F. CLARK

In addition to the description chart, we established visual guidelines to illustrate the spectrum from "partially concealed" to "entirely concealed by soil." We have photographs that make clear the distinction between a scratch and a chip. Standardizing the reporting categories to such detail informs future users of the collection, whether to provide a baseline of the objects' condition or to best inform fragments that may be of interest to subsequent research projects.

We tried to document as many boxes of fragments ourselves; however, we knew it was more important to document our process to provide continuity for the project. These precautions help ensure fidelity to the catalog descriptions, regardless of who continues documenting the fragments. The ASU Teotihuacan Research Laboratory plans to continue offering collections-focused summer internships to museum studies and archaeology graduate students to ensure this work continues.

Figure K.3. View of fragment in bowl. KRISTINE F. CLARK

Photography

At the beginning of the project, we photographed each fragment and altered our strategy as we encountered different obstacles. For example, we started with a table covered by white fabric set against a window to receive natural light. Eventually, we replaced the white fabric with black velvet to reduce dirt in the background and enhance the fragments' colors. One of the most difficult endeavors proved to be getting the camera to simultaneously focus on the fragment, the scale bar, and the label when all three components of the photo were at different heights. Ultimately, the solution for small to medium-sized fragments was to place them in a bowl with black sand.

Because each fragment needed at least two photos from different angles, it proved too time consuming to capture an image of every mural fragment. In order to make progress, we decided to photograph only larger fragments with well-defined iconographic representations in what we judged to be exceptional condition.

Next Steps

All the information about the various collections is currently being stored and updated on an Excel spreadsheet. We input the fragment descriptions directly into a portion of the spreadsheet that, after being reviewed, was added to the master document. While the metadata is transcribed in English, there are components of the spreadsheet that are in Spanish, such as transcription of box labels written in whichever language was used by the excavation crew. Photographs were saved multiple ways: uploaded into Dropbox, shared via a Team Google Drive, and downloaded onto an external hard drive. While the ultimate goal is to provide access to researchers, it is still unclear which software or web host will be selected for this purpose.

By the end of four weeks, we had cleaned, counted, and cataloged 1,650 fragments, representing roughly 20 percent of the collection. While still not complete, our work is analogous to beginning a jigsaw puzzle. We have found the edges of the puzzle, making it easier for others to fill in and eventually complete. We hope these mural fragments will inform future studies of the history and culture of Teotihuacan and that our catalog work is an important first step in making such work feasible.

Notes

1. George Cowgill, *Ancient Teotihuacan: Early Urbanism in Central Mexico* (New York, NY: Cambridge University Press, 2015).
2. Oralia Cabrera Cortés, email to author, September 11, 2018.
3. Harry S. Parker, "Preface," in *Feathered Serpents and Flowering Trees: Reconstructing the Murals of Teotihuacan*, ed. Kathleen Berrin (San Francisco, CA: Fine Arts Museums, 1988), 7.
4. Kathleen Berrin, "San Francisco, Mexico, and the Teotihuacan Murals," *Museum International* 235 (2007): 9–21.
5. René Millon, "Where Do They All Come From: The Provenance of the Wagner Murals from Teotihuacan," in *Feathered Serpents and Flowering Trees: Reconstructing the Murals of Teotihuacan*, ed. Kathleen Berrin (San Francisco, CA: Fine Arts Museums, 1988), 78–113.
6. Berrin, "San Francisco, Mexico, and the Teotihuacan Murals."

~

Case L

Helping Heritage Survive: An Inventory Project in Postwar Kosovo

Helen Merrett, Alex Cantrill-Lankester, and Miriam Orsini

Introduction

The project to introduce an electronic inventory system at the City Museum of Mitrovica (Kosovo) for the first time started in 2014. The project took three years and began within the context of a two-week conservation and collections care training program, organized by the Swedish NGO Cultural Heritage without Borders (CHwB). CHwB was founded in 1995 as an independent Swedish NGO dedicated to rescuing and preserving cultural heritage affected by conflict, neglect, or human and natural disasters.[1] CHwB has been operating in the Balkans for more than twenty years through a number of satellite offices in Bosnia and Herzegovina, Kosovo, and Albania, each running a range of projects aiming to rescue and protect local heritage.[2] CHwB is guided by the belief that heritage can be used as a tool to bring communities together, facilitate democratic processes, and generate economic development.[3]

CHwB Albania has been running Regional Restoration Camp (RRC) training programs since 2007 as part of their Balkans-wide push to encourage interaction between divided communities in the region and promote the valuing and care of local heritage.[4] Over the course of two weeks, participants, including students and young professionals from across the Balkans, take part in a conservation intervention on historic monuments in Albania, Bosnia and Herzegovina, Kosovo, and Serbia.[5] The camps combine theory with practical hands-on activities and directly assist local residents with the repair of local immovable heritage.[6] Each intervention offers participants the opportunity to learn skills to preserve traditional crafts and techniques and provides a new means of understanding and interpreting the local heritage, while also helping participants to build relations and create networking opportunities.[7]

In 2013, CHwB decided to trial a new style of restoration camp focusing on the interpretation and conservation of moveable objects. For this, they partnered with Heritage without Borders (HwB). HwB was established as a social enterprise in 2010 by three conservation graduates from University College London (UK) and became a registered charity in 2012.[8] Similar to CHwB, HwB's aim was to build conservation capacity in countries lacking resources and expertise, in situations of poverty, and following conflict and disaster. From this partnership, the Conservation of Museum Artefacts and Interpretation Camp was born.

Museum Background

The Kosovo War (1998–1999) deeply impacted the relationships between communities living in the country and destroyed and displaced much local heritage. CHwB identified the need to aid with the rescue of the country's heritage and encourage a new unity among the local communities through caring for their joint heritage.[9] In October 2012, a Memorandum of Understanding for the Program "Local Cultural Heritage Plans 2012–2015" was signed between CHwB and the Kosovo Ministry of Culture, Youth and Sports; Ministry of Environment and Spatial Planning; and the Kosovan municipalities of Dragash/Dragaš, Gjakova/Đakovica, Gjilan/Gnjilane, Kaçanik, Parteš/Partesh, Rahovec/Orahovac, and Vushtrri/Vučitrn.[10] The program aimed to help strengthen the role of the municipalities, NGOs, and communities through the revival of local cultural and natural heritage, while also aiding sustainable local economic development in the seven municipalities.[11] Their three main goals were (a) the protection and conservation of cultural and natural heritage;[12] (b) the integration of cultural and natural heritage in contemporary life and local development;[13] and (c) education, training, and awareness of cultural and natural heritage.[14]

CHwB established Local Cultural Heritage Forums for each partner municipality.[15] A forum consisted of twenty members, generally from the respective municipality, including representatives of central institutions, local authorities, international organizations, and civil society.[16] Between November 2012 and January 2013, 190 project ideas emerged from the forum discussions, and in May 2013, these ideas were put to public consultation within the seven municipalities.[17] The results helped CHwB to assess priorities and plan and implement its program of projects in the region.[18]

As part of this process, the City Museum of Mitrovica was selected as the host museum, which had been heavily affected by the war. Mitrovica had become a major flashpoint in postwar Kosovo and is still a very divided city. Once a model city of multicultural harmony, Mitrovica, located in the northwest of Kosovo, has become a living symbol of the segregation of Albanians and Serbs in postwar Kosovo. Here, the two communities are physically divided by the Ibar River, which runs through the city. For all practical purposes, they live under different systems with different languages, currencies, and infrastructure such as telecommunications systems.

The City Museum of Mitrovica was established in 1952 and was originally split between two sites, one on either side of the Ibar. It is now housed in the former Yugoslavia Army House in the city center. The museum's collection is organized into four sections: archaeology, ethnology, history, and geology. Objects range from traditional costume to archaeological ceramics, jewelry, and coins, dating back to the Illyrian civilization. The collection reflects the cultural diversity of the region, including Albanian, Turkish, Serbian, Bosnian, Catholic, and Orthodox collections.

Figure L.1. Example of textile objects in the collection at the City Museum of Mitrovica. CITY MUSEUM OF MITROVICA

Figure L.2. Display of regional costume at the City Museum of Mitrovica. CITY MUSEUM OF MITROVICA

Because the museum was previously located in two sites on opposite sides of the river and in what became opposing municipalities, many objects became disassociated from their documentation as a result of the war. Objects and documentation also suffered damage or were lost completely, most notably in a particularly severe flare-up of violence in 2009. At the time of the team's arrival, it appeared the museum had no clear documentation system in place for the collection and any existing documentation was in paper format.

Starting a New Inventory

The first camp in 2013 was developed and run by a core team of conservators and focused largely on collections care and conservation. Guest lecturers touched on other topics, such as access and interpretation.

The experience of the first year highlighted that given the loss of documentation and the lack of a clear documentation system, the museum needed support in this area. CHwB and HwB felt that recruiting a documentation specialist and adding "documentation" as a focus of the course would benefit the museum and offer a more holistic approach to the training. Therefore, in 2014, a museum registrar was recruited to join the team for the second camp to lead the documentation sessions and enrich the core program with collections management expertise.

Training sessions on the basics of museum documentation were given at the beginning of the course. The aim was to expand on conservation documentation by first discussing the fundamentals of collections documentation, from acquisition to loans and disposals. The sessions also covered topics such as ethical practices behind collecting and conserving and why documentation is key to a well-functioning museum.

Through these sessions, the team sought to build the knowledge, skills, and confidence of the participants to tackle problems commonly faced by museums worldwide, such as backlogs; limited information; damaged, missing, or destroyed information; and lack of funds for a database. The sessions demonstrated how simple record keeping can be achieved with Microsoft Excel and basic photography equipment and recommended utilizing the Collections Trust's Spectrum Standards[19] as well as ICOM's guidelines and standards,[20] which can be used by institutions of all sizes and offer a wealth of information for free.

Throughout the sessions, participants learned to document objects in the museum's collection in a variety of ways, including basic cataloging, drawing, photographing, and describing conditions pre- and post-conservation. The *Inventory of Movable Cultural Heritage*, a Microsoft Word document issued by the Kosovan government and used by local museums to record catalog information, such as the object's name, the collection it is part of, description, materials, measurements, condition, and who recorded the information, was also used in practical exercises.

Alongside these sessions, the team worked with the museum staff to help them solve problems with the documentation side of collections care. The government form was a good basis for recording object information, and the team looked at how to convert this information into an easily searchable database. A simple Excel database was created and translated into Albanian for museum staff. In addition, a system for location control using tickets, also designed in Excel, was recommended.

What Was Included in the Database and Why

The *Inventory of Movable Cultural Heritage* form and Spectrum Standards were used as a starting point to design the database. The focus was on key identifying factors, such as unique record number, object name, physical description, materials, dimensions, and images. The goal was to include object entry and ownership information, location and movement, and key catalog information so that objects could be identified from their records. It was recommended that a temporary numbering system be put in place to track objects that had become disassociated.

A guide was also created for each cell in the database to describe the type of data that should be entered. It was important to discuss terminology with museum staff and jointly decide what was essential to record. Translation was a challenge, for instance, describing to colleagues the definition of words such as "provenance" and finding an equivalent in Albanian. Albanian and Kosovan dialects differ; therefore, the team had to ensure the database and guide would be understood by everyone.

Challenges

The biggest challenge the project faced was the lack of funds and resources. The team came into the project fully aware that both the museum and CHwB had limited resources. There is no formal conservation or collections care training available locally. In a region recovering from conflict and a city that has become a major flashpoint in postwar Kosovo, it can be difficult to know where to begin when people have lost so much. Building and maintaining a relationship with the museum was crucial. The team's previous experience working with other museums with limited resources and only with Microsoft Excel or Access as a collections database helped to demonstrate to museum staff that it is possible to start to improve standards without considerable funds. As many museums worldwide face similar issues and backlogs, it felt important to highlight that the problems they find themselves tackling are not unique to their museum or indeed the Balkan region.

The short timeframe of the project presented another challenge for the team. The training lasted two weeks, with setup and orientation for the core team a few days before the participants arrived. During the first year, there had been time for a previsit to assess conservation needs and the work space available at the museum. Unfortunately, there was no time to schedule a previsit to assess documentation needs at the museum the second year, and preparation was based on guidance from the team who visited the previous year.

There was also limited time to focus on inventory with the museum staff. The project had a complex range of objectives and was trying to achieve a number of goals in the time the team was there. During the first two years, the team was given limited access to stored collections, and only limited details about collection documentation were made available. Building trust and confidence was a key project aim and assisted the inventory of the collections during the last two camps in Mitrovica. Each year, the team was given increased access to stored collections and available documentation, which gave better insight into how best to tackle collections care issues and undertake an inventory.

Table L.1. Guide for Database Cells and Data Descriptions

Cell Name	*Description*
Temporary number	MM (Museum of Mitrovica) number given to the object that has lost its number (e.g., MM0001)
Object number	Original museum number
Collection	Type of collection (e.g., archeology, ethnography, photography)
Category	Category within the collection, (e.g., costume, weapons, furniture)
Object name	Simple name describing the object (e.g., dress, belt, shoes)
Maker	The person who created the object if known
Place	The region or place where the object was used (e.g., Bulgaria, Kosovo)
Country of origin	Place where the object was found (e.g., Mitrovica, Kosovo)
Materials	Materials that make up the object (e.g., metal, wood, silver, cotton)
Dimensions	Full dimensions of the object at length or height, width, depth
Physical description	Detailed description of the object that includes shape, color, material by parts
Date	The period when the object was made or used
Object history	Detailed description of the path of the object (e.g., where is it found and when, where it has moved and when)
Notes	Additional information
Location	Where the object is usually stored or displayed
Temporary location	The position of the object if it moves from the initial position
Person who updated location	Name of the person who last located object
Date of movement	Date location was changed
Ownership	If the object is not owned by the museum and is temporarily located, there is a need for a number other than the other objects (with another code)
Condition	Description of the object's condition
Condition date	Date condition was assessed
Photographed by	Who took the image of the object
Date photograph taken	Date image taken
Place photograph is located	Place or folder in the computer where the object's picture is located
Value	The monetary value of the object
Date of valuation	Date when object was valued
Recorded by	The person who created the object record
Date recorded	Date the object record was created
Updated by	Person who has updated the record
Date updated	Date it was updated

Conclusion

Returning for a third year, the benefits of the Excel database were evident. In May 2018, a Museum of Mitrovica staffer reported, "Since the new database was created, we are continuously fulfilling [sic] the database with information from our collections. The database helped digitalizing [sic] data from the collections that didn't have digital documentation." In addition, the museum had been linking object images to the database and modifying it to suit their needs for different collections, particularly the numismatic collection. The hope is that a database will soon be set up by the Ministry of Culture of Kosovo, leading to a standard system for all museums in Kosovo, and that our work of the past four years will prove to be a valuable asset.

Acknowledgments

City Museum of Mitrovica for working with us on the project

Cultural Heritage without Borders, in particular Miri Black and Nedi Petri for support on the project and translating the database

Heritage without Borders, in particular Dominica D'Arcangelo and all the trainers involved in the project from 2013–2015

All the participants who took part in the RRC 2013–2015

Horniman Museum and Gardens, London, and Birmingham Museums Trust for supporting the project by allowing Helen Merrett and Alex Cantrill-Lankester time to volunteer

Notes

1. Cultural Heritage without Borders, "Who We Are," November 22, 2018, http://chwb.org/kosovo/about-us/.
2. Ibid.
3. Ibid.
4. Cultural Heritage without Borders, "The Regional Restoration Camps," June 6, 2018, http://chwb.org/albania/activities/rrc/.
5. Ibid.
6. Ibid.
7. Ibid.
8. Heritage without Borders, "Heritage Conservation Archaeology Museum Developing World Professionals Volunteers Volunteering Resources and Information," June 6, 2018, http://www.heritagewithoutborders.org.
9. Cultural Heritage without Borders, "CHwB Kosovo Strategic Plan 2013–16," http://chwb.org/kosovo/wp-content/uploads/sites/3/2014/02/CHwB-Kosovo-Strategic-Plan-2013-16.pdf.
10. Cultural Heritage without Borders, "Local Cultural Heritage Plans in 7 Municipalities of Kosovo," June 2018, http://chwb.org/kosovo/activities/activity-2/.
11. Ibid.
12. Ibid.
13. Ibid.
14. Ibid.
15. Ibid.
16. Ibid.
17. Ibid.
18. Ibid.
19. Collections Trust, "Spectrum," June 6, 2018, https://collectionstrust.org.uk/spectrum/.
20. International Council of Museums, "Standards & Guidelines-ICOM," June 6, 2018, http://icom.museum/professional-standards/standards-guidelines/.

~

Case M

I've Seen It All—Inventory at The Children's Museum of Indianapolis

Jennifer Noffze, Collections Manager

In September 2012, our new director of collections arrived at The Children's Museum of Indianapolis. One of his first questions for collections management staff concerned the date of our last inventory. It had been over twenty years ago, 1990 to be exact. He asked me, as the then registrar and archivist, to create an inventory plan. With a collection of over 130,000 objects representing the arts and humanities and natural sciences, I knew this project would take several years to complete. I started by creating a five-year plan to conduct a rolling inventory of the collection organized by storage area. By approaching the inventory this way, we will be able to plan for future inventories at roughly ten-year intervals. For example, by 2022, it will be time to inventory our textile collection again, almost ten years after the previous inventory, and we will continue with each storage area based on this pattern. Table M.1 details the original plan.

One area not included in this initial plan was our textile collection, which consists of approximately 9,000 items. This is because in 2012, we received an IMLS grant to upgrade our textile collection storage. We were therefore already underway with the inventory, digital photography, and condition reporting of this portion of the collection; in addition to our regular staff, the grant allowed us to hire two part-time personnel to assist with this work. Another area I excluded was our 2007 and 2008 acquisitions of over 20,000 comic books, as these two collections already had photographs and current locations recorded. With strong documentation in these areas, I focused on the remainder of the collection for the first five years. I knew I wouldn't be able to hire additional staff and that meant embarking on a multiyear collections management internship program!

Table M.1. Original five-year inventory plan.

Year	*Storage Area*	*Number of Artifacts*
2013	Archives	8,982
2014	American materials	8,559
2015	Ethnographic materials	11,097
2016	Toy storage	13,044
2017	Caplan collection	28,600
2017	Oversize storage	456
2017	Natural science	6,582

During the first year of the archives inventory, I supervised two interns. The archives consist of posters, maps, books, magazines, audiovisual materials, and various other documents. Our process was very analog and continued to be throughout the process. At the beginning, we didn't have laptops for direct data entry. We used location lists printed from our database to do the work. We would then go back to the computer and update the following fields in our database, KE-EMu:

- Inventory date
- Current location (the storage location)
- Condition
- Dimensions
- Multimedia (digital image)

If an item wasn't found, the storage location was deleted (there is a movement history for tracking storage locations), and the item was added to a group list titled "Not Found in Inventory," which is saved in the database. Inspecting the condition of objects allowed us to upgrade housing for some artifacts that required it. We also identified items for deaccession consideration. Re-

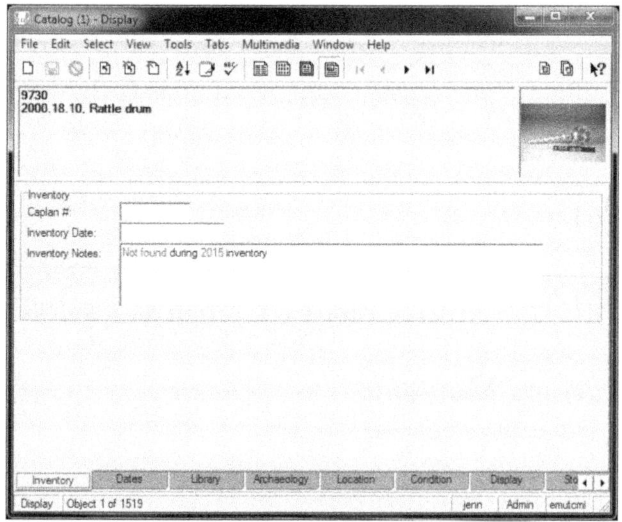

Figure M.1. Screenshot of database fields used to indicate whether an object has been located in inventory. JENNIFER NOFFZE

cording artifact dimensions was imperative because they are always helpful for exhibit prep. Digital photography was also a definite priority; only 2 percent of our artifact records had images when we embarked on our inventory. Photographs were uploaded to a shared network file. To name files, we used the accession number and object name. Photographs were then edited, resized, and added to catalog records. The original photographs are stored on an external hard drive and uploaded to InDiPres, a meta-archive cooperative established to assist Indiana cultural organizations with preserving digital content.

Remarkably, I was able to stay on track with my initial inventory plans. Our collections management interns helped us achieve our goal, as did our director's commitment and support to complete the inventory. The five-year inventory plan end date coincides with the museum's AAM reaccreditation in 2018. This is significant because we completed a Museum Assessment Program assessment in 2014 that highlighted the need for a full-scale inventory, and the assessment helped garner institutional support for the inventory project.

Before the five-year rolling inventory is truly complete, we need to finish inventorying the Caplan Collection, a folk art collection featuring objects from around

Figure M.2. The natural science collection storage area at The Children's Museum of Indianapolis. JENNIFER NOFFZE

the world as well as the natural science specimens. In 2003, we moved the natural science collection to a new storage area, and during this move, we completed an inventory. The work for this collection therefore shouldn't be as intensive as the other areas.

Throughout the inventory, we located artifacts with incorrect numbers, illegible numbers, or no database records. We took photographs of these objects and noted their location. One of the last projects will be trying to determine the status of these objects. To aid this process, we have been scanning photographs from old card catalog files and adding them to database records without images attached. We hope that these older photographs will help us identify the problem objects we came across.

I cannot emphasize enough how important this inventory work has been. It is wonderful to have images in our database along with updated condition information and dimensions. Plus, we're able to engage in database cleanup as we proceed. It is very satisfying to correct misspellings; capitalize proper names; and apply our specific nomenclature, for example, for dolls, stuffed toys, and toy trains. This work provides us with a solid foundation as we continue with our rolling inventory, which will hopefully go more quickly with the incorporation of mobile devices, which we hope to implement in 2020.

It's crazy to think that over the past five years, I have personally inspected close to 80,000 artifacts and specimens in the collection. I've truly seen it all. Well, almost!

Case N

Inventory at the Aanischaaukamikw Cree Cultural Institute

Laura Phillips, Coordinator of Collections and Exhibitions

Since opening in 2011, the permanent collections at Aanischaaukamikw Cree Cultural Institute (ACCI)[1] have expanded to include about 500 objects, with close to 1,000 objects on loan from Eeyouch[2] entities, Eeyouch community members, and individuals and organizations from outside the region. The Eeyou Istchee region, a self-governing territory of the Eeyouch peoples located on the east side of James Bay in what is now known as northern Quebec, spans some 5,000 kilometers.[3] Some Eeyouch choose to live in one of the nine communities[4]—Whapmagoostui, Chisasibi, Wemindji, Eastmain, Waskaganish, Waswanipi, Nemaska, Ouje-Bougoumou, and Mistissini—as well as spending part of the year on the land. The idea for the regional cultural center existed for decades, with some collections being formed in advance of the opening of the center. We have the highest ranking for cultural property facilities within Canada,[5] equivalent to national and provincial museums.

The collections gathered prior to the building of the facility were located in various storage locations in the region. Some collections were selected as loans from major museums in urban centers by the team working on the first incarnation of the permanent exhibit entitled *Aa Chiiwaaschaaniwich: Reclaiming the Ways of Our Ancestors*.[6] Some of these collections were stored in Montreal at the McCord Museum and transferred to the facility in 2011. For this transfer, simple Excel inventory lists were used for tracking objects. All permanent collections were registered once on-site, using a bound paper accessions register. We used the numbering system of yyyy.collection.item, indicating the year of acquisition, the sequential collection within that year, and unique object numbers. All objects were tagged and physically labeled using standard museological reversible methods. Collections not installed in the gallery were stored in the "Vault," a secure, climate-controlled room in the collections wing of the facility with access restricted to collections staff. Paper catalog records were created for each object following the Canadian Heritage Information Network guidelines, which we adapted as needed. These object files were organized in filing cabinet drawers by collection and object number. The shelving and drawer units within storage areas were assigned unique locational reference numbers. Display cases, visual storage areas, and exhibit spaces were also assigned unique locational identifiers.

Figure N.1. Aanischaaukamikw Cree Cultural Institute, Ouje Bougoumou, Eeyou Istchee.
AANISCHAAUKAMIKW CREE CULTURAL INSTITUTE

While the institute was preparing for opening, the MINISIS database was selected to manage the collections, which has a registration module (MINT) as well as modules for archives (M2A), library (M2L), and museum (M3) collections. The database purchase and implementation were funded with a Museums Assistance Program (MAP) grant from Heritage Canada. Additional funding from MAP supported the online component of the database (cree.minisisinc.com). The library and archive module customization was complete by 2013, with data entry beginning around this time. Cataloging is done primarily in English, though the database can accommodate French accents and the Cree syllabic alphabet. The archives module uses the standard Rules for Archival Description hierarchical arrangement, which we adapted as needed to meet our needs. The library classification system we selected was the Brian Deer system, which is designed specifically for Indigenous library collections and is in use at other Indigenous centers across this land.[7] The museum cataloging module required additional customization before we could begin data entry, which was completed for the full permanent collection using the MINT and M3 modules in 2018.

Prior to the implementation of our database, Excel spreadsheets were used to track object movements. In 2014, we started a full inventory and collections survey to record the locations of all objects in storage and on display. We used an Excel spreadsheet for this task, with fields for the recently appointed conservator to record basic condition information as she familiarized herself with the collection. Inventory fields included object number, registration comments, storage location, display location, display from date, display to date, collection status, number of items, and dimensions.

The conservator, collections officer, and registrar worked together to complete the inventory in approximately three dedicated weeks. Once complete, the inventory was used as the master object locational reference, with location information updated as movements occurred. Despite the relatively small number of objects in the collection and the brevity of time the institute was collecting, we still found orphaned and unknown objects in our storage areas. These were addressed individually and as time permitted by researching documentation to determine their status. Most turned out to be objects deposited for "acquisition consideration" very soon after the institute opened, when collections staff were extremely busy dealing with the final aspects of the exhibit, or objects that needed paperwork completed to finalize the acquisition. Fortunately, the status of most mystery objects was relatively easy to determine with focused research and enquiries made to staff who were working at the institute around the time of opening. This research consumes valuable time, so our lesson to share with other emerging or expanding institutions is to have basic acquisition and object entry processes in place from the very start, even if they are not perfect or comprehensive. Having signatures on transfers of title and details about why an object entered the building, as well as contact details for the owner, is essential.

One of the surprising moments during the inventory was when our collections officer, Paula Menarick, discovered that we had a beaded bowl made by her late grandmother Gracie Orr while she was living in Moose Factory in the 1960s. This was part of a collection of Eeyouch material donated by Dr. Richard Preston, an anthropologist who Eeyouch community members worked with in the late twentieth century.[8] The bowl was donated as part of a larger collection of objects and

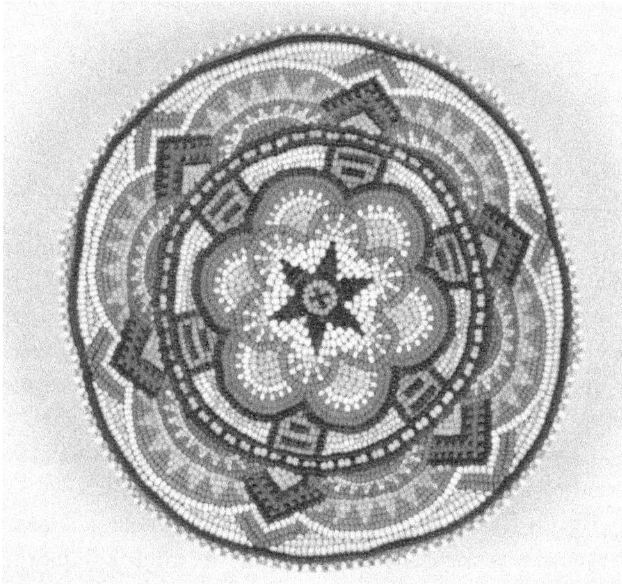

Figure N.2. Beaded bowl made by the late Gracie Herodier Orr of Chisasibi. Object #2011.01.49. From the Richard Preston Collection. AANISCHAAUKAMIKW CREE CULTURAL INSTITUTE

Figure N.3. Beaded bowl made by the late Gracie Herodier Orr of Chisasibi. Object #2011.01.49. From the Richard Preston Collection. AANISCHAAUKAMIKW CREE CULTURAL INSTITUTE

archives in 2011 when ACCI opened. This bowl had been made by Gracie to commemorate the centennial of the Canada dominion in 1967. Paula had an emotional response to being in the presence of this incredibly detailed beaded bowl because she had seen similar beaded bowls as a child and had been told family stories of the crafts her grandmother made. Paula's family members still make the bowls today, with their own designs.

In 2017, the customization of the museum collection module (M3) was complete, along with detailed pick lists, authority tables, and data entry guidelines. We chose not to use an existing classification or nomenclature system for our collection because we felt most existing standards reduce objects by their function in a way that was not a good fit for our needs, which required a method that would reflect our community members' expertise about our collections. At present, core collection data is in English, but most Eeyouch researchers are trilingual (Cree, English, and French), and we are working to expand Cree language content to maximize search functionality. A multientry authority table for the database's object name field is representative of objects in the region, including transliterated Cree words when English is deficient for the specificity required. For example, "makaahiikan" is used for the shovel/scoop/walking stick tool that has no English equivalent. For broader

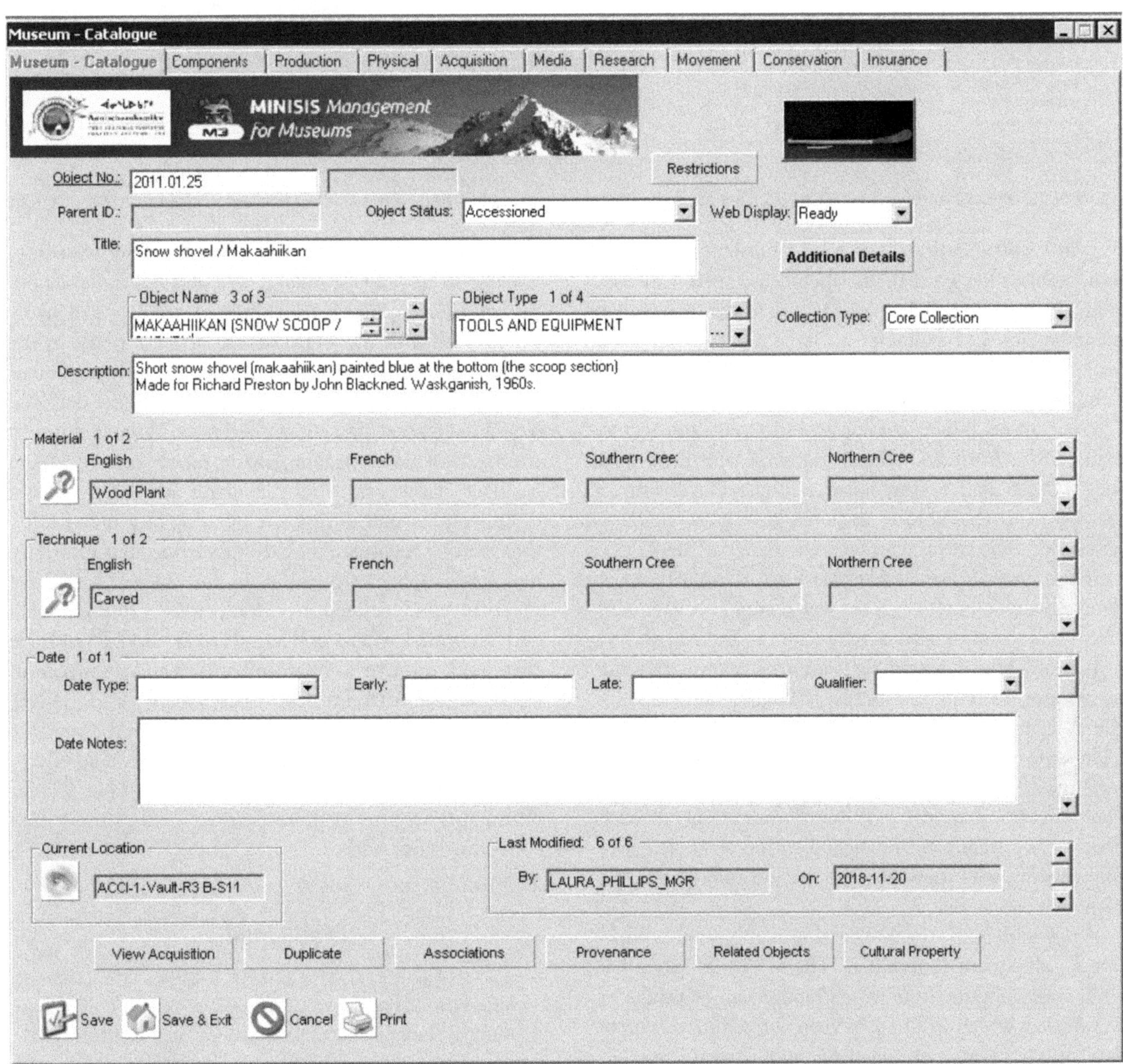

Figure N.4. Screenshot of M3 database record record for object #2011.01.25. AANISCHAAUKAMIKW CREE CULTURAL INSTITUTE

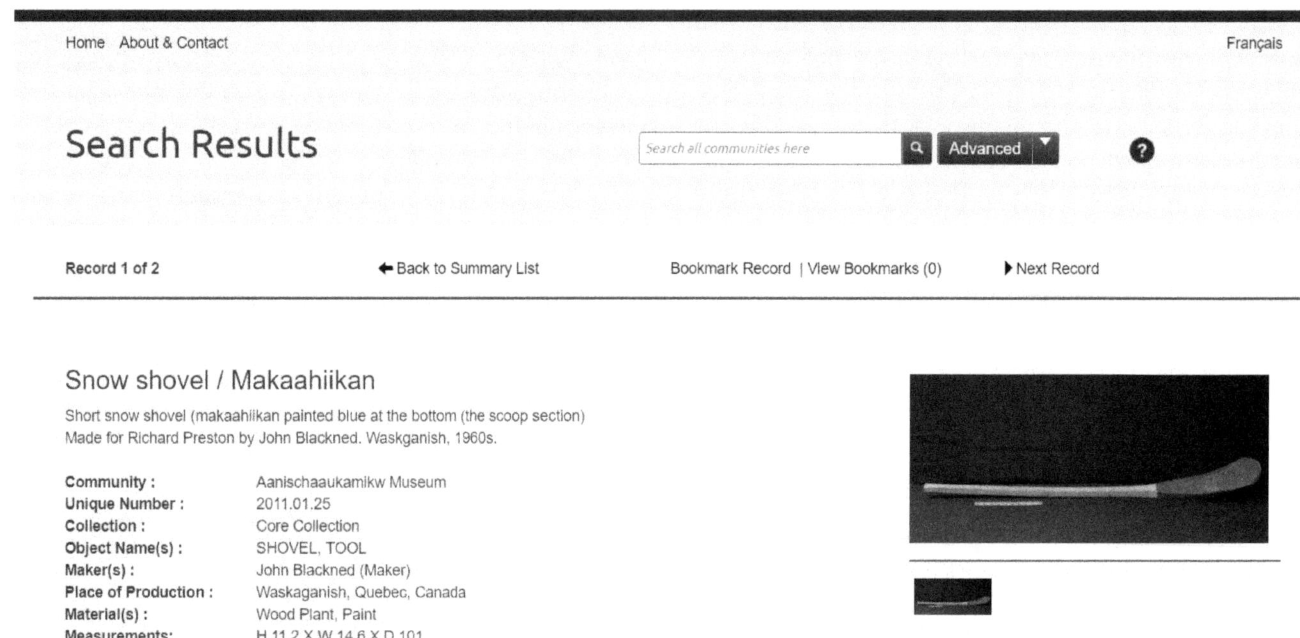

Figure N.5. Record for object #2011.01.25 from our online database: cree.minisisinc.com. AANISCHAAUKAMIKW CREE CULTURAL INSTITUTE

thematic classifications, we use a multientry authority table subject/keyword field, where catalogers can link objects to the multiple roles they play within Eeyouch communities. For example, we have a subject/keyword term for "moose hunt," which will retrieve objects related to the annual autumn hunt.

Our online public catalog website (cree.minisisinc.com) is the front end for our database and presents a selection of data for public searching and viewing of records from the library, archives, and museum databases. Because our primary target audience is the 17,000 Eeyouch community members, it was essential that our database cataloging match the way community members might search for objects as they relate to their lives.

It took approximately eight months to enter the full registration information and basic cataloging details for the 500 objects in the permanent collection while also addressing our regular duties. Data entry was done by the registrar, coordinator of collections and exhibitions, and two collections interns. As the information about each object was entered, the physical location was verified by the registrar, who then recorded the location data in the current location field.

As of mid-2018, the M3 catalog is the primary location for all our collections data. The MINISIS system has a full audit module, from which reports can be produced as required, which will help us keep our inventories up to date. We have not had time to design many reports, but this is the next step in our overall MINISIS implementation project that will ensure our collections inventory is kept up to date. We keep all copies of our previous inventories in printed paper formats, which will likely be ingested into the M3 database at some point in the future perhaps as an event record that will document the details of the project. In an ideal world, the database would have been fully customized prior to the opening of the institute, with accompanying procedural workflows in place. However, with the many activities required of collections staff during the opening of a new facility that features a permanent exhibit with regular rotations, this was simply not possible. In the interim, our 2014 inventory and collections survey were comprehensive and identified where collections staff should prioritize their work in order to have collections and their records organized for entry into M3 in the years that followed. This project and our current inventory were the result of many years of ongoing work by a dedicated team of collections staff, and we are extremely proud of our accomplishments in this little-recognized behind-the-scenes area of museum work.

Bibliography

Aanischaaukamikw Cree Cultural Institute. *Aa Chiiwaas-chaaniwich: Reclaiming the Ways of Our Ancestors*. Ouje Bougoumou: Aanischaaukamikw Cree Cultural Institute, 2011.

Bosum, Annie, and Ashley Dunne. "Implementing the Brian Deer Classification Scheme for Aanischaaukamikw Cree

Cultural Institute." *Collection Management* 42, no. 3–4 (2017): 280–93. https://doi.org/10.1080/01462679.2017.1340858.

Government of Canada. "Designation of Institutions and Public Authorities—Movable Cultural Property." Moveable Cultural Property. Modified May 8, 2018. https://www.canada.ca/en/canadian-heritage/services/designation-institutions-cultural-property.html.

Pashagumskum, Sarah, Paula Menarick, Laura Phillips, Geraldine Laurendeau, and Katherine Scott. "Seeing Ourselves: The Path to Self-Curation, Cultural Sovereignty and Self-Representation in Eeyou Istchee." In *Survivance and Reconciliation: 7 Forward / 7 Back: 2015 Canadian Indigenous Native Studies Association Conference Proceedings*, edited by Karl S. Hele, 60–87. Manitoba: Aboriginal Issues Press, 2016.

Notes

1. See Sarah Pashagumskum, Paula Menarick, Laura Phillips, Geraldine Laurendeau, and Katherine Scott, "Seeing Ourselves: The Path to Self-Curation, Cultural Sovereignty and Self-Representation in Eeyou Istchee," in *Survivance and Reconciliation: 7 Forward / 7 Back: 2015 Canadian Indigenous Native Studies Association Conference Proceedings*, ed. Karl S. Hele (Manitoba: Aboriginal Issues Press, 2016), 60–87, for a discussion of the development of ACCI and the exhibit programming.

2. Eeyou means "the people" in the James Bay dialect of Cree and is used interchangeably with Cree and Eenou, another regional dialect. The plural form is Eeyouch/Eenouch.

3. This is a drastic reduction to the original territory, which spanned some 450,000 kilometers. "Eeyou Istchee," Eeyou Istchee, Wikipedia, modified October 4, 2018, https://en.wikipedia.org/wiki/Eeyou_Istchee_(territory).

4. Washaw Sibi is a tenth community under the Grand Council of the Crees, but it does not have a village site at present.

5. Government of Canada, "Designation of Institutions and Public Authorities—Movable Cultural Property," modified May 8, 2018, https://www.canada.ca/en/canadian-heritage/services/designation-institutions-cultural-property.html.

6. Aanischaaukamikw Cree Cultural Institute, *Aa Chiiwaaschaaniwich: Reclaiming the Ways of Our Ancestors* (Ouje Bougoumou: Aanischaaukamikw Cree Cultural Institute, 2011).

7. Annie Bosum and Ashley Dunne, "Implementing the Brian Deer Classification Scheme for Aanischaaukamikw Cree Cultural Institute," *Collection Management* 42, no. 3–4 (2017): 280–93, https://doi.org/10.1080/01462679.2017.1340858.

8. In Paula's own words, "I was really happy once we confirmed that yes Gracie did make the bowl and how she made it for Preston. He shared with me through email of how my late grandmother Gracie was once found sewing under the table hiding from her mother because she was not allowed to touch her mother's sewing supplies yet because she was told she was too young. The beaded bowls Gracie made are beautiful treasures she's left behind for us to treasure and we're lucky we get to visit the one at ACCI! The beadwork of the bowl is mesmerizing! I love the colours she chose for the design. The embroidery on the outside has the finest stitches. Kuukuum Gracie was an amazing artist who shared her love of crafting with everyone." Paula Menarick, personal comment, June 15, 2018.

~

Case O

Inventory Interrupted: Turning a Challenge into an Opportunity

Linda Endersby, Registrar and Collections Manager

In 2006, the Missouri State Museum, a unit of Missouri State Parks, began the first full inventory of its collection. But in three years, staff managed to inventory only about 5 percent of the collection due to a lack of staff. Despite owning PastPerfect software for five years, staff had simply entered information into the database from catalog cards with no physical inventory to verify information. The location of most objects was uncertain. Adding to poor documentation, collections were stored in the basement of the ninety-year-old stone capitol building. Some were stored in dusty, moldy areas behind a door marked "High Voltage Do Not Enter" past the building's main transformer. Pipe leaks damaged some significant museum objects. Whether any other important objects were at risk was unknown. Improving collections storage conditions was therefore a priority alongside the inventory. After three years of struggling with inventory progress, museum staff developed a plan for moving the project forward and received a two-year Institute of Museum and Library Services (IMLS) grant to help complete the project.

In the midst of the IMLS-funded stage of the inventory, staff learned they would have to move their collection to a new storage facility. While a new facility was very much desired, it came at an inconvenient time. However, good planning for the inventory turned this challenge into an opportunity. By the end of the project, staff managed to significantly increase public awareness of the collections and overall support of the museum.

The inventory plan was developed through a collaborative approach, including administration, collections and exhibits staff, and the Missouri State Parks Registrar from our parent organization. The group outlined specific needs, desired outcomes, and short- and long-term needs.

A major decision to be made was the extent of information that would be captured: did we need full cataloging and a high-resolution digital image for every object? Though exhibits and other staff argued for this, the group decided on a limited approach. The priority was to know what the museum had and where it was. We chose a limited amount of information to be gathered/verified during the physical inventory—identification-only images and staged data reconciliation. This enabled the museum to complete the inventory quickly and efficiently, which became of great importance later. Only limited object rehousing was done during the process; however, staff documented rehousing needs to be addressed in the future.[1]

Checklists, written procedures, and standards assured speed, efficiency, and consistency despite several different staff performing inventory activities. A procedure was also developed for saving and naming digital images taken during the inventory. For some collections, such as a large shell collection, the curator created a shell identification and description guide. This assured not only consistency and accuracy but also brevity by specifying the identifying characteristics required. Museum staff also wrote a data entry standards manual to be used for all data entry into PastPerfect during the inventory and going forward.

Another effective practice involved developing strategies for dealing with problems or "snags" that could slow down the inventory's progress. For instance, staff created a "problem" cabinet to hold objects with odd circumstances or documentation issues. Rather than impeding progress for time-consuming research, these objects were tagged and placed in the cabinet to be addressed by the curator of collections or curator coordinator. Sometimes, the problems simply rectified themselves later in the inventory because of found documentation.

Only a few months into the IMLS-funded portion of the inventory project, the museum learned that almost all of the collection would need to be moved to a new storage facility, which was a mile away from the main building, and within six months.[2] Because of the detailed planning, organization, and setup of the inventory project, the move and the inventory worked hand in hand. By adjusting what sets of objects were inventoried in what order, no objects were moved before being inventoried. In turn, the move went smoothly because we knew what we were moving. Without the inventory, the move would have caused severe disruption and would not have been completed within the short time frame.

The inventory included good use of a variety of resources, particularly human. The positions funded by IMLS included one full-time inventory team leader and multiple part-time positions. Thus, at least two people worked on inventory at any time.[3] Even while museum staff were moving the collection, others were able to maintain inventory progress. Because the museum negotiated additional assistance with the move from Museum State Parks, staff could simultaneously work on the move and keep the inventory from getting too far behind. Certain components of inventory work, such as data entry from old catalog cards, were self-contained and could be accomplished by interns and done consistently because of the written procedures and checklists.

Regular meetings also contributed to the success of the inventory project. During the thick of the inventory, the team had weekly meetings to coordinate. Meetings sometimes lasted only five minutes, sometimes an hour. Regularity was critical. Meetings confirmed that all objects moving out of the building were inventoried first. In addition, any issues that arose could be quickly addressed.

The team approach, which included regular museum and inventory-specific staff, produced inventory success as well as wider benefits. Because the curator of exhibits and the curator coordinator participated in the inventory process, they increased their knowledge and expertise of the collection, resulting in much richer exhibits. For example, during the inventory, staff discovered a petticoat and spinning wheel. A Missouri woman and people enslaved by her used the spinning wheel to spin the thread used to make the petticoat. Because staff were now able to display historically significant objects such as these and tell their incredible stories, they could make a much more powerful argument for better storage conditions and collections care funding.[4]

The inventory also dramatically increased the use of collection items in quality interpretive programming. For example, the museum began the Museum after Hours programming series featuring parts of the collection, some of which were discovered by interpretive staff while participating in the inventory. Two of the Museum after Hours programs were "Trunkful of Treasures" and "Marching through Time," which featured notable miniatures by artist Florence Klusman and a collection of right shoe samples from a shoe factory salesman.

Additionally, at the new collections storage facility, staff held a behind-the-scenes event that would have been impossible without the inventory. At the event, staff spoke about the inventory and its importance for the preservation of the collection. The initial event became a series that brought the public into a new relationship with the museum. The inventory, the move, and these events ultimately led to the formation of a not-for-profit museum support group with the goal of raising funds and assisting with museum activities.

The primary lesson—never go so long without a collections inventory! To prevent this from happening again, museum staff wrote a new section into the collections management policy outlining a procedure for periodic partial inventories. Every object in the collection will now be physically inventoried at least once every ten years.

Another important lesson was to plan a flexible project. The inventory was divided into stages and self-contained projects, many of which were interchangeable. Flexibility to adjust mid-course improved procedures and quality of output. Dividing up the project into small pieces and following written procedures, documentation, and communication methods allowed for the addition of other team members to assist with the project as needed.

The museum accepted and managed its inventory challenges. This resulted in better storage conditions for collections, a full inventory of the collection, and a considerably heightened awareness of the collection by our parent organization and the public. Our case shows there is hope for other very unorganized collections.[5]

Notes

1. At the end of the inventory, staff determined the scope of materials needed for rehousing and identified funding.

2. A renovation of the building in which we were located required an overhaul of the electrical system. This work required space, and our storage area was identified as ideal because of its proximity to the old transformer. To keep the renovation project on schedule, the museum had to vacate its space within six months.

3. A side benefit of this use of resources was that six individuals gained significant work experience. Five got full-time positions after their work, with the sixth gaining admission to a graduate program.

4. Because of these finds, funds were made available to ensure good environmental conditions in storage areas that became accessible as a result of the inventory. Additional funds were also allocated to install compact shelving in 2018 as a result of storage needs identified during the project.

5. A recent publication provides some very practical tips and suggestions. Angela Kipp, *Managing Previously Unmanaged Collections: A Practical Guide for Museums* (Lanham, MD: Rowman & Littlefield, 2016).

~

Case P

The First Full Inventory and Cataloging of the Collection of the Daum Museum of Contemporary Art

Matthew Clouse, Former Registrar and Exhibitions Coordinator

The Daum Museum of Contemporary Art functions as a department of State Fair Community College in Sedalia, Missouri. Opened in 2002, the collection was formed around the donation of over 200 works of art from Dr. Harold F. Daum, who was a radiologist and local philanthropist. Dr. Daum was also integral to the building and financing of the museum, a treasure unto itself. Unique in its rural setting, it boasts an impressive collection of over 1,600 works by major local, national, and international artists, including ceramics, prints, photography, sculpture, and paintings, much of which is nonobjective and conceptually challenging.

In 2013, I was hired as the registrar and exhibitions coordinator, with the unique challenge of being the first person to hold my title and with the understanding that I would begin to fully catalog and inventory the entire collection in addition to the other duties associated with my dual roles.

While the museum's small staff had done their best to document the collection, there was work to be done before the inventory project could begin. Because of the collection's relatively small size, it was easy for staff to have a more intimate knowledge of their holdings; in fact, several had been employed there from the beginning and had even helped Dr. Daum acquire his collection. There was no collections management database, however, and record keeping was intermittent. I put together a loose outline of the way I thought the project would play out; however, the way things came together in the end was not exactly how I had envisioned. Yet having a plan was helpful to the extent that I allowed it to be as flexible as possible.

At the outset, I planned to begin with the physical inventory, matching what I found in storage to documentation and working one step at a time. As I moved forward, it became apparent that a more multidimensional approach was necessary, and I concluded it was best to start by evaluating each object from every possible aspect, from basic measurements all the way to provenance and date of acquisition.

Thus, for each object, I reviewed existing records, gathering together as much documentation as I could locate, which included acquisitions committee meeting minutes, documents from the foundation office, hard-copy object and artist files, Excel spreadsheets, and any digital files that appeared to have promising or enlightening information. I made sure not to discount any shred of evidence that might lead me in the right direction, although I wasn't always sure which direction I should have been going. Since I was going on only what I discovered and the institutional memory of those who came before me, I tried to take nothing at face value, and I assumed that what I was seeing was accurate only to the extent that it could be proven by my own verification methods.

I then began reassigning object ID numbers, and while many collections managers advise against this, for good reason, there were only 500 or so objects that had been given numbers, using an unorthodox system. Since the numbers didn't link to a database and were not always used consistently in cross-references, it wasn't especially difficult to implement the new system while simultaneously updating other records. I used the acquisitions committee meeting minutes to retroactively assign numbers (archiving the old numbers, of course), which helped tremendously in establishing a consistent system. However, the minutes were not comprehensive and, in some cases, were inaccurate. This is where culling information from other sources, such as old checklists, Excel sheets, and assorted object and artist files, helped to fill in the gaps.

At the time, it seemed as though centralizing all this information in a database was key to keeping everything in order as I began to work with greater and greater amounts of information. PastPerfect had already been purchased but never utilized, so we settled on getting the newest version and starting there. While I stand by this decision, I think that it may have complicated the process for several reasons. First, a database demands a certain amount of data to make it useful. Admittedly, there was a bit of a chicken-or-the-egg situation. How do you manage data when you aren't certain of the data you have or will have, and how do you simultaneously decide on the structure of the database while at the same time populating it with data you need to access, ad nauseum? I admit to scouring the database more than once with a fine-tooth comb, as new information would come to light, requiring many records to be modified. Reflecting on the process at the end of the project, my workload may have been reduced had I gathered the majority of my information first or as much as I could find and then embarked on a mass data-entry phase, for example, by creating Excel spreadsheets to hold information that would eventually be used to migrate data to the database. Yet having easily searchable digital records certainly made my day-to-day workflow outside of the inventory project much easier. PastPerfect also became a repository for loan and exhibitions records, constituent contacts, and digital document storage. As the project moved forward, it became more and more important to have one source of information.

Alongside the gathering of documentation, the establishment of the database structure, and the physical inventory, the hard-copy object records were being restructured. Originally organized alphabetically by artist, with corresponding object files grouped accordingly, refiling by object ID number helped create space in the cabinets. Artist files were also separated out, and new donor files created. For some objects that had very little documentation, it was necessary to populate the files with basic information, such as an information sheet from the database, a condition report, and a photograph at the least.

At the end of the project, we were able to properly accession over 200 unaccessioned (meaning that they did not appear in acquisitions committee meeting minutes) and found-in-collection works and even discovered a few pieces that were considered missing. With all collection information now in the database, future inventories can be conducted by running reports according to object location or medium, allowing staff to focus in one area and reducing the margin for error.

Powder-coated steel bins for two-dimensional framed works were designed and purchased, which enabled 130 plus artworks to be relocated from the floor. A new pallet rack, additional shelving, and two new off-site storage

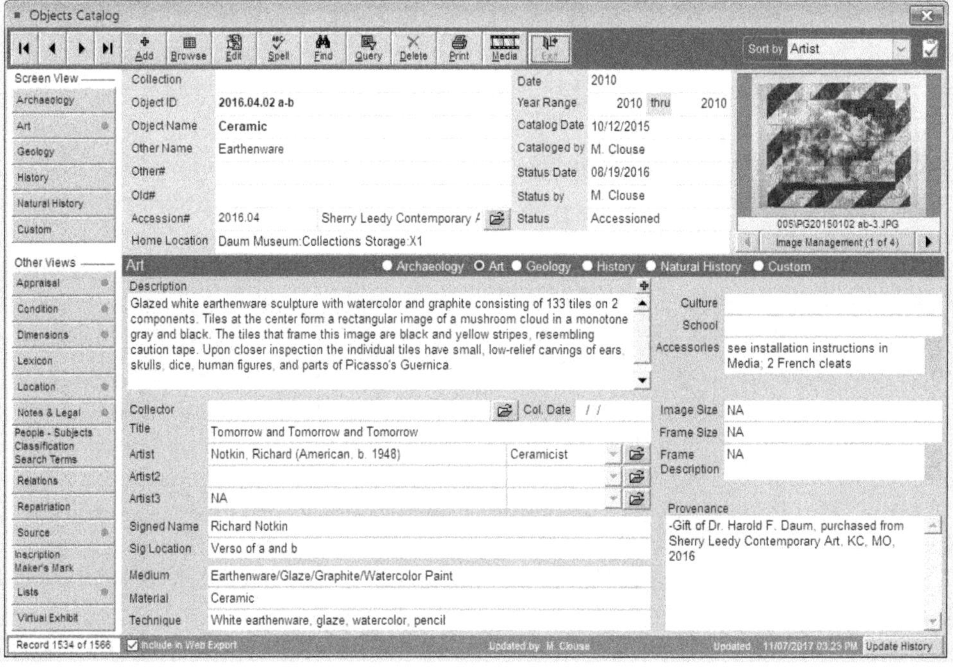

Figure P.1. Screenshot showing a completed database record for an artwork titled *Tomorrow and Tomorrow and Tomorrow* by Richard Notkin. MATTHEW CLOUSE

Figure P.2. Photograph of flatwork storage bins. A fully-inventoried collection allows for successful storage planning.
MATTHEW CLOUSE

spaces further decluttered the vault and allowed for the growth of the collection. The more changes we made in storage, the more important having all permanent collection objects marked, tagged, cataloged, and correctly located in the database became.

The full project spanned roughly four and a half years, yet as work was carried out in between other registration duties and exhibition installations, it's nearly impossible to give an accurate duration; when we were not working on the inventory or exhibitions, we were also writing a collections management policy, disaster plan, and additional policies and procedures and implementing environmental monitoring.

Summer interns and on-call contract staff played a key role in much of the physical inventory, as they were able to assist with condition reporting, measuring, handling, rehousing, relocating, and photographing many of the larger objects. I would be remiss if I didn't thank them and the amazing regular staff for much of what I was able to accomplish. My overarching mantra throughout the entire process was, "Will what I'm doing at this moment make sense to people working here in fifty years?" Human errors aside, I feel confident that the collection is fairly well documented and better preserved and that current and future staff will appreciate our efforts.

~

Case Q

Stealth Inventories at the TECHNOSEUM

Angela Kipp, Collections Manager

Certainly, one major reason for not doing inventories is that they require something even large institutions can seldom afford: collections staff being allowed to work through the collection with concentration, undisturbed by other duties. One way to work around this issue is to tie inventories to a task that fits into the broader scope of the institution's mission, for instance, exhibition planning.

In 2010, the TECHNOSEUM launched a new format for exhibitions. Interchanging with the customary theme-based exhibitions, the new format presents entire portions of the collection. Instead of showing just a few significant objects, the concept of these exhibitions is to show everything, or nearly everything, the museum owns, using a presentation style that resembles a museum storage area. For visitors, this creates a feeling of exploring a hidden area of the museum and getting a peek of behind-the-scenes museum work. This was done in 2011 with the exhibition *The Collection: 1001 Objects to Listen To and Look At*, with the museum's collection of radios, TV sets, record players, tape recorders, and other home entertainment objects, and in 2014, with *The Collection 2: The Electrical Household*, featuring vacuum cleaners,

Figure Q.1. Fans on display in the exhibition, *The Collection 2: The Electrical Household.* ANGELA KIPP

washing machines, refrigerators, fans, hair dryers, pressing irons, or, in short, everything that has a power cable. Now, we are in the midst of preparing *The Collection 3: Advertising and Selling*, which will open in 2019.

It goes without saying that if a museum wishes to present whole collections in this way, it needs to make sure the information provided to visitors is accurate. It is quite natural, then, to do an inventory of the objects slated for exhibition to capture and verify information. Preparing for upcoming exhibitions in this way is made a top priority, and there is a whole exhibition team to do it.

The TECHNOSEUM's approach is the following: staff assign responsibility for one or more collections to a team member. For example, team member X will inventory the coffee makers. They can get help from a student assistant, apprentice, or intern if one is available.

1. They will first search for the museum's coffee makers in the database and also search for alternative names, such as "coffee machine" or "percolator," as the use of thesauri and nomenclatures has not been consistent over the past thirty years
2. They then print out a list with object locations and check that the locations of objects are correct. As it is with institutions that have some history of collecting and haven't conducted an inventory for quite some time, this will reveal the following: a vast number of objects in the correct location, some objects that can't be found at the listed location, and some objects that are on the shelf but aren't listed as being there in the database.

In carrying out step two, the TECHNOSEUM may receive help from non-German-speaking assistants. The TECHNOSEUM is very keen on international exchange, so it often hosts colleagues from its partner museum, the Shanghai Science and Technology Museum, as well as other museums from around the world. However, especially when working in the collections department with a German-language database, the language barrier can be a limiting factor. Because step two mainly involves checking accession numbers and locations, this task can be done without knowing a single word of German. It can also be done by colleagues who don't come with a background in collections management but only basic art-handling training, thus making it an ideal task for our international colleagues.

3. Next, they will do a thorough check to confirm that what was found in each location is correct, as there may be objects with an incorrect number or two objects bearing the same number.
4. They will then change the location entry for objects not found to "location unknown." Some of these objects will show up in other locations.
5. The next step is to review the database entries for any additional objects found to determine why they didn't appear in the original database search. Most of the time, they have an incorrect location entry. In other cases, there are spelling errors in the record that made the object invisible in the original search. Any errors identified in the records are corrected.
6. Finally, there may be a small percentage of objects whose records still can't be found in the database. If these objects can't be reconciled with their numbers after searching the database for every bit of identifying information, such as serial number, and reviewing similar collections and paper documentation, these objects will receive new accession numbers and a note that they were "found in collection."

Once all objects have a correct number and location, the next step is to bring all database entries to the same standard. Because the main goal is preparing for the exhibition, staff had to agree on a limited set of database fields to be reviewed and corrected if needed. These are as follows:

- Object type
- Object name
- Manufacturer
- Place of manufacture
- Manufacture date or time span
- Serial number if existent
- Keywords

Staff can't always incorporate every object in a collection into the exhibition. For instance, while the museum did show all of its approximately 200 coffee makers, staff had to select from the museum's 700-plus vacuum cleaners. Staff ensure, however, that they correct the database entries for all objects in a collection. With this work complete, exhibition labels can be printed directly from the database.

Along with the completion and correction of database entries, every object gets a photograph from the front side; back side; and if existent, the nameplate. If we come across an object in need of conservation assessment, it goes directly to the conservation team.

The exhibition planning process goes on with the preparation of the object layout, but the inventory process is considered complete. Once all the objects relevant for the exhibition have gone through this process and the data is considered clean enough for publishing, the objects are published in the online catalog of the TECHNOSEUM (https://technoseum.faust-iserver.de/), where it is available for research and sharing by the general public.

Anybody who has done an inventory will probably have some questions about the museum's processes, such as the following:

- Why aren't dimensions included in the required fields list?

  While dimensions are valuable, measuring correctly takes time and is done most efficiently if one person takes measurements while another person types them into the database. This would mean an investment of more staff time, thus slowing down the whole process. For exhibitions featuring entire collections, dimensions don't particularly matter because staff always test the layout of displays beforehand in storage. For other exhibitions, dimensions will certainly matter, but no responsible curator has ever trusted a measurement purely from the database and always measures the object again—and this is the moment staff add this information to the database.

- Why isn't object condition reviewed?

  In a cursory way, staff do review condition, but they don't invest time to add this information to the database. If there is a need for condition assessment, staff send the object to the conservation department, whose staff document any work done.

- Why are lists printed rather than entering information directly into the database?

  TECHNOSEUM has Wi-Fi access throughout its storage areas, allowing staff to work with the database with a notebook everywhere, and they do. However, for the inventory, it has proven easier to keep an overview of what has been located on a shelf if one has a paper list for checking off what has been found. When all has been checked, it is much easier to see what is missing on paper rather than in a search result of the database.

- What kind of photographs are taken?

  Staff strive to take high-quality photographs that can also be used by the museum's marketing department. While these don't quite reach the quality that would be needed for a tabletop art book, they are just fine for all other uses, such as sharing on social media, printing advertising materials, or sharing with the press or researchers. Though a downside for documentation, we don't add a scale or the accession number to the photographs so that they can be used without further editing. We do, however, name the images after our accession number so that this information is not lost.

~

Case R

Venturing into New Territory: Inventorying Born-Digital Objects in the AIGA Design Archives at the Denver Art Museum

Kate Moomaw, Associate Conservator of Modern and Contemporary Art

The AIGA Design Archives came to the Denver Art Museum through an agreement between AIGA and the museum in 2006. AIGA, founded in 1914 as the American Institute for Graphic Arts and now known as "AIGA, the professional association for design," is the largest and oldest membership organization for the communication design profession in the United States.[1] The AIGA Design Archives arose from AIGA's annual design competitions celebrating the best of design in a variety of disciplines, industries, and formats. The archive is composed of winning competition entries from 1980 to 2012.[2]

Having demonstrated a major commitment to building one of the premier modern and contemporary design collections in the United States, the Denver Art Museum was selected as the permanent home for the AIGA Design Archives. The museum intends to make the collection accessible to scholars and designers as well as to the public through interactive exhibitions.

The AIGA Design Archives are made up of approximately 12,000 physical artifacts and include a wide variety of formats, from posters and books to food and toiletry packaging materials (often with their contents) to electronic media formats, such as video, digital graphics, and websites.

Beginning in 2008, the collection was sent to the museum incrementally, requiring dedicated staffing over several years to perform numbering, cataloging, and rehousing. Much of the collection was relatively straightforward to process, particularly the bound and unbound paper materials. However, the roughly 260 born-digital objects were new territory. Few museums employ specialists in digital media, and the Denver Art Museum was no different at that time. Digital files had been stored by AIGA on removable media, such as CDs, DVDs, USB flash drives, and floppy disks. Initial processing of the collection reflected that these materials were treated more like physical objects than born-digital content. For instance, medium description was that of the storage device with little information captured about the digital files themselves. Still, records were created at this time for each born-digital competition winner, which formed a strong basis for a more detailed inventory.[3]

The museum's conservation department initiated further work on the AIGA born-digital materials beginning in 2014. Broader awareness of the specific preservation needs of audio, video, and born-digital materials was beginning to coalesce within the field, and the conservation department had made assessment and preservation actions for these collections a priority. Conservation staff sought out professional development opportunities to gain a grasp of basic audiovisual and digital preservation principles.

A primary guiding resource came from the National Digital Stewardship Alliance. "Levels of Digital Preservation" summarizes a progressive approach to digital preservation.[4] Presented in table format, preservation actions are divided into five functional areas: storage and geographic location, file fixity and data integrity, information security, metadata, and file formats. The conservation and technology departments collaborated on infrastructure related to the first three areas. At the same time, conservators developed a plan to inventory and survey the AIGA born-digital materials to work toward recommendations in the areas of metadata and file formats, such as storing technical and descriptive metadata and inventorying file formats. These steps build toward more advanced practices for monitoring file format obso-

Figure R.1. Examples of removable media storage devices from the AIGA Design Archives, including 3.5" floppy disks, a Zip disk, CD-ROMs, a DVD-R, and a VHS videotape. KATE MOOMAW

lescence and in response, migrating or emulating digital objects to remain accessible via contemporary systems.

To accomplish these goals, the museum used internal funds to create a summer internship opportunity for a graduate student in the field of digital archiving or preservation. An intern from the New York University Moving Image Archiving and Preservation program was hired to focus on the AIGA born-digital materials in June 2015.

The department envisioned an inventory of the digital files that would result in further preservation recommendations. Our intern suggested going a step further to address the vulnerability of the files as stored on fragile and unstable removable media. If files were going to be accessed to document technical metadata, this would be an opportune time to copy them to a centralized, dedicated storage array at the museum, thereby creating crucial backups and allowing them to be managed together with other digital objects in the collection. Centralized storage would also provide accessibility for curators, educators, and scholars to study and utilize the collection.

To process and ingest the files, Archivematica, digital preservation software that automates the processing and packaging of digital files following the Open Archival Information System reference model, was employed. The BitCurator digital forensics software suite, a read/write blocker, and the KryoFlux floppy disk controller were employed to ensure safe and archival transfer of digital files.

In order to make certain that the metadata would be accessible and useful in the future, the museum's collections management database Argus.net was selected as the metadata repository. Working with the registration department, new fields were added to facilitate this: variable media format, storage device, status, and element creator. Variable media format was intended to capture the most critical piece of technical metadata, the file format. The format field is lexicon-controlled to provide consistency in terminology and data entry. The database's lexicon was eventually built out to include the full array of digital file formats found in the collection. (The hierarchy of and terms in the Getty Art and Architecture Thesaurus [AAT] were employed as a starting place.[5]) The other three fields are not lexicon controlled but utilize a controlled vocabulary. The status field refers to the generation or purpose of the file and uses the terms *master*, *preservation master*, *exhibition copy*, and *reference copy*. *Source* refers to the origin of the file: artist provided, gallery provided, donor provided, and museum produced. Finally, *storage device* refers to the device on which the file is stored and includes terms such as *data disk*, *external hard drive*, *floppy disk*, and *digital repository* (referring to the museum's centralized digital storage location for collections materials).

These four fields capture what was considered the most critical metadata for preservation planning across all digital and audiovisual formats in a controlled, consistent, and searchable manner. The existing free-text description field in the database is the designated location for more extensive technical metadata and production history if known.

With this framework in place, seventy AIGA born-digital objects were successfully inventoried and stored in the course of the summer internship. Based on this success, the conservation department devised a larger project to inventory, survey, digitize, and store the remainder of the AIGA audiovisual and born-digital materials as well as similar materials within the greater collection. In 2015, the project was proposed to the Institute of Museum and Library Services Collections Stewardship program, and a grant was awarded in 2016. Our intern returned as the project conservator, and the twenty-two-month project successfully concluded in October 2018.[6]

Results include the collection of significant technical and descriptive metadata needed to monitor and address the threat of file-format obsolescence for the entire collection. Additionally, the project identified works for which content is incomplete, of poor quality, already

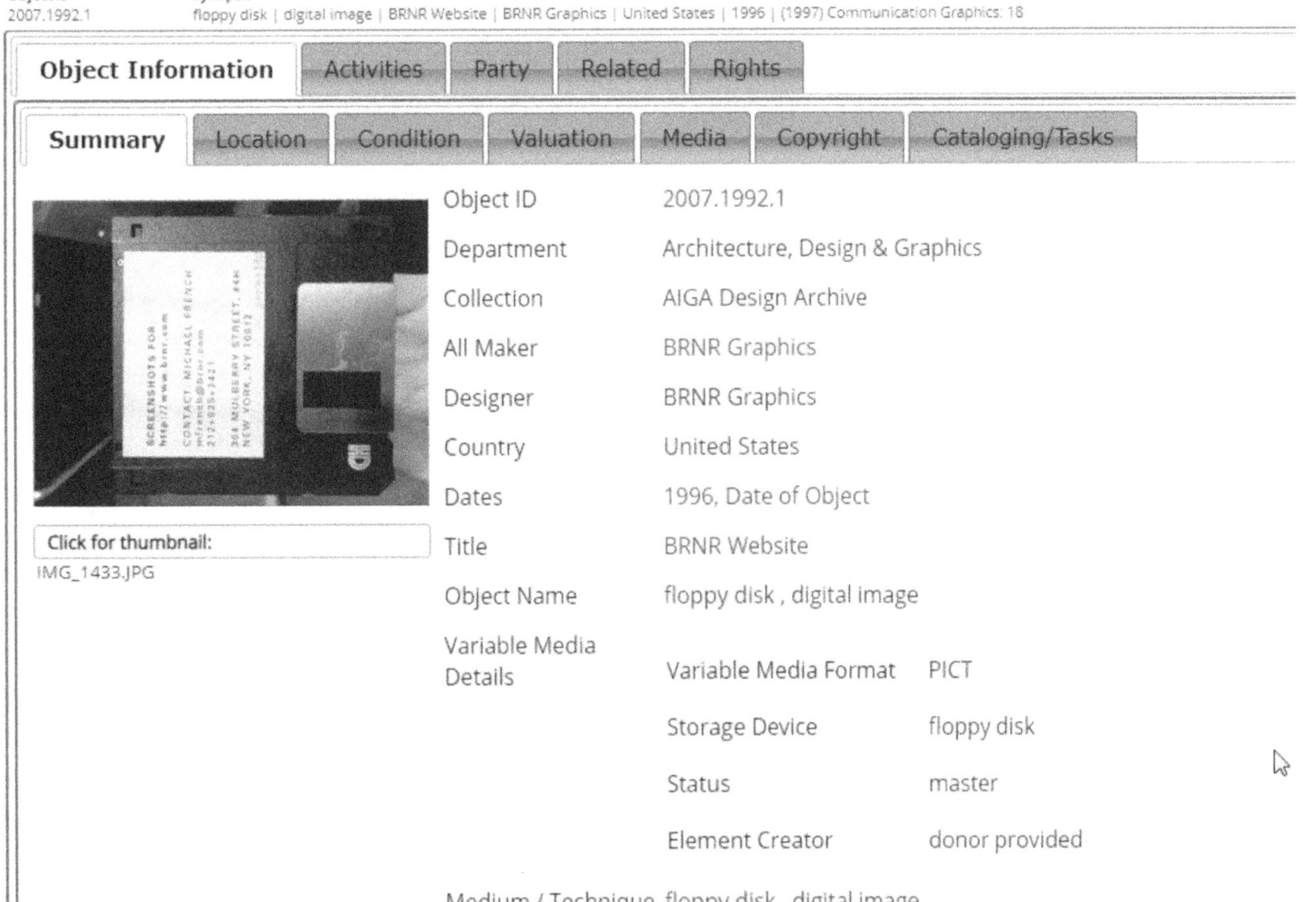

Figure R.2. Argus.net record for the floppy disk containing digital image screenshots of BRNR Graphics, *BRNR Website* (1996). The Variable Media Details fields were added to the Denver Art Museum's instance of Argus.net to better document audiovisual and born-digital materials in the collection. KATE MOOMAW

inaccessible, or in need of supporting software or hardware infrastructure. Periodic curatorial input ensured that understanding of the collection is now much more complete both technically and thematically. Critical to next steps, there now exists a road map for future use and preservation of the collection.

Bibliography

AIGA. "About AIGA." Accessed October 4, 2018. https://www.aiga.org/about/.

AIGA Design Archives. "About the AIGA Design Archives." Accessed October 4, 2018. https://designarchives.aiga.org/#/about.

Alfred, Darrin, Sarah Melching, and Kate Moomaw. "Exploding Sodas, Shrinking Fruit and Yesterday's CD-ROMs: Content and Conservation of the AIGA Design Archives at the Denver Art Museum." In *Future Talks 015. Processes. The Making of Design and Modern Art Materials, Technologies and Conservation Strategies*, edited by Tim Bechthold, 11–19. Munich: Die Neue Sammlung, 2016.

Colloton, Eddy, and Kate Moomaw. "Rewind, Pause, Playback: Addressing a Media Conservation Backlog at the Denver Art Museum." *Electronic Media Review* 5. https://resources.culturalheritage.org/emg-review/volume-5-2017-2018/colloton/.

Getty Research Institute. "Art and Architecture Thesaurus Online." Accessed October 4, 2018. http://www.getty.edu/research/tools/vocabularies/aat/.

National Digital Stewardship Alliance. "Levels of Digital Preservation." Accessed October 4, 2018. https://ndsa.org//activities/levels-of-digital-preservation/.

Notes

1. AIGA, "About AIGA," accessed October 4, 2018, https://www.aiga.org/about/.

2. AIGA Design Archives, "About the AIGA Design Archives," accessed October 4, 2018, https://designarchives.aiga.org/#/about.

3. Darrin Alfred, Sarah Melching, and Kate Moomaw, "Exploding Sodas, Shrinking Fruit and Yesterday's CD-ROMs: Content and Conservation of the AIGA Design Archives at the Denver Art Museum," in *Future Talks 015. Processes. The Making of Design and Modern Art Materials, Technologies and Conservation Strategies*, ed. Tim Bechthold (Munich: Die Neue Sammlung, 2016), 11–19.

4. National Digital Stewardship Alliance, "Levels of Digital Preservation," accessed October 4, 2018, https://ndsa.org//activities/levels-of-digital-preservation/.

5. Getty Research Institute, "Art & Architecture Thesaurus Online," accessed October 4, 2018, http://www.getty.edu/research/tools/vocabularies/aat/.

6. Eddy Colloton and Kate Moomaw, "Rewind, Pause, Playback: Addressing a Media Conservation Backlog at the Denver Art Museum," *Electronic Media Review* 5, https://resources.culturalheritage.org/emg-review/volume-5-2017-2018/colloton/.

Index

Page references for figures and tables are italicized.

~

About the Authors

Sandra Vanderwarf earned an MA in conservation from Fashion Institute of Technology and a BA in criminal justice from John Jay College. Inventory illustrates one way these disciplines have converged during her fifteen years of practice in cultural heritage preservation. Most recently, in collaboration with the National Museum of Mongolia and the U.S. Department of State, she provided expertise to enhance inventory protocols as part of Mongolia's self-determined strategy to deter unlawful trafficking and sale of heritage. Prior to that, her seasoned perspective was honed through intersecting roles of conservator, registrar, and collections manager at a corporate archive, the Smithsonian, American Museum of Natural History, and Brooklyn Children's Museum. Sandra's varied contributions—as inventory taker, author of winning (and rejected) inventory grant proposals, inventory project manager, and researcher referencing historic inventories—engendered a multifaceted appreciation for inventory. Through her presentations at CIDOC-ICOM'S International Committee for Documentation and the Association of Registrars and Collections Specialists and her continued partnerships with the U.S. Ambassador's Fund for Cultural Preservation, she has emphasized the significance of inventory as preventive conservation. Sandra's favorite part of inventory is witnessing humankind's boundless creativity for expressing beauty, ingenuity, and humor as well as our deeply flawed nature.

Bethany Romanowski is head registrar at the National September 11 Memorial & Museum. She holds a BA in anthropology from Indiana University and an MA in social sciences from the University of Chicago. She has over fifteen years' experience managing collections at New York City institutions, including the South Street Seaport Museum and the Cooper Hewitt Smithsonian Design Museum. Bethany recently oversaw the 9/11 Memorial Museum's first wall-to-wall inventory of tangible collections. She is interested in the intersection of inventory and digital preservation practices and is making plans with her colleagues to perform a full inventory of the museum's digital collections.

CPSIA information can be obtained
at www.ICGtesting.com
Printed in the USA
BVHW052105150222
629033BV00002B/5